Understanding the informal economy in Africa, Asia and Latin America is an important step towards poverty reduction. This book helps academics, the development community and policy-makers along that path.

Melanie Khamis, *Wesleyan University, USA*

# The Informal Economy in Developing Countries

The informal economy plays a predominant role in developing countries. It is a domain that remains largely ignored by researchers, and is neglected and often negatively perceived by public policy makers. A better understanding of how their economies work thus implies a better understanding of the informal economy. This book takes a fresh look at research in this domain and covers Asia, Africa and Latin America.

One key message that stands out in this book is that the principal characteristics of the informal economy are relatively similar in all developing countries, with highly precarious contracts and mediocre salaries and working conditions. This does not exclude variations depending on the development levels of each country, as well as the existence of great heterogeneity within each country. In spite of this heterogeneity, another key message – which derives from the first one, is that working in the informal economy is mostly imposed upon workers in countries studied in the book, rather than resulting from free choice.

In so far as the informal economy is condemned to continue, even in emerging countries, defining of support policies constitutes a major development challenge. Based on empirical results presented, this book proposes a three-pronged strategy. First, the informal economy must be officially recognized and defined. This will help to measure it, to reduce the grey area of legal rights and to give "voice" to the informal. Second, incentive policies towards formalization must be put into place. Third, support to informal firms is required, as most of them will remain informal in the medium term.

**Jean-Pierre Cling**, economist, Ministry of Foreign affairs, Paris, and associate member of DIAL (mixed research unit IRD/University Paris Dauphine), Paris, France.

**Stéphane Lagrée**, coordinator of the Bureau for Francophone Cooperation, Vietnam Academy of Social Science, Hanoi, Vietnam.

**Mireille Razafindrakoto**, senior research fellow at the Institut de Recherche pour le Développement (IRD) and a member of DIAL (mixed research unit IRD/University of Paris Dauphine), Paris, France.

**François Roubaud**, senior research fellow at the IRD and a member of DIAL, Paris, France.

# Routledge Studies in Development Economics

# The Informal Economy in Developing Countries

Edited by Jean-Pierre Cling,
Stéphane Lagrée,
Mireille Razafindrakoto and
François Roubaud

Routledge
Taylor & Francis Group

LONDON AND NEW YORK

First published 2015 by Routledge

2 Park Square, Milton Park, Abingdon, Oxfordshire OX14 4RN
52 Vanderbilt Avenue, New York, NY 10017

*Routledge is an imprint of the Taylor & Francis Group, an informa business*

First issued in paperback 2018

*British Library Cataloguing in Publication Data*
A catalogue record for this book is available from the British Library

*Library of Congress Cataloging in Publication Data*
The informal economy in developing countries / edited by Jean-Pierre Cling, Stéphane Lagrée, Mireille Razafindrakoto, François Roubaud.
   pages cm
   Includes bibliographical references and index.
   1. Informal sector (Economics)–Developing countries. 2. Labor market–Developing countries. 3. Small business–Developing countries.
   I. Cling, Jean-Pierre.
   HD2346.5.I525 2014
   330–dc23                                                                  2014004365

ISBN: 978-0-415-73034-1 (hbk)
ISBN: 978-0-367-17881-9 (pbk)

Typeset in Times New Roman
by Wearset Ltd, Boldon, Tyne and Wear

En la memoria de nuestro colega y amigo Francisco Verdera, alias Pancho. Te extrañamos.

# Contents

# Figures

# Tables

# Contributors

## Editors

**Jean-Pierre Cling** is an economist at the French Ministry for Foreign Affairs, Paris and an associated researcher at the mixed research unit DIAL (IRD/University Paris Dauphine) and at the CEPN (CNRS/University Paris Nord). He is a graduate of the École nationale de la statistique et de l'administration économique (ENSAE, Paris), has a PhD in economics (University Paris Dauphine) and is an administrator of the Institut National de la Statistique et des Études Économiques (INSEE). His research work concerns development economics, with a special interest in Africa, as well as in Vietnam, where he was posted between 2007 and 2010 within the framework of the Institut de recherche pour le développement (DIAL-IRD). He co-edited with M. Razafindrakoto and F. Roubaud a special issue of the *Journal of the Asian and Pacific Economy* devoted to the informal economy in Asia (vol. 17, no. 4, October 2012); he is also a co-author of *The Informal Sector in Vietnam: A Focus on Hanoi and Ho Chi Minh City* (2010, Hanoi: The Gioi Publisher; published in English and Vietnamese).

**Stéphane Lagrée** has been working and living in Vietnam since 1993. He defended his geography doctorate thesis on political and agricultural strategies in the north of Vietnam at the university of Bordeaux 3 in 2001; over the last fifteen years his work has concerned research and development problematics. Since 2009, he has been mandated by the École française d'Extrême-Orient (ÉFEO) and the Agence Française de Développement (AFD) to conceive, organise and develop "Tam Dao Days", a regional social sciences summer school university (continental South-East Asia). It is within the framework of this platform for the strengthening of capacities for the analysis of social and economic changes that different university courses have been proposing a reflection on informal economy issues (www.tamdaoconf.com). Also, he was behind the creation, in 2010, of the Francophone Cooperation Unit at the Training institute of the Vietnam Academy of Social Sciences.

**Mireille Razafindrakoto** is senior researcher at the IRD and a member of DIAL, Paris. She is a graduate of the ENSAE (ENSAE/CESD, Paris) and has a PhD in economics (École des Hautes Études en Sciences Sociales, EHESS). Her research into development economics particularly concerns questions of labour markets, poverty and inequalities, as well as governance. She was posted to Madagascar (1994–1999) and Vietnam (2006–2011) within the framework of research programmes carried out by the DIAL-IRD team (she was responsible for the scientific coordination of this last programme). She has acquired substantial experience in the conception and analysis of labour force surveys and the informal sector within the framework of these programmes.

**François Roubaud** is senior researcher at the IRD and a member of the UMR DIAL; he is a graduate of the ENSAE and has a PhD in economics (University of Paris Nanterre). In the statistics domain he was one of the pioneers in carrying out mixed (household/enterprise) surveys and the designer of 1-2-3 surveys that aimed to measure the informal economy and were implemented in numerous African, Asian and Latin American countries. His research in development economics particularly concerns the labour market and the informal economy, and the governance and the political economy of development policies. He has been posted to several countries (Mexico, Madagascar and Vietnam) where he worked with national public institutions on long duration programmes. He is, with Philippe De Vreyer, scientific editor of *Urban Labor Markets in Sub-Saharan Africa* (2013, Washington, DC: World Bank and AFD, which has also been published in French, Marseille: IRD Editions).

## Chapter authors

**François Bourguignon**, Ecole des Hautes Etudes en Sciences Sociales, Paris School of Economics, France.

**Paulette Castel**, Independent employment consultant, Washington DC, United States.

**Jean-Pierre Cling**, UMR DIAL and Centre d'Economie de l'Université Paris Nord, Paris, France.

**Sylvie Fanchette**, Institut de Recherche pour le Développement, UMR CEPED, Paris, France.

**Michael Grimm**, International Institute of Social Studies, Erasmus University, Rotterdam, Netherlands.

**Flore Gubert**, Institut de Recherche pour le Développement, UMR DIAL, Paris, France.

**Isabelle Guérin**, Institut de Recherche pour le Développement and French Institute of Pondicherry, India.

**Javier Herrera**, Institut de Recherche pour le Développement, UMR DIAL, Paris, France.

**Nancy Hidalgo**, National Institute of Statistics, Lima, Peru.

**Ousman Koriko**, Economic and Statistical Observatory for Sub-Saharan Africa, Bamako, Mali.

**Stéphane Lagrée**, Vietnam Academy of Social Sciences, Cellule de coopération francophone, Hanoi, Vietnam.

**Emmanuelle Lavallée**, Université Paris Dauphine, UMR DIAL, Paris, France.

**Jann Lay**, German Institute of Global and Area Studies and University of Gottingen, Germany.

**Roxana Maurizio**, Universidad Nacional de General Sarmiento and Consejo Nacional de Investigaciones Científicas y Técnicas, Buenos Aires, Argentina.

**Pierre Nguetse Tegoum**, Ministry for the Economy, Planning and Regional Development, Yaounde, Cameroon.

**Xuân Hoan Nguyen**, Centre of Research and Development for Agrarian Systems, Hanoi, Vietnam.

**Christophe J. Nordman**, Institut de Recherche pour le Développement, UMR DIAL, Paris, France.

**Xavier Oudin**, Institut de Recherche pour le Développement, UMR DIAL, Paris, France.

**Laure Pasquier-Doumer**, Institut de Recherche pour le Développement, UMR DIAL, Paris, France.

**Faly Hery Rakotomanana**, National Institute of Statistics and UMR DIAL, Antananarivo, Madagascar.

**Mireille Razafindrakoto**, Institut de Recherche pour le Développement, UMR DIAL, Paris, France.

**François Roubaud**, Institut de Recherche pour le Développement, UMR DIAL, Paris, France.

**Francisco Verdera**, Pontificia Universidad Católica del Perú and International Labour Organization, Lima, Peru.

**Jean-Michel Wachsberger**, Université Lille 3 and UMR DIAL, Paris, France.

# Abbreviations

| | |
|---|---|
| AAP | Active Age Population |
| AFD | Agence Française de Développement (France) |
| AFRISTAT | *Observatoire Economique et Statistique d'Afrique Subsaharienne* (Mali) |
| ATT | Average Treatment on the Treated |
| CASEN | *Encuesta de Caracterización Socioeconómica Nacional* (Chile) |
| CELS | Centre for Education and Labour Studies (Thailand) |
| CEPN | *Centre d'Économie de l'université Paris Nord* (France) |
| CIEM | Central Institute for Economic Management (Vietnam) |
| CNRS | *Centre National de la Recherche Scientifique* (France) |
| DEA | Data Envelopment Analysis |
| DIAL | *Développement, Institutions et Mondialisation* |
| EAP | Economically Active Population |
| EESI | *Enquête sur l'emploi et le secteur informel* (Cameroon) |
| ÉFEO | *École française d'Extrême-Orient* (France) |
| EFS | Employment in the Formal Sector |
| EHESS | *École des Hautes Études en Sciences Sociales* (France) |
| EIS | Employment in the Informal Sector |
| ENAHO | *Encuesta Nacional de Hogares sobre Condiciones de Vida y Pobreza* (Peru) |
| ENAMIN | *Encuesta Nacional de Micronegocios* (Mexico) |
| ENEU | *Encuesta Nacional de Empleo Urbano* (Mexico) |
| EPH | *Encuesta Permanente de Hogares* (Argentina) |
| EPZs | Export Processing Zones |
| FAR | Female Activity Rate |
| FE | Formal Employment |
| FEQR | Fixed Effects Quantile Regressions |
| FS | Formal Sector |
| FSLC | First School Leaving Certificate |
| GCE-OL | General Certificate of Education, Ordinary Level |
| GDP | Gross Domestic Product |
| GNP | Gross National Product |
| GSO | General Statistical Office |

| | |
|---|---|
| HBs | Household Business |
| ICLS | International Conference of Labour Statisticians |
| IE | Informal Employment |
| IHBs | Informal Household Businesses |
| IIA | Independence of Irrelevant Alternatives |
| ILO | International Labour Organisation |
| ILSSA | Institute of Labour Science and Social Affairs (Vietnam) |
| INSEE | *Institut National de la Statistique et des Études Économiques* (France) |
| IPU | Informal Production Units |
| IRD | *Institut de Recherche pour le Développement* (France) |
| IS | Informal Sector |
| ISS | Institute of Statistical Science |
| IVM | Instrumental Variables Method |
| JICA | Japan International Cooperation Agency |
| LFS | Labour Force Survey |
| MARD | Ministry of Agriculture and Rural Development (Vietnam) |
| MOLISA | Ministry of Labour, Invalids and Social Affairs (Vietnam) |
| MSEs | Micro and Small Enterprises |
| NGO | Non-governmental Organization |
| NSO | National Statistical Office |
| OECD | Organization for Economic Co-operation and Development |
| OLS | Ordinary Least Squares (method) |
| PNAD | *Pesquisa Nacional por Amostra de Domicilios* (Brazil) |
| PREALC | Regional Employment Program for Latin America and the Caribbean |
| QR | Quantile Regression |
| SE | Self-employed |
| SFA | Stochastic (Statistical) Frontier Analysis |
| SMEs | Small and Medium Entreprises |
| SSA | Sub-Saharan Africa |
| UICs | Unobserved Individual Characteristics |
| UIS | Urban Informal Sector |
| UMR CEPED | *Unité Mixte de Recherche "Centre population et développement"* |
| UMR DIAL | *Unité Mixte de Recherche "Développement, institutions et mondialisation"* |
| UNDP | United Nations Development Programme |
| VASS | Vietnam Academy of Social Sciences (Vietnam) |
| VHLSS | Vietnam Household Living Standard Survey (Vietnam) |
| VSIIS | Voluntary Social Insurance for the Informal Sector (Vietnam) |
| VSS | Vietnam Social Security |
| WAEMU | West-African Economic and Monetary Union |
| WTO | World Trade Organization |

# Acknowledgements

This book is a collective work. Our special thanks go to all the authors for giving their best and answering our numerous demands, often at short notice. We would also like to thank the translators, especially Diane Bertrand for top quality translation as usual. We express our deep gratitude to Bui Thu Trang for her endless and invaluable support during the preparation of this book.

This book consists of a selection of papers presented during an international conference organized in May 2010 in Hanoi, Vietnam by the Vietnam Academy of Social Sciences and the Institut de Recherche pour le Développement, with the support of the Agence Française de Développement (AFD) and several international organisations: the World Bank, the International Labour Organisation, the United Nations Development Programme and the Department for International Development. The selected papers have been augmented and updated after a scrupulous refereeing process. Furthermore, the book has been enriched with a few original chapters. We would like to thank all the institutions which contributed to support the Conference. We are very grateful to the team led by Philippe Cabin at Agence Française de Développement in particular, for the publication in French of a condensed version of the proceedings. It topped the list of online consultations on the AFD website in 2013.

Last of all, many thanks to the small informal restaurants and coffee shops in Hanoi in which we spent long hours and had many informal meetings when preparing this book.

# Introduction

Most jobs in developing countries are found in the informal economy which plays a predominant role within the economy. One may even think that the world economic crisis would add more weight to the informal economy because of job losses in other sectors of economic activity. Better understanding of how the economies of these countries work thus requires a better knowledge of the informal sector. This knowledge is also indispensable in the fight against poverty which is at the heart of political development preoccupations. Understanding the informal sector is of utmost importance from a political, economic and social point of view. Let us not forget that the "Arab springs" of 2011 began in Tunisia with the immolation of an informal street seller of fruit and vegetables who was ill treated by the police. At the same time, the informal economy remains largely unrecognized by researchers, is neglected by politicians and is even negatively perceived, as the emblematic drama of the Tunisian revolution evoked above testifies.

In spite of the efforts made in this domain by the International Labour Organisation (ILO) over the last decades, the vagueness which continues to surround the informal economy remains a big obstacle which prevents it being taken into account in economic policies. In conformity with international recommendations, the informal sector is defined in this work as the whole of non-agricultural and non-registered individual enterprises which produce goods and services for the market.[1] Informal employment is, for its part, defined as work without any social protection. Several characteristics can be considered in this regard for a precise definition: social protection, written contracts, pay slips, redundancy pay, etc. On account of these definitions, informal employment comprises two distinct principal components, namely employment in the informal sector, as well as unprotected employment in the formal sector. In conformity with the definitions of the ILO (2003), the informal sector and employment together make up what is designated as the informal economy.

The lack of precise statistical data concerning the formal economy is also to be remarked. Several factors result from this: a haziness of definitions outside the statistical community; a lack of interest on behalf of the authorities towards a sector which operates on the fringe of the economy and pays no taxes; and, finally, there is the preconceived idea according to which the informal sector is a mark of underdevelopment which is expected to disappear with the development of the country. Whatever the case, the lack of accurate data limits the pertinence of the analyses presented in international reports on this subject (cf. in particular those produced by the ILO the WTO and the OECD in 2009; Bacchetta *et al.*, 2009; Jutting and de Laiglesia, 2009). Furthermore, the economic studies on this subject are generally restricted by the absence of data adequate enough to adopt an ad hoc ("small and medium-size enterprises" for example) and very rough definition (Guha-Khasnobis and Kanbur, 2006).

Beyond the problem of the availability of adequate data, the prevailing confusion is very much linked to the multi-form nature of the informal sector and the work motivations therein. In economic academic work, three dominant approaches are used concerning the origins and causes of informality (Roubaud, 1994; Bachetta *et al.*, 2009):

- The "dualist" approach is a continuation of the studies by Lewis (1954) and by Harris and Todaro (1970); this approach is based on the model of a dual labour market, where the informal sector is considered as a residual component of the informal market without any link with the formal economy. It is a subsistence economy which only exists because the formal economy is incapable of offering a sufficient number of jobs.
- Unlike the preceding approach, the structuralist one highlights the interdependences between the formal and informal sectors (Moser, 1978; Portes *et al.*, 1989); according to this approach of Marxist inspiration, the informal sector is integrated into the capitalist system according to a relation of subordination; by providing cheap labour and products to formal enterprises, the informal sector increases economic flexibility and competitiveness.
- Finally, the "legalist" approach considers that the informal sector is constituted of micro-entrepreneurs who prefer to operate informally in order to escape from economic regulations (de Soto, 1989); this liberal approach contrasts sharply with the two preceding ones in so much as the choice of informality is voluntary and linked to the excessive costs of the legalization process associated with registering and obtaining a formal status.

This book aims to present "state of the art" research on the informal economy, to propose, in the hope of them being adopted, policies aimed at the informal sector and finally to suggest some common approaches to define and measure the informal employment sector in developing countries. Almost half of the contributors come from developing countries: they work either in universities, research institutions, international organizations (ILO, AFRISTAT, etc.) or in government. The research questions are studied in developing countries covering Asia, Africa and Latin America. For the most part, the different contributions adopt similar methodologies and econometric instruments. But the use of qualitative approaches alongside the quantitative ones also brings added value to the analysis. In many cases (nine chapters out of fifteen), the analysis is based on the results of surveys which have been conducted using comparable questionnaires and survey techniques. Regarding this last point, this work is the first of its type to take into account direct observations of the informal economy using international definitions. The *1-2-3 surveys* which were developed by the DIAL research unit to measure the informal economy have provided the base for the studies presented here about West Africa, Cameroon, Madagascar, Peru and Vietnam. All too often, comparative studies are based on disparate measurement instruments, which ultimately risk marring the validity of the findings. It then becomes hard to know whether the differences observed between countries are to be ascribed to real differences in informal economy functioning or to differences in the measurement instruments, if not to differences in the concepts themselves. This book provides the possibility, unique to date, to take a comparative approach to the informal economy using this set of perfectly comparable empirical basis. It extends the recent work by De Vreyer and Roubaud (2013), focused on labour markets in Sub-Saharan Africa.

This book comprises three parts preceded by an interview with F. Bourguignon which presents a global view of the principal problematics relating to the informal sector. The first part is concerned with factors of the sectorial allocation of employment and poses questions about the reasons for which workers seek employment in the informal sector and about the satisfaction they gain from this. The second part analyses the economic, institutional and social constraints which weigh upon the informal sector in developing countries: corruption, factors of productive efficiency and integration into the economy. The third part deals with the micro and macro dynamics of the informal sector, which leads us to study mobility between the formal and informal sectors and the link between informal employment, income and poverty. We shall present below the problematic studied in each part and the principal results obtained.

A key message comes out of the chapters presented. The principal characteristics of the informal sector testify to some profound similarities between developing countries, a fact already pointed out by Cling *et al.* (2010): low qualifications and precariousness of jobs, mediocre incomes and working conditions, atomization of production units and lack of articulation with the formal economy, etc. In the absence of a sufficient number of job creations, the informal sector essentially constitutes a refuge for workers seeking a job or leaving agriculture, in accordance with the dual approach of the labour market which seems to play a predominant role whatever the level of development of the developing countries. In this respect, we share the conclusions of Banerjee and Duflo (2011), according to which the poor create their own enterprises by default rather than by choice. This general conclusion is not contradictory with the observation of a high level of heterogeneity in the sector and in informal employment within each country, confirmed by several chapters in this work. Finally, the drawing up of support policies appears to be of paramount importance, in spite of the difficulties such a task presents.

## Sectorial allocation of employment between the formal and informal sectors

This first part concerns the determinants of the sectorial allocation of employment in the informal economy (informal sector and employment). The principal question is the following: why do workers find themselves in the informal sector and does this situation result from a choice or is it forced upon them? Answering this question might allow us verify the validity of the "dualist", "structuralist" and "legalist" approaches of the informal sector defined above. The study of these compared characteristics of formal and informal workers as well as their working conditions and incomes shows that the informal economy welcomes the least qualified workers (and migrants) by offering the least well-paid jobs (except for agriculture); finally, employment in the informal economy is generally considered as temporary while waiting for something better to turn up in the formal sector, which shows that this type of employment is forced upon workers and not chosen freely given the surplus workforce in developing countries. This result, however, contradicts the conclusions of several authors who advanced the "legalist" thesis in the case of Latin America (de Soto, 1989; Maloney, 2004).

Roxana Maurizio (Chapter 1) examines the link between informality, job precariousness and the segmentation of incomes as well as the relation between informality and poverty. The study involves four Latin American countries (Argentina, Brazil, Chili and Peru). The author shows that there is a positive correlation between informality and poverty. Informal workers (including informal sector workers and non-declared salaried workers) have, on average, a lower level of education than formal workers; they are characterized by a greater presence of the young and women, and they are to be found more in commercial activities, construction and home services than their formal counterparts. This "composition effect" is unfavourable to informal incomes. The salary gaps can also be explained by the different outputs obtained from formal and informal workers for each considered characteristic, particularly in Argentina and Peru. These gaps seem to indicate the presence of a segmentation of the labour market as informal workers do not have access to better remunerated formal jobs.

Mireille Razafindrakoto *et al.* (Chapter 2) analyse labour determinants in the informal sector (chosen/not chosen) in Vietnam from job satisfaction and mobility projects towards other types of employment. This original approach allows us to go beyond only taking remuneration into account and also a certain number of working conditions, to include all the dimensions linked to the exercise of a job, including the link with outside work activities. Jobs in the informal sector are both less well remunerated (except for agriculture) and those which provide the least satisfaction (on a par with the agricultural sector). This is why numerous workers in this sector, whether they be entrepreneurs or especially employees, wish to change job, with a marked preference for protected posts in the public sector.

Laure Pasquier-Doumer (Chapter 3) completes the analysis of the employment choice determinants in the informal sector from an inter-generational perspective. The author takes as a starting point the observation that there is a strong correlation of the informal entrepreneur status between generations. The study shows that contrary to what was observed in developed countries, this correlation cannot be explained by the handing down of management competences, physical capital or even social capital from parents to children. Consequently, having an entrepreneur father does not generally provide a comparative advantage for the performances of the enterprise. On the other hand, the heads of informal enterprises who benefit from a family tradition do have such a comparative advantage. It can be thus deduced that entry into the informal sector corresponds to a voluntary choice for entrepreneurs who have inherited or can rely on the support of family tradition.

The integration of the informal sector into the formal economy is studied by Sylvie Fanchette and Xuân Hoan Nguyen through the example of the craft villages in the Red River delta (Hanoi region) in Vietnam (Chapter 4). By taking an essentially qualitative geographical approach to this question, the authors highlight the hazy character of the frontier between the formal/informal on account of the close integration of micro-enterprises in the craft villages. This integration allows small enterprises to participate through sub-contracting in the export of industrial products (clothing textiles, furniture, pottery, etc.). Here we find ourselves in a classical case described in the "structuralist" approach. All the same, this formal/informal sectorial integration appears to be rather marginal in Vietnam beyond the emblematic case of the craft villages (Cling *et al.*, 2010), while it was traditionally believed that in the case of Asian countries with high growth the informal sector fully participated in the emergence process by its sub-contracting links with export enterprises.

Finally, Paulette Castel (Chapter 5) deals with social protection (health and retirement) in Vietnam, but her conclusions have a wider impact. In this country which entered into the category of middle-income countries in 2010, this question has become critical (because of the demographic transition) but also realistic because of the rise in incomes and thus in the number of potential contributions. Given the definition of informal employment (employment without social protection), the widening of social protection would *ipso facto* reduce informal employment. The study deals with both formal and informal enterprises, that is to say, the two components of informal employment. Many of the former tend to under-declare salaries paid in order to reduce and even nullify social contributions. Empirical analyses show that salaried workers often accept this situation because the relationship cost/benefit of the contributions does not encourage them to participate. One of the proposed solutions consists of providing subsidies to incite participation in social protection.

## Economic, institutional and social constraints

Recent studies have highlighted the heterogeneity of the informal sector which is composed of a great variety of individual enterprises differing totally according to their size, economic performances, working conditions, etc. (Guha-Khasnobis and Kanbur, 2006). A multi-segmentation of the informal sector was thus observed where an upper segment comprising big, successful individual enterprises coexists with a lower segment (the majority) of small enterprises operating in precarious conditions to stay alive. The latter are theoretically trapped in extreme conditions by barriers preventing their entry to the upper segment, barriers which are linked to the imperfections of capital markets in particular (difficulties with credit access) and training. To these economic constraints can be added institutional ones according to the "legalist" approach (corruption, for example) which dissuades informal entrepreneurs from declaring themselves in order to escape from legislation which is too restrictive or from corruption. This part also establishes a link between the informal sector and social capital, a question which has only been addressed until now by anthropologists but has been hardly looked at by economists. Social links can play a role which is both positive (if the networks help to compensate the imperfections in the labour and capital markets) or negatively in the case of forced solidarities imposed within the family for example. This second part explores the heterogeneity of the informal sector in relation to economic, institutional and social constraints.

The study of technical efficiency in the informal sector in Madagascar lead by Faly Hery Rakotomanana (Chapter 6) using quantile regressions highlights the low level of efficiency of informal production units (IPUs): by mobilizing the same resources, it would be possible to triple production on condition that demand constraints (credit access, access to adapted professional premises, etc.) and training constraints be lifted. Commercial enterprises and those managed by women are the least competitive. The results appear to be very stable over the two years of estimations (2001 and 2004).

Pierre Nguetse Tegoum (Chapter 7) focuses on this last aspect, by measuring the returns on education in the non-agricultural informal sector in Cameroon with the help of matching methods and selection models which take into account unobservable characteristics. The estimations show that education has a big impact on workers' incomes in the informal sector. Successfully completing basic education (before entering employment or returning to school) increases income by between 20 and 30 per cent. Furthermore, completing the first cycle of secondary education increases the income of the workers in the informal sector by roughly 30 per cent.

Emmanuelle Lavallée and François Roubaud (Chapter 8) show that few informal enterprises are globally concerned by corruption in West Africa. However, this percentage rises to 37 per cent if we limit ourselves to entrepreneurs who have been in contact with state services. Large sized informal enterprises and more particularly those in the transport sector are the most affected by corruption. Their estimations suggest that corruption has a negative impact on firms economic outcomes. Conversely, paying taxes[2] in exchange for public services allows informal enterprises to improve their performances. Finally, non-registering is especially linked to an ignorance of the laws rather than to the deliberate will to escape corruption, contrary to what is suggested by the "legalist" approach.

Michael Grimm *et al.* (Chapter 9) study the influence of family ties on the informal sector in West Africa through social networks. The idea that family and kinship ties may imply adverse incentive effects (and not positive effects as put in evidence in Chapter 3) is often mentioned in the anthropological and socio-logical literature. However, there is very little empirical backup for the existence of such negative effects of social networks on entrepreneurial activities. The authors analyse more precisely the impact of the "forced solidarity" imposed by the families who have remained in the village on informal entrepreneurs who have migrated to towns. The distance between the place of residence and the place of birth is used as a proxy for the amount of financial transfers to the family. According to the study, the less close the ties, the more intensive the use of physical capital. Conversely, family ties within a town or city tend to increase the use of capital and the quantity of work and thus function as a mutual support.

The chapter by Isabelle Guerin (Chapter 10) questions the widely promoted positive impact of micro-credit for self-entrepreneurs. It presents the results of a long-term on-going research programme conducted in India, looking at labour and finance in various districts of north and coastal rural Tamil Nadu. It brings together researchers from various origins and backgrounds, some of which live on site. It relies on a wide range of methods, including semi-directive interviews, case studies, detailed analysis of villages, value chains and markets and house-hold surveys. The chapter starts by locating self-employment into the broader labour landscape, first at the Indian level and then in the region under study. It then details the multiple barriers that micro-entrepreneurs may face in starting a business, by shedding light on the very unequal structure of power that underlies markets and the key role of social institutions such as caste and gender.

## Micro macro dynamics and poverty

In the long term, as François Bourguignon remarked in the interview following this introduction, it is expected that a country's development will be accom-panied by a progressive reduction of the weight of the informal economy. The example of developed countries where the informal economy occupies a mar-ginal place supports this theory. A first question of a macro-economic nature thus concerns the link between economic growth and the dynamics of the informal sector. The multi-segmented analysis of the labour market may be quite naturally extended to employment dynamics by establishing a link between these formal/informal dynamics and the macro-economic environment (Bacchetta *et al.*, 2009). Segmentation implies that certain workers cannot obtain sufficient remuneration to take care of their own and their family's needs. Informality thus constitutes a characteristic factor of a situation of poverty for households and the link between informality and poverty is studied here using an approach which is both macro- and micro-economic.

Christophe J. Nordman *et al.* (Chapter 11) study informal sector income dynamics vis-à-vis the formal sector. They assess the magnitude of various formal/informal sector earnings gaps while addressing heterogeneity issues at three different levels: the worker, the job (wage employment vs self-employment) and the earnings distribution. The questions asked are the following. Is there an informal sector job earnings penalty? Do some informal sector jobs provide pecuniary premiums? Which ones? Do possible gaps vary along the earnings distribution? Standard earnings equations are estimated at the mean and at various conditional quantiles of the earnings distribution, focusing particularly on heterogeneity within both the formal and informal sector categories. The results suggest that the informal sector earnings gap highly depends on the workers' job status and on their relative position in the earnings distribution. Penalties may in some cases turn into premiums. By comparing the results with studies in other developing countries, the conclusions highlight the Madagascar's labour market specificity.

Francisco Verdera (Chapter 12) analyses employment dynamics in the urban informal sector in South America (ten countries) between 1970 and 2008. To our knowledge this is the first solid study of its type based on temporal data for the whole continent. It highlights the very big progression of the share of employment in the informal sector during the 1990s, a period of low economic growth following structural adjustments. On the other hand, the second half of the last decade up to the international crisis saw the informal sector retreat in percentage points in relation to strong growth of the GDP. The econometric estimations show the negative correlation between employment in the informal sector and growth of the GDP, and the positive correlation between the growth of the working population, the (mainly female) activity rate and productivity. As François Bourguignon remarked (ibid.), it is first and foremost the lack of economic growth which triggered the rise of informality in South America during the 1970s.

Xavier Oudin (Chapter 13) analyses the dynamics of the labour market in Thailand over a long period (1970–2005). Throughout this phase of high growth and industrialization which was interrupted at the moment of the 1997 crisis, an underlying fall of employment in the informal sector was observed. Since the crisis, the relative weight of the informal sector has stabilized in relation to the slowing down of growth. This correlation between economic growth and employment in the informal sector conforms to the results presented for Latin America in this part. Nevertheless, the biographical surveys carried out by the author show the high level of mobility of workers (informal sector ones in particular), as well as the high number of inter-sectorial transitions between the formal and informal, particularly high in this direction. According to these surveys, the Thais continue to express a great deal of aversion to salaried work and a desire for independence which is very much conditioned by their life cycle that the activity of independent entrepreneur can help to satisfy.

The study by Javier Herrera and Nancy Hidalgo (Chapter 14) about Peru continues and goes deeper into the preceding chapter by dealing with transitions on the labour market. It takes a micro-economic approach using long-term panel data from household surveys. Using data from the 2002–2010 period, it throws light upon the high level of heterogeneity of informal sector enterprises, with a certain number of quite high income enterprises but also a high proportion of poor ones. As we have already seen on the scale of the South American continent in general, the share of the informal sector in employment diminished in the

2000s (while remaining higher in 2010 than its level in 2002). On a more macro-economic level the failure and creation rates of IPUs appears to be very high (about 35 per cent in 2010) given that the entry into poverty of a head of an IPU is correlated with the disappearance of his/her production unit, according to the estimated multinomial logit model. This result which establishes a strong link between poverty and the informal sector implies that development policies should be more concerned with making easier transitions between informal and formal sector and increasing the productivity of the former. This point of view which is still largely ignored even today in public policies is explored in more detail in the last part of this work.

Jean-Pierre Cling *et al.* (Chapter 15) show that in spite of rapid economic growth in Vietnam the informal sector is there to stay. It represents the first source of non-agricultural employment and its weight is tending to increase with the agrarian transition. The authors also demonstrate the vulnerability of the informal economy to macro-economic shocks through the impact of the international crisis. The informal sector helped to reduce pressure on the labour market, particularly through a rise in employment in the sector; under-employment and multi-activity also increased. In spite of the difficulties this sector faces, economic support policies implemented after the crisis totally ignored it. The authors recommend an official consideration of the informal sector (which implies particularly defining it in a manner acceptable to every-body). A greater transparency and simplicity of the rules for registering, as well as the implementation of targeted policies of which the most significant will be conceived on the basis of precise information.

## Notes

1 In accordance with national circumstances, other definitions of the informal sector can also be retained: no written accounts; size (number of employees) beneath a certain threshold.
2 Because they are not declared, informal sector enterprises do not pay taxes on profits or turnover. However, they pay local taxes (if they have fixed premises).

## References

Bacchetta, M., Ernst, E. and Bustamante, J.P. (2009) *Globalization and Informal Jobs in Developing Countries*, Geneva: ILO and WTO.

Banerjee, A. and Duflo, E. (2011) *Poor Economics: A Radical Rethinking of the Way to Fight Global Poverty*, New York: Public Affairs.

Cling, J.P., Nguyen, T.T.H., Nguyen, H.C., Phan, T.N.T., Razafindrakoto, M. and Roubaud, F. (2010) *The Informal Sector in Vietnam: A Focus on Hanoi and Ho Chi Minh City*, Hanoi: The Gioi Publisher.

de Soto, H. (1989) *The Other Path: The Invisible Revolution in the Third World*, New York: Harper Collins (original edition published in Spanish in 1986).

De Vreyer, P. and Roubaud, F. eds (2013), *Urban Labor Markets in Sub-Saharan Africa*, Washington, DC: World Bank/AFD.

Guha-Khasnobis, B. and Kanbur, R. eds (2006) *Informal Labor Markets and Development*, London: Palgrave Macmillan.

Harris, J.R. and Todaro, M.P. (1970) "Migration, unemployment and development: A two-sector analysis", *American Economic Review* 60(1): 126–42.

Jutting, P. and de Laiglesia, J.R. eds (2009) *Is Informal Normal? Towards More and Better Jobs in Developing Countries*, Paris: OECD Development Centre.

Lewis, W.A. (1954) "Economic development with unlimited supplies of labour", *Manchester School* 28(2): 139–91.

Maloney, W. (2004) "Informality revisited", *World Development* 32(7): 1159–1178.

Moser, C.O. (1978) "Informal sector or petty commodity production: Dualism or dependence in urban development", *World Development* 6(9/10): 1041–64.

ILO (2003) "Guidelines concerning a statistical definition of informal employment", 17th International Conference of Labour Statisticians, ILO, 24 November to 3 December.

Portes, A., Castells, M. and Benton, L.A. (1989) *The Informal Economy: Studies in Advanced and Less Developed Countries*, Baltimore, MD: The Johns Hopkins University Press.

Roubaud, F. (1994) *L'économie informelle au Mexique : de la sphère domestique à la dynamique macro-économique*, Paris: Karthala/Orstom.

# Interview of François Bourguignon[1]

*Introduction*: I am very pleased to have with us today Professor Francois Bourguignon. Professor Bourguignon is a global authority in development economics. Among others, he was the Chief Economist of the World Bank between 2003 and 2007, years during which he brought several issues to the forefront of the world in development, including work on inequalities and especially on assessing the impact of development policies. Both of them were really pushed ahead in their field. Professor Bouguignon is also very well known in academic circles. He founded the prestigious DELTA in Paris and he is at present leading the Paris School of Economics. He was also the editor of the *European Economic Review* and has published very numerous articles on economic issues and development issues. So it is a privilege for us to have Professor Bourguignon to share his views on issues related to the informal sector.

*Question*: Professor Bourguignon, in order to characterise the informal sector we can say that initially the informal sector was more of an empirical concept and was considered as a residual, backward and disconnected sector, which is supposed to disappear with industrialisation and development. But nowadays different views prevail. At the micro-level, some authors claimed that working in the informal sector can be a real and deliberate choice, not necessarily a constrained choice due to a lack of job opportunities in the modern formal sector. So how do you explain these very different views?

*F. Bourguignon*: Informality is a topic which has been present in development economics forever. We have to remember that, basically, informality is the reserve army that we find in Marx and it is the unlimited supply of labour that we find in this very well known model by Arthur Lewis. What is important in this concept of informality that it is associated with poverty and the idea is really that fighting informality somehow should be fighting poverty. Reducing informality should somehow be reducing poverty. Now, when you say that this is an empirical concept, I am not completely convinced by that. It seems to me that the reserve army that I was mentioning before, all the Lewis definition of duality or dualism, is more of an intellectual construct, which is making a lot of sense and which corresponds obviously to some reality. But those people never ask themselves what will be the empirical content of this. Now that we have data to try to characterise informality – and then I guess that in the discussion we will get back to the issue of how do we define informality – but now that we have some data, we are realising that things are not as simple as we would like them to be.

We realise, in particular, that informality does not seem to be declining systematically with growth. This is really problematic because we think about growth as the first solution or the most important way we can get rid of poverty and if we associate poverty and informality then we would like to see growth systematically reducing informality. Then we find this is not completely the case – again, maybe we will come back to that issue a little later with the definition of informality – but what we observe today is that there is a change that corresponds to what development economists always thought, which is that there is a shift in economic activity from the rural sector to the urban sector. And to the extent that we can consider that in many developing countries rural sector is informal, from that point of view we have declining informality. But at the same time – and this is what is troublesome in what we observe today – we have an increase in the informality of the urban sector or at least we have growth in the urban sector where we see growing at the same both the formal and informal sector. The kind of interrogation that we have in front of us is really this part, the urban informality more than rural informality and then your analysis saying that in informality we have both two types of behaviour: people who decide that they would be better in the informal sector to do whatever they can do or have to do and then you have people who cannot get a job in the formal sector and take anything that is available, which is in the informal sector. And it is very difficult, as we know, to make a distinction between those two cases. But we know that they are present and the most important question, I would say, in analysing informality is trying to answer that question.

*Question*: I think you addressed already the question of the dynamics of the informal sector, but I don't know if you still want to elaborate on this because many people think that the informal sector is going to progressively disappear when a country has developed. But this is not what is actually happening in many developing countries. That is the case of Vietnam. We made some projections and these projections suggest that the share of the informal sector of total employment will increase in the next few years, knowing that the informal sector is already the first employer in Vietnam out of agriculture. So how do you analyse this situation?

*F. Bourguignon*: What are the dynamics of informality, what can we expect, what is happening, and how can we explain what we observe? What we expect, ideally, is of course that economic growth will progressively eliminate the informal sector. This is more or less what we observed in today's developed countries. In History, we could see that there was an informal sector in Europe, there was an informal sector in the United States and progressively with economic growth these sectors have disappeared. We could say there still are – and many sociologists in particular say that there still are informal sectors in those countries – but they are of a very tiny size. Now, why would this not work? Why is it the case that apparently in many developing countries there is some growth – I will not say that we have fast growth but some growth – yet the informal sector remains in relative terms more or less constant? At the same time, the urban population is growing. Now there are various explanations for that. One explanation is to say that at the same time that growth is taking place, there is technical change. There are the imports of foreign technologies coming from developed countries that are less intensive in labour, which means that growth is taking place in the non-agricultural part of the economy but with less and less employment content, which means that the formal sector is growing in output but much less quickly in terms of employment. We have observed that in many countries. For example, if we look at China, we observe that at the beginning just after the reforms in the 1980s, the development of the Chinese manufacturing sector was accompanied by a big increase in formal employment. At some stage the employment creation by the export manufacturing sector in China dropped considerably and today the elasticity between employment and output in manufacturing in China is very low. What is behind that is this kind of substitution that I was mentioning before.

But then there are other possible explanations. Another explanation in many countries in particular in Latin America would be that growth simply has not been fast enough to eliminate informality. Again, if we refer to the case of Europe, if we look at Europe after the Second World War there is definitely an informal sector in Europe in those days. It virtually disappeared during the twenty years after the world war but at the same time we must admit that the rate of growth has been extremely high for twenty-five to thirty years in a row. So this is what is explaining the disappearance of the informal sector. In Latin America and in many countries, growth has been very sluggish over the last twenty years, then because of that informality is remaining something important.

Then the final possible explanation is what we were saying before about for some people it is in those societies something which is quite attractive to be in the informal sector because you are avoiding paying taxes, paying contributions to social security, etc. Informality is attractive because it is another type of organisation of production. This is not for all types of production. Of course, if you have a big company, it is very difficult to imagine that you will not be in the formal sector. But for a small production unit, yes, this is definitely a choice and, again, in some countries we seem to observe that the persistence of the informal sector is associated with that choice. Let me finish that by saying that I read the book that was mentioned on informality in Vietnam[2] and I saw it was a very nice book, which was in particular summarising very well the basic questions about formality and informality. I thought that the Vietnamese story about this was quite interesting. But one big issue in that book and in some other work in Asia on informality is really the issue of empirical definition of what is the informal sector.

*Question*: Your referring to the definition brings us to a question that we were keen to ask, which is given the heterogeneity of the informal sector, which you referred to, the fact that at one end you have people who voluntarily choose to be part of it and you have other people who are constrained, it is difficult to know what is driving different people into the informal sector. That also has implications for the definition. It is quite striking that, while there is some consensus on international definitions of, say, the unemployment rate – even if we can discuss what is the meaning of the unemployment rate in different countries – we do have consistent data across countries, we do not have anything defensible in relation to the informal sector. So the question is given this fuzziness or this heterogeneity of the informal sector, how do we go about a definition and what are the implications for policy and research?

*F. Bourguignon*: This is something that is absolutely central to the whole debate. The other day I was trying to get some views about informality in several countries in the world, recent work which had been done on informality. Then I found this paper on China where the story was, basically, that most job creation in China was informal. The proportions, which we are given, were absolutely huge and I could not believe that it was the case that the informal sector was so big. Then I looked into the definition that was used. In the definition, it was essentially non-state-owned corporations and companies that are not publicly traded. So this gives you a definition of the formal sector that is extremely restrictive. Now it is the case in China that the initial situation was state-owned companies and no companies at all – the rest was completely informal. Then they moved into more and more private companies, which are incorporated, etc., but which are not necessarily publicly traded, which means that the definition of informality in all this work does not compare with the definition of informality in other countries: for example in Latin America where the definition is more based on the size of the production unit where people are being employed, with most of the self-employed is considered as people being informal and family work being considered as informal and then all the others.

Now there is always the problem with what is the threshold in terms of size. Is it two employees, five employees? What do we do with small retail stores that are completely formal but have a small number of employees? This field is extremely difficult. But I would say that, from that point of view, there may not be good ways of making international comparisons. What really matters I would say is simply the analysis of the evolution of informality within a country making or maintaining the definition of informality constant. So if you have labour force surveys, like you have in the case of Vietnam, and if those surveys are taken at regular points of time, then it is possible to follow the evolution of the informal sector. But it is quite essential that we have this kind of consistency in the way in which data are being collected. I remember that I started working a long time ago (twenty-five years ago or maybe more) on the informal sector in Columbia and I was using a labour force survey and then one day the Statistical Office decided not to ask any questions anymore about the size of companies.

So I was not able to continue my analysis to have the complete series of evolution of the informal sector in Columbia because of that. So it is quite important.

Now, there is a lot of debate about this. I know that – and, again, this is something you have in the Vietnam book – some people are considering whether there is a labour contract or not is the definition of informality, whether there are payments or contributions to social security is part of it. All this is debatable. I simply want to conclude this by mentioning one definition that we worked on with our colleague Martin Rama and my colleague when I was in the World Bank Stefano Scarpetta. We wrote a paper which was called "Good Jobs, Bad Jobs", where – I mean this is an old ILO story – but where we thought that the right and interesting concept was to look at it in terms of the earnings associated with the job and to consider that a good job was a job that the earnings which you would get would allow you, if you were living in a typical household, to get out of absolute poverty; and a bad job would be a job, the earnings of which would not allow you to do that. We thought that it was a nice way to look at formality–informality because you have bad jobs in the formal sector and good jobs in the informal sector but the correspondence is quite strong between formality–informality and good jobs–bad jobs. This is a concept that you can follow over time in a rather easy way and, if you want to get into international comparisons, it is possible to get international comparisons.

*Question*: So we have talked about economic facts, micro and macro behaviour and we have talked about definitions. Let's now go to policy because even if we don't know exactly what is the informal sector – there is some debate on the definition – I think that at least one point is clear that the jobs in this sector are precarious jobs. So we got the key issue of protection and social protection for the informal sector workers. In Vietnam, in particular, but many countries in the region have embarked on a programme of universal coverage protection scheme. The question here is probably we know how to do to protect people when they are wage workers, but what to do with the self-employed people which are the bulk of the informal sector? So my question is related to this. Vietnam will get a mandatory scheme for the wage workers and a voluntary scheme for the self-employed and it's not functioning at this first time very well. So what is your advice on this, your ideas, and do you have some examples of countries which have succeeded in this field?

*F. Bourguignon*: You're right that, at the end, this really is the important question. Is it possible to do something about this informality and is it possible to think of policies that would indeed reduce the precariousness of those jobs? I think this is a kind of paradoxical question, in the sense that if you think about policy which is addressing the issue of informality, at the same time you might be increasing informality: because for many people informality is a kind of natural reaction to imposing some regulations in the labour market, in the kind of relationship between an employer and an employee – even in the case where the employer and the employee are the same person – and because of that any change in the policy environment will have an impact on informality and formality. I must say that I don't know exactly the way in which this issue has to be raised in the case of Vietnam and Asian countries. I know a little better the case of Latin American countries, in particular the case of Mexico where this issue has really been at the centre of the public debate for quite some time. The debate has really been on what is explaining why. I mean: what explains why somebody would prefer to be informal than formal and the answer to that is because there are extra costs to being formal that are not paid by informal employees and because of that people would prefer to go to the informal sector. Now, what are those costs? The costs are, in the general, the contribution to social security, in particular for example to health insurance. So you cannot say really that this is a pure cost. When a formal worker is paying or the employer, which is more or less the same thing when there is no minimum wage legislation, when the formal employee is paying a contribution to get health insurance there is a benefit which corresponds to that contribution. So from that point of view you could say that if the health insurance system was completely neutral from an actuarial point of view – if everybody was paying exactly what is the expected cost of health care – then there would be no problem. This would be a completely neutral operation. Somebody is paying for an insurance and gets the health care when this person is getting sick. Now, there are two problems with that. One problem is that it may be the case that the payment is too high and in that case the cost is too high with respect to the benefit and therefore you are better off in the informal sector. Or it may be the case that the cost is much lower than the benefit, in which case many people would be attracted by formal employment but because the cost of labour for the employers will be high many people will not be accepted in the formal sector. So whatever the situation, any kind of disequilibrium between cost and benefit of protection insurance – the case of health insurance is probably the simpler case – is producing this informality whether it is voluntary informality or whether it is forced informality.

So if you think, to describe in those terms, what would be the solution? The solution probably is to offer health insurance to everybody, to make health insurance universal. To say from now on everybody will have access to health care. This will be publicly funded, as in many countries in the world. Let's take the case of the United Kingdom. For many decades this has been the case in the UK. This is funded by the tax collected by the state. This is universal and because of that one source of informality or one source of segregation of the labour market into formal–informal is disappearing. Now, if in the formal sector, employers want to offer their employees more, they can always take an additional insurance that will pay for or cover some risks that are not paid for by the universal system. So in other words if we believe and in some countries – I am not saying that this is the case in all countries – but in some countries the issue of all these fringe benefits which come with formal employment are the cause for this formality–informality distinction. If we believe that it is the major cause for that then probably the solution is to try to universalise as quickly as possible some basic services and if you do that to some extent the concept itself of informality might simply disappear. Then you are back to formality being more what is the kind of labour contract, what are the rules when a worker is being laid off, what is the compensation, etc. Informality will be at another level of the dimension of the employer–employee relationship, but it seems to me that at least in some countries one important cause will have been removed. But I am absolutely convinced that this is very country specific and I don't think it is a general recipe. But this means that at least this is a kind of issue that has to be looked at in order for policy to be able to address the issue of informality.

## Notes

1 The interview was conducted in April 2010 by Martin Rama (then World Bank, Hanoi), Jean-Pierre Cling, Mireille Razafindrakoto and François Roubaud through a video conference prepared for the "International conference on the informal sector and informal employment" organized in Hanoi, 6 and 7 May 2010 by the editors of this book. The interviewers wish to thank the World Bank teams in Hanoi and in Paris for organising the video conference. Special thanks to Nicolas Meyer (World Bank Institute, Paris).
2 Cling, J.-P., Nguyen Thi Thu Huyen, Nguyen Huu Chi, Phan Thi Ngoc Tram, Razafindrakoto M. and Roubaud F., 2010. *The Informal Sector in Vietnam: A Focus on Hanoi and Ho Chi Minh City*, Hanoi: The Gioi Publisher (also published in Vietnamese).

# Part I

# Sector allocation between formal and informal employment

# 1 Labor informality and poverty in Latin America

## The case of Argentina, Brazil, Chile and Peru

*Roxana Maurizio*

Latin America continues to be characterized by inequality and poverty. A highly precarious labor market in the context of a very limited social protection system lies behind this situation. In turn, the meager coverage of unemployment insurance compels individuals who do not have a job in the formal sector to quickly resort to other labor alternatives such as precarious jobs or own-account activities, since they are not able to undertake an extensive job search.

At the same time, given the lack of an extended social protection system, a strong link between the individuals' labor situation and the poverty situation of the households they belong to is verified. In fact, poor labor insertion – in terms of the amount of working hours and the quality of the job – constitutes the "working poor" phenomenon that prevails in Latin American countries suggesting that having a job is no reassurance against poverty.

Hence, in a region with a high incidence of informality and poverty, it is relevant to analyze how these phenomena relate to each other. This chapter aims at analyzing two aspects associated with informality from a comparative point of view. The first one is the association between informality and income segmentation. The second one is the relationship between informality and poverty and, especially, the direct and indirect mechanisms through which this association is verified.

Four Latin American countries, whose labor informality is significantly different from each other in its size and characteristics, were selected. On the one hand, Argentina and Chile whose informal sectors are relatively small in the Latin American context; on the other hand, Brazil and Peru, where the opposite is verified. Data used in this chapter come from household surveys with the most recent available information.

The first section of this chapter follows with a review of different conceptual frameworks on informality and income segmentation. The second section details the alternative criteria for measuring informality as well as the estimation methods used. The third section describes the sources of information. The fourth section presents an initial outlook on informality incidence and its characteristics in the countries selected. The two following sections show the econometric results: in the fifth section those related to the existence of labor income gaps associated with informality; in the sixth section those related to the independent impact of the latter on poverty incidence. Finally, the seventh section concludes.

## Informality, income segmentation and poverty: some theoretical issues

### Employment in the informal sector and informal employment

Labor informality is one of the categories of analysis that has greatly contributed to the characterization of labor conditions in Latin America. There are at least two different approaches to informality.

The concept of informal sector (IS) emerged in the early 1970s, in the International Labour Organisation's documents for African countries (ILO, 1972). It was then developed in Latin America by the Regional Employment Program for Latin America and the Caribbean (PREALC for its acronym in Spanish), with the objective of explaining the growth of wide sectors of the population that were not able to participate in the processes of productive modernization through a formal labor market. Under this "productive approach", informality reflects the inability of these economies to generate sufficient employment in the formal sector in comparison to the growth of the labor force. The IS is usually associated with small productive units with low levels of productivity and where the aim is survival more than accumulation. Jobs generated in this sector constitute employment in the informal sector (EIS).

Along with this conceptualization based on a "productive approach", informal employment (IE) is another concept that has developed in more recent years. Based on a "legal approach", informal employment refers to a different dimension of informality because it focuses directly on job conditions. In particular, this approach associates informality with the evasion of labor regulations, defining informal employment as that of workers not covered by labor legislation.

In this chapter both the "productive approach" and the "legal approach" will be considered so as to identify the distinctive characteristics of each dimension and the interrelation between them. Table 1.1 details the classification of workers taking both approaches into account.

*Table 1.1* Classification of workers according to the "productive" and "legal" approach of informality

|  | *Formal employment (FE)* | *Informal employment (IE)* |
|---|---|---|
| Employment in the formal sector (EFS) | • Formal wage earners (registered wage earners) in the formal sector (FS)<br>• Formal non-wage earners | • Informal wage earners (non-registered wage earners) in the formal sector (FS) |
| Employment in the informal sector (EIS) | • Formal wage earners (registered wage earners) in the informal sector (IS) | • Informal wage earners (non-registered wage earners) in the informal sector (IS)<br>• Informal non-wage earners – unpaid family workers |

## *Informality and income segmentation*

The concept of income segmentation is used here to refer to labor income differentials that are not explained by the workers' individual attributes: that is to say, income gaps associated with certain characteristics of the job. In particular, this chapter evaluates whether two workers with equal personal attributes obtain different remunerations because one works in the formal sector (FS) and the other in the informal sector (IS). The same way of reasoning is applied to labor income differentials between informal employment (IE) and formal employment (FE).

Informality defined according to any of the two approaches – productive and legal – is consistent with both situations with and without income segmentation. In the latter case, for example, under the "productive approach" it could be argued that were there no restrictions, the excess of labor that cannot enter the formal sector and thus goes to the informal sector with its lower levels of productivity, would cause a global fall in wages, both in the formal and informal sectors. In the "legal approach", informality without segmentation could take place if formal and informal wage earners ended up receiving equal net remunerations even when in the second case the employers face additional costs related to labor regulations.

On the contrary, there are other arguments that account for the existence of income segmentation associated with informality even when there are no restrictions on labor mobility or other restrictions generated by labor institutions. One of them states that small firms – typical of the informal sector – usually operate with lower productivity levels, and therefore pay lower average remunerations. Likewise, the non-fulfillment of tax obligations could make the firms work with lower levels of efficiency and productivity, which would once again result in lower wages for informal workers than those obtained by formal workers (Beccaria and Groisman, 2008). However, the mere existence of productivity differentials is not sufficient to produce wage segmentation. Therefore, it is necessary to explain why the equalizing forces of the market do not operate and why some companies – those of higher productivity – pay higher wages than the rest of the firms.

One hypothesis is based on the Efficiency Wages theory, which states that employers may decide to pay wages above the market reference as an instrument to reduce labor turnover, or to encourage higher work efforts. Income segmentation could arise if firms in the formal sector use this mechanism more often than firms in the informal sector. At the same time, the existence of internal labor markets within the firms of the formal sector can isolate workers from external competition, especially the more educated workers, thus creating a wage gap with informal workers.

In addition, under the "legal approach", it could be said that the fulfillment of labor norms not only affects total labor costs but also the net wages paid to workers. The impact of minimum wages, collective bargaining and unions on wage structure are examples of the latter. Therefore, an additional source of wage segmentation may be the fact that certain workers are protected by labor legislation or unions while others with equal attributes are not.

Lastly, if the two approaches overlap and the non-fulfillment of labor legislation is greater in informal firms, the mentioned factors will complement each other to explain the presence of segmentation. For example, one worker with certain personal attributes working in a small firm could get a lower wage than another worker with equal characteristics working in a larger firm, both due to lower productivity levels and because the small firm faces, in general, less union pressure or does not abide by labor institutions, such as the minimum wage.

On the workers' side, an important condition for these results to manifest is the presence of a deficit in the creation of formal jobs or within the formal sector, which makes them accept lower remunerations or more precarious working conditions. This behavior is, in turn, encouraged by the lack or weakness of social protection mechanisms. To a greater or lesser extent, this is the case of Latin American countries.

### Informality and poverty

It is possible to identify a relationship between informality and poverty that may or may not be mediated by segmentation. In the former case, as long as segmentation implies that certain workers are not able to obtain sufficient remuneration to meet the needs of the households they belong to, informality will constitute an independent factor related to the households' poverty situation.

The case without segmentation associated with informality may occur when the situation of poverty is a result of workers not being able to obtain sufficient remunerations in any of the two circumstances, formality and informality, due to some personal characteristics. But, if these characteristics are more frequent in informal than in formal workers (or in the IS than FS), then this different composition of employment would mean that informal sector workers (EIS) would obtain, on average, lower remunerations than formal sector workers (EFS) and would thus face a higher probability of falling into poverty.

By taking all these different arguments into account, this chapter aims at evaluating the presence of possible associations between informality, segmentation and poverty in four Latin American countries.

## Approach and methodology

### Measurement of informality

The ILO's 15th and 17th International Conference of Labour Statistics (ICLS) have established the classification criteria for formal and informal workers. According to the "productive approach", the EIS is defined as the group of workers employed in small productive units that are not legally registered as firms, use a reduced amount of capital and make limited use of technology.

However, given that household surveys do not inquire in depth into the characteristics of the firms, the ILO suggests adopting a measurement criterion based on the combination of occupational categories, occupation groups defined according to job qualifications and the size of the firm. In this way, it is possible to identify the two major components of the IS: (1) family units comprising own-account workers and family workers; and (2) microenterprises made up of employers and wage-earners in establishments of fewer than five employees. In the case of independent workers, only those with no professional skills are considered as part of the IS, as an operational way to leave only independent workers with low productivity in this sector. Finally, the public sector is excluded from the IS.

On the other hand, as mentioned, IE is defined as the occupational group for which labor regulations are not fulfilled: non-registered wage earners, and own-account workers and employers that do not fulfill their tax obligations.

Also on the ILO's recommendation, given the lack of enough information from household surveys, in the case of independent workers, their formal/informal character is directly determined by the characteristics of their enterprises: informal own-account and employers are those working in enterprises of the IS. Therefore, the classification of workers according to whether they belong to the IS or the FS being, simultaneously, part of the EIS or the EFS is more interesting in the case of wage earners given that for non-wage earners both classifications coincide. Finally, unpaid family workers are considered simultaneously as a part of IE and of the EIS.

### *The absolute poverty line approach to poverty identification*

The absolute poverty line approach to identify poverty is used in this chapter following each country's official methodology, with the exception of Peru. Specifically, a household is classified as poor if its total monetary income – as measured in the household survey – is below an absolute poverty line that takes the household's size and composition into account.[1] In Peru, instead, official poverty is calculated based on the comparison between the poverty line and the total expenditures of the household. In this case, in order to apply the methodology explained below, a new household poverty status comparing total income with the poverty line was built.

### *Methodology*

The analysis conducted in this chapter is structured in two major parts. In the first one, the objective is to estimate income gaps associated with informality. Under the hypothesis of segmentation related to informality, workers in the IS and/or informal workers should be getting lower wages than workers with similar personal characteristics working in the FS or as formal workers, respectively. In the second part of the analysis, the aim is to evaluate to what extent the income segmentation associated with informality is an independent factor related to poverty.

To do this, several parametric and non-parametric methods were performed in order to give greater robustness to the results. Each of these methods is described in detail below.

*Income gap, informality and segmentation*

1   First, average wage gaps between informal sector (EIS) and formal sector (EFS) are estimated by using Mincer Equations by OLS regression. This is the most common approach when analyzing the effect of one independent variable on labor income, while controlling for the rest of the covariates. In the case that matters in this study, the coefficient of the variable that identifies informality quantifies its independent impact on wage determination. The estimates are corrected for the sample selection bias using the Heckman Two Step Estimator.

2   OLS estimates the effects of the covariates only at the central part of the conditional distribution. However, it is relevant to identify the impact of the covariates along the entire conditional distribution of income. To do that, the Quantile Regression Model (QR)[2] is applied from which it is possible to evaluate whether wage gaps remain constant, grow or decrease along the conditional distribution.

3   From the estimates of wage equations, the Oaxaca-Blinder Decomposition Method allows the decomposition of average income gaps between formal and informal workers (or of the FS and IS) into three effects: the "Endowments effect", which is the part of the differential derived from the differences in the vector of characteristics of each group; the "Coefficient effect", which corresponds to the differences in the returns to those attributes; and the "Interaction effect". The segmentation hypothesis is verified if the second effect is statistically significant and positive, thus indicating that, given equal attributes, a formal worker (or worker of the FS) gets a higher wage than an informal worker (or worker of the IS). These estimates are also corrected by the sample selection bias.

4   Finally, the Matching Estimator Method is used as a non-parametric way to estimate the impact of informality on labor income. The parameter of interest is the Average Treatment effect on the Treated (ATT), which is defined as:

$$\theta_{ATT} = E(\tau \mid D = 1) = E[Y(1) \mid D = 1] - E[Y(0) \mid D = 1] \quad (1.1)$$

where $E[Y(1)|D=1]$ is the expected value for the treated group given that it was under treatment, and $E[Y(0)|D=1]$ is the expected value for the treated group had it not been treated.

Given that this counterfactual situation is not observed, it is necessary to resort to an alternative method in order to estimate the ATT. The most accurate way to identify what would have happened to the group under treatment had it not been treated, is by considering the situation of the non-treated individuals with equal (or similar) characteristics (control group). One of the methods used to build the control group is the Propensity Score Matching Estimator,[3] in which the propensity score of participation for the whole sample is estimated and the individuals of the treated group and the control group with similar scores are matched. In the case we are analyzing, the IE (and the EIS) is considered as being the treated group, whereas the FE (and the EFS) is the control group.

There are different ways to determine which individuals in the control group will be the counterpart of the group under treatment. One of them, which is used here, is the Kernel Estimator in which the outcome of the treated individual is associated with a matched outcome given by a kernel-weighted average of the outcome of all non-treated individuals. The ATT is estimated as follows:

$$ATT = \frac{1}{N_n} \sum_{i \in n} \left( w_i - \sum_{j \in f} \kappa_{ij} w_j \right) \tag{1.2}$$

where $w_i$ and $w_j$ indicate the wage of each formal and informal worker, respectively, $\kappa_{ij}$ is the Kernel and $N_n$ is the quantity of informal workers.

*Informality and poverty*

As mentioned, one of the objectives of this study is to evaluate to what extent the income segmentation associated with informality is a relevant factor to explain the poverty situation of households.

Hence, after estimating the wage gaps associated with informality, the independent impact of informality on poverty is computed. In order to do so, micro-simulation exercises that simulate what poverty rate would result if the IE received the same remuneration as the formal workers (or if the EIS were paid as the EFS) were performed. A counterfactual total family income is calculated by multiplying the actual monthly remuneration of informal workers by the value of the ratio between the estimated income of a formal worker and that of an informal worker with equal attributes.[4] It is assumed that the rest of the family incomes remain constant. Finally, the counterfactual total family income is compared to the poverty line value in order to estimate what the poverty would be in the absence of segmentation due to informality.

**Source of information**

Data used in this chapter come from the regular household surveys of each country considered. For each case, the most recent microdata base available at the time of writing was used.

* Argentina: *Encuesta Permanente de Hogares* (EPH), second semester 2006.
* Brazil: *Pesquisa Nacional por Amostra de Domicilios* (PNAD), 2006.
* Chile: *Encuesta de Caracterización Socioeconómica Nacional* (CASEN), 2006.
* Peru: *Encuesta Nacional de Hogares sobre Condiciones de Vida y Pobreza* (ENAHO), 2007.

As mentioned before, non-registered employees are those wage earners not covered by labor legislation. The empirical identification of the wage earners' registration condition in each of these countries was based on the availability of information derived from these databases. In Argentina, a wage earner is considered as registered in the social security system if his/her employer pays social security contributions. In Chile and Brazil, a wage earner is considered as registered if he/she has signed a labor contract. In Peru, registered workers are those who are affiliated to a pension system.

Given the strong heterogeneity between urban and rural labor markets and due to the fact that the Argentine household survey only covers urban areas, this chapter will concentrate only on this zone.

## An overview of informality in four Latin American countries

The aim of this section is to present a general outlook of the importance and characteristics of IE and EIS in each of the four countries under study. Table 1.2 shows that employment in the informal sector and informal employment represent more than one-third of total workers in these countries. Peru is placed in one extreme, where EIS (including domestic workers) represents 56 percent of the employed workforce whereas IE (including informal domestic workers) reaches 67 percent of total workers. On the other extreme, in Chile these figures fall to 35 and 38 percent respectively.

In all cases IE is higher than EIS. If domestic service is excluded, the reduction of the relative importance of EIS is bigger in Argentina – due to the higher proportion of these activities in total employment – than in other countries. The difference between Argentina–Chile on one side and Brazil–Peru on the other becomes, thus, more evident.

*Table 1.2* Share of informality in the urban labor market, 2006/2007

| Categories | Argentina | Peru | Brazil | Chile |
|---|---|---|---|---|
| Formal non-wage earners | 4.4 | 5.6 | 2.8 | 3.7 |
| Informal non-wage earners | 21.6 | 31.1 | 22.6 | 20.6 |
| Formal wage earners in FS | 38.4 | 24.8 | 36.2 | 51.8 |
| Informal wage earners in FS | 10.4 | 13.5 | 10.3 | 9.1 |
| Formal wage earners in IS | 3.8 | 2.2 | 5.6 | 4.0 |
| Informal wage earners in IS | 10.6 | 10.7 | 8.7 | 3.8 |
| Formal domestic service | 0.8 | 0.6 | 2.5 | 2.3 |
| Informal domestic service | 8.7 | 5.0 | 6.4 | 3.9 |
| Unpaid familiar workers | 1.3 | 6.4 | 4.9 | 0.9 |
| Total employment | 100 | 100 | 100 | 100 |
| Employment in the IS (includes domestic services) | 46.8 | 56.1 | 50.6 | 35.4 |
| Employment in the IS (excludes domestic services) | 37.3 | 50.5 | 41.8 | 29.3 |
| Informal employment (includes informal domestic services) | 52.6 | 66.8 | 52.9 | 38.3 |
| % Informal wage-earners in the total wage earners | 40.8 | 51.5 | 36.5 | 22.4 |

Sources: author's calculations based on data from Household Surveys.

Different categories that arise from the double classification of informality also indicate important discrepancies among countries. For example, the larger participation of informal non-wage earners stands out in Peru, where they represent approximately one-third of total employment. In Chile half of the total workers are formal wage earners of the formal sector, while that figure diminishes to around 40 percent in Argentina and Brazil (although they still represent the majority) and to 25 percent in Peru. In all countries the most important groups are informal non-wage earners (due to the importance of independent workers) and formal wage earners of the formal sector. Formal wage earners in the informal sector and formal non-wage earners are of little importance in all cases.

Nevertheless, beyond these differences, this general overview shows the importance that the informal sector, informal employment and wage earners not registered in the social security system have in the occupational structure in all countries analyzed.

As for the composition of informality in terms of different attributes, some common patterns arise (annex: Table 1.A.1). In all cases a very high proportion of workers who have not finished secondary school is observed among informal workers (for example, it reaches 69 percent in Brazil). The incidence of low skilled workers in the informal sector is even higher. The opposite situation is verified among formal workers and workers of the formal sector. A similar scenario arises if the analysis is restricted to the group of wage earners. For example, in Brazil workers without a secondary education represent almost 70 percent of total non-registered wage earners (40 percent among registered) while that figure drops to 4 percent for workers with a university degree (16 percent of registered wage earners).

Women have a higher proportion in informality than in total occupation. This is particularly evident for the case of Peru, where while they concentrate almost one-half of IE and EIS, their share decreases to 37/39 percent of FE and EFS, respectively. In Argentina and Brazil, although the general bias of women to informality is also observed, differences in the distribution of IE and EIS between men and women are less important than in the two remaining countries. If the analysis is restricted to wage earners, the differences in occupational insertion according to sex widen. However, given the strong predominance of men in the labor markets in these countries, they are the majority in informality in almost all cases, even though their specific informality rate is lower than that of women (annex: Table 1.A.1).

It is also observed that the share of young workers and the elderly is higher in IE and EIS (except for the case of the elderly in Peru) than in total employment. In the case of young workers these findings intensify among wage earners, since their share in non-registered jobs more than doubles that corresponding to jobs registered in the social security system. On the contrary, this divergence decreases if the composition of the formal and the informal sectors is observed. The opposite occurs with the elderly, where the differences in favor of the informal sector are clearly higher than those observed between FE and IE. This is in part explained by the higher incidence of independent workers among adult workers (annex: Table 1.A.1).

Additionally, the importance of IE and EIS varies across industries. In general, informality has a higher relative incidence in commercial activities, construction and domestic service, while the opposite is verified in the case of manufacturing, the public sector, financial services and – to a lesser extent – personal services. A similar picture arises among wage earners, where the former three industries concentrate more than 60 percent of informal activities in Argentina and Brazil or around 50 percent in Peru and Chile (annex: Table 1.A.1).

It is also relevant to point out the close correlation between being a non-registered wage earner and a worker in the informal sector (Table 1.3). Approximately 45 percent of the total non-registered wage earners work in the informal sector in Chile and Peru whereas this figure increases to 65 and 68 percent in Argentina and Brazil, respectively. On the other hand, more than half of wage earners in the informal sector in Chile are not registered in the social security system reaching almost 90 percent in Peru. This suggests the precarious character of the jobs generated in the informal sector where, probably, the combination of low productivity and non-fulfillment of labor regulation derive in low wages.

Finally, there is a positive correlation between informality and poverty. The incidence of poverty among workers in informal jobs or the informal sector is between two and five times higher that observed among formal workers. This leads to the fact that, for example, around one-third of informal workers are poor

*Table 1.3* Employment in the informal sector and non-registered wage earners

| | Argentina | | | Peru | | |
|---|---|---|---|---|---|---|
| | Registered | Non-registered | Total | Registered | Non-registered | Total |
| Formal sector | 78.7 | 21.3 | 100 | 58.3 | 41.7 | 100 |
| | 89.3 | 35.2 | 67.2 | 92.0 | 53.6 | 70.8 |
| Informal sector | 19.4 | 80.6 | 100 | 12.3 | 87.7 | 100 |
| | 10.7 | 64.8 | 32.8 | 8.0 | 46.4 | 29.2 |
| Total | 100 | 100 | 100 | 100 | 100 | 100 |
| | Brazil | | | Chile | | |
| | Registered | Non-registered | Total | Registered | Non-registered | Total |
| Formal sector | 85.1 | 14.9 | 100 | 84.4 | 15.6 | 100 |
| | 82.6 | 31.9 | 66.8 | 88.4 | 54.4 | 80.5 |
| Informal sector | 36.0 | 64.0 | 100 | 45.9 | 54.1 | 100 |
| | 17.4 | 68.1 | 33.2 | 11.7 | 45.6 | 19.5 |
| Total | 100 | 100 | 100 | 100 | 100 | 100 |

Sources: author's calculations based on data from Household Surveys.

in Argentina and Brazil, while only 5 and 10 percent of formal workers are in that situation, respectively (annex: Table 1.A.1).

Therefore, the results presented in this section allow us to conclude that informal workers (also workers in the informal sector and non-registered wage earners) have – on average – a lower educational level than the formal workers, they show a higher presence of young people and women, and are more frequent than formal workers in commercial activities, construction and domestic service.[5] This differential structure suggests a priori that *informals*[6] will have lower average incomes than *formals* because these workers have a vector of personal characteristics that are usually less remunerated; that is to say, there is a "composition effect" against *informals*. The next section analyzes to what extent the wage gaps are explained, also, by differences in the returns obtained by *formals* and *informals* for each of the considered characteristics.

## Empirical evidence about informality and income segmentation

The results obtained from the parametric and non-parametric methods are presented in this section. In particular, Table 1.4 shows the income gaps obtained from OLS method for all workers. These figures correspond to the dummy variables that identify informality – IE and EIS – in the income equations. The dependent variable is, alternatively, the log of monthly or hourly incomes. The complete regressions are shown in the annex (Table 1.A.2).

A statistically significant "penalty" due to informality is verified in the four countries, both for being an informal worker (IE) and for being employed in the

*Table 1.4* Labor income gaps; Mincer equations by OLS

|  | Argentina | Peru | Brazil | Chile |
|---|---|---|---|---|
| *IE/FE* | | | | |
| Monthly wages | −0.655*** | −0.324*** | −0.245*** | −0.103*** |
|  | [0.00733] | [0.0181] | [0.00374] | [0.00465] |
| Hourly wages | −0.517*** | −0.258*** | −0.200*** | −0.0140*** |
|  | [0.00676] | [0.0177] | [0.00382] | [0.00468] |
| *EIS/EFS* | | | | |
| Monthly wages | −0.486*** | −0.390*** | −0.179*** | −0.0109** |
|  | [0.00798] | [0.0175] | [0.00405] | [0.00479] |
| Hourly wages | −0.387*** | −0.298*** | −0.135*** | 0.0724*** |
|  | [0.00725] | [0.0171] | [0.00413] | [0.00480] |

Sources: author's calculations based on data from Household Surveys.

Notes
Standard errors in brackets.
*** $p < 0.01$.
** $p < 0.05$.
* $p < 0.1$.

informal sector (EIS). The gaps are wider between monthly incomes than between hourly incomes. This indicates that informal workers obtain lower remunerations not only because of a lower income per hour, but also because they work fewer hours. Beyond this general picture, the magnitude of the gap is clearly different across countries. Specifically, the gap of monthly labor income between IE and FE is near 66 percent in Argentina, 32 percent in Peru, 25 percent in Brazil and 10 percent in Chile.

The labor income gaps are also statistically significant if the comparison is made between workers of the informal and the formal sectors. However, except for Peru, a narrower gap is observed in this case, indicating that informality measured through the labor relationship (IE) seems to be more important than informality measured through the "productive approach" (EIS). In this case, the "penalty" of monthly labor income is 48 percent in Argentina, 39 percent in Peru, 18 percent in Brazil and 1 percent in Chile. In the latter case, the gap between EIS and EFS seems to arise only because of the difference in the working hours because for the hourly income the gap reverts its sign.

As has been mentioned before, OLS estimates the effects of the covariates only in the center of the conditional distribution. For this reason it is of interest to know, additionally, the impact of the covariates along the whole conditional income distribution. To do that, QR are applied both to monthly and hourly labor incomes. The results shown in the annex (Table 1.A.3)[7] suggest that the gap associated with informality is not constant through income distribution but it is wider in the lower extreme.[8] In particular, in Chile and Brazil the difference reverses at the top of the conditional distribution. This result is verified both for monthly and for hourly incomes.

Very interesting findings arise from the decomposition of the differences of monthly incomes obtained applying the Oaxaca-Blinder procedure for both approaches of informality (Table 1.5).

First, in all cases the total difference of mean incomes is significantly larger than that found using OLS and QR. Second, when this difference is decomposed in the three above-mentioned components, in all cases the "Coefficient effect" is statistically significant and negative. Therefore, the segmentation hypothesis is verified again thus indicating that, given equal attributes, an informal worker (or a worker in the informal sector) gets a lower wage than a similar formal worker (or a worker in the formal sector). However, in all cases (with the exception of Chile when comparing the FS and the IS) the wage gap seems to be smaller than that obtained through the value of the dummy for informality in the OLS regressions.

Third, the "Endowments effect" also proves to be significant and negative. This effect is, in most cases, the factor explaining the highest proportion of the income gap. This reflects the fact that formal workers (workers in the formal sector) have a vector of characteristics that is more favorable than that of informal workers (workers in the informal sector), as described in the previous section. Specifically, it has been shown that *formals* have more human capital and a lower proportion of women – who are usually discriminated in the labor market and thus receive lower wages than men with similar attributes. Thus,

Table 1.5 Oaxaca-Blinder decomposition

| | Monthly income | | | | | | | |
| --- | --- | --- | --- | --- | --- | --- | --- | --- |
| | Argentina | | Peru | | Brazil | | Chile | |
| | IE/FE | EIS/EFS | IE/FE | EIS/EFS | IE/FE | EIS/EFS | IE/FE | EIS/EFS |
| Difference | −1.019*** [0.00765] | −0.848*** [0.00829] | −0.900*** [0.0151] | −0.855*** [0.0151] | −0.476*** [0.00440] | −0.678*** [0.00451] | −0.350*** [0.00562] | −0.262*** [0.00542] |
| Endowments | −0.335*** [0.00683] | −0.322*** [0.0335] | −0.417*** [0.0186] | −0.480*** [0.0377] | −0.207*** [0.00344] | −0.367*** [0.00405] | −0.229*** [0.00324] | −0.214*** [0.00352] |
| Coefficients | −0.544*** [0.0125] | −0.296*** [0.0516] | −0.279*** [0.0222] | −0.313 [0.306] | −0.162*** [0.00411] | −0.160*** [0.0351] | −0.100*** [0.00611] | −0.0643*** [0.00575] |
| Interaction | −0.140*** [0.0123] | −0.230*** [0.0610] | −0.204*** [0.0253] | −0.0627 [0.308] | −0.106*** [0.00375] | −0.151*** [0.0351] | −0.0207*** [0.00467] | 0.0163*** [0.00435] |

Sources: author's calculations based on data from Household Surveys.

Notes
Standard errors in brackets.
*** $p < 0.01$.
** $p < 0.05$.
* $p < 0.1$.

total labor income gaps between *formals* and *informals* are explained not only because the former have a more favorable endowment vector, but also because the returns to their attributes are higher than those of *informals*.

Finally, the non-parametric estimates based on the Matching Estimator Method (Table 1.6) are consistent with previous results and confirm again the existence of a "penalty" for informality. Specifically, the value of the ATT is significant and negative in all cases, even when the magnitude of the differences tends to be larger than those found with the previous methods.

Also, in line with previous results, income gaps seem to be more intense in Argentina and Peru than in Brazil and Chile. This is an important result because it does not seem to be completely related to the size of informality. In particular, even if it is possible to think that the wider wage gap in Peru and the lower wage gap in Chile would be accounting for a direct relationship between the relative weight of informality and the magnitude of the wage gap, this does not seem to be the case in Argentina and Brazil where the share of the informal sector is very similar in both countries but the penalty is significantly higher in the former than in the latter case.

Up to this point the gaps have been estimated for informality defined by the two approaches (informal sector and informal employment). However, it might be the case that both dimensions combine in the determination of labor incomes, which would make identification of the independent effect of each of them difficult. For example, the "penalty" suffered by informal workers might be due to the fact that a large proportion of them work in the informal sector, as shown previously. In that case, low productivity – and not the labor relationship – might be the factor that determines the lower wages. It could also be that workers in the formal sector earn higher wages because there is a higher proportion of formal workers in this sector. This, in turn, could be a consequence of certain labor regulations as, for example, legal minimum wages or collective bargaining, which are less likely to be observed in the case of informal workers.

*Table 1.6* Matching Estimator Method

|  | Monthly income | | | |
|  | Argentina | Peru | Brazil | Chile |
| --- | --- | --- | --- | --- |
| Informal employment | −0.759*** | −0.666*** | −0.416*** | −0.147*** |
|  | [0.00819] | [0.00968] | [0.000713] | [0.00326] |
| Informal sector | −0.287*** | −0.560*** | −0.301*** | −0.0296*** |
|  | [0.0414] | [0.00809] | [0.00225] | [0.000947] |

Sources: author's calculations based on data from Household Surveys.

Notes
Standard errors in brackets.
*** $p<0.01$.
** $p<0.05$.
* $p<0.1$.

In order to measure the independent effect of each dimension, OLS regressions have been performed for monthly incomes, but this time incorporating all categories arising from the combination of both approaches. The baseline group is comprises formal workers in the formal sector. As shown in Table 1.7, in Argentina all categories suffer a "penalty" in relation to those workers. It is also possible to observe that the labor relationship is more relevant than the sector in the labor income differentials.

Chile and Brazil show similar results. In those countries the gaps are also wider between formal and informal workers than between workers in the formal and the informal sectors. Anyhow, and consistently with previous results, the gaps are not as wide as in Argentina. Moreover, informal non-wage earners in Chile have higher incomes than the baseline group. Likewise, both in Chile and Brazil formal non-wage earners obtain the highest remunerations.

As in Argentina, formal workers in the formal sector in Peru obtain the highest wages. However, in the case of wage earners the sector (formal/informal) seems to be more important than the labor relationship. Finally, in all cases both dimensions combine in such a way to produce larger income differences than those corresponding to each dimension separately, with the group of informal workers in the IS obtaining the lowest incomes (when controlling for all remaining characteristics).

Therefore, the different estimates (parametric and non-parametric) point to the existence of significant income gaps in favor of formality that are not explained by differences in the observed attributes of workers. This brings us to the conclusion that there is income segmentation associated with informality in the four countries analyzed.

The question arising is which factors explain the differences in the magnitude of the income gap across countries and, especially, the wage gap among wage earners (registered and non-registered) in the FS. One hypothesis might relate these results to the role of labor institutions such as, minimum wage, collective bargaining or unions. Specifically, the difference between registered and

*Table 1.7* Labor income gaps between categories; Mincer equations by OLS – monthly income

| Categories | Argentina | Peru | Brazil | Chile |
|---|---|---|---|---|
| Formal non-wage earners | −0.2161*** | −0.6887*** | 0.3246*** | 0.6556*** |
| Informal non-wage earners | −0.7271*** | −0.6095*** | −0.1422*** | 0.2271*** |
| Informal wage earners in FS | −0.5730*** | −0.2969*** | −0.2016*** | −0.2754*** |
| Formal wage earners in IS | −0.2233*** | −0.5177*** | −0.1021*** | −0.146*** |
| Informal wage earners in IS | −0.8012*** | −0.6703*** | −0.4172*** | −0.5081*** |

Sources: author's calculations based on data from Household Surveys.

Notes
Standard errors in brackets.
*** $p<0.01$.
** $p<0.05$.
* $p<0.1$.

non-registered wage earners could positively depend on how "binding" these labor institutions are. As long as the minimum wage is relatively high in comparison with average wages or the bargaining power of unions is high, it could generate a wider wage gap between workers who are subject or not to these labor institutions.

Additionally, these results might be affected by variables that are not observable and, thus, not included in the estimates. For example, other non-monetary advantages that compensate the lower wages of informality might exist, which make these jobs more attractive to certain individuals. But, given that a close link seems to exist between informality and poverty (as has been shown in the previous section and will be verified in the following), the arguments suggesting that informality is a voluntary choice of workers is not likely to apply to all workers in the region. On the contrary, the high levels of unemployment and labor precariousness experienced by these countries suggest that the insertion in informality could be the only choice for a big group of people.

## Informality and poverty

With the aim of evaluating the independent impact of informality on poverty incidence, microsimulation exercises have been carried out. These exercises allow us to estimate a counterfactual household income that would result if family members who work as *informals* worked as *formals* (considering the two approaches of informality).

As shown in Table 1.8, in all cases the "formalization" of informal workers would imply a reduction of poverty rates. However, the size of this reduction differs across countries. The dissimilar results are related, at least in part, to the different magnitudes of the income gap between *formals* and *informals*. For example, in Argentina and Peru, where the income gap is wider, the reduction of poverty in individuals due to the formalization of workers is also larger; in Argentina this reduction is about 34 percent. In Peru, the decrease in poverty is

*Table 1.8* Microsimulation of the reduction of poverty associated with formalization of workers

|  | Argentina | Peru | Brazil | Chile |
|---|---|---|---|---|
| Initial poverty rate | 26.85 | 34.68 | 29.96 | 13.7 |
| Initial poverty gap | 0.4171 | 0.3792 | 0.4249 | 0.3179 |
| *Counterfactual* |  |  |  |  |
| FE/IE | 17.81 | 24.44 | 26.35 | 13.12 |
| EFS/EIS | 22.59 | 20.69 | 26.32 | 13.61 |
| *Reduction* |  |  |  |  |
| FE/IE | −34% | −30% | −12% | −4% |
| EFS/EIS | −16% | −40% | −12% | −1% |

Sources: author's calculations based on data from Household Surveys.

also significant, around 30 percent of the initial rate. But given the fact that in these countries the initial incidence of poverty is very high, even if all workers were formal the percentage of poor people would remain high. The low impact of "formalization" in Chile was, in part, expected given the fact that the informality gap is narrower. Finally, in Brazil the reduction is also important but clearly lower than in Peru and Argentina.

In Table 1.8 the poverty gap was also included given that it is likely to be another important factor, since the probability of exiting poverty depends not only on the absolute increase in the total family income after "formalization", but also on the initial distance to the poverty line. Brazil is the country with the higher poverty gap, which contributes, additionally, to the lower impact of "formalization".

The fact that in some countries a high poverty incidence persists even when eliminating informality suggests that other factors also have an important influence on poverty. High unemployment and underemployment, the low educational levels deriving in insufficient incomes even for formal workers (or workers in the formal sector), and the high dependency rates are factors probably associated with poverty as well. Additionally, the low average labor income goes hand in hand with high income inequality which also contributes to increased levels of poverty.

Lastly, it is important to mention that these microsimulations should be interpreted as analytical exercises while the results should be interpreted as indicators of the relevance of informality in the incidence of poverty because they do not show what would really happen in the absence of informality. The *ceteris paribus* assumption behind these partial equilibrium exercises does not account for the fact that an important reduction of informality would surely be accompanied by other changes in the labor market – for example in the unemployment rate or in the average wages – that could also have an important impact on poverty levels.

## Final remarks

The aim of this chapter was to analyze the links between informality, income segmentation and poverty from a comparative perspective in four Latin American countries: Argentina, Brazil, Chile and Peru.

The results suggest that informality is a very important phenomenon in the four countries, even when its relevance is not the same in all cases. The share of non-registered wage earners is also significant in all cases, even in Chile where it represents about 22 percent of the total wage earners. In the rest of the countries this figure reaches 40–50 percent. This suggests a very high level of labor precariousness given that the lack of registration in the social security system does not only imply lower wages than the rest of wage earners but the lack of other social benefits, like health insurance or future pensions.

Informality proved to be an independent source of lower incomes, even if controlled by an extended vector of personal and job characteristics, indicating the presence of income segmentation. Additionally, a positive relationship between informality and poverty was proved. Nevertheless, it has also been shown that the elimination of informality does not allow the eradication of poverty, suggesting the presence of other factors that affect it. The high incidence of unemployment and low educational levels deriving in insufficient incomes even for formal workers (or workers in the formal sector), together with a very unequal income distribution, are also factors associated with poverty.

Therefore, these results suggest the need to carry out different public policies in order to reduce inequality and poverty, both through labor market policies and others of more universal character. A central issue is to reduce the share of informal and precarious employment. It implies acting both at the supply and at the demand side of the problem: i.e., stimulating the creation of formal jobs suitable for those workers and assisting them in increasing their chances of getting these kinds of jobs (through training and/or better employment services, for example). The level of wages also has to be considered as an objective when trying to reduce poverty, as being employed does not always ensure leaving poverty, especially due to the high incidence of informal occupations.

On the other hand, the scope and coverage of unemployment insurance in Latin America has historically been limited. Even in those few countries that do have these kinds of programs, coverage rates among the unemployed are very low. Therefore, it is essential to extend some kind of unemployment assistance to those leaving non-regular jobs. However, even if extended benefits to the unemployed are implemented, households with low and unstable labor incomes will still be facing difficulties. Therefore, and in parallel with other policies, it is necessary for these countries to reinforce cash transfer programs aimed at low income households, at least until the labor market is able to generate enough jobs with incomes that allow households to escape poverty.

Table 1.A.1 Characteristics of informality

| Variables | Argentina | | | Peru | | | Brazil | | | Chile | | |
| --- | --- | --- | --- | --- | --- | --- | --- | --- | --- | --- | --- | --- |
| | Formal | Informal | Total | Formal | Informal | Total | Formal | Informal | Total | Formal | Informal | Total |
| *Gender* | | | | | | | | | | | | |
| Men | 57.8 | 56.4 | 57.1 | 62.8 | 50.3 | 54.5 | 56.7 | 56.0 | 56.4 | 61.2 | 55.4 | 59.0 |
| Women | 42.2 | 43.6 | 42.9 | 37.2 | 49.7 | 45.5 | 42.6 | 42.8 | 42.7 | 38.9 | 42.5 | 40.3 |
| Total | 100 | 100 | 100 | 100 | 100 | 100 | 100 | 100 | 100 | 100 | 100 | 100 |
| *Age* | | | | | | | | | | | | |
| Younger than 25 | 9.4 | 19.4 | 14.7 | 7.7 | 26.2 | 20.0 | 18.2 | 24.0 | 20.8 | 12.3 | 13.8 | 12.9 |
| 25–45 | 56.7 | 43.9 | 50.0 | 57.9 | 44.6 | 49.0 | 57.3 | 44.3 | 51.4 | 55.4 | 41.4 | 50.0 |
| Older than 45 | 33.9 | 36.7 | 35.4 | 34.4 | 29.2 | 30.9 | 24.5 | 31.8 | 27.8 | 32.3 | 44.7 | 37.1 |
| Total | 100 | 100 | 100 | 100 | 100 | 100 | 100 | 100 | 100 | 100 | 100 | 100 |
| *Educational level* | | | | | | | | | | | | |
| Less than complete secondary | 29.27 | 61.4 | 46.1 | 10.6 | 43.9 | 33.2 | 38.5 | 69.2 | 52.6 | 28.2 | 53.8 | 38.0 |
| Complete secondary/ incomplete university | 38.01 | 33.1 | 35.4 | 35.9 | 46.6 | 43.2 | 42.3 | 27.4 | 35.5 | 44.6 | 40.6 | 43.1 |
| Complete university | 32.72 | 5.6 | 18.5 | 53.5 | 9.4 | 23.6 | 19.1 | 3.3 | 11.9 | 27.2 | 5.6 | 18.9 |
| Total | 100 | 100 | 100 | 100 | 100 | 100 | 100 | 100 | 100 | 100 | 100 | 100 |

continued

Table 1.A.1 Continued

| | Argentina | | | Peru | | | Brazil | | | Chile | | |
|---|---|---|---|---|---|---|---|---|---|---|---|---|
| | Formal | Informal | Total | Formal | Informal | Total | Formal | Informal | Total | Formal | Informal | Total |
| *Industry* | | | | | | | | | | | | |
| Agriculture | – | – | – | – | – | – | – | – | – | 7.9 | 7.2 | 7.6 |
| Manufacture | 15.0 | 12.2 | 13.5 | 15.8 | 14.1 | 14.7 | 21.5 | 12.8 | 17.7 | 14.0 | 13.7 | 13.9 |
| Construction | 3.9 | 13.5 | 8.9 | 4.6 | 6.4 | 5.8 | 3.9 | 12.3 | 7.6 | 8.7 | 9.6 | 9.0 |
| Trade | 16.4 | 32.0 | 24.6 | 17.1 | 37.0 | 30.0 | 21.0 | 30.1 | 25.0 | 17.0 | 27.9 | 21.2 |
| Transport | 6.2 | 6.5 | 6.4 | 6.8 | 11.6 | 9.9 | 5.9 | 5.6 | 5.8 | 7.3 | 8.2 | 7.6 |
| Financial services | 12.4 | 7.4 | 9.8 | 12.5 | 4.1 | 7.1 | 11.8 | 5.5 | 9.1 | 9.8 | 4.1 | 7.6 |
| Personal services | 9.7 | 3.7 | 6.5 | 6.4 | 3.1 | 4.3 | 6.6 | 3.0 | 5.0 | 13.4 | 15.4 | 14.2 |
| Domestic services | 1.7 | 16.6 | 9.5 | 1.8 | 8.2 | 6.0 | 4.8 | 13.9 | 8.7 | 3.7 | 10.1 | 6.1 |
| Public sector | 27.6 | 2.0 | 14.1 | 26.3 | 3.2 | 11.4 | 19.0 | 2.9 | 12.1 | 16.6 | 3.0 | 11.4 |
| Other | 7.2 | 6.3 | 6.7 | 8.8 | 12.2 | 11.0 | 5.4 | 13.8 | 9.1 | 1.8 | 0.9 | 1.5 |
| Total | 100 | 100 | 100 | 100 | 100 | 100 | 100 | 100 | 100 | 100 | 100 | 100 |
| *Poverty status* | | | | | | | | | | | | |
| Non-poor | 95.04 | 73.3 | 84.1 | 93.2 | 76.8 | 84.1 | 89.7 | 73.7 | 82.4 | 94.6 | 89.9 | 92.8 |
| Poor | 4.96 | 26.7 | 15.9 | 6.8 | 23.2 | 15.9 | 10.3 | 26.3 | 17.6 | 5.4 | 10.1 | 7.2 |
| Total | 100 | 100 | 100 | 100 | 100 | 100 | 100 | 100 | 100 | 100 | 100 | 100 |

| | FS | IS | Total | FS | IS | Total | FS | IS | Total | FS | IS | Total |
|---|---|---|---|---|---|---|---|---|---|---|---|---|
| *Gender* | | | | | | | | | | | | |
| Men | 59.7 | 54.1 | 57.1 | 60.9 | 49.4 | 54.5 | 59.4 | 52.8 | 56.4 | 63.6 | 50.6 | 59.0 |
| Women | 40.3 | 45.9 | 42.9 | 39.1 | 50.6 | 45.5 | 40.5 | 47.2 | 42.7 | 36.4 | 49.4 | 40.3 |
| Total | 100 | 100 | 100 | 100 | 100 | 100 | 100 | 100 | 100 | 100 | 100 | 100 |
| *Age* | | | | | | | | | | | | |
| Younger than 25 | 12.8 | 16.7 | 14.7 | 16.5 | 22.8 | 20.0 | 21.2 | 20.4 | 20.8 | 14.7 | 9.6 | 12.9 |
| 25–45 | 55.7 | 43.5 | 50.0 | 56.6 | 43.1 | 49.0 | 55.5 | 46.6 | 51.4 | 54.4 | 42.0 | 50.0 |
| Older than 45 | 31.5 | 39.8 | 35.4 | 27.0 | 34.0 | 30.9 | 23.3 | 33.0 | 27.8 | 30.8 | 48.4 | 37.1 |
| Total | 100 | 100 | 100 | 100 | 100 | 100 | 100 | 100 | 100 | 100 | 100 | 100 |
| *Educational level* | | | | | | | | | | | | |
| Less than complete secondary | 31.2 | 63.2 | 46.1 | 14.1 | 47.6 | 33.2 | 36.8 | 70.9 | 52.6 | 27.5 | 57.0 | 38.0 |
| Complete second/incomplete university | 37.6 | 32.9 | 35.4 | 40.2 | 45.5 | 43.2 | 43.3 | 26.5 | 35.5 | 45.2 | 39.3 | 43.1 |
| Complete university | 31.2 | 3.9 | 18.5 | 45.7 | 6.9 | 23.6 | 19.9 | 2.7 | 11.9 | 27.3 | 3.7 | 18.9 |
| Total | 100 | 100 | 100 | 100 | 100 | 100 | 100 | 100 | 100 | 100 | 100 | 100 |
| *Industry* | | | | | | | | | | | | |
| Agriculture | – | – | – | – | – | – | – | – | – | 8.96 | 5.16 | 7.61 |
| Manufacture | 16.0 | 10.6 | 13.5 | 18.2 | 11.6 | 14.7 | 23.5 | 10.4 | 17.7 | 14.4 | 13.0 | 13.9 |
| Construction | 5.4 | 13.0 | 8.9 | 4.4 | 6.9 | 5.8 | 4.7 | 11.3 | 7.6 | 9.6 | 8.0 | 9.0 |
| Trade | 16.1 | 34.2 | 24.6 | 17.6 | 40.9 | 30.0 | 21.2 | 29.8 | 25.0 | 17.0 | 28.8 | 21.2 |
| Transport | 7.1 | 5.5 | 6.4 | 6.1 | 13.2 | 9.9 | 6.3 | 5.1 | 5.8 | 7.7 | 7.5 | 7.6 |
| Financial services | 11.9 | 7.4 | 9.8 | 11.3 | 3.4 | 7.1 | 11.9 | 5.5 | 9.1 | 9.5 | 4.0 | 7.6 |
| Personal services | 10.0 | 2.6 | 6.5 | 7.3 | 1.6 | 4.3 | 7.0 | 2.6 | 5.0 | 13.5 | 15.5 | 14.2 |
| Domestic services | – | 20.4 | 9.5 | – | 11.2 | 6.0 | – | 19.8 | 8.7 | – | 17.3 | 6.1 |
| Public sector | 26.5 | – | 14.1 | 24.3 | – | 11.4 | 21.6 | – | 12.1 | 17.6 | – | 11.4 |
| Other | 7.0 | 6.4 | 6.7 | 10.8 | 11.0 | 11.0 | 4.0 | 15.5 | 9.1 | 1.8 | – | 1.5 |
| Total | 100 | 100 | 100 | 100 | 100 | 100 | 100 | 100 | 100 | 100 | 100 | 100 |

*continued*

Table 1.A.1 Continued

|  | Argentina |  |  | Peru |  |  | Brazil |  |  | Chile |  |  |
|---|---|---|---|---|---|---|---|---|---|---|---|---|
|  | FS | IS | Total | FS | IS | Total | FS | IS | Total | Registered | Non-regist. | Total |
| *Poverty status* |  |  |  |  |  |  |  |  |  |  |  |  |
| Non-poor | 92.7 | 73.3 | 84.1 | 90.2 | 76.0 | 82.3 | 89.3 | 74.5 | 82.4 | 93.8 | 91.1 | 92.8 |
| Poor | 7.3 | 26.7 | 15.9 | 9.8 | 24.0 | 17.8 | 10.7 | 25.6 | 17.6 | 6.2 | 8.9 | 7.2 |
| Total | 100 | 100 | 100 | 100 | 100 | 100 | 100 | 100 | 100 | 100 | 100 | 100 |
|  | Registered | Non-regist. | Total | Registered | Non-regist. | Total | Registered | Non-regist. | Total | Registered | Non-regist. | Total |
| *Gender* |  |  |  |  |  |  |  |  |  |  |  |  |
| Men | 58.2 | 48.3 | 54.2 | 64.6 | 52.0 | 58.1 | 56.4 | 49.8 | 54.5 | 61.0 | 48.3 | 58.2 |
| Women | 41.8 | 51.7 | 45.8 | 35.4 | 48.0 | 41.9 | 42.8 | 46.3 | 43.9 | 39.0 | 51.7 | 41.8 |
| Total | 100 | 100 | 100 | 100 | 100 | 100 | 100 | 100 | 100 | 100 | 100 | 100 |
| *Age* |  |  |  |  |  |  |  |  |  |  |  |  |
| Younger than 25 | 10.1 | 26.0 | 16.6 | 8.5 | 38.2 | 23.7 | 18.9 | 36.5 | 24.0 | 13.0 | 22.2 | 15.1 |
| 25–45 | 58.0 | 47.6 | 53.7 | 58.6 | 47.6 | 53.0 | 57.7 | 44.4 | 53.9 | 55.8 | 45.6 | 53.5 |
| Older than 45 | 31.9 | 26.4 | 29.6 | 32.9 | 14.2 | 23.3 | 23.4 | 19.2 | 22.2 | 31.2 | 32.3 | 31.5 |
| Total | 100 | 100 | 100 | 100 | 100 | 100 | 100 | 100 | 100 | 100 | 100 | 100 |
| *Educational level* |  |  |  |  |  |  |  |  |  |  |  |  |
| Less than complete secondary | 32.0 | 62.3 | 44.4 | 12.1 | 35.4 | 24.4 | 40.1 | 69.9 | 48.5 | 29.6 | 49.8 | 34.1 |
| Complete second/ incomplete university | 41.3 | 30.3 | 36.8 | 42.4 | 49.5 | 46.1 | 43.7 | 26.5 | 38.8 | 46.7 | 40.6 | 45.3 |
| Complete university | 26.8 | 7.3 | 18.9 | 45.6 | 15.1 | 29.5 | 16.3 | 3.7 | 12.7 | 23.8 | 9.6 | 20.6 |
| Total | 100 | 100 | 100 | 100 | 100 | 100 | 100 | 100 | 100 | 100 | 100 | 100 |

| Industry | | | | | | | | | | | | |
|---|---|---|---|---|---|---|---|---|---|---|---|---|
| Agriculture | – | – | – | – | – | – | – | – | – | 8.07 | 8.93 | 8.27 |
| Manufacture | 15.7 | 11.5 | 14.0 | 17.0 | 16.9 | 17.0 | 21.9 | 11.0 | 18.8 | 14.1 | 11.8 | 13.6 |
| Construction | 3.8 | 11.3 | 6.9 | 4.6 | 7.8 | 6.2 | 4.0 | 8.5 | 5.3 | 8.7 | 8.4 | 8.7 |
| Trade | 16.2 | 21.5 | 18.4 | 12.8 | 23.2 | 18.1 | 20.7 | 21.3 | 20.8 | 17.0 | 16.8 | 16.9 |
| Transport | 6.5 | 7.2 | 6.8 | 5.9 | 7.7 | 6.8 | 6.0 | 3.4 | 5.3 | 7.2 | 7.1 | 7.2 |
| Financial services | 10.3 | 6.2 | 8.6 | 11.3 | 5.6 | 8.4 | 10.9 | 6.1 | 9.5 | 8.8 | 5.1 | 8.0 |
| Personal services | 8.1 | 4.0 | 6.4 | 6.2 | 4.8 | 5.5 | 6.2 | 3.6 | 5.4 | 12.8 | 11.4 | 12.5 |
| Domestic services | 1.9 | 29.2 | 13.0 | 2.1 | 16.2 | 9.3 | 5.0 | 27.9 | 11.6 | 3.9 | 23.0 | 8.2 |
| Public sector | 30.4 | 3.5 | 19.4 | 31.6 | 6.7 | 18.9 | 20.0 | 5.9 | 15.9 | 17.6 | 6.9 | 15.2 |
| Other | 7.3 | 5.7 | 6.6 | 8.6 | 11.1 | 9.9 | 5.4 | 12.5 | 7.4 | 1.7 | 0.6 | 1.5 |
| Total | 100 | 100 | 100 | 100 | 100 | 100 | 100 | 100 | 100 | – | – | – |
| *Poverty status* | | | | | | | | | | | | |
| Non-poor | 94.9 | 73.5 | 86.5 | 93.4 | 78.7 | 85.9 | 89.3 | 69.9 | 83.7 | 94.4 | 85.3 | 92.4 |
| Poor | 5.1 | 26.5 | 13.6 | 6.6 | 21.3 | 14.1 | 10.7 | 30.1 | 16.3 | 5.6 | 14.7 | 7.6 |
| Total | 100 | 100 | 100 | 100 | 100 | 100 | 100 | 100 | 100 | 100 | 100 | 100 |

Table 1.A.2 Mincer equations, OLS

| Covariates | Argentina | | | | Peru | | | |
| --- | --- | --- | --- | --- | --- | --- | --- | --- |
| | Informal employment | | Informal sector | | Informal employment | | Informal sector | |
| | Monthly | Hourly | Monthly | Hourly | Monthly | Hourly | Monthly | Hourly |
| Informality | -0.655*** [-0.00733] | -0.517*** [-0.00676] | -0.486*** [-0.00798] | -0.387*** [-0.00725] | -0.324*** [-0.0181] | -0.258*** [-0.0177] | -0.390*** [-0.0175] | -0.298*** [-0.0171] |
| Men | 0.185*** [0.00937] | 0.126*** [0.00871] | 0.177*** [0.00981] | 0.117*** [0.00902] | 0.403*** [0.0208] | 0.356*** [0.0205] | 0.399*** [0.0207] | 0.354*** [0.0205] |
| Head of household | 0.0425*** [0.0103] | 0.0295*** [0.00955] | 0.0457*** [0.0108] | 0.0315*** [0.00989] | 0.147*** [0.0297] | 0.0995*** [0.0293] | 0.137*** [0.0296] | 0.0911*** [0.0293] |
| Age | 0.0434*** [0.00144] | 0.0367*** [0.00132] | 0.0548*** [0.00150] | 0.0453*** [0.00136] | 0.0629*** [0.00270] | 0.0605*** [0.00262] | 0.0688*** [0.00267] | 0.0652*** [0.00260] |
| Age* Age | -0.000408*** [-1.69e-05] | -0.000320*** [-1.56e-05] | -0.000521*** [-1.76e-05] | -0.000405*** [-1.60e-05] | -0.000733*** [-3.18e-05] | -0.000700*** [-3.09e-05] | -0.000774*** [-3.15e-05] | -0.000732*** [-3.07e-05] |
| Worked hours | 0.00741*** [0.000130] | -0.0135*** [0.000171] | 0.00781*** [0.000136] | -0.0126*** [0.000176] | -0.404*** [0.0252] | -0.393*** [0.0247] | -0.390*** [0.0251] | -0.384*** [0.0247] |
| Incomplete primary or less | -0.206*** [-0.0133] | -0.181*** [-0.0123] | -0.236*** [-0.0139] | -0.203*** [-0.0127] | -0.147*** [-0.0299] | -0.150*** [-0.0290] | -0.160*** [-0.0297] | -0.160*** [-0.0289] |
| Incomplete secondary | 0.0906*** [0.0101] | 0.0909*** [0.00930] | 0.0941*** [0.0106] | 0.0929*** [0.00962] | 0.0989*** [0.0284] | 0.111*** [0.0276] | 0.101*** [0.0282] | 0.113*** [0.0275] |
| Complete secondary | 0.272*** [0.00975] | 0.249*** [0.00895] | 0.318*** [0.0102] | 0.284*** [0.00923] | 0.208*** [0.0271] | 0.205*** [0.0263] | 0.203*** [0.0270] | 0.203*** [0.0263] |
| Incomplete university | 0.317*** [0.0119] | 0.342*** [0.0109] | 0.338*** [0.0125] | 0.360*** [0.0113] | 0.349*** [0.0315] | 0.362*** [0.0307] | 0.343*** [0.0314] | 0.359*** [0.0306] |
| Complete university | 0.538*** [0.0119] | 0.568*** [0.0110] | 0.595*** [0.0124] | 0.614*** [0.0113] | 0.560*** [0.0328] | 0.526*** [0.0318] | 0.541*** [0.0325] | 0.516*** [0.0316] |

| | | | | | | | |
|---|---|---|---|---|---|---|---|
| Construction | 0.0159 [0.0135] | -0.0193 [0.0123] | -0.0365*** [0.0141] | -0.0572*** [0.0127] | 0.184*** [0.0333] | 0.147*** [0.0324] | 0.219*** [0.0332] | 0.174*** [0.0324] |
| Trade | -0.0662*** [-0.0111] | -0.0733*** [-0.0102] | -0.0640*** [-0.0117] | -0.0714*** [-0.0106] | -0.121*** [-0.0226] | -0.0771*** [-0.0219] | -0.0697*** [-0.0227] | -0.0386* [-0.0221] |
| Financial services | 0.0487*** [0.0142] | 0.0685*** [0.0131] | 0.0647*** [0.0149] | 0.0825*** [0.0135] | -0.00635 [-0.0283] | 0.0628** [0.0275] | 0.0616** [0.0285] | 0.113*** [0.0278] |
| Transport | 0.103*** [0.0154] | 0.108*** [0.0142] | 0.0756*** [0.0161] | 0.0838*** [0.0146] | 0.166*** [0.0332] | 0.199*** [0.0324] | 0.179*** [0.0330] | 0.210*** [0.0323] |
| Personal services | -0.116*** [-0.0165] | 0.00332 [0.0153] | -0.111*** [0.0173] | 0.00969 [0.0159] | 0.0507 [0.0427] | 0.127*** [0.0417] | 0.00536 [0.0426] | 0.0935** [0.0417] |
| Domestic services | -0.405*** [-0.0151] | -0.199*** [-0.0139] | -0.368*** [-0.0162] | -0.160*** [-0.0147] | -0.287*** [-0.0361] | -0.223*** [-0.0349] | -0.154*** [-0.0366] | -0.122*** [-0.0355] |
| Public sector | 0.0221* [0.0122] | 0.0738*** [0.0113] | 0.0663*** [0.0128] | 0.111*** [0.0117] | 0.321*** [0.0286] | 0.210*** [0.0282] | 0.272*** [0.0287] | 0.173*** [0.0284] |
| Other | 0.0419*** [0.0143] | 0.0905*** [0.0132] | 0.0391*** [0.0150] | 0.0905*** [0.0136] | -0.129*** [0.0267] | -0.0671** [0.0261] | -0.133*** [0.0266] | -0.0709*** [0.0260] |
| Region | Yes | Yes | Yes | Yes | Yes | Yes | Yes | Yes |
| Lambda | -0.273*** [-0.0184] | -0.249*** [-0.0170] | -0.305*** [-0.0192] | -0.272*** [-0.0176] | -0.127* [-0.0666] | -0.213*** [-0.0652] | -0.164** [-0.0664] | -0.243*** [-0.0651] |
| Constant | 5.564*** [0.0409] | 2.895*** [0.0379] | 5.174*** [0.0424] | 2.572*** [0.0388] | 4.137*** [0.0936] | 1.849*** [0.0913] | 3.995*** [0.0915] | 1.729*** [0.0894] |
| Observations | 92,492 | 91,172 | 92,492 | 91,172 | 31,753 | 31,311 | 31,753 | 31,311 |

continued

Table 1.A.2 Continued

| Covariates | Brazil | | | | Chile | | | |
| --- | --- | --- | --- | --- | --- | --- | --- | --- |
| | Informal employment | | Informal sector | | Informal employment | | Informal sector | |
| | Monthly | Hourly | Monthly | Hourly | Monthly | Hourly | Monthly | Hourly |
| Informality | -0.245*** [0.00374] | -0.200*** [0.00382] | -0.179*** [0.00405] | -0.135*** [0.00413] | -0.103*** [0.00465] | -0.0140*** [0.00468] | -0.0109** [0.00479] | 0.0724*** [0.00480] |
| Men | 0.278*** [0.00612] | 0.278*** [0.00624] | 0.274*** [0.00617] | 0.275*** [0.00628] | 0.254*** [0.00958] | 0.240*** [0.00964] | 0.252*** [0.00961] | 0.241*** [0.00963] |
| Head of household | 0.111*** [0.00663] | 0.121*** [0.00677] | 0.116*** [0.00668] | 0.126*** [0.00680] | 0.144*** [0.00996] | 0.164*** [0.0100] | 0.142*** [0.00999] | 0.159*** [0.0100] |
| Age | 0.0545*** [0.000720] | 0.0548*** [0.000735] | 0.0581*** [0.000724] | 0.0576*** [0.000737] | 0.0324*** [0.000909] | 0.0312*** [0.000915] | 0.0333*** [0.000911] | 0.0312*** [0.000913] |
| Age*Age | -0.000539*** [8.78e-06] | -0.000538*** [8.96e-06] | -0.000578*** [8.81e-06] | -0.000570*** [8.98e-06] | -0.000271*** [1.03e-05] | -0.000254*** [1.03e-05] | -0.000286*** [1.03e-05] | -0.000259*** [1.03e-05] |
| Worked hours | 0.0149*** [0.000133] | -0.0166*** [0.000135] | 0.0156*** [0.000133] | -0.0160*** [0.000135] | 0.0711*** [0.0141] | 0.0640*** [0.0142] | 0.0816*** [0.0141] | 0.0695*** [0.0142] |
| Incomplete primary or less | -0.191*** [0.00575] | -0.190*** [0.00587] | -0.203*** [0.00579] | -0.199*** [0.00590] | -0.182*** [0.00706] | -0.186*** [0.00710] | -0.187*** [0.00708] | -0.187*** [0.00709] |
| Incomplete secondary | 0.0769*** [0.00732] | 0.0795*** [0.00747] | 0.0743*** [0.00737] | 0.0774*** [0.00751] | 0.117*** [0.00762] | 0.122*** [0.00766] | 0.118*** [0.00764] | 0.126*** [0.00766] |
| Complete secondary | 0.286*** [0.00692] | 0.285*** [0.00706] | 0.303*** [0.00696] | 0.300*** [0.00709] | 0.314*** [0.00826] | 0.319*** [0.00831] | 0.324*** [0.00828] | 0.327*** [0.00830] |
| Incomplete university | 0.618*** [0.00896] | 0.608*** [0.00915] | 0.621*** [0.00903] | 0.612*** [0.00920] | 0.560*** [0.0123] | 0.581*** [0.0124] | 0.568*** [0.0123] | 0.593*** [0.0124] |
| Complete university | 1.135*** [0.0100] | 1.139*** [0.0102] | 1.158*** [0.0101] | 1.160*** [0.0103] | 1.086*** [0.0123] | 1.087*** [0.0124] | 1.111*** [0.0124] | 1.116*** [0.0124] |

| | (1) | (2) | (3) | (4) | (5) | (6) | (7) | (8) |
|---|---|---|---|---|---|---|---|---|
| Construction | 0.0176** [0.00762] | -0.00590 [0.00778] | 0.00380 [0.00771] | -0.0211*** [0.00786] | 0.142*** [0.00810] | 0.137*** [0.00815] | 0.140*** [0.00812] | 0.136*** [0.00814] |
| Trade | -0.0121** [0.00545] | 0.0188*** [0.00557] | -0.0132** [0.00554] | 0.0151*** [0.00564] | 0.0782*** [0.00682] | 0.128*** [0.00686] | 0.0673*** [0.00687] | 0.112*** [0.00689] |
| Financial services | 0.0825*** [0.00721] | 0.0746*** [0.00736] | 0.0920*** [0.00727] | 0.0820*** [0.00740] | 0.170*** [0.00946] | 0.218*** [0.00951] | 0.162*** [0.00948] | 0.211*** [0.00950] |
| Transport | 0.123*** [0.00833] | 0.162*** [0.00850] | 0.118*** [0.00840] | 0.156*** [0.00855] | 0.198*** [0.0114] | 0.213*** [0.0115] | 0.208*** [0.0114] | 0.215*** [0.0115] |
| Personal services | -0.0311*** [0.00909] | -0.0178* [0.00928] | -0.0328*** [0.00916] | -0.0188*** [0.00933] | 0.0127** [0.00614] | 0.0374*** [0.00618] | 0.0195*** [0.00616] | 0.0335*** [0.00617] |
| Domestic services | -0.228*** [0.00762] | -0.197*** [0.00778] | -0.182*** [0.00800] | -0.166*** [0.00816] | 0.247*** [0.0177] | 0.300*** [0.0178] | 0.264*** [0.0178] | 0.316*** [0.0178] |
| Public sector | 0.115*** [0.00674] | 0.0853*** [0.00688] | 0.0930*** [0.00687] | 0.0706*** [0.00700] | 0.152*** [0.0181] | 0.170*** [0.0182] | 0.171*** [0.0181] | 0.186*** [0.0181] |
| Other | -0.219*** [0.00626] | -0.203*** [0.00639] | -0.267*** [0.00623] | -0.245*** [0.00635] | 0.0558** [0.0164] | 0.0414** [0.0165] | 0.0675*** [0.0164] | 0.0534*** [0.0164] |
| Region | Yes | Yes | Yes | Yes | Yes | Yes | Yes | Yes |
| Lambda | -0.0687*** [0.0159] | -0.0487*** [0.0162] | -0.0644*** [0.0160] | -0.0458*** [0.0163] | -0.0132 [0.0186] | 0.00790 [0.0187] | -0.0262 [0.0187] | -0.00527 [0.0187] |
| Constant | 4.288*** [0.0217] | 1.873*** [0.0222] | 4.134*** [0.0217] | 1.743*** [0.0221] | 10.14*** [0.0323] | 7.619*** [0.0325] | 10.06*** [0.0323] | 7.581*** [0.0323] |

Notes
Standard errors in brackets.
*** $p<0.01$.
** $p<0.05$.
* $p<0.1$.

*Table 1.A.3* Mincer equations; quantile regression

| Argentina | Taus | | | | |
|---|---|---|---|---|---|
| | q10 | q25 | q50 | q75 | q90 |
| IE monthly | −0.977*** | −0.757*** | −0.602*** | −0.475*** | −0.364*** |
| | [0.00795] | [0.000253] | [0.0141] | [0.00864] | [0.0170] |
| IE hourly | −0.795*** | −0.635*** | −0.495*** | −0.393*** | −0.292*** |
| | [0.000147] | [0.0116] | [0.00370] | [0.00539] | [0.0107] |
| IS monthly | −0.651*** | −0.563*** | −0.468*** | −0.386*** | −0.293*** |
| | [0.0426] | [0.00303] | [0.0103] | [0.00287] | [0.000241] |
| IS hourly | −0.560*** | −0.476*** | −0.388*** | −0.316*** | −0.239*** |
| | [0.00677] | [0.0111] | [0.00375] | [0.0200] | [0.000349] |
| **Peru** | **Taus** | | | | |
| | q10 | q25 | q50 | q75 | q90 |
| IE monthly | −0.494*** | −0.433*** | −0.403*** | −0.403*** | −0.440*** |
| | [0.00863] | [0.000660] | [0.0135] | [0.000915] | [0.0176] |
| IE hourly | −0.445*** | −0.390*** | −0.343*** | −0.334*** | −0.352*** |
| | [0.0389] | [0.0149] | [0.0228] | [0.0143] | [0.00583] |
| IS monthly | −0.724*** | −0.568*** | −0.424*** | −0.326*** | −0.272*** |
| | [0.0147] | [0.0195] | [0.00751] | [0.0210] | [0.0259] |
| IS hourly | −0.644*** | −0.452*** | −0.337*** | −0.231*** | −0.162*** |
| | [0.0550] | [0.0424] | [0.00853] | [0.00374] | [0.00811] |
| **Brazil** | **Taus** | | | | |
| | q10 | q25 | q50 | q75 | q90 |
| IE monthly | −0.555*** | −0.354*** | −0.211*** | −0.107*** | −0.0241*** |
| | [0.00314] | [0.00417] | [0.00957] | [0.00766] | [0.00211] |
| IE hourly | −0.489*** | −0.300*** | −0.168*** | −0.0632*** | 0.0215*** |
| | [0.00457] | [0.00410] | [0.00224] | [0.000970] | [0.00663] |
| IS monthly | −0.453*** | −0.276*** | −0.145*** | −0.0411*** | 0.0569*** |
| | [0.00300] | [0.00140] | [0.00381] | [0.0123] | [0.0145] |
| IS hourly | −0.395*** | −0.228*** | −0.108*** | 0.0100 | 0.117*** |
| | [0.00374] | [0.00698] | [0.00745] | [0.0158] | [0.0139] |

*continued*

*Table 1.A.3* Continued

| Chile | Taus | | | | |
|---|---|---|---|---|---|
| | *q10* | *q25* | *q50* | *q75* | *q90* |
| IE monthly | −0.584*** [0.00899] | −0.318*** [0.000870] | −0.0880*** [0.000634] | 0.121*** [0.00359] | 0.263*** [0.00572] |
| IE hourly | −0.477*** [0.00934] | −0.230*** [0.0113] | −0.0132 [0.0114] | 0.207*** [0.00798] | 0.368*** [0.0128] |
| IS monthly | −0.363*** [0.003 14] | −0.195*** [0.00939] | −0.0244*** [0.00426] | 0.181*** [0.0128] | 0.318*** [0.0173] |
| IS hourly | −0.273*** [0.0102] | −0.125*** [0.00115] | 0.0430*** [0.00390] | 0.268*** [0.0101] | 0.418*** [0.0192] |

Notes
Standard errors in brackets.
*** $p<0.01$. ** $p<0.05$. * $p<0.1$.

# Notes

1 The value of a normative food basket satisfies nutritional requirements considering the consumption pattern of a "reference population". The overall poverty line is computed by multiplying the value of the normative food basket by the inverse of the Engel coefficient observed in the reference population.
2 Koenker and Bassett (1978).
3 Developed by Rosenbaum and Rubin (1983).
4 The estimated labor incomes are those previously obtained by OLS.
5 Similar results for Argentina are presented in Ministry of Labour (2007).
6 *Informals* refers both to IE and EIS. In a similar way, *formals* is used to refer to the group of FE and EFS.
7 Only coefficients of informality are shown.
8 Tannuri-Pianto and Pianto (2002) also find that the wage gaps between formal and informal workers in Brazil are wider at low conditional quantiles than at high quantiles.

# References

Beccaria, L. and Groisman, F. (2008) *Argentina Desigual*, Los Polvorines: Editorial Universidad Nacional de General Sarmiento.
ILO (1972) *Employment, Income and Equality: A Strategy for Increasing Productive Employment in Kenya*, Geneva: International Labour Office.
Koenker, R. and Bassett, G. (1978) "Regression quantiles", *Econometrica*, 46: 33–50.
Ministry of Labour (2007) *La informalidad Laboral en el Gran Buenos Aires, Una nueva mirada, resultados del módulo de informalidad de la EPH*, Buenos Aires: Ministry of Labor.
Rosenbaum, P. and Rubin, D. (1983) "The central role of propensity score in observational studies for causal effects", *Biometrika*, 70(1): 41–55.
Tannuri-Pianto, M. and Pianto, D. (2002) "Informal employment in Brazil: A choice at the top and segmentation at the bottom: a quantile regression approach", Paper presented at the XXIV Brazilian Econometrics Meeting, Rio de Janeiro, Brazil.

# 2 Working in the informal sector

## A free choice or an obligation? An analysis of job satisfaction in Vietnam

*Mireille Razafindrakoto, François Roubaud and Jean-Michel Wachsberger*

Two antagonistic visions of the informal sector in developing countries can be schematically opposed. According to the first which is more specifically economic, this sector could be the mark of a segmentation of the labour market caused by a structural abundance of labour and the insufficient capacity of absorption of the peripheral economies of the modern sector. It thus constitutes a simple reservoir of labour for the formal sector and a dominated form of production within which prevail low salaries, precarious working conditions and a high level of under-employment. The second vision, historically defended by sociologists and anthropologists alike, tends to consider on the contrary the informal sector as a popular and family economy anchored in traditional moral values, a place of solidarity and conviviality, or even a nursery of poor but inventive entrepreneurs proud of their independence. More recently, economists have examined the intrinsic heterogeneity of the informal sector, which would allow the reconciliation of the two above-mentioned approaches. Thus, it would be necessary to distinguish two components within the informal sector: the first consisting of subsistence activities whose economic performances are mediocre and without any prospect of accumulation, this category includes the least qualified and the least integrated in the labour market; the second regrouping dynamic entrepreneurs capable of generating huge profits, who have decided to work in this sector less by constraint but as a choice.

This chapter aims at contributing to this debate using an original method. We are interested in the satisfaction that these informal sector jobs bring to those who do them. In the tradition of recent work carried out by Razafindrakoto and Roubaud (2013) about the labour market in eight African capitals, we put forward here the hypothesis that job satisfaction constitutes a good indicator to evaluate the quality of these jobs. The comparison of degrees of job satisfaction in the informal sector with that of jobs in other sectors may then be a key element to reflect on the nature and the function of the informal sector.

We mainly use in this study data from the Labour Force Survey carried out by the General Office of Statistics in 2009 with a sample group of 16 000 households representative of the national population. By checking the socio-demographic characteristics of the individuals, the incomes generated by their work and their working conditions, the study intends to evaluate the value these informal sector jobs have to those who do them, particularly when compared to other types of job (public sector, etc.). To our knowledge, this is the first study of its kind in Asia, and one of the very rare ones to be carried out in developing countries.

This chapter is composed of four sections. In the first, we shall give a panorama of existing academic work and at the same time attempt to put together two traditionally independent fields: one which examines the informal sector (in DCs) and the other which concentrates on job satisfaction (principally in developed countries). The second section is devoted to the presentation of data as well as the main results from descriptive statistics. The analysis of econometric estimates is the object of the third section. Finally, in the fourth section, we propose a few elements for the interpretation of the mechanisms at work and the subjacent logic.

## A brief review of previous academic work

The informal sector, and more widely informal work, today represents the most usual way of entering the job market in DCs (Bacchetta *et al.*, 2009). Contrary to all prognostics, this sector has not disappeared with economic growth and development. The informal economy has not only maintained its position over the last decades, but it has also grown in many countries affected by globalization, a phenomenon which has been all the more apparent following the international financial crisis starting in 2008. In a publication giving a synthesis of the issue, the OECD even asked the question about whether participating in the informal sector does not, when all is said and done, constitute the normal "mode" of professional insertion for the great majority of workers in developing countries (Jütting and de Laiglesia, 2009).

What might be the reason for such a state of affairs? In the tradition of research into dualism (see for example Harris and Todaro, 1970), the dominant voice held as a truth that poor workers were obliged to work in the informal sector, because of the formal sector's insufficient capacity to absorb the existing supply of labour. More recently, those in the structuralist school arrived at the same conclusions (see for example Portes *et al.*, 1989) but for very different reasons: strategies to minimize costs and global competition lead formal enterprises to externalize and subcontract a growing part of their production to the informal sector whose labour force is over exploited and excluded from the workers' protection system.

From the end of the 1980s, a new school called the "legalists" suggests that many informal workers "choose" to avoid public regulations which they judge to be too constraining and inefficient (De Soto, 1989). In the same vein, other authors also underline that entering the informal sector can be a deliberate move done according to individual preferences and the respective attributes of each kind of job (Perry *et al.*, 2007).

For about 30 years now, the question about the voluntary or forced nature of informal work is at the heart of the debate. To settle this debate, researchers focused on the analysis of remunerations, following a logic of declared preferences. While it was generally accepted that salaries were lower in the informal sector, reinforcing the idea that it was a question of lower quality work, more recent studies, based on panel data, at least partially contradicts these findings (Bargain and Kwenda, 2011; Nguyen *et al.*, 2013; Nordman *et al.*, this volume; Demenet *et al.*, 2010; Nguyen *et al.*, 2010) showing that there are big transition flows in both directions and that the probability of working in a given sector is systematically higher when an individual has worked in this sector in the preceding period. However, neither of these two approaches (remuneration or transition analysis) allows us to decisively reply to the question regarding whether the choice to work in the informal sector is voluntary or not. The former because monetary reward is not the only criterion against which to measure to what extent a job is appreciated. The latter because persisting in a given state (formal or informal) may also result from a positive strategy rather than from the force of circumstance.

In order to remove these limitations, a third way which we have adopted here, consists of approaching directly the question of the utility and desirability of the job. Rather than concentrating uniquely on financial reward, job satisfaction allows us to take into account all the criteria associated with job quality while at the same time synthesizing the information in a one-dimensional indicator. This approach nevertheless assumes that a subjective measure of well-being at work has a sense, a hypothesis which has been refuted for a long time, but which is nowadays largely accepted, particularly in developing countries (Razafindrakoto and Roubaud, 2013).

In existing academic work, we have identified only a very limited number of studies concerned with the case of developing countries or countries in transition which have adopted our approach. The overwhelming majority of these studies concerns Latin America, where data about informality at work are more complete and research is more advanced. Pagés and Madrigal (2008) show for example that, mainly in Honduras, but also in Guatemala and Salvador, there is globally less job satisfaction in the informal sector. However, it is clearly less so for salaried workers, whereas the diagnosis is less clear for independent workers. Perry *et al.* (2007) confirm these results for Argentina and the Dominican Republic. In both countries, independent workers consider themselves to be, everything else being equal, as poor as formal salaried workers, while informal salaried workers consider their level of poverty to be higher in the first country, but not in the second. In the case of Columbia, Raquel Bernal (2009) shows that the two categories of informal workers (independent and salaried) are less satisfied than formal salaried workers.

Some studies have been undertaken in Africa and in Asia on this topic. Razafindrakoto and Roubaud (2013) show that in the case of eight African countries, the informal sector is not less appreciated than the private formal sector, the public sector systematically appearing to be the most desirable job sector to work in. Their interest variable is not however a real scale of job satisfaction, but the desire to change job. Mobilizing the same data, but this time using a classical score of satisfaction, Rakotomanana (2011) confirms these preceding conclusions for Madagascar. Analysing panel data, Falco *et al.* (2011) propose what is probably the most complete study establishing a link between job satisfaction and informality in the case of Ghanaian workers. Their results are partially convergent with the two above-mentioned studies: informal workers do not seem to be less satisfied than their formal counterparts, whereas the existence of a bonus awarded for working for oneself is extremely robust.

Azalea *et al.* (2009) have studied the job satisfaction of Indonesian and Malaysian graduates in a comparative perspective in order to stress the influence of specific cultural factors. Tolentino (2007) analyses job satisfaction of workers in micro and small enterprises (MSEs) in the Philippines and shows that the sources of satisfaction are rather linked to the quality of social relationships (interaction between employees and with clients), while economic factors (remuneration, working hours and workload) constitute obstacles to happiness in the workplace.

Two principal conclusions can be drawn from this rapid glimpse of essentially economic academic work. On the one hand, analysis of job satisfaction represents an original way, both fecund and little explored, to make a diagnostic about job quality. It allows us to go beyond the traditional theoretical framework which sees financial remuneration as the only indicator to measure the utility of a job. On the other hand, it appears that the relative position (in terms of satisfaction) of the informal sector (and of its different constituents) varies noticeably from one country to another, depending on the context and local characteristics of the labour market, thus making any type of generalization impossible. It is therefore an open question that only empirical analysis will allow us to answer. This is what we propose to do in the following sections for the case of Vietnam, a country for which no study has previously ever been carried out on this subject.

## Description of the data and first descriptive analyses

### The data

This study relies principally on data from the official Labour Force Survey (LFS 2009), representative at a national level and carried out by the Vietnam Office of statistics (GSO, 2010). Outside the standard indicators on the labour market (activity, unemployment, under-employment, work status, branch of activity, multi-activities, etc.) two sets of questions, essential for this study, have been introduced into the questionnaire, at the authors' instigation, in the framework of a joint research project between the GSO and the French Institute for Research and Development (IRD).

First of all, the survey was especially conceived to measure employment in the informal sector and more widely informal employment (for more details, see Razafindrakoto *et al.*, 2008; Cling *et al.*, 2010a). Following international recommendations, the *informal sector* is defined as all private unincorporated enterprises that produce at least some of their goods and services for sale or barter, are not registered (no business licence) and are engaged in non-agricultural activities. This stands for wherever the activity is carried out (on professional premises, in the street or at home). In accordance with the terminology in use in Vietnam, we shall call these production units "informal household business" (informal HBs), in contrast with those which are registered called "formal household business".

This definition of the formal sector has the advantage of falling within the larger context of institutional sectors, which constitute the preferred point of departure for our analysis. Thus, we distinguish six institutional sectors according to the nature of the capital of the enterprises: the public sector (administration and public enterprises), enterprises with foreign capital, domestic enterprises (the two latter ones having a different legal status from that of their managers), the formal household businesses, the informal sector (all informal HBs) and agriculture. This opening approach according to institutional sector allows us to go beyond the binary and over-simplified contrast of the situation of the informal sector which only distinguishes formal/informal.

Second, a specific question about job satisfaction, inspired by international experience in this field, has been introduced into the questionnaire: "All things considered, to what extent are you satisfied with your job?" Five different types of ordered answers are proposed: "Very dissatisfied", "Rather dissatisfied", "Neither satisfied nor dissatisfied", "Rather satisfied", "Very satisfied". The question was asked to all employed workers over the age of 15 and refers to their main job. This general question can provide a synthetic indicator of the different advantages and disadvantages linked to each type of job. The multiple recent studies (see Razafindrakoto *et al.*, 2012) demonstrated the relevance and robustness of this measure. In our case, the very low rate of non-response (0.4 per cent) demonstrates that the exercise did not present a major constraint to the interviewees.

### Descriptive analysis of the principal stylized facts

We shall begin our analysis by presenting the principal characteristics of the informal sector, and we shall continue by studying the job satisfaction associated with different posts occupied on the job market.

With more than 11 million jobs, that is to say nearly one-quarter (24 per cent) of the workforce, the informal sector is the second biggest source of jobs after agriculture in Vietnam, and by far the first if the non-agricultural jobs are considered (Table 2.1). It is before the public sector (10 per cent), domestic enterprises and individual formal enterprises (8 per cent each), with foreign enterprises arriving last with less than 3 per cent. This preponderance of the informal sector is a long-lasting phenomenon: whatever the economic growth hypotheses of these last years, employment projections show that the informal sector is forecast to grow because of the double effect of the urbanization and industrialization of the country (Cling *et al.*, 2010b).

Table 2.1 Characteristics of the workforce by institutional sector in Vietnam, 2009

| Institutional sector | Number of jobs (1,000) | Structure (%) | Rural (%) | Female (%) | Ethnic minorities (%) | Age (years) | Higher education (%) |
|---|---|---|---|---|---|---|---|
| Public sector | 4,615 | 9.7 | 42.8 | 47.1 | 8.9 | 37.6 | 48.0 |
| Foreign enterprise | 1,376 | 2.9 | 63.4 | 64.7 | 5.1 | 26.8 | 8.0 |
| Domestic enterprise | 3,669 | 7.7 | 48.1 | 39.1 | 5.8 | 31.6 | 15.3 |
| Formal HBs | 3,688 | 7.8 | 46.4 | 46.0 | 7.2 | 36.4 | 3.6 |
| Informal sector | 11,313 | 23.8 | 63.2 | 48.0 | 5.7 | 38.4 | 1.0 |
| Agriculture | 22,838 | 48.0 | 91.7 | 51.1 | 27.2 | 39.8 | 0.6 |
| Total | 47,548 | 100 | 72.6 | 49.1 | 16.5 | 38.0 | 6.8 |

Sources: Labour Force Survey 2009, GSO; authors' calculations.

The informal sector does not constitute an atypical segment, which concentrates secondary labour from the labour market, as is often argued: the proportion of heads of household here is the highest of the whole of institutional sectors (including the public sector); inversely, migrants and ethnic minorities are less well represented. In fact, the principal singularity of workers in the informal sector is their low level of education, agriculture being the only sector to employ less qualified workers: only 1 per cent have been in tertiary education compared to an average of 7 per cent and near to 50 per cent in the public sector.

The attributes of the jobs in the informal sector are generally of worse quality than in the other sectors (except agriculture). The rate of wage workers is low (27 per cent) and the forms of wage work clearly more precarious (Table 2.2): more than 99 per cent have at best a verbal contract (25 per cent are without any contract), compared to only 3 per cent in the public sector, 10 per cent are paid monthly (which is the norm in the other sectors), the majority being paid by day, by the hour, for piecework or on commission. For all the workers in this sector, social protection is negligible (0.1 per cent), whereas it reaches 87 per cent in the public sector and foreign enterprises. Besides, in spite of long working hours (46 hours a week compared to an average of 43), and a long average length of service (almost eight years), the average monthly salary (1.7 million VN dong, i.e. about €75) is 50 per cent less than in the formal sector. The informal sector thus occupies an intermediary position between the non-agricultural formal sector (at the top of the distribution) and agriculture (at the bottom).

If we now begin to examine job satisfaction, relying on the distributions of answers and the balance of satisfaction indicator,[1] Figure 2.1 highlights a very clear hierarchy depending on institutional sector. The public sector is found at the top of the ladder: nearly three-quarters (72 per cent) of employees in the

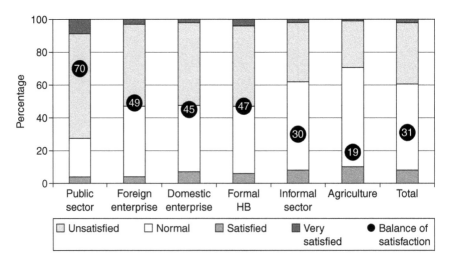

*Figure 2.1* Job satisfaction levels by institutional sector in Vietnam, 2009 (sources: Labour Force Survey 2009, GSO; authors' calculations).

*Table 2.2* Job characteristics by institutional sector in Vietnam, 2009

| Institutional sector | Seniority (years) | Wage workers (%) | Social protection (%) | Hours/week | Real remuneration* (1,000 VND/month) |
|---|---|---|---|---|---|
| Public sector | 10.5 | 99.7 | 87.4 | 44.0 | 1,964 |
| Foreign enterprise | 3.5 | 99.9 | 86.9 | 53.0 | 1,735 |
| Domestic enterprise | 4.4 | 93.6 | 48.5 | 51.8 | 2,093 |
| Formal HBs | 7.1 | 36.4 | 1.3 | 51.8 | 1,805 |
| Informal sector | 7.7 | 26.7 | 0.1 | 45.9 | 1,273 |
| Agriculture | 15.8 | 9.6 | 1.5 | 37.0 | 703 |
| Total | 11.4 | 33.6 | 15.6 | 42.6 | 1,185 |

Sources: Labour Force Survey 2009, GSO; authors' calculations.

Note
* Including non-remunerated family help workers (income=0).

public sector (civil servants or salaried workers in public or para-public enterprises) declare themselves to be satisfied or very satisfied with their job. Then come workers from the private formal sector, of which a little more than half (52 per cent) show themselves to be at least satisfied, without any significant difference between those who work in foreign, domestic or individual enterprises. Finally, workers in the informal sector and in agriculture are the most critical, the proportion of those declaring themselves satisfied being around one-third, with an advantage to the former (38 and 29 per cent respectively).

The hierarchy of job satisfaction according to institutional sector partially respects working conditions and average remuneration offered in each sector. As they benefit from higher salaries, shorter working hours and better welfare protection (social security, long-term contracts, paid holidays, etc.), public service employees are by far the most satisfied. Finally, the stylized facts taken from this first descriptive analysis of job satisfaction seem to validate the hypothesis of the queue before the gates leading to the formal sector: vulnerability and precariousness entail low level of satisfaction in the informal sector.

However, given the constitutive heterogeneity of the informal sector, it is necessary to go beyond averages alone and break down each institutional sector in considering employment status. Indeed, ever since the work of Maloney (1999) in Mexico, two categories of job are distinguished in academic work: salaried workers and independent workers (managers and self-employed workers). The former generally earn less than those in the formal sector, who in turn are less well remunerated than independent workers in the informal sector, at least in the higher part of income distribution, as was confirmed in Vietnam by Nguyen *et al.* (2013).

If job status is considered (Figure 2.2), on average, salaried workers are more satisfied than independent workers: half of the former declare themselves to be satisfied in their job compared to one-third of the latter. But this result might only be a structural effect. Indeed, as soon as the results are broken down according to institutional sector, the order of satisfaction levels is systematically in favour of independent workers. For the informal sector, managers register a balance of satisfaction of 54 per cent, that is to say, a higher rate than the average one observed in the private formal sector. Then follow self-employed workers and family workers (30 and 32 per cent respectively); while salaried workers come in last (21 per cent).

Beyond these averages, it is however advisable to control the level of satisfaction by remuneration. Indeed, out of all the results exhibited in academic work, the most robust is the positive role of income on satisfaction. This stylized fact is also found as much in macro studies (in cross-section or in panel countries data) as in micro ones (on an individual level), whether it be about job satisfaction, or more widely about the effect of income on general happiness. Vietnam is no exception to this rule. Whether it is in the informal sector or for all the workers, the level of satisfaction increases with the level of remuneration, even though the effect of income appears slightly less pronounced in the informal sector, as shown in Figure 2.2a.

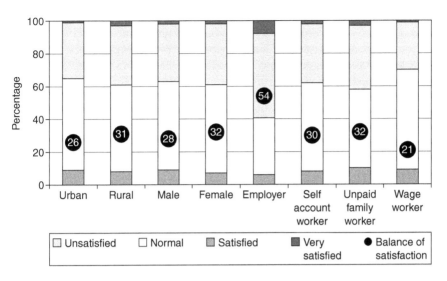

*Figure 2.2* Job satisfaction levels in the informal sector by subgroup, 2009 (sources: Labour Force Survey 2009, GSO; authors' calculations).

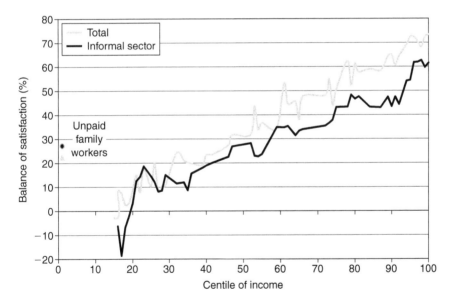

*Figure 2.2a* Job satisfaction levels according to remuneration in Vietnam, 2009 (sources: Labour Force Survey 2009, GSO; authors' calculations).

A calculation equivalent to that in Figure 2.2a can be made for each institutional sector. Given the size of the sample groups, we shall proceed by remuneration quintile. The improvement of satisfaction with income is observed in each sector (Figure 2.2b). However, hierarchy between sectors is globally respected at each level of remuneration, which shows that remuneration is not the only determinant of satisfaction.

## Modelling and discussion of econometric results

To go further, ordered probit or logit type models are mobilized to calculate the conditional probability of finding oneself in a given state of satisfaction. We shall proceed by successive stages, by beginning with the most simple model (by institutional sector) and by progressively adding sets of variables, respectively corresponding to the characteristics of the jobs, the enterprises and the workers. A fixed effect household model is considered in order to attempt to control certain unobservable characteristics and validate our results. The stability of estimated coefficients, whatever the specification used, attests the robustness of our conclusions.

First of all, the simple model (model 1) confirms the hierarchy of the institutional sectors obtained in the preceding section (Table 2.3a). The introduction of variables to control their influence changes nothing globally to the order: the informal sector is always negatively connoted, which is particularly true when incomes are controlled (model 3). Thus, for a given income, the satisfaction it procures is not significantly different from that in agriculture, which leads us to suppose that informal sector jobs are associated with negative properties that our

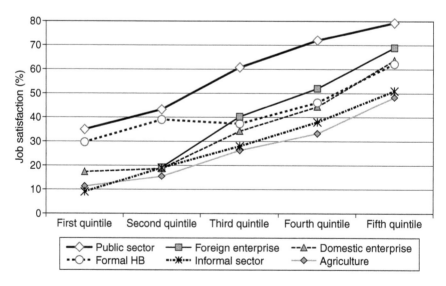

*Figure 2.2b* Job satisfaction levels according to remuneration and institutional sector, 2009 (sources: Labour Force Survey 2009, GSO; authors' calculations).

Table 2.3a  Job satisfaction determinants (ordered logit)

| | (1) | (2) | (3) | (4) | (5) | (6) | Logit model (satisfied or not) |
|---|---|---|---|---|---|---|---|
| | | (1) + job status | (2) + income | (3) + character of job | (4) + character of the enterprise | (5) + individual characteristics | Fixed effect household |
| *Institutional sector (ref. = informal sector)* | | | | | | | |
| Public sector | 1.4*** | 1.7*** | 1.4*** | 0.7*** | 0.6*** | 0.5*** | 0.8*** |
| | (15.59) | (14.37) | (12.25) | (5.286) | (3.807) | (4.127) | (3.341) |
| Foreign enterprise | 0.8*** | 1.1*** | 0.9*** | 0.4** | 0.5*** | 0.4** | 0.5* |
| | (6.289) | (6.776) | (5.946) | (2.539) | (2.609) | (2.075) | (1.773) |
| Domestic enterprise | 0.6*** | 0.8*** | 0.5*** | 0.2** | 0.1 | 0.1 | 0.3 |
| | (8.852) | (9.025) | (6.946) | (2.163) | (1.124) | (0.937) | (1.443) |
| Formal household business | 0.6*** | 0.6*** | 0.5*** | 0.4*** | 0.3*** | 0.3*** | 0.6*** |
| | (10.97) | (10.22) | (7.161) | (7.166) | (4.808) | (5.582) | (4.218) |
| Agriculture | -0.3*** | -0.3*** | -0.1 | -0.2*** | -0.0 | -0.1* | -0.2 |
| | (-3.811) | (-4.191) | (-1.444) | (-2.713) | (-0.514) | (-1.815) | (-0.937) |
| *Job status* | | | | | | | |
| Salaried worker | | -0.3*** | -0.3*** | -0.3*** | -0.3*** | -0.2*** | -0.4*** |
| | | (-4.888) | (-4.648) | (-3.998) | (-3.189) | (-2.793) | (-3.087) |
| *Remuneration* | | | | | | | |
| Log (income) | | | -0.6*** | -0.5*** | -0.5*** | -0.6*** | -0.9*** |
| | | | (-9.946) | (-8.730) | (-8.820) | (-10.69) | (-12.40) |
| Log (income)² | | | 0.1*** | 0.1*** | 0.1*** | 0.1*** | 0.1*** |
| | | | (12.00) | (10.39) | (10.52) | (12.97) | (14.36) |
| Log (income other household members) | | | 0.0 | 0.0 | 0.0 | 0.0** | -0.0 |
| | | | (1.049) | (0.722) | (0.676) | (2.001) | (-0.374) |
| Observations | 35,528 | 35,528 | 35,224 | 35,018 | 35,018 | 35,018 | 10,267 |
| pseudo R² | 0.04 | 0.04 | 0.07 | 0.09 | 0.09 | 0.10 | 0.24 |

continued

Table 2.3a Continued

|  | (1) | (2) | (3) | (4) | (5) | (6) | Logit model (satisfied or not) Fixed effect household? |
|---|---|---|---|---|---|---|---|
|  |  | (1) + job status | (2) + income | (3) + characteristics of the job | (4) + characteristics of the enterprise | (5) + individual characteristics |  |
| *Job characteristics* |  |  |  |  |  |  |  |
| Part-time job | – | – | – | -0.1* (-1.900) | -0.1** (-1.963) | -0.2*** (-2.983) | -0.1 (-0.920) |
| Log (number of hours) | – | – | – | -0.0 (-0.823) | -0.0 (-0.789) | -0.0 (-0.415) | 0.1 (0.431) |
| Wish to work longer hours | – | – | – | -1.1*** (-16.55) | -1.1*** (-16.18) | -1.1*** (-19.63) | -0.8*** (-4.563) |
| Log (seniority) | – | – | – | 0.1*** (5.837) | 0.1*** (6.186) | 0.1*** (6.413) | 0.1*** (5.763) |
| Social security | – | – | – | 0.2** (2.096) | 0.2** (2.105) | 0.2** (2.078) | 0.4*** (3.804) |
| Work contract: indeterminate length (ref.=no contract) | – | 0.5*** | 0.5*** | 0.5*** (4.226) | 0.8*** (3.915) | – (4.659) | – (4.857) |
| Work contract: determinate length (ref. = no contact) | – | 0.2 | 0.2 | 0.3** (1.642) | 0.5*** (1.434) | (2.174) | (3.525) |
| *Characteristics of the enterprises* |  |  |  |  |  |  |  |
| Size [21–300] people (ref.=size<=20) | – | – | – | – | 0.0 (0.526) | 0.0 (0.897) | 0.0 (0.239) |
| Size [300 or +] people (ref. = size<=20) | – | – | – | – | -0.2* (-1.786) | -0.1 (-1.283) | 0.0 (0.233) |
| Manufacturing (ref. = service) | – | – | – | – | -0.0 (-0.682) | -0.0 (-0.854) | -0.0 (-0.425) |

| | | | | | | | |
|---|---|---|---|---|---|---|---|
| Commerce (ref. = service) | – | – | – | – | 0.1*** | 0.1** | 0.2*** |
| | | | | | (2.826) | (2.161) | (3.036) |
| Professional premises (ref. = in the street) | – | – | – | – | 0.3*** | 0.4*** | 0.3*** |
| | | | | | (3.723) | (5.486) | (2.822) |
| Domicile (ref. = in the street) | – | – | – | – | 0.3*** | 0.3*** | 0.4*** |
| | | | | | (5.602) | (6.831) | (5.449) |
| | *(1)* | *(2)* | *(3)* | *(4)* | *(5)* | *(6)* | *Model logit* |
| | | *(1) + job status* | *(2) + income* | *(3) + job characteristics* | *(4) + workplace* | *(5) + socio–demo* | *(satisfied or not) fixed-effect household* |
| *Socio-demographical characteristics* | | | | | | | |
| Female | – | – | – | – | – | 0.1*** | 0.3*** |
| | | | | | | (4.740) | (5.684) |
| Log (age) | – | – | – | – | – | 0.2*** | 0.3*** |
| | | | | | | (4.050) | (3.241) |
| Head of household | – | – | – | – | – | 0.1** | 0.1 |
| | | | | | | (2.356) | (1.623) |
| Education: higher | – | – | – | – | – | 0.4*** | 0.4*** |
| | | | | | | (7.110) | (2.926) |
| Migrant | – | – | – | – | – | –0.0 | –0.4 |
| | | | | | | (–0.462) | (–1.077) |
| Ethnic minority | – | – | – | – | – | 0.1 | 0.4 |
| | | | | | | (1.019) | (1.408) |
| Rural | – | – | – | – | – | 0.3*** | – |
| | | | | | | (5.531) | |

*continued*

Table 2.3a Continued

| | (1) | (2) | (3) | (4) | (5) | (6) |
|---|---|---|---|---|---|---|
| | + job status | (1) + income | (2) + job characteristics | (3) + workplace | (4) + socio-demo | Model logit (satisfied or not) fixed-effect household |
| **Region (ref. = Central Highlands)** | | | | | | |
| Hanoi | — | — | — | — | −0.7*** | — |
| | | | | | (−9.882) | |
| Ho Chi Minh City | — | — | — | — | 0.1 | — |
| | | | | | (0.431) | |
| Mekong Delta | — | — | — | — | 0.4*** | — |
| | | | | | (4.974) | |
| Red River Delta | — | — | — | — | 0.4*** | — |
| | | | | | (5.419) | |
| South-east | — | — | — | — | 0.2*** | — |
| | | | | | (2.806) | |
| Central coast and central-south | — | — | — | — | 0.1 | — |
| | | | | | (1.193) | |
| Northern mountains | — | — | — | — | 0.2*** | — |
| | | | | | (4.303) | |
| Observations | 35,528 | 35,224 | 35,018 | 35,018 | 35,018 | 10,267 |
| pseudo R² | 0.04 | 0.07 | 0.09 | 0.09 | 0.10 | 0.24 |
| Log (pseudo likelihood) | −35,516 | −34,167 | −33,363 | −33,312 | −32,827 | −2,936 |

Sources: Labour Force Survey 2009, GSO; authors' calculations.

Notes
Robust z statistics in brackets.
*** $p < 0.01$.
** $p < 0.05$.
* $p < 0.1$.

models do not allow us to identify. We shall attempt to examine more thoroughly this question in fourth section of the chapter.

Nevertheless, the relative situation of two other institutional sectors merits attention. On the one hand, the "satisfaction bonus" awarded to jobs in domestic enterprises falls considerably when the remunerations and the job characteristics are taken into consideration (models 3 and 4), and disappear if the characteristics of the enterprises and the workers are added (models 5 and 6). Therefore, there is no advantage in working in this sector, beyond the variables taken into account in our models. On the other hand, the "satisfaction bonus" awarded to formal household businesses remains at a high level, whichever model is considered (including the fixed effect household estimation). For an entrepreneur, not being registered thus weighs negatively on his/her satisfaction, either directly (if he is the victim of harassment by state agents or if he is socially disparaged for example), or indirectly, as a marker of negative characteristics linked to the jobs (with less access to public services for example, or being concentrated in insalubrious zones) which are not taken into account in our models.

Second, the status of salaried worker is always devalued compared to non-salaried workers, in spite of the fact that it provides on average higher remunerations and better job protection. To be independent (being one's own boss, not having to obey someone) remains a dream which is massively pursued by the majority of Vietnamese workers (see fourth section, below). The level of remuneration has also a significant influence on job satisfaction.

In terms of job characteristics, time spent at work also plays a role (models 4 and 5). Rather than the number of hours as such, what seems decisive is whether one works full or part time (less than 35 hours a week), the latter case reducing satisfaction. This result tends to show that part-time work is an imposed choice.[2] In a country like Vietnam, visible under-employment, unlike unemployment, is thus a measure of the tensions on the labour market (Razafindrakoto *et al.*, 2011). Besides, job protection as well as social security affiliation or being covered by a formal work contract are also benefits which are held in high prestige by workers. This result thus qualifies the criticism aimed at the labour legislation system in force in Vietnam (Castel and To, 2012). Eventually, the positive correlation between seniority and satisfaction reveals that job stability is appreciated.

If the enterprise characteristics are considered, size (number of employees) does not seem to be a preponderant factor in satisfaction, except on the fringe, to the detriment of the bigger establishments (models 5, 6 and 7). On the reverse, the type of activity counts. Indeed, the Vietnamese have a preference for commercial activities, to the detriment of manufacturing activities. Finally, the existence of fixed premises is a source of satisfaction whereas ambulant activities, in the streets or fields, exposed to the elements, severely test the workforce.

Finally, the role of the socio-demographic control variables reinforces a certain number of intuitions corroborated by our descriptive analyses. For a given type of job, rural workers, women and the elderly get more satisfaction from their job than their young, male urban counterparts. This result appears all the more robust as it resists the fixed effect household equation estimation. The question of aspirations and the above-mentioned phenomenon of preference attrition are found again here. The traditionally dominated categories satisfy themselves with lower quality jobs, doubtlessly because they have more limited ambitions.[3]

It is also interesting to note that having a higher level of education also translates into extra satisfaction. Beyond the substantial gains it allows one to obtain, a diploma is perhaps synonymous with promotion and career prospects and perhaps also has its own intrinsic value which gratifies those who possess one. As for the region variables introduced into the regressions (model 6) in order to better control the specific conditions of local labour markets (prices, competition, specialization etc.), they are generally significant. The big cities in particular, Ho Chi Minh City and especially Hanoi, are associated with lower levels of satisfaction, which might be tied with growing urban disturbances (urban traffic jams, pollution, etc.).

In order to take into account the heterogeneity of the informal sector, we separate, within the informal sector, salaried and non-salaried workers.[4] Indeed, numerous studies quoted in the first section conclude that independent workers in the informal sector choose this sector, unlike salaried workers who would be obliged to work in this sector for lack of any alternative. Our estimations only partially confirm this thesis (Table 2.3b). Admittedly, salaried workers in the informal sector show less job satisfaction than non-salaried workers in this sector, and this is true whatever specification is retained. However, their level of satisfaction is always lower than those who have non-agricultural jobs in other

*Table 2.3b* Job satisfaction determinants (ordered logit)

|  | *(1)* | *(3)* | *(4)* | *(5)* | *(6)* | *Fixed effect household* |
|---|---|---|---|---|---|---|
| *Institutional sector (ref. = non-salaried workers in informal sector)* | | | | | | |
| Public sector | 1.4** | 1.1** | 0.5** | 0.5** | 0.4** | 0.5** |
|  | (14.67) | (13.20) | (4.32) | (2.98) | (3.14) | (2.71) |
| Foreign enterprise | 0.8** | 0.5** | 0.3 | 0.4* | 0.3 | 0.3 |
|  | (5.54) | (4.01) | (1.57) | (1.99) | (1.56) | (1.03) |
| Domestic enterprise | 0.5** | 0.2** | 0.1 | −0.0 | −0.0 | 0.0 |
|  | (7.06) | (3.87) | (0.61) | (0.01) | (0.17) | (0.26) |
| Formal household business | 0.5** | 0.3** | 0.3** | 0.3** | 0.3** | 0.5** |
|  | (8.89) | (5.61) | (5.72) | (3.65) | (4.62) | (3.20) |
| Informal sector (salaried) | −0.3** | −0.3** | −0.3** | −0.2** | −0.2** | −0.4** |
|  | (5.95) | (5.86) | (4.08) | (3.58) | (2.68) | (2.62) |
| Agriculture | −0.4** | −0.2* | −0.2** | −0.1 | −0.2* | −0.2 |
|  | (4.66) | (2.14) | (3.16) | (0.92) | (2.25) | (1.32) |

Sources: Labour Force Survey 2009, GSO; author's calculations.

Notes
For the different models, see Table 2.3a. Control variables not reported.

sectors, even for the same remuneration. It is only when the other characteristics of jobs, enterprises and workers are integrated that the latter are not less satisfied than certain categories in the formal sector, namely salaried workers in foreign and domestic enterprises. In all cases, public service salaried workers and workers in individual formal enterprises are systematically happier at work. Heterogeneity is therefore not a specificity of the informal sector only: it also affects the formal sector.

## Some elements of interpretation

At this stage of analysis, we can firmly conclude that on average the informal sector provides less job satisfaction than all the other institutional sectors (with the exception of agriculture), particularly when one is employed as a salaried worker. But this result far from exhausts the question, and here we arrive at the limits of our modelling. On the other hand, this "on average" reasoning flattens out the diversity of the situations. It does not account for the heterogeneity of the informal sector and the motives which drive people to work there. On the other hand, our quantitative analysis does not allow us to understand the mechanisms which drive individuals to enter the informal sector and remain there.

To go further into the motivations leading workers to enter the informal sector, we shall use information derived from the two waves of surveys representative of the informal sector carried out by us in Hanoi and Ho Chi Minh City between 2007 and 2010, complemented by a series of in-depth interviews with 60 or so informal operators in these two agglomerations.

First, regarding the motivations which led them to create their own business, more than half of the heads of informal establishments say that they made the choice for positive reasons (Table 2.4). The prospect of earning a higher income (especially in Hanoi), the desire to be one's own boss (especially in Ho Chi Minh City) or even a family tradition constitute big incentives to set up in the informal sector. In fact, only a minority (31 per cent in Hanoi and scarcely 6 per cent in the economic capital) started their own business because they failed to find salaried work in the formal sector. If it is not necessary to exclude the possibility of an a posteriori rationalization of an above all constrained choice, the standard hypothesis of a queue at the gates of the formal sector appears to be at best a superficial approximation of the sectional allocation of jobs. Salaried work in the formal sector thus far from constitutes the ultimate, impassable objective of the workforce in Vietnam. Oudin (see Chapter 13 in this book) finds similar results in the case of Thailand.

Nevertheless, informal operators are far from being optimistic about the prospects of their production units. Only 45 per cent in Hanoi and 29 per cent in Ho Chi Minh City declare that their activity has a future (Table 2.5). Even more worrying, scarcely 20 per cent affirm that they would like their children (if they had any, for those without) to take over their business.

Such pessimism appears to be absolutely specific to the case of Vietnam. In the context of African countries, where identical studies have been carried out,

*Table 2.4* Principal reason for creating an individual enterprise according to the head (% of HBs)

| | Did not find salaried work (big enterprise) | Did not find salaried work (individual enterprise) | To obtain higher revenue | To be independent | By family tradition | Other | Total |
|---|---|---|---|---|---|---|---|
| *Hanoi* | | | | | | | |
| Informal HB | 30.6 | 11.9 | 28.8 | 14.2 | 2.6 | 11.8 | 100 |
| Formal HB | 13.8 | 6.5 | 33.9 | 31.0 | 10.5 | 4.4 | 100 |
| Household business | 27.3 | 10.9 | 29.8 | 17.5 | 4.2 | 10.4 | 100 |
| *Ho Chi Minh City* | | | | | | | |
| Informal HB | 18.9 | 11.1 | 14.7 | 34.1 | 7.4 | 13.7 | 100 |
| Formal HB | 6.4 | 2.4 | 18.3 | 54.4 | 12.5 | 6.1 | 100 |
| Household business | 15.7 | 9.0 | 15.7 | 39.2 | 8.8 | 11.7 | 100 |

Sources: HB&IS survey; Hanoi (2007), Ho Chi Minh City (2008) surveys; GSO-ISS/IRD-DIAL; authors' calculations.

*Table 2.5* Informal sector prospects according to the head of enterprise (% of informal HBs)

| | Vietnam (2007, 2009) | | Cameroon (2005) | | Madagascar (2004) | WAEMU (2001–2003) |
|---|---|---|---|---|---|---|
| | Hanoi | HCMC | Douala | Yaoundé | Antananarivo | – |
| Enterprise has a | 2007 42.2 | 30.9 | 64.0 | 70.6 | 60.4 | 83.1 |
| future | 2009 45.0 | 29.3 | | | | |
| Wish to see | 2007 19.5 | 17.2 | 39.8 | 43.5 | 37.1 | 65.2 |
| children take over | 2009 23.9 | 14.7 | | | | |
| the household | | | | | | |
| business | | | | | | |

Sources: *Surveys 1-2-3*, Phases 2; Cameroon (2005), Madagascar (2004), UEMOA (2001–2003) and Vietnam (surveys HB&IS, Hanoi (2007, 2009) & Ho Chi Minh City (2008, 2010)); authors' calculations.

the informal sector is much more often considered as the natural way of entering on to the labour market. Thus, 40 per cent in Cameroon and in Madagascar, and nearly two-thirds in French-speaking West Africa would like their children to inherit their business. The recent dynamism of the Vietnamese economy doubtlessly explains this contrasted result (Cling *et al.*, 2010a).

In order to explain these partially contradictory results, we can propose the following elements of interpretation: setting up one's own business outside agriculture remains the desired objective of a great many Vietnamese, on the one hand in order to escape the miserable conditions of the greater part of agricultural activities and, on the other hand, because salaried work, which is still limited in spite of its noteworthy recent progress, is far from being the norm as it is the case in developed countries. It appears as a less than enviable prospect because of its servitudes: remuneration which is not always attractive and above all hierarchical dependency which is not to the taste of many local workers.

The qualitative interviews clearly illustrate the tensions between aspirations and fulfilment which informal operators must face up to. If the desire to be independent (synonymous with prestige and autonomy) is recurrent and working-hour flexibility greatly appreciated whereas the financial advantages of the formal sector are far from being systematically assured, the insecurity of demand and income weighs heavily on the well-being of informal sector workers, and giving clients satisfaction is a source of constant stress, to such a point that there is a wish to return to the formal salaried job (Razafindrakoto, 2010).

The results of the HB&IS survey of 2009/2010 confirm these hypotheses. In this survey, we asked heads of informal enterprises if they wanted to change jobs and, if so, for which institutional sector and, second, in which sector they would like to see their children work. In response to the first question, only a minority declared a wish to seek new activity. Among the others, both in Hanoi and in Ho Chi Minh City nearly 60 per cent wished to set up a new individual enterprise (without it being possible to distinguish between formal and informal sectors), a little more than 20 per cent wished to be hired by a domestic enterprise and about 10 per cent wished to enter the public services (Table 2.6). On the other hand, as far as children are concerned the replies are very different. Not only is the immense majority not in favour of handing down their activity to their children, but they all hope that their children will find a job as salaried workers in the public sector (65 per cent in Hanoi and 51 per cent in Ho Chi Minh City), percentages which are totally unrealistic when compared to the present (and future) employment structure. In second place are domestic and foreign enterprises. In summary, if informal operators consider that it is probably too late (in life) to hope for a favourable insertion, the great majority of them dream of a better future for their descendants outside this sector.

## Conclusion

This chapter set out to explore the question of the *raison d'être* of the informal sector in Vietnam, a component of the country's economy which is as massive and long lasting as it is misunderstood. Are the jobs carried out in this sector appreciated by the workforce or, on the contrary, do they represent a stopgap to escape unemployment? To this day the debate remains open. Rather than confining ourselves to indirect job quality measures, and above all to the remunerations jobs provide, we have focused on the job satisfaction question. This study comes within the framework of a very recent field of research into DCs, to which we are attempting to make an original contribution.

Our results clearly demonstrate the low level of satisfaction provided by informal sector jobs. The latter are situated at the bottom of the ladder, with the exception of agricultural jobs, which provide by far the least satisfaction. The level of remuneration is an important factor but is not a sufficient explanation. At equal income, non-agricultural jobs continue to be more attractive than jobs in the informal sector. On the other hand, the latter are situated at the same level

*Table 2.6* Wish to change of heads of enterprise by institutional sector (% of informal HBs)

| | Wish for personal change | | Wish for change for their children | |
|---|---|---|---|---|
| | *Hanoi* | *HCM City* | *Hanoi* | *HCM City* |
| Public sector | 13.2 | 9.6 | 65.3 | 50.9 |
| Foreign enterprise | 0 | 0.8 | 12.6 | 15.5 |
| Domestic enterprise | 2.9 | 24.2 | 14.9 | 26.3 |
| Individual enterprise | 58.3 | 57.5 | 3.9 | 4.9 |
| Agriculture | 3.7 | 1.4 | 0.2 | 0 |
| Other, does not know | 3.9 | 6.5 | 3.1 | 2.4 |
| *Total* | *100* | *100* | *100* | *100* |

Sources: HB&IS surveys, Hanoi (2007, 2009) and Ho Chi Minh City (2008, 2010); authors' calculations.

as agricultural jobs, showing that these jobs are preferred only because they are better paid. The relative dissatisfaction provided by jobs in the informal sector persists beyond the many job and enterprise characteristics which are rather unfavourable to the informal sector. Once these monetary and non-monetary elements are taken into account, all the institutional non-agricultural sectors remain implacably preferred to the informal sector, with the exception of private domestic enterprises.

In order to take into account the heterogeneity of the informal sector, the usual distinction between salaried and non-salaried jobs was considered. Contrary to classical results in academic work, according to which the former type of job is "forced upon" workers and the latter a personal choice, in the case of Vietnam both types seem to correspond to second rate jobs. Admittedly, salaried jobs in the informal sector are the least valued, but informal independent jobs are hardly more appreciated. In spite of all this, once we have eliminated the structural effects (remuneration and protection levels), they are on an equal footing with jobs in private formal enterprises.

In conclusion, this chapter confirms that a job satisfaction approach is a fruitful one to appreciate the quality of jobs in Vietnam, and more widely in other developing countries. It helps bring some original answers to researchers' questions, but also some new ideas for a better elaboration of economic policy. For example, well-being derived from social protection and preference for independent worker status should lead to the development of a social security system which is not reserved to wage-workers only. Such an option is all the more necessary as job creation in the formal sector is (and will be in any case) insufficient to absorb massive flows of new entrants in the labour market.

## Notes

1  The balance of satisfaction (per cent of satisfied workers to per cent of dissatisfied workers) is a technique widely used in the analysis of opinion surveys.
2  Furthermore and logically, wanting to work more is an indicator of decisive dissatisfaction in one's current job.
3  However, this characteristic is not true for the ethnic minorities and migrants. For a discussion of this result see Razafindrakoto *et al.*, 2012.
4  Family workers have been incorporated with independent workers after verifying that there was no difference in terms of satisfaction with whichever model specified.

## References

Azalea, A., Omar, F., Mastor, K.A. (2009) "The Role of Individual Differences in Job Satisfaction Among Indonesians and Malaysians", *European Journal of Social Sciences* Vol. 10, 4; 496–11.

Bacchetta, M., Ernst, E., Bustamante, J.P. (2009) *Globalization and Informal Jobs in Developing Countries*, Geneva: ILO and WTO.

Bargain, O., Kwenda, P. (2011) "Earnings Structures, Informal Employment, and Self-Employment: New Evidence from Brazil, Mexico and South Africa", *Review of Income and Wealth*, Vol. 57, Special Issue, May; 100–22.

Castel, P., To, T.T. (2012) "Informal Employment in the Formal Sector Wages and Social Security Tax Evasion in Vietnam", in Cling, J.P., Razafindrakoto, M. and Roubaud, F. eds, The Informal Economy in Asia, special issue of the *Journal of the Asia and Pacific Economy*, Vol. 14, 4, October.

Cling, J.-P., Nguyen Thi Thu Huyen, Nguyen, Huu Chi, Phan, T. Ngoc Trâm, Razafindrakoto, M., Roubaud, F. (2010a) *The Informal Sector in Vietnam: A Focus on Hanoi and Ho Chi Minh City*, Hanoi: The Gioi Publishers.

Cling, J.-P., Razafindrakoto, M., Roubaud, F. (2010b) "Assessing the Potential Impact of the Global Crisis on the Labour Market and the Informal Sector in Vietnam", *Journal of Economics and Development*, Vol. 38, June; 16–25.

de Soto, H. (1989) *The Other Path: The Invisible Revolution in the Third World*, New York: Harper Collins (original edition published in Spanish in 1986).

Demenet, A., Nguyen Thi Thu Huyen, Razafindrakoto, M., Roubaud, F. (2010) "Dynamics of the informal sector in Hanoi and Ho Chi Minh City 2007–2009", GSO-IRD Policy Brief, Hanoi.

Falco, P., Maloney, W.F., Rijkers, B. (2011) *Self Employment and Informality in Africa: Panel Evidence from Satisfaction Data*, processed.

GSO (2010) "Report on Labour force and Employment Survey in Vietnam 2009", National Statistical Publishing House, Hanoi.

Harris, J.R., Todaro, M.P. (1970) "Migration, Unemployment, and Development: A Two-sector Analysis", *American Economic Review*, Vol. 60, 1; 126–42.

Jütting, J.P., de Laiglesia, J.R., eds (2009) *Is Informal Normal? Towards More and Better Jobs in Developing Countries*, Paris: OECD Development Centre.

Maloney, W. (1999) "Does Informality imply Segmentation in Urban Labor Markets? Evidence from Sectoral Transitions in Mexico", *World Bank Economic Review*, Vol. 13, 2; 275–302.

Nguyen, Huu Chi, Nordman, C.J., Roubaud, F. (2010) "Panel Data Analysis of the Dynamics of Labour Allocation in Vietnam: The State Dependency Reconsidered", ASSV-IRD International Conference, "The Informal Sector and Informal Employment: Statistical Measurement, Economic Implications and Public Policies", Hanoi, Mai.

Nguyen, Huu Chi, Nordman, C.J., Roubaud, F. (2013) "Who Suffers the Penalty? A Panel Data Analysis of Earnings Gaps in Vietnam" *Journal of Development Studies*, Vol. 49, 12; 1694–710.

Pagés, C., Madrigal, L. (2008) "Is Informality a Good Measure of Job Quality? Evidence from Job Satisfaction Data", Inter-American Development Bank, Research Department Working Papers No. 654, Washington, DC.

Perry, G.E., Maloney, W.F., Arias, O.S., Fajnzylber, P., Mason, A.D., Saavedra-Chanduvi, J. (2007) *Informality: Exit and Exclusion*, Washington, DC: World Bank, World Bank Latin American and Caribbean Studies.

Portes, A., Castells, M., Benton, L.A. (1989) *The Informal Economy: Studies in Advanced and Less Developed Countries*, Baltimore, MD: The Johns Hopkins University Press.

Raquel Bernal, S. (2009) "The Informal Labor Market in Colombia: Identification and Characterization", *Desarrollo y Sociedad*, Primer Semestre de 2009: 145–08.

Rakotomanana, F. (2011) "Les travailleurs du secteur informel sont-ils plus heureux: le cas de l'agglomération d'Antananarivo, in Secteur informel urbain, marché du travail et pauvreté. Essais d'analyse sur le cas de Madagascar", Doctoral Thesis, Université Bordeaux IV, December.

Razafindrakoto, M. (2010) "Household Business and Informal Sector in Hanoi and Ho Chi Minh City: First Results from a Qualitative Survey (2009)", DIAL, Hanoi, June.

Razafindrakoto, M., Roubaud, F. (2013) "Job Satisfaction in Eight African Cities", in De Vreyer, P., Roubaud, F. eds, *Urban Labor Markets in Sub-Saharan Africa*, Washington, DC: World Bank/AFD: 109–34.

Razafindrakoto, M., Roubaud, F., Lê Van, D. (2008) "Measuring the Informal Sector in Vietnam: Situation and Prospects", *Statistical Scientific Information*, Special Issue on Informal Sector, Vol. 2008, 1–2; 15–29.

Razafindrakoto, M., Roubaud, F., Nguyen, Huu Chi (2011) "Vietnam Labor Market: An Informal Sector Perspective", in Nguyễn, Đức Thành ed., *Vietnam Annual Economic Report 2011: The Economy at a Crossroad*, Hanoi: Tri Thức Publishers: 223–58.

Razafindrakoto, M., Roubaud, F., Wachsberger, J.-M. (2012) "Travailler dans le secteur informel: choix ou contrainte? Une analyse de la satisfaction dans l'emploi au Vietnam", *document de travail DIAL*, DT 2012-8; 30.

Tolentino, C.M. (2007) "Job Satisfaction of SME Workers in Select Cities of Mindanao", *Philippine Journal of Labor and Industrial Relations*, Vol. 27, 1 & 2; 42–55.

# 3 Being an informal self-employed from one generation to the next

## A constrained choice or better income prospects? Evidence from seven West-African countries

*Laure Pasquier-Doumer*

Since the 1970s, research on the informal sector constitutes a growing part of the literature on labour markets in developing countries. The upsurge in interest is at least partly because most households in many developing countries, in particular poor households, derive a large part of their earnings from the informal sector. It constitutes an often unacknowledged contribution to national production levels as well. However, despite nearly four decades of research, no consensus has emerged on the origin and the persistence of the informal sector.

While there is no consensus on the voluntary nature of entry into informal self-employment, strong evidence points to a strong intergenerational transmission of the self-employed status in developed countries. For developing countries, there is almost no evidence on this issue. An exception is Pasquier-Doumer (2013a) who shows high social reproduction rates for the self-employed in West Africa. Starting from this observation, the present chapter addresses the following questions. First, do children of self-employed perform better than children of wage earners when they become informal self-employed? Second, which are the sources of this advantage in terms of firm value added? Do they have a better access to valuable human capital, physical or social capital? If they had such advantage, one could support the idea that children of self-employed would choose voluntarily to enter into the informal sector because they expect better incomes.

Addressing these questions is particularly relevant in the African context. Inequalities in Africa are very high and social mobility very low (Cogneau *et al.*, 2007). The intergenerational transmission of occupation is one possible cause of low social mobility. Furthermore, informal activities are the main provider of incomes and of jobs for most African urban dwellers (Brilleau *et al.*, 2005a). In addition, the informal sector is the prevalent place of professionalization and integration of young people into the labour market, in particular for those who drop out of school (Walther, 2007). Then, this chapter will shed light on the heterogeneity of the informal sector, by testing whether entrepreneurial familial background may be a source of success for informal businesses.

The next section presents the conceptual framework and the hypotheses to be tested. The second section provides an overview of the data and the main characteristics of the second generation of self-employed. The third section describes the estimation strategy. The fourth section examines the existence of a competitive advantage for the second generation of self-employed in terms of informal business outcomes. The fifth section analyses the composition of this advantage. The sixth section summarizes and concludes.

## Conceptual background and hypotheses

Some studies conducted in developed countries analyse the impact of having self-employed parents on the determinants of becoming self-employed rather than wage earner (Dunn and Holtz-Eakin, 2000; Colombier and Masclet, 2008; Laferrère and McEntee, 1996). They all conclude that there is a substantially higher probability to become self-employed among children of self-employed. Two main channels are identified. First, successful entrepreneurs may be more able and willing to transfer financial wealth to their children and thus allow them to relax capital market constraints. Second, parents transmit to their children valuable work experience, reputation or other managerial human capital.

To my knowledge, only two studies aim at understanding the impact of familial background on small businesses outcomes (Lentz and Laband, 1990; Fairlie and Robb, 2007). Again both relate to developed countries. Lentz and Laband (1990) suggest that individuals acquire general managerial skills while growing up in the context of family business through the continued exposure to the family business. Children of self-employed have then an advantage compared with children of wage-earners, who do not see their parents at work. The authors show that second generation self-employed have greater success compared with first-generation self-employed. Because second generation self-employed are found to start their businesses at a significantly younger age and to start their business careers with a significantly greater quantity of managerial human capital, the authors conclude that children of self-employed have a competitive advantage through early acquisition of managerial human capital, and that this advantage will predictably serve to motivate voluntary choice of being self-employed in children of self-employed.

Along similar lines, Fairlie and Robb (2007) identify three potential channels that can explain the better outcomes of the second generation of self-employed: the acquisition of general business or managerial experience in family owned businesses, the acquisition of industry- or firm-specific business experience in family owned businesses and inheritances of businesses. In the latter case, parents transmit capital as a reputation capital or an established clientele from one generation to the next. With another dataset than Lentz and Laband, the authors conclude that the second generation of self-employed has an advantage in terms of business outcomes compared with self-employed without self-employed family member, through the transmission of managerial experience and/or firm-specific business experience.

In developing countries, there is no study that specifically addresses the impact of familial background on informal business outcomes. However, some evidence can be found in the related literature on social capital, in particular on the effects of family kinship on businesses outcomes. For example, Fafchamps (2002) investigates whether social networks improve firm productivity among agricultural traders in Madagascar. The author finds that having close relatives in agricultural trade does not have a positive effect on productivity. Furthermore, productivity is higher among traders who learned the business on their own and did not receive coaching from relatives. However, Fafchamps' results may not be generalized to the whole informal sector and to West-African countries. First, the way of acquisition of skills in West-African countries is very different from that in Madagascar and, second, trade is a specific sector of activity in terms of acquisition of skills and level of capital required.

## Hypotheses

This chapter aims to fill the knowledge gap on developing countries by testing whether second-generation entrepreneurs have better business outcomes than first-generation entrepreneurs. I then attempt to identify the channels that can explain possible differences in business outcomes. Following the empirical literature on developed countries, two main channels are tested: physical capital transfers and human capital transfers. As in developed countries, having a self-employed family member may facilitate the acquisition of physical capital for two possible reasons: self-employed, at least successful ones, may have more capacity to invest than a wage earner. Alternatively, some of the second generation self-employed simply inherit a part or the whole enterprise from their family member.

Following Lentz and Laband (1990), I distinguish two types of human capital transfers, general-managerial and enterprise-specific skills. General administrative and personnel management skills fall into the former type, while information specific to the firm's production process characterizes the latter. I assume that growing up in a self-employed family may procure better endowments in general-managerial skills, as a by-product of the continued exposure to the family business. In addition, there is intergenerational transmission of enterprise-specific skills only if the sector of activity of the family business is closely related to the one of the respondent. For this reason, I consider two types of second-generation self-employed. First, those whose parents were self-employed in a business which could be or not related to the one of the respondent (*SE* hereafter), and second those whose parents or family members were owners of a highly similar business (*TRAD* hereafter).

Indeed, having a family member involved in the same type of activity (*TRAD*) can improve the acquisition of enterprise-specific skills, in particular in the West-African context where traditional apprenticeship is prevalent.[1] The choice of the master is essential for the transmission of skills. Some masters may take advantage of a high demand for training, multiplying the number of apprentices. Consequently, they do not have time to supervise the apprentices and they do not have enough turnover to make them practice (Charmes and Oudin, 1994). If one of the members of the family is involved in a certain type of business, it may be easier for the family to choose a master with high professional skills and sufficient turnover. Moreover, family ties continue to play an important role in the selection of apprentices in West Africa (Birks *et al.*, 1994). Having family members in the same activity may allow young people to be more easily accepted by a "good" master. In addition, because traditional apprenticeship training has its roots in socio-cultural traditions that restricted the transfer of skills to members of the family or the clan (Haan, 2006), one can think that the transmission of enterprise-specific skills may be better with a master related to the family.

In the case of acquisition of human capital through experience, having a self-employed family member may increase the opportunities to accumulate experience in his/her business. This experience may also be more valuable in terms of acquisition of skills because the owner may give more responsibility to a family member. Indeed, socio-cultural traditions facilitate transmission of skills inside the family, and the family could have a greater interest in the professional success of one of its members than in that of someone unrelated to the family.

For all these reasons, having a self-employed family member in the same type of activities may increase endowments in enterprise-specific skills but also return to these skills.

In their study, Lentz and Laband (1990) do not include social capital as a possible way of intergenerational transmission of self-employed status. Fairlie and Robb (2007) introduce it but very indirectly, as a component of the inheritance of a family enterprise. They do not formally test it. Because of imperfect markets, social capital plays a crucial role in the performance of informal businesses in developing countries (Bacchetta *et al.*, 2009). As shown by Fafchamps (2002), social capital and more precisely social networks improve the circulation of reliable information about technology and market opportunities as well as the blacklisting of unreliable agents. Social capital can also make it easier to build up a clientele through reputation and trust. In addition, as shown by Pasquier-Doumer (2014) a large part of the social network mobilized with the aim of improving professional activities is related to the family. I assume that family members involved in the same type of business may pass on valuable social capital because they are known in the sector of activity: their name may inspire trust, they have information on market opportunities and on reliable suppliers in this sector of activity, and they can convey this information to other family members. I thus assume that the potential advantage of *TRAD* entrepreneurs can be partly explained by better endowments in social capital but also by higher return to this capital. However, the advantage should be very weak if family members (as the father) are involved in a different sector of activity, because children of wage-earners also benefit from family social capital that is not specific to their sector of activity.

To sum up, I suppose that the channels that can explain possible competitive advantage of second generation self-employed are the intergenerational transmission of general-managerial skills and physical capital or higher return to these factors, as far as children of self-employed are concerned (*SE*). For entrepreneurs with a self-employed family member in the same type of activities (*TRAD*), one may add two other channels: transmission of enterprise-specific skills and social capital.

## Data and characteristics of second generation self-employed in the informal sector

### *The data*

In this study, I use a set of 1-2-3 surveys carried out between 2001 and 2002 in seven economic capitals of West-African Economic and Monetary Union (WAEMU) countries: Cotonou (Benin), Ouagadougou (Burkina Faso), Abidjan (Côte d'Ivoire), Bamako (Mali), Niamey (Niger), Dakar (Senegal) and Lomé (Togo). A 1-2-3 survey is a multi-layer survey organized in three phases and specially designed to study the informal sector (see Brilleau *et al.*, 2005b). For this chapter, I use the phases 1 and 2 of the surveys. Phase 1 is a representative labour force survey collecting detailed information about individual employment and socio-demographic characteristics, in particular the sector and status of activity of the father when the individual was 15 years old. Phase 2 is a survey which interviews a sub-sample of informal production units identified in Phase 1. It provides very detailed data on sales, investment and inputs of the informal enterprises and on the characteristics of the owner. The 1-2-3 surveys define informal enterprises as small production units that (a) do not have written formal accounts and/or (b) are not registered with the tax administration.

A major advantage of the 1-2-3 survey is its nested structure because Phase 1 ensures that Phase 2 delivers a representative picture of the informal sector. Another one is that it allows us to identify the second generation of self-employed. Second generation of self-employed is defined in two ways. In a broad definition, it includes the informal business owners, whose father[2] was self-employed when his child was 15 years old (*SE*).[3] In a narrow definition, informal entrepreneurs of the second generation of self-employed are defined as entrepreneurs who benefit from a familial tradition in the way to run a business in their sector of activity (*TRAD*).[4] It is important to note that *SE* and *TRAD* are not exclusive: an informal entrepreneur may have a father self-employed in a different sector of activity and another family member in the same sector of activity. Overlap may also exist when the father is self-employed in the same sector of activity.

The 1-2-3 survey also provides a number of useful proxies of skills, social capital and the intergenerational transmission of physical capital. To take into account general managerial skills, I have three variables at my disposal. The first one is whether the entrepreneur has had a managerial experience before becoming the owner of the informal business surveyed. A previous experience as entrepreneur in another business is supposed to increase the ability of the owner to manage the informal business. The second proxy is whether the owner knows micro-finance institutions. It reveals better access to information that could improve productivity, and better access to external finance as well. The last one is whether the owner keeps books. It implicates better organization in the way of conducting the business.

There are two proxies of enterprise-specific skills. The first one takes the value 1 if the owner learned his profession by traditional apprenticeship training and the value 0 otherwise, for the most part if he or she learned his profession on his own. Traditional apprenticeship training gives to the owner a previous experience in his sector of activity during which transmission of enterprise-specific skills may be high. The second proxy is the number of years of experience in his actual activity.

Social capital of the informal entrepreneur is approached by the membership to a professional association. Although the determinant of the membership to a professional association is very poorly documented, it is likely that knowing the way of joining a professional association and being accepted as member in the West-African context may be more linked with the level of social capital than with the size or outcomes of the enterprise. A way of convincing the reader is that the size of the enterprise measured by the log of the amount of capital or by the log of the value added is a very poor predictor of the membership to a professional association.[5] For these reasons, the exogeneity of this proxy may be assumed.

Inherited physical capital is taken into account using two variables: (i) the amount of physical capital obtained from the family, and (ii) a dummy that takes the value 1 if the physical capital obtained from the family is higher than half of the whole amount of physical capital.

For all countries, I have at my disposal 5718 informal enterprises surveyed with corresponding data of the phase 1, and thus, on average, 817 enterprises per economic capital. Unfortunately, the scarcity of entrepreneurs with family members involved in the same type of activity (on average 120 per capital city) does not allow me to conduct a separate analysis for each city. All the data are pooled and I use country dummies in the estimations.

### What distinguish second generation of self-employed?

The second generation of self-employed represents 66 per cent of the informal business owners. Among them, 61 per cent have a self-employed father and 16 per cent benefit from familial tradition (Table 3.1).[6] Second generation of self-employed has better average outcomes than the other informal business owners, but only when they are defined with the narrow definition (*TRAD*). Otherwise, differences are not significant.

Their enterprises are older, in particular when they benefit from a familial tradition and they are more homogeneous with regard to ethnic criteria and familial relationship. Informal businesses with familial tradition are in addition more labour intensive and less capital intensive (Table 3.1). Besides differences in the characteristics of their businesses, second generation of self-employed distinguish themselves by several personal characteristics (Table 3.2).

Table 3.1 Characteristics of informal businesses

| Informal business characteristics | (1) 2nd generation | (2) 1st generation | (2)–(1) | (3) With self-employed father (SE) | (4) Non-SE | (4)–(3) | (5) With familial tradition (TRAD) | (6) Non-TRAD | (6)–(5) |
|---|---|---|---|---|---|---|---|---|---|
| Value added (mean, Int. $) | 369.0 | 378.6 | NS | 368.8 | 377.8 | NS | 424.7 | 362.2 | ** |
| Sales (mean, Int. $) | 1,133.6 | 1,027.9 | NS | 990.8 | 959.9 | NS | 1,170.3 | 941.7 | *** |
| Capital (mean, Int. $) | 790.0 | 757.4 | NS | 790.2 | 761.6 | NS | 713.2 | 791.6 | NS |
| Paid labour (mean, monthly hours) | 247.6 | 243.4 | NS | 246.0 | 246.5 | NS | 271.7 | 241.3 | *** |
| Age of the enterprise (mean) | 7.5 | 5.9 | *** | 7.2 | 6.5 | *** | 9.9 | 6.4 | *** |
| Ethnic homogeneity in the enterprise (%) | 95.7 | 94.4 | *** | 95.7 | 94.6 | *** | 96.1 | 95.1 | *** |
| Share of the workers from the same family (%) | 92.0 | 90.4 | *** | 91.9 | 90.9 | ** | 93.6 | 91.1 | *** |
| *Sectors of activity (%)* | | | | | | | | | |
| Clothing and apparel | 9.7 | 11.0 | * | 9.7 | 10.7 | NS | 7.4 | 10.6 | NS |
| Other manufacturing and food | 11.5 | 13.4 | NS | 11.4 | 13.3 | NS | 11.6 | 12.2 | NS |
| Construction | 5.7 | 5.7 | NS | 5.8 | 5.6 | NS | 2.9 | 6.2 | *** |
| Wholesale/retail shops | 12.0 | 9.6 | NS | 12.0 | 9.9 | NS | 15.9 | 10.2 | *** |
| Petty traders | 35.0 | 33.4 | *** | 35.0 | 33.7 | *** | 33.8 | 34.6 | NS |
| Hotels and restaurants | 6.3 | 6.1 | NS | 6.3 | 6.2 | NS | 5.8 | 6.3 | NS |
| Repair services | 4.4 | 4.9 | *** | 4.4 | 4.8 | ** | 3.3 | 4.8 | *** |
| Transport | 3.8 | 3.6 | NS | 3.8 | 3.6 | NS | 1.9 | 4.1 | *** |
| Other services | 11.7 | 12.3 | NS | 11.7 | 12.3 | NS | 17.2 | 10.8 | *** |
| N obs | 3,571 | 2,147 | | 3,253 | 2,465 | | 843 | 4,875 | |
| Frequency | 66.2 | 33.8 | | 60.7 | 39.3 | | 16.2 | 83.8 | |

Sources: author's computation based on *1-2-3* surveys (Phases 1 and 2, 2001/02, AFRISTAT, DIAL, INS).

Notes

The column Sign test with t-test the significance of the difference between *SE* versus non-*SE* and between *TRAD* and non-*TRAD*.

*, **, ***, NS mean respectively that the difference is significant at the 10% level, 5% level, 1% level, not significant.

Table 3.2 Informal entrepreneurs' characteristics

| Owner characteristics | (1) 2nd generation of self-employed | (2) 1st generation of self-employed | (2)–(1) | (3) Self-employed father (SE) | (4) Non-SE | (4)–(3) | (5) With familial tradition (TRAD) | (6) Non-TRAD | (6)–(5) |
|---|---|---|---|---|---|---|---|---|---|
| Female (%) | 49.1 | 52.3 | *** | 54.2 | 60.6 | *** | 55.4 | 57.0 | NS |
| Years of education | 2.9 | 5.0 | *** | 2.8 | 4.6 | *** | 3.0 | 3.6 | *** |
| Literacy in French (%) | 40.1 | 59.9 | *** | 37.0 | 58.7 | *** | 40.7 | 46.4 | *** |
| Polygamous (%) | 18.2 | 14.0 | *** | 18.3 | 14.3 | *** | 19.2 | 16.3 | ** |
| Muslim (%) | 59.1 | 52.8 | *** | 58.4 | 54.7 | *** | 66.5 | 55.1 | *** |
| Has not migrated (%) | 31.3 | 56.6 | *** | 28.7 | 57.1 | *** | 40.8 | 39.6 | NS |
| Has migrated recently (%) | 10.4 | 5.9 | *** | 10.8 | 5.8 | *** | 11.2 | 8.4 | ** |
| Father has primary education (%) | 3.5 | 13.7 | *** | 2.8 | 13.3 | *** | 4.9 | 6.5 | ** |
| Father has secondary education or more (%) | 1.9 | 14.6 | *** | 1.0 | 14.3 | *** | 5.3 | 6.9 | ** |
| *Managerial skills* | | | | | | | | | |
| Prior management experience (%) | 19.0 | 16.0 | *** | 19.3 | 16.0 | *** | 14.5 | 18.6 | *** |
| Knowledge of MFI (%) | 34.1 | 40.4 | *** | 34.0 | 39.8 | *** | 31.7 | 37.1 | *** |
| Owner keeps books (%) | 30.1 | 40.8 | *** | 29.3 | 40.5 | *** | 35.1 | 33.4 | * |
| *Enterprise-specific skills* | | | | | | | | | |
| Traditional apprenticeship training (%) | 28.7 | 26.7 | NS | 28.0 | 28.2 | NS | 31.8 | 27.3 | *** |
| Years worked in this profession | 10.1 | 8.2 | *** | 10.1 | 8.6 | *** | 11.5 | 9.1 | *** |
| *Social capital* | | | | | | | | | |
| Member of a professional association (%) | 4.8 | 2.8 | *** | 4.6 | 3.3 | *** | 7.2 | 3.5 | *** |
| *Familial investment* | | | | | | | | | |
| Share of familial investment in total investment (%) | 40.0 | 40.6 | ** | 39.3 | 41.6 | NS | 44.8 | 39.3 | *** |

Sources and note: same as Table 3.1.

First, they are less educated and more experienced. They have on average two fewer years of schooling and two more years of experience in their profession. This result is similar to the one obtained by Lentz and Laband (1990) for the USA and by Colombier and Masclet (2006) for Europe. These authors explain this result by a relatively less need for second generation of self-employed to acquire formal training since they have the opportunity to accumulate equivalent training through the occupation of their father.

Then, the second generation of self-employed has a disadvantaged background, as shown by the weaker level of schooling of their father. Finally, children of self-employed are more often migrants.

If the results of Lentz and Laband (1990) stand in the West-African context, I expect that children of self-employed have more managerial skills and a higher familial investment in terms of physical capital. In this first descriptive approach, it seems not to be true. Although they have more often a prior experience as manager, they neither have a better knowledge of financial institutions nor a better managerial organization. Moreover, their family did not invest more in their business than the average of informal entrepreneurs.

As far as informal entrepreneurs with familial tradition are concerned, I expect that they are endowed with more enterprise-specific skills, social capital and familial investment. It seems at this first stage largely true. On average, they have accumulated more experiences that are likely to give them higher enterprise-specific skills. Their social capital seems to be larger through a more frequent membership of a professional association. Their family contributes more to the capital formation than the family of informal business owners as a whole.

### Estimation strategy

The first step is to test whether being second generation of self-employed affects firm performance. For the reasons mentioned above, I anticipate that *TRAD* has higher positive effects on the productivity of the factors than *SE*.

Let us consider a firm with labour, physical and human capital denoted by $L$, $K$ and $H$ respectively. The functional form used for regression analysis is basically a Cobb–Douglas production function and is estimated in log form. Given the Cobb–Douglas functional form, *SE* and *TRAD* potentially raise the efficiency of labour, physical and human capital out as a Hicks-neutral multiplicative term. I will then estimate the following equations:

$$V = (g_{SG}(SG)[L])^{\beta_L} (h_{SG}(SG)[K])^{\beta_K} (l_{SG}(SG)[H])^{\beta_H}$$
$$= f_{SG}(SG)L^{\beta_L} K^{\beta_K} H^{\beta_H} \tag{3.1}$$

where $V$ stand for the value added, SG indicates whether the owner is a second generation of self-employed with $SG = SE$, *TRAD*, $g_{SG}(SG)$, $h_{SG}(SG)$, $l_{SG}(SG)$ and $f_{SG}(SG)$ are functions that express the effect of *SE* or *TRAD* on the efficiency of labour $L$, physical capital $K$ and human capital $H$.

If *SE* or *TRAD* has a significant positive effect on *V*, this shows that businesses with owners belonging to the second generation of self-employed get higher return from their labour and physical and human capital. In that case, *SE* and *TRAD* enter the regression as a productivity shifter.

To estimate equation (3.1), I choose value added as the firm's performance measure. Value added is calculated as the difference between total sales and intermediary consumption. Intermediary consumption includes raw material and inventory purchases, rent and utilities, and other expenses. It represents the total returns to labour, management and capital. Price differences between countries are adjusted.

Labour (*L*) is defined as the number of monthly hours used in the informal business. Physical capital (*K*) includes buildings and other locations, machines, furniture, vehicles and tools. All items are evaluated at replacement costs. Like for value added, price differences between countries are adjusted. Human capital (*H*) is measured by the potential experience of the owner[7] in the labour market which reflects the gross time that entrepreneurs have spent while in the labour force, and by the owner's education.

In a second step, I examine the channels through which these variables raise owner productivity. As argued above, one possible channel is through intergenerational transmission of factors of production allowing a better access to these factors, in particular managerial skills, enterprise-specific skills, physical and social capital. Another possible channel is through higher total factor productivity. To test these hypotheses, I expand the estimation of equation (3.1) to include proxy of inherited physical capital $K_I$. I also split human capital into general managerial skills $H_{MS}$ and enterprise-specific skills $H_{ESS}$, and, following Faf-champs (2002), I introduce in the production function social capital as input, denoted *S*. The production function becomes:

$$V = F(L, K_I, K_{NI}, H_{MS}, H_{ESS}, S) \qquad (3.2)$$

I then identify which of these variables is the most able to capture the effect of having benefited from a familial tradition or of having a self-employed father.

## Does second generation of self-employed have a competitive advantage in the informal sector?

To test if having a self-employed father procures an advantage for informal business owners in terms of business performance, I estimate equation (3.1) where business performance is measured by the log of value added.[8] The regressors include a dummy that takes the value 1 if the owner has a father self-employed (*SE*), labour and capital in the log form, and human capital variables.

I introduce also some additional variables (*X*) to control for various background characteristics: owner's gender because women may face difficulties entering the upper-tier segment of informal sector for various reasons (household responsibilities, discrimination, restricted mobility); polygamous status, because redistributive pressure inside the family may be higher and thus capital accumulation more difficult (Morrisson, 2006); religion and ethnic group, because they may give access to different social networks; migration status, because recent migrants may have weaker knowledge about market opportunities.

Because of moral hazard consideration, family workers or workers from the same ethnic group as the owner may be more productive. For this reason, I include the share of family workers and the share of workers from the same ethnic group as the owner in the informal business' workforce as well. In addition, since old enterprises should be better established than young ones (they have survived), I introduce the age of the enterprise. Lastly, I control for the sector of activity and the country.

The equation to estimate is then:

$$\ln VA_j = \beta_0 + \beta_{SE} SE_j + \beta_L \ln L_j + \beta_K \ln K_j + \beta_H h_j + \beta_X X_j + \varepsilon_j \qquad (3.3)$$

The estimation of equation (3.3) is confronted with a number of potential biases. The first one is the well-known simultaneity bias (Marshak and Andrews, 1944). Capital and labour are generally chosen by the firm depending on unobserved productivity shocks. Thus, capital and labour would likely be correlated with residuals and their coefficients are consequently biased. Unfortunately, to correct for this bias I have at my disposal neither panel data nor good instruments. That is why I choose a very simple approach that just splits the sample into informal businesses with different levels of capital stock and labour, and I estimate equation (3.3) with and without introducing capital and labour in the regressors. But capital and labour coefficients have to be taken with caution. However, simultaneity bias should not impact the *SE* coefficient.

The second potential bias, more crucial for the purpose of this chapter, is due to unobserved characteristics of the owner that are correlated with both value added and having a self-employed father. These characteristics could be entrepreneurial ability, effort or motivation. Indeed, it is very likely that children of self-employed are more motivated than children of wage-earners because of a higher taste for autonomy. The omission of these unobserved characteristics would lead to an upward bias of the coefficient of *SE*.

Table 3.3 reports the main results from OLS regression. Contrary to expectations, having a father self-employed is shown to have no effect on value added. This result remains unchanged when I split informal businesses into different terciles of capital or of labour, or when I introduce interactions between *SE* and country dummies (not reported) to take into account potentially different effects of *SE* between countries. Another robustness check consists in introducing interactions between *SE* and production factors, because SE may have compensating effects on labour and capital productivity. I find that *SE* has no effect on productivity factors taking separately as interactions coefficients are not significant. Because omission bias leads to overestimate *SE* effect, I conclude that informal entrepreneurs who have a father involved in self-employed activities do not

*Table 3.3* Effect of having a father self-employed on value added and sales

| Variables | (1) | (2) |
|---|---|---|
| | Ln VA | Ln VA |
| Father was self-employed (SE) | **−0.0488** | **−0.0408** |
| | **(0.0439)** | **(0.0429)** |
| Owner's potential experience | 0.0307*** | 0.0203*** |
| | (0.00625) | (0.00614) |
| Owner's potential experience squared | −0.000447*** | −0.000315*** |
| | (9.11e-05) | (8.94e-05) |
| Owner's education | 0.0137 | 0.00577 |
| | (0.0142) | (0.0139) |
| Owner's education squared | 0.00179 | 0.00209* |
| | (0.00110) | (0.00107) |
| Amount of capital in log | – | 0.0935*** |
| | | (0.0113) |
| Amount of labour in log | – | 0.256*** |
| | | (0.0203) |
| Constant | 6.215*** | 3.964*** |
| | (0.203) | (0.247) |
| Observations | 5,712 | 5,712 |
| R-squared | 0.223 | 0.259 |

Sources: author's computation based on *1-2-3* surveys (Phases 1 and 2, 2001/02, AFRISTAT, DIAL, INS).

Notes
Controls: owner's sex, polygamous status, religion, ethnic group, migration status; ethnic homogeneity inside the enterprise, share of family workers, age of the enterprise; sectors of activity and country dummies.
Standard errors in parentheses.
*** $p<0.01$.
** $p<0.05$.
* $p<0.1$.

benefit from an advantage, compared to informal entrepreneurs without a self-employed father. This result suggests that there is no intergenerational transmission of valuable managerial skills or physical capital for children of self-employed.

Regarding the other variables, results by and large conform with expectations: other things being equal, higher levels of labour, human and physical capital lead to higher performance (Table 3.3); men have better business outcomes than women; being born in the city is an advantage compared with migrants. However, marital status, religion and ethnic group are not significant and ethnic homogeneity and the share of family members in the enterprise has a significant but negative effect on outcomes (full table not reported). As in Fafchamps (2002), family members thus appear to work less hard than hired workers. This could be explained by a familial pressure to distribute work that leads to a number of workers uncorrelated with the necessary amount of work to produce.

We now consider the narrower definition of second generation of self-employed, that is informal entrepreneurs who benefit from a familial tradition (*TRAD*). To test if self-employed with familial tradition (*TRAD*) perform better than those without familial tradition, I estimate the following equation:

$$\ln VA_j = \beta_0 + \beta_{SE}SE_j + \beta_L \ln L_j + \beta_K \ln K_j + \beta_H h_j + \beta_X X_j + \varepsilon_j \tag{3.4}$$

As for equation (3.3), I also estimate the equation on subsamples, splitting informal businesses into different terciles of capital (models 7 to 9) or of labour (models 10 to 12). Results are presented in Table 3.4.

Table 3.4 shows that having benefited from a familial tradition has a positive and significant effect on informal businesses outcomes: other things being equal, value added of informal entrepreneurs with familial tradition is 13.6 per cent higher than value added of other informal entrepreneurs (model 5). The level and the significance of the effect are robust to the inclusion of capital and labour variables. It remains unchanged for informal businesses with high level of production factors as well. But having benefited from a familial tradition has no significant effect for low level of production factors. For these informal entrepreneurs, having benefited from a familial tradition provides no advantage. As far as heterogeneity of informal businesses is concerned, we can conclude that such entrepreneurial familial background is irrelevant when informal businesses represent a form of urban subsistence production.

## What is the source of advantage?

After having established the positive effect of having benefited from a family tradition with the same choice of activity,[9] I would like to highlight the channels through which this familial tradition provides an advantage. I then estimate which of the identified potential channels is the most able to capture the effect of *TRAD* in the production function. To this end, I introduce step-by-step proxies of these channels in equation (3.4), first one by one (not reported) and then by pairs (Table 3.5).

I find that when I introduce only one of these factors, the effect of *TRAD* is still significant. All proxies are significant, except the dummies of informal apprenticeship and of prior management experience. The effect of *TRAD* disappears only when I introduce factors by pairs. More precisely, Table 3.5 shows that the effect of having benefited from a familial tradition disappears only when I jointly introduce proxies of enterprise-specific skills and social capital. The other combinations do not allow capturing the whole effect of *TRAD*.

Taken together, these results suggest that more valuable social capital and higher enterprise-specific skills contribute to why informal business owners with family members involved in the same sector of activity have better outcomes.

Table 3.4 Effect of inheriting a familial tradition on value added

| Variables | (5) All | (6) All | (7) K<q33 | (8) q33<K<q66 | (9) K>q66 | (10) L<q33 | (11) q33<L<q66 | (12) L>q66 |
|---|---|---|---|---|---|---|---|---|
| Enterprise with familial tradition (TRAD) | **0.128**** | **0.0905*** | **0.108** | **0.147*** | **0.137** | **-0.0208** | **0.0372** | **0.247**** |
| Familial tradition (TRAD) | **(0.0585)** | **(0.0573)** | **(0.0923)** | **(0.0897)** | **(0.122)** | **(0.114)** | **(0.0936)** | **(0.0971)** |
| Owner's potential experience | 0.0312*** | 0.0207*** | 0.0347*** | 0.0322*** | 0.0125 | 0.0302*** | 0.0277*** | 0.0236** |
|  | (0.00625) | (0.00615) | (0.00891) | (0.0106) | (0.0132) | (0.0110) | (0.00979) | (0.0116) |
| Owner's potential experience, sqd | -0.0004*** | -0.0003*** | -0.0005*** | -0.0005*** | -0.0002 | -0.0004** | -0.0004*** | -0.0003** |
|  | (9.11e-05) | (8.94e-05) | (0.000127) | (0.000154) | (0.000198) | (0.000164) | (0.000140) | (0.000168) |
| Years of education | 0.0162 | 0.00773 | 0.0258 | -0.0116 | -0.00397 | 0.0425* | -0.00297 | 0.00529 |
|  | (0.0141) | (0.0138) | (0.0259) | (0.0245) | (0.0266) | (0.0254) | (0.0233) | (0.0241) |
| Years of education, sqd | 0.00177 | 0.00206* | 0.00169 | 0.00280 | 0.00242 | 0.000507 | 0.00239 | 0.00278 |
|  | (0.00110) | (0.00107) | (0.00187) | (0.00210) | (0.00187) | (0.00196) | (0.00187) | (0.00182) |
| Amount of capital in log | — | 0.0939*** | — | — | — | — | — | — |
|  |  | (0.0112) |  |  |  |  |  |  |
| Amount of paid labour in log | — | 0.254*** | — | — | — | — | — | — |
|  |  | (0.0204) |  |  |  |  |  |  |
| Constant | 6.171*** | 3.940*** | 5.564*** | 6.030*** | 5.659*** | 4.736*** | 4.992*** | 5.828*** |
|  | (0.202) | (0.246) | (0.451) | (0.355) | (0.407) | (0.467) | (0.356) | (0.361) |
| Observations | 5,712 | 5,712 | 1,865 | 1,925 | 1,922 | 1,736 | 1,993 | 1,983 |
| R-squared | 0.224 | 0.259 | 0.174 | 0.184 | 0.154 | 0.108 | 0.177 | 0.194 |

Sources: author's computation based on 1-2-3 surveys (Phases 1 and 2, 2001/02, AFRISTAT, DIAL, INS).

Note
Controls: idem models (1) to (4).
Standard errors in parentheses.
*** $p < 0.01$.
** $p < 0.05$.
* $p < 0.1$.

Table 3.5 Effect of inheriting a familial tradition on VA introducing social capital, two types of skills and inherited physical capital

| Variables | (21) | (22) | (23) | (24) | (25) | (26) |
|---|---|---|---|---|---|---|
| | Ln VA | Ln VA | Ln VA | Ln VA | Ln VA | Ln VA |
| Enterprise with familial tradition (TRAD) | 0.125** | 0.115** | 0.143** | 0.0957 | 0.124** | 0.114* |
| | (0.0580) | (0.0580) | (0.0578) | (0.0585) | (0.0584) | (0.0583) |
| *Proxies of managerial skills* | | | | | | |
| Prior management experience | 0.000463 | −0.00866 | −0.0124 | — | — | — |
| | (0.0538) | (0.0536) | (0.0535) | | | |
| Knowledge of MFI | 0.0912** | 0.0821* | 0.0815* | — | — | — |
| | (0.0443) | (0.0443) | (0.0442) | | | |
| Owner keeps books | 0.617*** | 0.612*** | 0.629*** | — | — | — |
| | (0.0585) | (0.0585) | (0.0583) | | | |
| *Proxies of enterprise-specific skills* | | | | | | |
| Owner was informal apprentice | 0.0427 | — | — | 0.0492 | 0.0445 | — |
| | (0.0495) | | | (0.0499) | (0.0499) | |
| Experience in this profession (years) | 0.00969*** | — | — | 0.00942*** | 0.00940*** | — |
| | (0.00284) | | | (0.00286) | (0.00286) | |
| *Proxies of social capital* | | | | | | |
| Owner is member of a business association | — | 0.435*** | — | 0.459*** | — | 0.470*** |
| | | (0.0934) | | (0.0941) | | (0.0937) |

*Proxies of familial investment*

| | (1) | (2) | (3) | (4) | (5) | (6) |
|---|---|---|---|---|---|---|
| Share of familial invesment in total investment | — | — | -0.325*** | — | -0.309*** | -0.314*** |
| | | | (0.0504) | | (0.0509) | (0.0508) |
| Constant | 5.762*** | 5.826*** | 5.969*** | 6.524*** | 6.687*** | 6.731*** |
| | (0.183) | (0.180) | (0.180) | (0.167) | (0.167) | (0.164) |
| Observations | 5,712 | 5,712 | 5,712 | 5,712 | 5,712 | 5,712 |
| R-squared | 0.238 | 0.239 | 0.242 | 0.225 | 0.227 | 0.229 |

Sources: author's computation based on *1-2-3* surveys (Phases 1 and 2, 2001/02, AFRISTAT, DIAL, INS).

Note

Controls: owner's sex, education level, education level squared, polygamous status, religion, ethnic group, migration status; ethnic homogeneity inside the enterprise, share of family workers, age of the enterprise; sectors of activity and country dummies.

Standard errors in parentheses.

*** $p<0.01$.

** $p<0.05$.

* $p<0.1$.

## Conclusion

This chapter has shown that, for West-African informal entrepreneurs, having a self-employed father does not provide any advantage in terms of value added or sales, as far as the business activity is different from that of the father. Children of self-employed generally do not have better access to valuable human, physical or social capital. In contrast to the USA or European countries, there is thus no intergenerational transmission of general managerial skills, which would explain such a competitive advantage for children of self-employed. This specificity of West-African countries with regard to the USA or European countries might be due to a different way of being exposed to the business of the father.

This implies that the strong correlation of self-employment status across generations cannot be explained by the existence of such a competitive advantage. Alternative determinants of this correlation can then be put forward: the conveyance of taste for autonomy, a self-limitation of professional aspirations or a segmented structure of the labour market that constrains children of self-employed to be themselves self-employed in the informal sector. However, we do not have evidence to justify acceptance of one hypothesis over another. Further research is needed.

A second important result of this chapter is that having family members involved in the same type of activity is important for informal businesses, in particular for businesses with high level of production factors. The informal entrepreneurs with familial tradition have a competitive advantage in terms of value added or sales.

These findings are important from a policy perspective. Most policies currently in place aiming at improving efficiency of the informal sector are targeted towards alleviating financial constraints. Other programmes focus on reinforcing general business human capital, for example management and financial skills. My findings suggest that providing opportunities for work experience in informal businesses and developing professional networks through associations may be effective policies. They might allow would-be informal entrepreneurs to acquire enterprise-specific skills and develop their social capital. They would then contribute to improving informal sector efficiency and reduce intergenerational inequalities in business ownership patterns. However, these issues deserve further investigation on the effectiveness of these types of policies, especially evidence from impact evaluations of experimental programmes.

Moreover, this chapter casts a new light on the heterogeneity of the informal sector, by identifying social background, in particular entrepreneurial familial background, as a source of heterogeneity in terms of performance.

# Notes

1 In the capital of seven West-African countries, 28 per cent of the informal business owners have learned their profession through traditional apprenticeship training.
2 The activity of the mother was not included in the Phase 1 questionnaire. This is the reason why I had to limit the analysis to the activity of the father.
3 The data do not allow to identify whether self-employed fathers were formal or informal entrepreneurs. We suspect that the bulk of self-employed fathers is informal as 97 per cent of self-employed surveyed aged 40 and more are informal. But we can not say it for certain because of the structural evolution of the West-African labour markets, characterized by an informalization process in recent decades (Calves and Schoumaker, 2004 for the case of Burkina Faso).
4 More precisely, *TRAD* takes the value 1 if the owner says:

- she or he has created the informal business by familial tradition; and/or
- she or he has chosen the informal business' product/services by familial tradition; and/or
- one of his/her family members has created the informal business.

5 When I estimate a logit model, where membership to a professional association is the dependent variable, the log of the amount of capital and the age of the enterprise are the regressors, and where sex, level of schooling, migration status, religion, ethnic group, polygamous status of the owner are introduced as controls, I am able to predict correctly the membership to a professional association in only 0.3 per cent of cases.
6 In total, 16 per cent of second generation of self-employed have both a self-employed father and have benefited from a familial tradition. Among *SE* entrepreneurs, 17.6 per cent are *TRAD* as well. Among *TRAD* entrepreneurs, 66.3 per cent have a father self-employed (*SE*).
7 Age minus years of schooling minus seven, the legal age at school entry.
8 More precisely, the variable used is the log of value added (respectively sales) plus one to avoid losing observations with value added (respectively sales) equal to 0.
9 For a discussion on the omission bias, see Pasquier-Doumer (2013b).

# References

Bacchetta, M., Ernst, E. and Bustamante, J.P. (2009) *Globalization and Informal Jobs in Developing Countries: A Joint Study from the International Labour Organization and the WTO*, Geneva: ILO/WTO.

Birks, S., Fluitman, F., Oudin, X. and Sinclair, C. (1994) *Skills Acquisition in Micro-enterprises: Evidence from West Africa*, Paris: OECD Publications.

Brilleau, A., Coulibaly, S., Gubert, F., Koriko, O., Kuepie, M. and Ouedraogo, E. (2005) "Le secteur informel: Performances, insertion, perspectives, enquête 1-2-3, phase 2", *Statéco*, 99: 65–88.

Brilleau, A., Ouedraogo, E. and Roubaud, F. (2005) "Introduction générale au dossier, l'enquête 1-2-3 dans les principales agglomérations de sept Etats membres de l'UEMOA: la consolidation d'une méthode", *Statéco*, 99: 15–19.

Calves, A.E. and Schoumaker, B. (2004) "Deteriorating economic context and changing patterns of youth employment in urban Burkina Faso: 1980–2000", *World Development*, 32(8): 1341–1354.

Charmes, J. and Oudin, X. (1994) "Formation sur le tas dans le secteur informel", *Afrique Contemporaine*, 4: 230–238.

Colombier, N. and Masclet, D. (2006) "Self-employment and the intergenerational transmission of human capital", *CIRANO Scientific Series*, 2006s-19.

Colombier, N. and Masclet, D. (2008) "Intergenerational correlation in self employment: Some further evidence from French ECHP data", *Small Business Economics*, 30: 423–437.

Cogneau, D., Bossuroy, T., De Vreyer, P., Guénard, C., Hiller, V., Leite, P., Mesplé-Somps, S., Pasquier-Doumer, L. and Torelli, C. (2007) "Inequalities and equity in Africa", *Notes et Documents*, 31, AFD.

Dunn, T.A. and Holtz-Eakin, D.J. (2000) "Financial capital, human capital, and the transition to self-employment: Evidence from intergenerational links", *Journal of Labor Economics*, 18(2): 282–305.

Fafchamps, F. (2002) 'Returns to social network capital among traders', *Oxford Economic Papers*, 54(2): 173–206.

Fairlie, R.W. and Robb, A.M. (2007) "Families, human capital, and small business: Evidence from the characteristics of business owners survey", *Industrial and Labor Relations Review*, 60(2): 225–245.

Haan, H.C. (2006) *Training for Work in the Informal Micro-Enterprise Sector: Fresh Evidence from Sub-Sahara Africa*, Dordrecht: Springer.

Laferrère, A. and McEntee, P. (1996) "Self-employment and intergenerational transfers: Liquidity constraints of family environment?" CREST Working Paper.

Lentz, B.F. and Laband, D.N. (1990) "Entrepreneurial success and occupational inheritance among proprietors", *Canadian Journal of Economics*, 23(3): 563–579.

Marschak, J. and Andrews, W.H. (1944) "Random simultaneous equations and the theory of production", *Econometrica*, 12(3,4): 143–205.

Morrisson, C. (2006) "Structures familiales, transferts et épargne", OECD Development Centre Working paper, 255.

Pasquier-Doumer, L. (2013a) "Reducing inequality of opportunities in West African urban labor markets: What kinds of policy matter?" In De Vreyer, P. and Roubaud, F. (eds), *Urban Labor Markets in Sub-Saharan Africa*, Washington DC: World Bank/AFD, 251–270.

Pasquier-Doumer L. (2013b) "Intergenerational transmission of self-employed status in the informal sector: A constrained choice or better income prospects? Evidence from seven West-African countries", *Journal of African Economies*, 22(1): 73–111.

Pasquier-Doumer, L. (2014) "Le rôle des réseaux sociaux dans les parcours de vie." In Boyer, F. and Delaunay, D. (eds), *Peuplement de Ouagadougou et développement urbain*, forthcoming.

Walther, R. (2007) "La formation professionnelle en secteur informel", *Notes et Documents*, 33, AFD.

# 4 Integration of formal and informal sectors in craft villages of the Red River Delta (Vietnam)

*Sylvie Fanchette and Xuân Hoan Nguyen*

Industrialization in the Red River Delta has developed in craft villages over the last centuries. Small scale craftwork carried out at the same time as agriculture was, until *Doi Moi* (Renewal), restricted to the interior of village dwellings. This type of activity expanded because irrigated agriculture, although very intensive, cannot sustain a very dense population (more than 1000 inhabitants per km$^2$) which remains under-employed for part of the year. These villages produce articles and services for daily life (food processing, religious objects, industrial products and building materials, commercial services and transport, etc.). Since *Doi Moi*, there has been rapid growth and a diversification of production, an extension of the production surface and employment of many villagers for sub-contract work.

Provincial People's Committees have implemented policies to promote SMEs in rural areas and have especially encouraged small enterprises to formalize. However, this rural industrialization, which grew from "nothing" with local capital and specific technical innovations, is having difficulties in doing so.

First of all, state and regional policy concerning the support of rural SMEs contradicts land ownership and industrial policies, in the context of the expansion of the city of Hanoi and of the implementation of the future Master Plan 2010. The "small is beautiful" period is apparently over and the state, in its desire to modernize the country with the help of foreign capital, is now turning to heavy industry and the construction of big industrial estates while continuing to subsidize state enterprises. It is becoming more and more difficult for small village enterprises to get land because of land liberalization and the abolition of grants for industrial sites in craft villages. There thus exists a contradiction: heavy mechanized industry with a limited potential for job creation receives more support from the authorities, particularly for land acquisition. On the other hand, the small labour-intensive enterprises with little capital, operating in the craft villages, benefit from very little aid in spite of the good intentions of the numerous resolutions decreed in their favour.

Furthermore, the formal/informal approach does not provide an explanation for the situation of the non-agricultural work market in the over-populated areas of the Red River Delta because the limits between these two sectors are unclear on account of the very strong integration between the multitude of undeclared micro and small family enterprises and the formal enterprises of the craft villages.

Indeed, most craft villages are organized in clusters interlinked within trade and family networks and within production chains which are becoming more and more complex. In the context of a very dense population and rural under-employment, craft villages offer to numerous villagers with little capital to invest and participate to the craft production chain.

We will here present local production system of craft village clusters and the nature of the links between declared and undeclared enterprises. We will develop the hypothesis according to which the strength of the cluster depends on the complementary nature of the different types of enterprise and the flexibility of these relationships in terms of use of workforce, space and markets. The policy for the formalization of SMEs put at risk the dynamic of clusters and of intensifying competition between formal enterprises.

## Craft village clusters: a local production system providing many informal jobs

### Employment and craft villages: did you say informal?

*Numbering craft villages with different sources and various criteria*

The number of permanently and temporarily employed workers in the craft villages varies greatly according to different sources. Everything depends on how one defines a craft village. Several organizations have carried out exhaustive studies based on a more or less restrictive definition of the term.

*The MARD (Ministry of Agriculture and Rural Development)/JICA (Japan International Cooperation Agency)* study carried out in 2002 gives the following criteria to describe a craft village:

- At least 20 per cent of the active population devoting their full time to the craft.
- Local authorities recognize the importance of the craft production for the village.

According to this study, in 2004 there were more than 1.3 million workers in 2017 craft villages in the whole country, that is to say 2.5 per cent of villages. The former province of Ha Tây has the higher number of craft villages (409 villages and 337 000 workers). In spite of giving such a wide definition of the term, the number of villages remains relatively low and the number of workers too.

However, in reality this study underestimates the most industrialized villages and also those specialized in construction materials not considered to be craftwork. Bắc Ninh province has in fact 62 craft villages, whereas the JICA- MARD study counted only 32. What is more, one can add to these workers, countless family workers and occasional labourers who temporarily participate in the activities and family help.

*The study of the Association of Craft Villages in Vietnam.* This study takes into account villages which have been carrying out a craft for more than 50 years of which at least 50 per cent of the production is craftwork and in which at least 30 per cent of the population is devoted to the craft.

According to this definition, Vietnam has 2790 craft villages and 11 million craftworkers. This association counts the total number of country folk devoted to craftwork, whether they are seasonal workers or not. This wider definition of the craft village can be explained by the association's wish to show the importance of this local production system in the countryside and to persuade the administration to promote them.

*Provincial services for rural development.* Each province has its own definition of what is a craft village. According to the People's Committee of the former Hà Tây province, a craft village should have at least 50 per cent of its active workforce involved in full-time craftwork and the profits from this work should represent 50 per cent of the village's total income. In 2006, 260 villages corresponded to this definition. Each province tries to define a craft village in an attempt to better target them and implement policies for the promotion of craftwork.

The differences between these definitions and the resulting estimated number of craft villages reveal the diverging political and economic interests of the organizations responsible for them. These differences are symptomatic of the fragmentation of the rural development policy between various ministries and provincial services.

### Craft villages: the reign of informality and small units of production

The enterprises are mostly small and undeclared. Only a minority of them are registered as companies, firms, cooperatives or private enterprises with issuing tax invoices. According to the People's Committee of Bắc Ninh, in 2005, 89 per cent of craftworkers worked at home and only 11 per cent worked in companies or in cooperatives.

However, each type of activity (textile, paper-making, wickerwork, craft furniture) has its own specificities: production chain length, division of labour, possibility of mechanizing certain parts of the production process and maintaining other parts manual. These specificities shape the relationships between the

*Table 4.1* Number of units and employees according to status

| Types of enterprise | Number of units | Number of employees |
| --- | --- | --- |
| Companies and firms | 308 | 8,061 |
| Private enterprises | 202 | |
| Cooperatives | 214 | |
| Undeclared households | 18,415 | 72,608 |

Sources: People's Committee of Bac Ninh province, 2005.

various enterprises with different statuses working in the clusters. Furthermore, most formal businesses only declare a minority of their employees and have a multitude of informal subcontracted craftsmen working at home.

## Cluster organization: how to integrate villages and enterprises of various production capacities and status into the production chain

A cluster of craft villages is a local production system grouping a vast array of declared and undeclared enterprises, of various size, status, production methods and techniques. The way these clusters operate depends on their activity. The geographical concentration of small enterprises can be associated with the development of commercial networks: this concentration contributes to the development of economies of scale, a better use of supply networks and the dissemination of technical know-how within a profoundly rustic society where several generations live together under the same roof. Thus, the geographical proximity between the enterprises operating within the cluster contributes to the rapid linking together of a multitude of households and enterprises within a network of knowledge of workers with complementary know-how.

### The division of labour and specialization of villages within the production chain: the cluster cohesion

These clusters are structured on three levels:

#### BETWEEN VILLAGES

A cluster of villages is composed of a central village (the mother-village) and of secondary villages. At the centre are the major producers and placers of orders, official businesses, often mechanized and concentrated within a designated craft park. Several types of inter-village relations can be found within clusters. Each village specializes in one type of product but relies on others for:

- Supply of raw materials (trade, sorting, recycling): for villages using recycled products, there is a long processing chain for these materials. In the case of paper-making, there exist different types of sorting (quality paper offcuts, used paper, cement sacks, etc.). Workshops that carry this kind of work generally belong to poorer secondary villages of the cluster that have a numerous workforce and scant means to set up mechanized workshops. In the most dynamic villages the elderly and the children participate in this type of work.
- Know-how: some villages have had a craft specialization for centuries and take part in the making of luxury articles or artwork (woodcarving, mother of pearl inlaying, carpentry, etc.). These are often villages where the artisans are not businessmen or salesmen and rely on more dynamic villages to market their products.

- Production space: large-scale contractors in the mother-villages have big workshops and lacking sufficient land in their villages, they rent plots of land in neighbouring villages in order to build workshops and shops there.
- Services: transportation, shops, raw materials markets, workshops for repairing machines and other related activities linked to the main craft (packaging, dyeing and sewing services for textile villages).
- Supply of manpower: subcontracting, workers or apprentices. The extension of the employment area of clusters takes place in two directions: the closest communes for subcontracting and the hiring of some temporary workers, and the provinces on the fringes of the Red River Delta for longer-term workers, without experience, but working for lower wages and bad working conditions.

### AT VILLAGE LEVEL

Work is divided up between complementary businesses, each responsible for one stage of production, or which may also specialize in one type of product. Mechanization and diversification have extended the production chain and generated an increase in the division of labour between households. Recycled raw materials (paper or metal) are traded down a long line of collectors (in the case of paper), then processed by craftspeople who have invested in machines – smelters sell recycled metal in the form of ready-to-use sheets, which can then be cut to make pots, trays and gongs.

### BETWEEN VILLAGE BUSINESSES AND FORMAL SECTOR COMPANIES ON INDUSTRIAL SITES

Large-scale companies established on urban industrial sites subcontract the production of spare parts to specialized workshops in craft villages. This type of relationship can be found in the metalworking industry.

*A system of subcontracting and of integrating the informal sector into the formal sector which is inseparable from the notion of clusters*

The division of labour between the cluster villages is mostly based on workforce subcontracting within a hierarchy of villages. The most dynamic ones are linked to their neighbours' family businesses by contractual relationships. These villages are the source of the activity that they have disseminated in their neighbourhood, either during the collectivist period through cooperatives or since *Doi Moi* by apprenticeship. There exist three types of subcontracting:

- Subcontracting of manual work on items not requiring special know-how: weaving rattan and bamboo in the case of basketwork. Large formal businesses sign orders with foreign clients and subcontract them to heads of workshops of neighbouring villages of the cluster specializing in one type of product. The latter then redistribute the work to a multitude of households which carry out the manual part of the production process.

- Subcontracting of work carried out by simple machines to mechanized workshops managed by unskilled workers.
- Subcontracting of the crafted parts of an item requiring specific know-how.

*A growing division of labour and a lengthening of the production chain*

The production chain is globally divided into several stages:

- Preparing raw materials: certain ones are recycled, such as paper or metals, and must be sorted and then smelted into ingots, in the case of metals, others must first undergo a transformation stage or treatment for pest control, in the case of bamboo or rattan. This stage is often carried out in independent family workshops which sell the ready-to-use raw materials, either to the contractors or to other family workshops.
- Items manufactured by crafts people or part of the process carried out by subcontractors (manual or mechanical).
- Finishing touches made in the workshop that holds the contract (quality control, assembly, finishing, packaging, etc.).

Subcontracting workers at home induces an extreme division of labour and rationalization of the production system. Each worker makes the best use of his know-how, his machines etc. Furthermore, he works within a very limited production space as the contract-holders do not have sufficient space. As far as the workforce is concerned, it is a very flexible system and subcontractors only work when there are orders.

This extreme division of labour in the workshop and among subcontractors also stems from the managers' and contract-holders' desire to protect their production methods, which had to be kept secret, in the context of the opening of their workshops to the outside world. Indeed, owners are scared that workers who know how to carry out all the production stages of an article will set up on their own and steal their business. Only the owner knows all the machines in his workshop. Until recently, techniques in a village, or even in a family, were kept secret and even young girls were not initiated to these secrets for fear that they might marry a man from another village and reveal the secret know-how. With the increase in production and the geographical extension of the employment area of clusters, numerous villagers in the surrounding areas share, in a disconnected way, the everyday life and know-how of the workers in the mother-villages.

The small enterprises with a small capital can thus participate in the production process without workshops and machines to meet orders.

*A relationship of trust between contract-holders and subcontract*
*workers*

The contracting enterprises are linked by non-binding relationships to their sub-contract workers, the latter being undeclared. One might question the nature of the trust which links these two different players for the respect of deadlines and for the quality of products. Art furniture businesses, for example, which use expensive raw materials (such as precious woods), supply the subcontractors. In the case of a failure to meet demand, the contractor must be reimbursed. In this sector, different types of relationships have been observed:

- family and neighbourhood links;
- technical know-how (ownership of machines);
- specific know-how (carving, mother of pearl inlaying);
- networks established during apprenticeship: some workshop owners in Dong Ky train workers from other villages. The latter set up their own businesses at home and are then specifically subcontracted by their former employer.

At La Phu (knitting), the subcontract workers are introduced to the contract-holders by acquaintances, by craftworkers employed in their homes or by people from a village which usually works for the mother-village.

In order to test their ability, the new subcontract workers are given both wool and a pattern by the contractor and they are required to leave a deposit for the first order. If their work is deemed satisfactory, no deposit is required for the second order. Big, formal enterprises oblige employees to sign a "contract" whose validity is not guaranteed because the subcontract worker is not registered.

Networks exist between certain villages which provide the workers and the villages which hire them. The multiplicity of links between the villages and the length of time the relationship has existed are guarantees of trust.

### The variability of the system of integration between enterprises and villages depending on the type of work

Relationships between enterprises depend on the nature of the work carried out (length of production chain, export or domestic markets).

*The fine cabinetmaking cluster managed by Dong Ky village: a very*
*long production chain which demands various types of know-how*

THE PRODUCTION CHAIN

The production chain for fine furniture is made up of eight stages: from cutting up the wood, first treatment of these pieces, carving, mother-of-pearl inlaying or varnishing, through to assembling. These specialized workshops have a geographic dimension that depends both on their needs in terms of production space and on the harmful effects that they generate (Dubiez and Hamel, 2009). A part of the production chain is carried out in village workshops or in other villages of the cluster, while other parts are made in the contract-holder's workshop:

*The subcontracted parts*
- The manual parts do not require a lot of know-how.
- Entrepreneurs in Dong Ky subcontract the workers in their own village and those of the neighbouring village, Lang Cho, who set up their own businesses about ten years after finishing their apprenticeships there.
- The stages of the fabrication of the article requiring the use of machines (sanders, electric saw, planing machine, drills, etc.). In Dong Ky, each workshop is specialized in a stage of production, each one being determined by a type of machine.
- The stages require specialized skills.
- Large businesses in Dong Ky, subcontract the most ornate and carved parts of pieces of furniture to the cluster's specialized artisans:

  - The commune of Huong Mac specialized in statues, chairs and ancestors altar-carving.
  - The commune of Phu Khê used to be specialized in religious objects and in carved carpentry for more than 1000 years.
  - The village of Thiêt specializes in Buddha, phoenix and turtle sculptures.
  - The commune of Chuyên My (Ha Tây, about 60 km away) specializes in mother-of-pearl inlaying. A total of 500 inlayers have temporarily settled in Dong Ky and produce there most of the elaborate parts of furniture and control the mother-of-pearl trade.

Although they are some very talented artisans, most craftworkers in the neighbouring villages do not have enough income and enough social and commercial contacts to enable them to set up their own businesses. They have neither the same business network as their Dong Ky counterparts, nor the financial means to buy wood. Only five or six enterprises in Phu Khê and as many in Huong Mac are declared and capable of exporting directly to China.

*The stages carried out in the contractor's workshop*
The enterprises in Dong Ky hire unqualified workers in their workshops to assemble subcontracted pieces, carry out final stages cut wood and take care of small orders.

In 2006, about 5200 regular and undeclared workers from surrounding villages and neighbouring provinces were working in Dong Ky workshops. A temporary work market exists for the hiring of daily workers.

*Raw material markets*

The internationalization of Dông Ky came about thanks to the emergence of "export agents" controlling the cluster's relations with the outside world. For the most part, heads of family businesses that have become officially declared, integrated into many networks, such as military, political, commercial and familial, they have succeeded in penetrating the entire sub-regional networks of trade in wood and fine furniture.

A SOCIAL SPACE OF PRODUCTION

Know-how and proximity count in the production of an object. Owing to the length of the production chain in the art furniture sector whose parts to assemble are generally very heavy, and the extreme division of labour between different enterprises, the work spaces need to be organized and the correct proximity between the workshops is necessary (Dubiez and Hamel, 2009).

- Workshops for the cutting of wood are found on the main roads of the village. There are only 20 of them because they take up a lot of space (surface occupied by one machine: $24\,m^2$) and cost a lot of money (VND300 million). These workshops are open only at daytime because they are not allowed to open at night because of noise pollution.
- Other workshops do not require much space and are found in small houses which have been abandoned by workers who have settled in craft zones and are found along secondary roads.
- Certain activities are in great demand and the workshops in which these skills are practised are found in each hamlet so that craftworkers can benefit from their services.

This spatial repartition of skills changes according to the varying price of land, market fluctuations and demand and the degree to which environmental laws are enforced.

Thus, specialized workshops in such a craft equipped with such a type of machine will be found in each hamlet so that manufacturers can have easy access to their services.

*La Phu: a cluster specializing in knitting and confectionary with limited know-how*

The knitting craft opens out on to two markets:

- The international market: East European countries (the former cooperative markets of the collectivist period) are the concern of declared enterprises. This market is limited by season for the European winter.
- The national market: poor quality pullovers for the mountain regions, socks and the edges of collars and cuffs for national textile enterprises. To avoid

competition from China or from more modern national textile enterprises, the La Phù cluster targets the low-price market and is attempting to diversify its production.

The subcontracting system varies according to the two types of markets.

In the case of the international market, declared contract-holders subcontract the knitting of pullovers' parts to a multitude of small family workshops which are equipped with simple machines. They manufacture either the sleeves or the body of the garment. The contractors provide them with wool and sometimes rent or lend them a machine. These workshops are in the surrounding poorer villages and do not have a lot of know-how or capital. In the contractors' enterprises the workers only manufacture the most profitable items requiring special machines and they also carry out finishing, assembly and packaging.

A limited number of temporary workers from the contracted villages operate in the workshops in the cluster centre. These workers generally prefer to be their own boss and work at home. They no longer accept the hard working conditions and low wages of the large businesses. Most of the workers are from remote provinces.

In the case of the domestic market, the workers are either subcontracted to iron and pack the socks, for example, or they carry out a stage of the production chain on specialized machines. They buy their own wool, have invested in sophisticated machines to which the subcontract workers will have no access and, unlike the latter, are totally independent. They subcontract the wool dyeing to specialized workshops.

Numerous small workshops have specialized in basic knitting in long tubes of wool, a stage carried out before the dyeing process. Once dyed, these tubes of wool are unravelled and the wool is wound on to bobbins. Their profit margins are very small but they can work from home and there is very little financial investment.

Making good use of the seasonality of the two markets and also of the two activities (textiles and confectionary for the domestic market) makes the system more simple, particularly in the context of a crisis in textile exports.

## Characteristics and complementariness of formal and informal enterprises

In the craft villages, the majority of enterprises belong to the informal sector (80 per cent); this figure varies depending on the feasibility of industrializing the manufacturing process of the products and on the types of market targeted (domestic or export). The enterprises, whatever their legal statute, function with others in the clusters and occupy a particular place within the production chain. It is not therefore fair to examine them separately. However, each legal statute has its own characteristics, its advantages and disadvantages, and, in the present context of under-employment in the countryside, difficult access to capital and to international markets and a lack of space, the informal sector continues to dominate.

**The numerical importance of different types of enterprises and characteristics depending on the clusters**

*The difficulty of localizing clusters in space*

The analysis of clusters is first based on fieldwork and on statistics of economic activity mapping in order to localize groups of villages. The relationships between these villages are not always easy to establish because they change in time and in space.

The employment area extends, the biggest declared enterprises recruit in more and more distant provinces to pay these workers lower salaries. This is not without an impact on local hiring, whether it is seasonal, permanent or home subcontract work.

Furthermore, the extension of the production space of mother villages into neighbouring communes is accelerating: because of lack of space, big enterprises relocate in the neighbourhood or move to farther away communes and provinces where land is easier to find.

All these factors show the variability in the shape of clusters and their geographical extension beyond the limits of neighbouring communes. This makes it more and more difficult to delimit the cluster and count the number of enterprises and workers.

We opted for a local definition of a cluster, with the exception of Dong Ky, whose dimensions are regional, even international (it spreads to south China).

Furthermore, the estimated number of villages belonging to a cluster is to be accepted cautiously. First, certain communes comprise just one large-sized village while others comprise several small ones, a factor which distorts the size of the clusters. Furthermore, the satellite villages of the cluster do not take part in the activity in the same way (labour, subcontracting, land, services, know-how, etc.).

*A varying participation of declared enterprises depending on type of activity*

Large enterprises' contract-holders are open to international markets, innovative at a technical level and capable of investing in the purchase of raw materials whose prices fluctuate greatly; they are the base upon which other enterprises function and the means by which small enterprises can indirectly participate in international markets. Their share in the market varies according to the type of activity carried out; everything hinges on the production system, the length of the production line and the number of subcontract workers. It is necessary to strike a balance between these declared enterprises and the multitude of small, informal, family workshops.

The clusters which have benefitted from a bigger concentration of capital and a rapid evolution of industrialization, such as the papermakers in Phong Khê, have a larger share of declared enterprises. They are better developed, they

Table 4.2 Characteristics of the clusters studied in the provinces of Bac Ninh and Ha Tây

| Activities | Dong Ky cluster | Duong O cluster | La Phu cluster | Phu Nghia cluster |
| --- | --- | --- | --- | --- |
| | Craft Furniture | Paper | Knitting Confectionary | Basketwork rattan and bamboo |
| Number of villages in the cluster | 12 | 5 | 7 | 26 |
| Number of declared workshops | 246 | 110 | 130 | 62 |
| • firms and companies | 99 | 19 | 33 | 60 |
| • private, declared enterprises | 85 | 73 | 95 | 2 |
| • cooperatives | 62 | 28 | 2 | 0 |
| Undeclared craft households | 5,038 | 630 | 3,078 | 7,580 |
| Total number of workshops | 5,284 | 740 | 3,208 | 7,642 |
| Percentage of declared workshops | 4.6 | 14.8 | 4 | 0.8 |
| Households in the service sector | 322 | 65 | 1,500 | 2,170 |
| Workers in the craft industry | 23,186 | 8,200 | 14,741 | 18,159 |
| Number of workers inside cluster | 15,386 | 4,160 | 7,541 | 17,259 |
| Number of workers outside cluster | 7,800 | 4,040 | 7,200 | 900 |

Sources: Survey carried out by Xuan Hoan Nguyên, Casrad (with the Popular Committees of the communes), 2006, authors' calculations.

innovate technically and are more open to markets. They have larger workshops to install their machines and invest even more capital in an activity which has become heavily mechanized.

On the other hand, the basket-weaving industry, which is mostly manual, has fewer declared enterprises. These enterprises are generally commercial, export enterprises which distribute the biggest share of the work to a few dozen production groups who, in turn, subcontract the work to small workshops. These declared enterprises have large-sized workshops, as the stages of production carried out there (quality control, varnishing, packaging, etc.) need a lot of space. These enterprises are among the biggest in the former Hà Tay province. They invest in market research and communication (10 per cent of their expenses), have internet sites and belong to professional associations when they exist (Mekong-Economics, 2008). They are generally located along departmental roads or in craft zones.

The furniture and knitting activities find themselves in an intermediate position. They require a high number of formal enterprises able to export but, at the same time, they need a very long production chain involving numerous subcontract craft-workers with a varying degree of qualifications. Cabinetmaking requires a large capital as wood, mother-of-pearl and drying machines are very expensive.

### The complementariness of enterprises with different legal statutes: a guarantee of flexibility within the system of production

*Declared companies: the locomotives of clusters with diversified markets*

There exist different types of legal statutes for businesses, each one having a different degree of responsibility for its members and their financial participation in the capital. These enterprises have legal ability to sign contracts with national and international partners. They have easier access to bank credit at preferential rates and are allowed to borrow greater sums of money. They have special access to land, particularly in industrial zones, which enables them to increase their scale of production, innovate and diversify their products. They can open bank accounts more easily (crucial for export), and they benefit from official stamps and invoices. Companies can open subsidiaries in other provinces of the country to improve control of access to raw materials and improve market penetration. Finally, they can take part in events for the commercial promotion of their products (trade fairs, promotion days, etc.).

However, formalization has quickly transformed into disillusionment in certain clusters. Indeed, the cost of becoming formal is very high for entrepreneurs:

- there are a lot of long administrative procedures for managers who have received very little management training;

*Table 4.3* Characteristics of the companies studied in the clusters in 2006

| Cluster name | Surface area + residence + production (m²) | Part of surface area rented (industrial zone + private) (%) | Total invested capital/limited company (million VND) | Total land capital/limited company (million VND) | Working capital (million VND) | Average turnover (million VND) | No. of enterprises questioned | Average no. of permanent workers in 1 limited company | No. of subcontract workers in 1 limited company |
|---|---|---|---|---|---|---|---|---|---|
| Dong Ky | 2,081.56 | 72 | 8,232.56 | 751.56 | 6,982.88 | 7,593.75 | 16 | 161 | 22 |
| Phong Khê | 3,566.66 | 54 | 13,044.16 | 5,816.66 | 2,184.30 | 14,400.00 | 6 | 36 | 0 |
| La Phu | 1,401.80 | 68 | 6,539.70 | 1,836.00 | 2,434.80 | 10,200.00 | 10 | 104 | 261 |
| Phu Nghia | 4,421.25 | 92 | 5,866.25 | 742.50 | 4,615.40 | 12,600.00 | 8 | 50 | 0 |

Sources: Survey carried out by Xuan Hoan Nguyên, Casrad (with the Popular Committees of the communes), 2006, authors' calculations.

- according to the provisions of the "Enterprise Law", they must:

  - hire an accountant from outside the family and declare him;
  - declare the totality of their profits and pay a tax of 28 per cent on this amount;
  - pay VAT at 10 per cent;
  - respect workers' rights and declare at least ten workers and insure them.

The strict and costly management to which they are subjected by the administration discourages numerous small companies struggling to make profits. Few managers have received real management training and don't have the required competences. In the province of Bac Ninh, where there are a total of 59 600 workers in the craft villages, only 2.3 per cent have college or university diplomas, only 3.1 per cent have a professional education and only 2.3 per cent have had technical training (Bac Ninh DPI, 2005).

Some enterprises went bankrupt soon after changing statute. Cooperatives play an intermediary role between declared private enterprises and the multitude of small family workshops. They have the same obligations as other declared enterprises (tax payment, respect of labour regulations, etc.) but they permit the joining together of the interests of family workshops which do not have the means to become formal individually. They pool together their capital, their know-how and their labour. Thanks to the financial contributions of their members, the cooperatives are capable of equipping themselves and innovating technically. In the textile villages the cooperatives have played an important role in the renovation of looms and in the installation of equipment and electricity. They have participated in the training of new craftworkers or in the improvement of their members' skills.

However, the cooperative system does not receive the support from craftworkers from the small enterprises that could benefit of economy of scale by merging their capital. The bad memories and experiences of the collectivist era have definitely stopped their development.

UNDECLARED FAMILY WORKSHOPS

Informal family enterprises are not governed by commercial law, are not subject to labour regulations and production taxes and do not issue bills. Commercial and management activities are carried out by family members who are often not remunerated. This form of organization allows all family members to participate and to make better use of working time and residential space for production and makes labour more flexible to meet varying demand. Employment is flexible and is adapted to the market or to production conditions. During the rice harvest, workers abandon the workshops (Fanchette and Nguyen, 2009).

Even when undeclared, these workshops have an appreciable capacity for hiring and they also subcontract a large reserve of labour. On average, each workshop employs 27 people on a regular basis and recruits eight to ten seasonal workers. The workshops carry out textile work, sewing and embroidery, which is very labour intensive and they can hire up to 30 or 50 people – and certain others employ hundreds of workers (Nguyen Quy Nghi, 2009).

Furthermore, the biggest undeclared enterprises nonetheless succeed in exporting in return for the payment of a tax of 10 per cent paid to the intermediary enterprises whose export licences they use.

Different types of undeclared enterprises exist and their place in the production line alters depending on their activities and the required level of expertise.

• Workshops that have a specific know-how or that own machines to carry out specific tasks.
• Sub-contracting workshops that carry out unskilled tasks.
• They accept a big order from a contractor but must, in turn, either subcontract a part of this work to other smaller enterprises or hire home workers to carry out the work.
• They are subcontracted by declared enterprises who work for export a part of the year. They subcontract in turn small workshops during the period of production for the domestic market.
• They only hire members of their own families because of a lack of means (lack of space and lack of money to feed workers and buy raw materials).

A survey carried out by Xuân Hoan Nguyen in Dong Ky in 2006 among 50 enterprises with different statutes demonstrates their specificity:

• Declared enterprises have large sized workshops (more than 800 m²), in the industrial site or at the limits of the residential area. Family workshops, whether they be declared or not, are generally localized within the residential area.
• Undeclared family workshops have very limited capital for investment or working capital. They do not have access to low-interest loans from banks and have difficulty acceding to land on industrial sites.
• Co-operatives: median characteristics in terms of floor space, capital and turnover in relation to other declared companies and to family workshops.
• When a family workshop becomes formal, it gains a greater ability to borrow capital and rent land, without turnover being more than that of undeclared family entreprises. The cost of formalization (declaring profits, paying taxes) is high for these small companies.

BUT AN INCOMPLETE FORMALIZATION OF THE COMPANIES AND A
SERIOUS COMPETITION

According to the study carried out by Mekong-Economics (2008), out of the 21 joint-venture enterprises and limited liability companies which participated in the Ha Tây province, only eight had a working capital of more than three billion VND (€120 000). The biggest, a joint-venture company had €900 000.

These declared companies are subject to two types of competition: from state companies which benefit from numerous advantages/private sector, in terms of land and credit access and other things and also by informal sector workshops whose production costs are a lot less as they pay no taxes, use under-paid family labour and are not subject to labour regulations.

Informal work in formal enterprises is high: few employees are declared. Only the accountants and some other qualified employees have national insurance and work contracts. Each employer negotiates hiring conditions. For the most dangerous type of work, wages are higher. Employers should pay insurance for all their employees, but they take advantage of the seasonality of the work to avoid doing so.

The hard working conditions in some declared enterprises force numerous workers to change employers frequently. Hence the big problem of worker turnover that makes enterprises more fragile, particularly during periods of big orders. The lack of flexibility in working hours discourages workers from the surrounding villages, most of the permanent workers originate from the remote areas where the opportunities to find work are limited.

Certain entrepreneurs are conscious of the bad working and living conditions they offer to their workers and would like to improve them. According to regulations, they are supposed to conform to norms of formal companies (employment law, hygiene and public health) but they have not the means either in capital or space to do so. Most employers from rural areas, having no other training other than the experience and know-how transmitted from generation to generation, have little awareness of environmental and sanitary risks. The high level of competition between formal businesses forces them to pressurize both labour and work quality. So the subcontracted workers attempt to work longer than they are legally permitted in order to earn more and thus work at a tiring pace. Employers hire young unqualified teenagers from distant areas.

## Conclusion

In the craft villages of the Red River Delta a large workforce has devoted itself to crafts and industry for several hundred years. These villages, which are organized in clusters, are part of a production chain whose length depends on the nature of the craft and the degree to which the techniques are mechanized. The fragmentary nature of the production process can be explained by the limited financial and technical capacity of the workers – who mostly work on an informal basis – the lack of space in the workshops, the pursuit to improve the know-how of the most talented workers and the increased mechanization of certain stages in the production process. Workshops fight off competition by specializing in one stage of a production process or by producing one type of product. At the top of the pyramid are the contractors – for the most part declared companies or enterprises – who subcontract the manual or the more elaborate parts of the fabricated article to a multitude of small, informal family businesses.

At the heart of the production chain, there exists a close relationship between the declared enterprises and the family workshops. This allows small enterprises to participate to the international market, to diversify their products and increase production through subcontracting.

However, this relationship between the two sectors is to the detriment of the working conditions of workers and of quality because most of the enterprises and their subcontracting links are informal. The guilds which controlled production quality and were responsible for training skilled workers were disbanded during the collectivist period and the cooperatives have not succeeded in filling the huge vacuum left behind. What is more, declared enterprises do not really abide by Labour Laws and laws concerning the environment and the quality of products.

The share of the formal sector in the craft villages cannot rise higher than a certain percentage; otherwise, too high a number of declared enterprises would create competition between them and limit the system of sub-contracting which guarantees the flexibility of this localized production system.

Furthermore, the increased mechanization of formal enterprises, which are seeking to standardize their production and increase output, is accompanied by a greater control of the whole production process and a reduction in the subcontracting of production stages.

## References

Dubiez, B. and Hamel, C. (2009) *Etude socio-spatiale de deux villages de metier: Les villages de Dong Ky et de Kiêu Ky*. Rapport de stage pour l'obtention de master en sociologie urbaine et en Urbanisme et aménagement, Hanoi IR: 123.

Fanchette, S. and Nguyen, Xuân Hoan (2009) "Un cluster en expansion: les villages de métier de meubles d'art de Dong Ky, réseaux sociaux, dynamiques territoriales et développement économique (delta du Fleuve rouge – Vietnam)", *Revue Moussons* 13–14 spécial "Vietnam: Histoire et perspectives contemporaines", Aix en Provence: 243–268.

JICA-MARD (2004) "The Study on Artisan Craft Development Plan for Rural Industrialization in the Socialist Republic of Vietnam, Final Report", Vol. 1. Almec, Tokyo.

Mekong-Economics (2008) "Survey on Advocacy Demand, Business Associations and Business Development Services in Crafts Sector in Ha Tây", Final Report prepared for Global Competitiveness Facility for Vietnamese Enterprises: 90.

Nguyen, Quy Nghi (2009) "La reconfiguration des districts industriels au Vietnam. Du monde local au monde global, une analyse sociologique des mutations d'un village de metier", Doctorat de Sociologie, Université Louis Lumière 2: 384.

# 5 Social insurance and informal economy in Vietnam

## The challenge of a universal coverage

*Paulette Castel*

In Vietnam, a large proportion of the population does not benefit from social or health insurance. This is not unusual for a low middle income country of around USD 1,200 income per capita. What is unusual is the government's mandate to rapidly develop "strong social insurance and health systems towards health and social insurances for all" (ILSSA, 2010). The approach appears original since, besides China, large coverage rates in developing countries have been mostly achieved through free public health care and the distribution of non-contributory pensions to the elderly.

Generally, when it comes to health and social insurance, policy makers believe in a natural growth-fueled progression of coverage and shrinking of informal employment with an expansion of wage employment and progress in public information and management systems. International experience does indeed indicate that countries with higher per capita gross domestic product (GDP) tend to have higher health and social insurance coverage of the labor force (Palacios and Pallares, 2000).

Expanding coverage might be considerably challenging. In Latin America, despite a long tradition of social security and extensive reforms since the 1980s, Rofman and Oliveri (2011) find that only three of 18 countries present coverage rates of the employed above 60 percent and, that only seven countries present coverage rates of salaried workers above 60 percent. Several factors explain these disappointing results. Besides the issues of affordability, health and social insurance programs are often not designed for all kinds of workers. Even in the formal sector, the coverage of part-time or seasonal employees is usually not mandatory. Some schemes impose long vesting periods for pension rights and these are difficult to fulfill when jobs are not stable. Loose links between contributions and benefits that prevail in many schemes fail to provide good incentives to participate. The systems' weak information management, unreliability and unfairness have a large influence as well (Forteza *et al.*, 2009). In Chile and Peru, Packard (2002) and Barr and Packard (2003) find that the self-employed – who can freely join social insurance – opt to remain out of social security when they perceive that retirement investments such as housing, household enterprise, education of children are "relatively less risky than saving in the reformed pension system". Behavioral economics also show that people's time inconsistency, psychological predisposition and cognitive limitations are all factors that prevent them from making sound life-cycle financial planning decisions (Berheim and Rangel, 2005).

With important social and economic changes due to the transition from a command to a market economy, public health and social insurance systems have grown fast in Vietnam over the past decades. Strong growth and the quick development of the private sector since 2000 have led to a rapid progression of Vietnam Social Security coverage from 3.2 million in 1996 to 9.4 million people in 2010. This number, however, is small in comparison to Vietnam's 48 million workers. State subsidies to large sectors of the population (children, students, the elderly and the poor) helped expand health insurance coverage to 55.9 percent of the entire population in 2008. The health insurance law of 2008 foresees mandatory participation for all in 2015. The actual take up rate of voluntary insurance, however, casts some doubt about the willingness to join of workers in the informal sector even if participation keeps being heavily subsidized. Regarding social insurance (pensions, disability, sick and maternity leave, etc.) no strategy has been developed yet. So far, government's policies have focused on enlarging access. In 1995, mandatory participation in Vietnam Social Security (VSS) initially reserved to public sector employees was extended to the employees of the private sector. The Social Insurance Law of 2006 expanded the system to the farmers and the self-employed on a voluntary basis. Subsidizing participation could help only partially. Pension rights require commitments over long periods, therefore, even if suddenly all the workers in the informal sector decided to join the pension system, most of these persons would be too old to accumulate enough rights for pension income at retirement or for their dependants in case of death. Universal coverage remains a challenge in the social insurance as well as in health insurance.

This chapter presents the results of several studies that have been done in Vietnam to understand non-salaried and salaried workers' participation and willingness to participate in health and social insurance in this country. These studies show that the extension of coverage is related to many issues beyond those that are usually discussed (affordability or benefit packages) and include: the attitude of health care providers, business competition in the labor market, public perception of the role of social security institutions, and the ability of the latter to protect today's elderly people.

## Health insurance

The 2008 Act mandates the progressive coverage by health insurance of the entire population. To overcome the issues of affordability, the government has set up an extensive system of subsidies. Thus, the poor, people of ethnic groups living in mountainous and remote areas, those living in the poorest communes, all children under six years and those over 80 years of age receive a free health insurance card. The latter is half price for those close to the poverty line and for students in primary and secondary schools. Access to care is also very broad. All health services (in registered establishments) are reimbursed up to a ceiling equivalent to 40 times the minimum wage. A deductible of 20 percent is, however, imposed on all visits. It is reduced to 5 percent for people under the poverty line and is removed for all children under six years of age. It varies according the region but most people are registered to their local health care facilities, which means that rural residents require referrals to access higher level of health care at provincial and central – overcrowded – hospitals.

As the figures reported in Table 5.1 show, coverage of health insurance in 2008 was already high (55.9 percent). If all the beneficiaries of government aid and their dependants joined, the health insurance system could enroll 17.3 million more people, and reach 76 percent of the population.

Expanding coverage to the remaining 20.7 million persons who work in the informal sector and are above the poverty line is a challenge. As shown in Figure 5.1, only a small share of these people are low income earners, even when they make their living through multiple occupations. More than two-thirds earn an income equal to or greater than the average income of the employed population in Vietnam. The lack of coverage of relatively better off workers is not specific to Vietnam. In Latin America, Da Costa *et al.* (2011) found that only 20 percent of workers not covered by social security systems belong to low income groups.

The general consensus in Vietnam is that extending health insurance coverage to these people is particularly difficult. On the one hand, the adverse selection problems hinder the administration from engaging in large affiliation campaigns since those who voluntarily join are mostly people who are sick and in need of care. Faced with a growing health insurance deficit, in 2007 the administration suspended the initiatives it had put in place, specifically those with the organization of the Women's Union and the Farmers Association to facilitate the enrollment of workers in the informal sector. Mandatory participation for all in 2015

*Table 5.1* Health insurance coverage, 2008 rate and simulations for 2014

|  | *Persons* | *Share in total* |
|---|---|---|
| *Situation in 2008* | | |
| Number of persons with health insurance | | |
|    Mandatory public | 30,682,798 | 35.55 |
|    Voluntary public | 17,148,210 | 19.87 |
|    Voluntary private | 401,102 | 0.46 |
| Population's coverage rate of health insurance in 2008 | | **55.88** |
| *Potential expansion 2008–2014* | | |
| Number of additional persons who can benefit from state's subsidies in 2014 | 17,351,459 | 20.10 |
| Population's coverage rate in 2014 if enrolled | | **75.98** |
| Population and workers in the informal sector who are not entitled to state's subsidies for health insurance | 20,728,688 | **24.02** |
| Total population | 86,312,257 | 100.0 |

Sources: VHLSS, 2008; GSO; author's calculations.

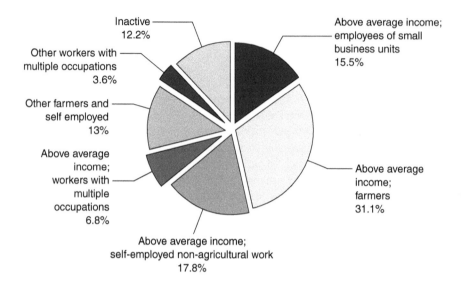

*Figure 5.1* Population in the informal sector not entitled to state subsidies for health insurance (sources: VHLSS 2008, GSO, author's calculations).

could solve the problem of adverse selection, if the government actually gets universal coverage. The low turnout so far among workers in the informal sector (12.5 percent in 2008 or 2.6 million people out of 20.7 million) casts doubts on the possibility of getting them all affiliated by that time because enforcement appears difficult to implement if people are not ready to participate. From a practical point of view, inspecting individual records on a yearly basis and enforcing participation of about 21 million informal workers is a cumbersome and expensive business.

The analysis of results of the GSO household survey of 2006 on health insurance (Castel *et al.*, 2011) indicates that, among the workers in the informal sector, the main reason cited for non-participation is not cost and affordability (20.7 percent), but the perception that health insurance is not useful (36.7 percent) and not accessible (24.1 percent) because, until the law of 2008, individual membership to health insurance was not possible in order to reduce the effects of adverse selection.

Their analysis of participation by region indicates that the participation in health insurance of non-subsidized workers in the informal sector is higher in areas where access to higher level of health care at hospitals is easier. In the South Central region where the insured in 2006 were more likely affiliated to a hospital (only 18 percent were affiliated to a communal health center against 32 percent nationally), the rate of new enrollments between 2006 and 2008 was higher than in other regions. Out-of-pocket amounts for hospital care when using the health insurance card were also lower than in other provinces.

The quality of care people expect to obtain plays also an important role in the perception the public has about the utility of being insured. One possible reason for which workers in the informal sector decide against joining health insurance is that, in some regions, it fails to eliminate horizontal inequalities in the provision of care. A study of individual health insurance claims was conducted in 2008 in the province of Kon Tum, where coverage is almost universal because of the large share of subsidized groups (ethnic minorities, poor, mountainous and remote communes, etc.). It shows that, among people of the same sex, age group and type of disease, the poorest and those belonging to ethnic minorities consistently received less expensive care (Castel, 2009). While in general better off individuals are more inclined to ask for non-essential care, poor patients in Vietnam are using the hospital only at the most critical moments. If health insurance smoothed inequalities, the direction of the gaps in health care spending between these two groups should be more randomly distributed and not, as the data show, be systematically to the detriment of the poorest people.

These observations suggest that information campaigns on health insurance will have little impact on the desire of workers in the informal sector to join the program. Policies focusing on affordability have likely reached their limits. While, understandably, most of current reforms primarily aim at resolving financing issues and controlling the expansion of health care spending, some innovations in health insurance could help boost the participation of the workers living in rural areas and reach universal coverage. Currently, health insurance reimburses health care providers based on fees for services payments. New policies, like the introduction of performance based arrangements under which providers are rewarded for meeting pre-established targets for delivery of health care services to under-served groups (poor, population in rural areas, etc.) could help improve the quality of care to those groups and improve public perception of health insurance usefulness.

## Social insurance – formal employment

Social insurance in Vietnam is made of a mandatory system and a voluntary system. The mandatory system covers only the wage employed with labor contracts of three months and above. The voluntary system, recently created with the Social Security Law of 2006, covers all the other workers. The mandatory system includes a large range of programs (short-term benefits, compensation for work accident and professional disease, old-age pension and survivorship). The voluntary system consists only of a pension system with survivorship benefits. Both systems require a minimum contribution calculated on the minimum wage.

In 2010, Vietnam Social Security had registered 9.4 million contributors. Figure 5.2 presents their distribution by type of enterprise. Because until 1995 the system was reserved for the military and the employees of public administrations and enterprises, those groups represent today slightly less than half of the participants (35 and 14 percent). Created in 2008, the voluntary scheme has attracted a very small number of participants.

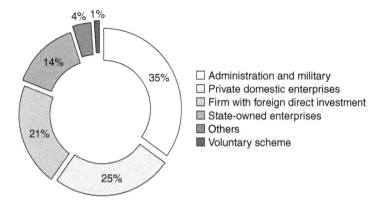

*Figure 5.2* Distribution of Vietnam social security participants (sources: VSS, MOLISA, author's calculations).

Vietnam social security does not provide any estimate of the corresponding size of formal employment. Using GSO information on individual health insurance registration and type of employment, Nguyen Thi Thu Phuong and Castel (2009) estimate that, in 2006, Vietnam Social Security covered only 12.9 percent of the working-age population or 16.2 percent of the employed (excluding working pensioners). More specifically, it covered 38.8 percent of the 17.5 million persons that were waged-employed. Evasion or the lack of employees' registration in violation of the social insurance law, although large, is not however the main issue in Vietnam. Actually, most households' units are exempt from business registration. According to the decree 88/2006/ND-CP only small business with a turnover above a minimum threshold (defined locally) need to register at the district Business Registration Office, and have to undertake the procedures to obtain a Tax Registration Certificate with a tax code (Cling *et al.*, 2010). These formal enterprises, moreover, only have to register employees that have a labor contract of three months or more in social security. Consequently, the authors find that the total number of employees in the formal sector that are required to register in Vietnam Social Security is relatively small, and the coverage of social insurance relatively high: 69.4 percent, particularly if we consider that VSS information and management systems are currently rather under-developed.

## Social insurance – informal employment in formal sector

Informal employment and informality in the formal sector are, by contrast, widespread. On the one hand, many small private companies do not contribute to social security. On the other hand, many companies in the formal sector contribute on wages well below those they actually distribute. The line that distinguishes formal and informal employment is, therefore, rather blurred in Vietnam since a large share of formal employment's income is in fact not reported to social insurance.

The GSO 2006 Census of Enterprises clearly reflects the situation. Based on those data reported in Table 5.2, Castel and To (2012) report high coverage rates of employees in state-owned enterprises (96.7 percent) and foreign direct investment enterprises (86.8 percent) but low rates in the other enterprises of the private sector (43.6 percent). More intriguing, among the companies that contribute the share of contributions in wages is abnormally low. According to the regulations, these payments should amount to 23 percent of the sum of the enterprises' registered employees' wages. These levels are much lower: even in the public sector, the share of contributions in the wage bill is largely below the expected rate (7.6 percent vs 23 percent).

Three factors explain these low levels. First, in Vietnam enterprises are not obliged to register short-term employees with labor contracts of three months or less. Second, subsidies, bonuses, and other allowances are not subject to social contributions. Third, a worker's level of contributions is calculated on the wage recorded in the worker's labor contract and enterprises do not adjust this value when wages are increased. As a result, the amount of contributions paid to social security gradually falls over time in relation to the wages workers effectively receive.

Cross-checking the data of the Census of Enterprises with the figures of Vietnam Social Security (VSS) the authors find that about 23.9 percent of the employees in the enterprise sector are employed under short-term contracts and that contributions are paid on wages equal on average to 46.4 percent of the wages actually paid in the sector of enterprises with foreign investment and 37.7 percent in the other private enterprises. Only 1,218 enterprises out of 58,906 report contributions high enough to fully cover all their employees and 100 percent of the wages they actually paid.

The use of short-term contracts and the payment of contributions not on the wages that are actually paid but on those reported in labor contracts are not illegal practices in Vietnam. Making them illegal will not deeply change this

*Table 5.2* Enterprise sector – participation in Vietnam Social Security, 2005

| | Total | Public sector | Foreign direct investment | Private sector |
|---|---|---|---|---|
| Number of firms | 129,208 | 3,366 | 4,142 | 121,699 |
| Total employment | 6,222,430 | 1,625,589 | 1,339,474 | 3,257,362 |
| Number of firms paying social contributions | 59,964 | 3,255 | 3,594 | 53,115 |
| Participation rate | 46.4 | 96.7 | 86.8 | 43.6 |
| Share in total employment | 79.0 | 98.7 | 95.6 | 62.4 |
| Share of contributions in wage bill[1] | 7.5 | 7.6 | 9.5 | 5.9 |

Sources: Enterprise Census, 2006; GSO; author's calculations.

Note
1 Only enterprises paying contributions.

*Table 5.3* Estimation of short-term contracts and wage evasion or under-reporting, 2005

|  | Total sector enterprise | Private sector | Foreign direct investment | Public sector |
|---|---|---|---|---|
| *Covered employment and short-term contracts* |  |  |  |  |
| Census total employment[1] (a) | 4,918,249 | 2,033,191 | 1,339,474 | 1,625,589 |
| Social Security covered employees[2] (b) | 3,742,119 | 1,374,261 | 1,124,566 | 1,291,915 |
| Employees with short-term contract (a–b) | 1,176,130 | 658,930 | 214,908 | 333,674 |
| Share of short-term contracts in employment | 23.9 | 32.4 | 16.0 | 20.5 |
| *Monthly average wage and wage evasion or under-reporting* |  |  |  |  |
| Census enterprises' average wage | – | 1,577,276 | 2,101,708 | – |
| Social Security average reported wage[3] | – | 594,259 | 985,243 | – |
| Share of wages reported to social security | – | 37.7 | 46.9 | – |

Sources: Enterprise Census 2006, GSO, VSS, author's calculations.

Notes
1 Enterprises reporting social security contribution.
2 VSS administrative data public sector employees and, army excluded.
3 Based on VSS administrative data.

situation. In Colombia, Kugler and Kugler (2003) also find an unexplained range of amount of contributions in wages between companies. In most countries, the under-reporting of wages disappears when social security institutions are sufficiently equipped to cooperate with the Directorate General of Taxation and ensure that contributions are calculated on companies' labor costs. The cost and complexity of these tasks explain that these control and enforcement systems are slow to implement. It is, however, impressive how much these procedures are widespread among enterprises in Vietnam. A recent enterprise survey conducted by the World Bank shows that, in 2010, temporary workers represented 35.8 percent of the surveyed firms' staff compared to an average of 7 percent in low and middle income countries and 9 percent in similar populated countries (IFC, 2011).

Using the variation of the share of social contributions in wages across enterprises, Castel and To (2012) show that workers in Vietnam are probably the ones who benefit the most from enterprises' evasion and under-reporting of wages through higher net wages. Like in many countries, firms in Vietnam can shift the burden of social contributions on workers in the form of lower wages. The data actually indicate that average wages in enterprises that fully comply are more likely to be lower than in enterprises of the same branch of activity that evade or under-report wages. On the other hand, the study does not find any evidence that the enterprises that evade or under-report wages realize higher profits or have greater turnover per worker. The under-reporting of wages could be a strategy for firms to pay higher wages and retain workers. A study by CIEM indicates that turnover reached a stunning 43.4 percent among foreign companies over the period from 2001 to 2003 (VDR, 2006, p. 94).

This situation is worrying for multiple reasons. First, lack of coverage and small contributions engender none or small social security benefits that do not adequately replace a worker's income in the event of sickness or during retirement. Second the system appears to be already locked into a status quo. On the one hand, workers are not showing interest in social security, for lack of understanding or preferences for higher wages over social security benefits. On the other hand, confronted with large employee turnover, enterprises seek to minimize or to avoid social contributions in order to pay higher wages and attract or retain workers. This reinforces workers' preconceptions that social insurance provides small benefits that are not very meaningful. Without public policies in coordination with workers and enterprises, the status quo will strengthen over time, and since the horizons of social security are very long, it is conceivable that distrust and misunderstanding will be ingrained in the minds of many workers and their families when future policy makers seek to resolve the issue of low coverage of social security system. At that time, changing behavior could be very difficult as the disappointing results in terms of coverage that the reforms of pension systems in Latin America suggest.

## Social insurance – informal sector

The two previous sections focus on the situation of the employees in the formal sector. Today, however, most workers in Vietnam belong to the informal sector. Based on the GSO Employment Survey of 2007, Cling *et al.* (2011) estimate that there are 34 million people who are informally employed (or 71.8 percent of total employment) of which 23 million are in the agricultural sector.

Three studies have looked at the willingness of the workers of the informal sector to participate in a voluntary pension scheme in Vietnam. Bales and Castel (2005) have conducted a survey in preparation of the 2006 Law on Social Insurance; based on the results, Castel (2008) analyzed the determinants of the willingness to participate of the workers in the informal sector. A second survey realized in 2007 studied the potential transition of the participants of the Farmers' Pension Fund in the province of Nghe An to the VSS new voluntary pension system created in 2008 (Castel, 2007). These three studies show that about half of the workers in the informal sector are willing to participate in a retirement system. However, the limitations of the current scheme such as a relatively high minimum contribution, and especially the non-eligibility for pension of all those who cannot contribute 20 years before reaching retirement age, significantly reduce the attractiveness of the current system. Without transition policies, the implementation of the new pension system risks being disappointing (low coverage, small benefits). Enrollment rates cannot take off if the lack of understanding of social insurance mechanisms and the perception that the pension system provides no significant benefits dampen the current interest for participation.

*Willingness to join a pension system*

To understand the willingness of workers in the informal sector to contribute to a retirement system, Bales and Castel conducted in 2005 a survey of 3,412 Vietnamese households with at least one member employed in the informal sector. The population of the surveyed households, representative of the Vietnamese informal sector above the poverty line, was composed mainly of unsalaried workers (77.7 percent) and wage-employees (14.9 percent) with no social insurance, and some salaried workers (7.4 percent) with social security; 30 percent of the households had only agricultural activities, 27 percent had only off-farming activities, and 43 percent combined these two types of activity.

Participants were asked to indicate their willingness to hypothetically join a pension system that would function like a long-term financial saving account that could finance annuities during retirement. In such a system, all respondents are proposed the same cost–benefit relationship. The amount of the pension depends on the savings accumulated by the insured. In the system proposed by the survey, the amount of pension income was the same for everyone and participants were, accordingly, invited to indicate their interest to accumulate the same amount of savings at retirement (age 60). The amount of the monthly premium that was hypothetically required in order to participate in the system, consequently, increased exponentially with the respondent's age (in order to save the same amount in a shorter period of time).

As shown in Table 5.4, just over half of the respondents (50.7 percent) showed some readiness to participate in the pension scheme. Only 34.6 percent, however, appeared to be ready to contribute an actuarially fair amount; 16.5 percent would participate if contributions were lower and, therefore, subsidized. The analysis of the determinants of participation indicates that, as expected, wealthier and more educated people are more likely to participate. Less obvious, households in rural areas are likewise more inclined to participate despite stronger family and relatives' network than urban residents. Participation is also sensitive to the cost–benefit relationship: it decreases with the contribution rate (ratio contributions to household income) and it increases with the replacement rate (ratio benefit to household income).

The results were used to predict the willingness of the respondents to participate in the voluntary pension system established in the Social Insurance Law of 2006. Figure 5.3 compares the contribution rates and the replacement rates of the VSS scheme with the one proposed in the 2005 survey. Participating in the new voluntary pension system is less costly than in the survey's scheme particularly for middle-aged people. The corresponding level of benefits is also, however, much lower because 20 years of contribution are required for pension eligibility in the VSS scheme. Those who enroll at ages of 45 and above and reach retirement age with shorter contributory periods are only entitled to a relatively small lump sum amount.

The results are presented in Table 5.5. The lower level of contributions results in greater potential youth participation in the VSS voluntary scheme. Youth

*Table 5.4* Distribution of respondents according to their readiness to participate[1]

|  | % in total respondents | % in total respondents' readiness adjusted for savings capacity[2] |
| --- | --- | --- |
| **Total ready to participate** | **51.5** | **50.7** |
| *Ready to pay actuarially fair amount of contributions* | | |
| Total | 37.1 | 34.6 |
| Minimum wage at age 60[3] | 17.2 | 13.3 |
| Half minimum wage at age 60 | 15.7 | 15.7 |
| Half minimum wage at age 65 | 4.2 | 5.6 |
| *Ready if the amount of contributions is lower than the actuarially fair level* | | |
| Total | 14.4 | 16.5 |
| Half minimum wage at age 65 (subsidized 20%) | 3.8 | 4.6 |
| Half minimum wage at age 65 (subsidized 40%) | 2.6 | 3.5 |
| Half minimum wage at age 65 (subsidized 60%) | 8.0 | 8.4 |
| **Not willing to participate** | **48.5** | **48.9** |
| Proposed benefits too low | 4.3 | 4.3 |
| Not interested in any option | 44.2 | 44.6 |
| Total respondents | 100.0 | 100.0 |

Sources: Survey on VSIIS in Vietnam, MOLISA, author's calculations.

Notes

1 An iterative bidding process was established in order to elicit participants' preferences. Respondents were asked, first, if they would agree to pay a determined amount of contributions in order to receive a pension income of about half the minimum wage at the age of 60. The amount of the proposed contribution exponentially increased with the age of the respondents in order to reflect the fact that older people would have to accumulate the same amount of savings over a shorter period. Respondents' reactions to this level were obtained through follow-up questions. Respondents that did not show interest in participating under the first option were proposed a lower amount of contribution for the same entitlement but at age 65, in case of refusal lower subsidized level were proposed afterward.

2 Participation is adjusted to ensure consistency between the level of contributions respondents accepted and the monthly household savings capacity they reported in the survey.

3 Participants that mentioned that a benefit of half the minimum wage was too low and showed readiness to pay higher contributions (actuarially fair amount) in order to receive a pension equal to the minimum wage.

*Table 5.5* Predicted participation in VSS voluntary pension system

| Age group | 15–19 | 20–24 | 25–29 | 30–34 | 35–39 | 40–44 | 45–49 | 50–54 | 55–60 | Total |
| --- | --- | --- | --- | --- | --- | --- | --- | --- | --- | --- |
| Participation rate | 60.6 | 87.7 | 86.3 | 84.0 | 72.2 | 41.5 | 8.1 | 0.4 | 0.2 | 48.8 |

Sources: Survey on VSIIS in Vietnam, MOLISA, author's calculations.

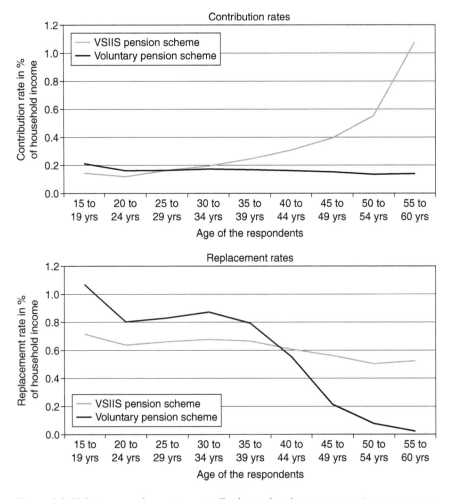

*Figure 5.3* Voluntary pension system contribution and replacement rates (sources: survey on VSIIS in Vietnam, MOLISA, author's calculation).

participation increases by less than 60 percent in the survey to more than 80 percent in the simulation. By contrast, the participation of persons 50 years and older falls from 40 percent in the survey to less than 10 percent. The sharp decline in the participation of older workers is due to the particularly unfavorable cost–benefit relationship of the new scheme that does not give them the opportunity to acquire pension rights.

### The participants of the Nghe An Farmers' Pension Fund

The Farmers' Pension Fund of the province of Nghe An was established in 1998. The fund was based on individual accounts but with pre-determined levels of return and, therefore, benefits above the levels that the Fund could finance over the long term (von Hauff and Knop, 2004; Castel, 2005). The fund was, consequently, closed in 2009 and members were offered to transfer to the VSS voluntary pension scheme that was created in 2008. A study was realized in 2007 to prepare the transition.

In March 2007, the Fund included 84,860 members. Most of the participants were farmers (74.3 percent) or worked in the service sector (15.5 percent). There is no clear evidence that the Fund's members were among the better off in the province: 49.1 percent reported individual income per capita lower than the minimum wage. However, when compared to the rest of the population of the province (VHLSS 2006) their level of education was higher than the average level of education of the farmers and self-employed of Nghe An province. The comparison also indicates that the Fund covered around 6.9 percent of the non-waged employed workers of the province.

The majority of the participants were 40 years or older and paid very low contributions. On average, members contributed VND25,843 per month and only 4.9 percent of them contributed an amount equal to or above the minimum level of contribution required in VSS pension schemes (VND72,000 or 16 percent of the minimum wage in 2007). Not surprisingly, since the levels of contribution were very low, the expected levels of the pension benefits were also very low. The average level of the pensions paid in 2009 was around VND76,000 (or around 17 percent of the 2007 minimum wage).

In order to understand participant's expectations and capacity to join the national pension scheme, ILSSA (Ministry of Labor) realized a survey in which respondents were precisely informed about the options they would most likely face when the Fund closed given the amount they had saved in it.[1] As the VSS voluntary pension scheme requires 20 years of contributions for retirement, the survey asked people aged 40 (women) or 45 years (men) and over if they would be willing to contribute an amount higher than the minimum in order to "buy" additional contributory years and complete the minimum requirement and get a pension.

Among the younger participants, 58.3 percent reported willing to join the voluntary pension system; 19.9 percent showed interest only if the contribution rate was reduced from 72,000 to 50,000 VND (or 16 to 11.1 percent of the minimum wage), even if the expected amount of the pension income would be accordingly lower. Among the older participants, 39.1 percent indicated their desire to participate and to contribute additional money in order to be entitled to pension income, 20.3 percent showed the same interest, but if the amount of required contributions was lower.

Based on these results and all members' characteristics, the study furthermore estimated that about 36.6 percent of the Fund's members could be willing to join the VSS voluntary pension scheme; 6.1 percent additional members could participate if the minimum amount of contribution was reduced and 30.7 percent could participate if the system gave them the opportunity to obtain a pension at retirement; 6.3 percent would refuse; 30.4 percent could not be classified. Figure 5.4 gives the distribution of these groups by age.

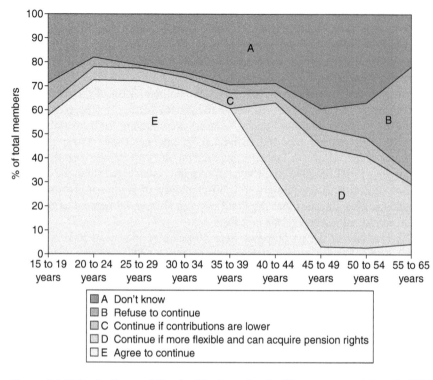

*Figure 5.4* Nghe An Farmers' Pension Fund members' willingness to participate in VSS voluntary pension system (sources: survey on VSIIS in Vietnam, MOLISA, author's calculations).

In 2009, the government decided to gradually close the Fund. Members were given the option to receive a lump sum based on the contributions they had paid to the Fund or to transfer their savings, translated in years of contributions, to the new VSS voluntary pension scheme created in 2008. In the latter case, members could realize extra transfers of money to acquire more pension rights but in a more restrictive way than in the variant envisaged in the survey: the number of contributory years acquired in the new system could not be higher than the number of years they had actually contributed in the Fund (that is at most ten years and often less excluding, therefore, the possibility for many middle-aged women and men to get a pension in the new system). According to the Fund's official documents, 25,650 persons of the 86,012 members registered in 2009 (29.8 percent) decided to join the national voluntary pension system.

## Conclusions and policy implications

While it has embarked since the 1980s in radical transformations of its economy from a control and command economy to a market economy, Vietnam has built up a vision of a universal social protection system also based on commercial principles through public insurance mechanisms in the fields of health care and pension income.

In the sector of health insurance the implementation of this vision led to strong participation by the state with the obligation, by law, to subsidize the participation of the poor, the most vulnerable groups and the youth. Coverage has progressed rapidly. Health insurance reached more than half of the population in 2008 and almost three-quarters of the population could be covered in 2014. Similar mechanisms, like matching contributions, could be implemented in the sector of social insurance. These policies that give access to social insurance to a large sector of the population are an important factor of integration of populations largely in the informal sector to systems that otherwise could be used only by the better off. Moreover, it increases public awareness of insurance mechanisms that are still very new for many people in Vietnam. In that sense subsidizing participation is an important milestone which can be used to further develop coverage.

In the sector of health insurance as well as in the sector of pension and social insurance, affordability, however, is currently not any more the main cause for non-participation. The perception among a large share of workers in the informal sector that both systems are not useful for them is also an important factor. Although health insurance gives access to a large range of attention and levels of care and social insurance provides relatively high benefits to those who have stable jobs and long contributory periods, a large share of the population does not think that these systems are serving them well. Health insurance does not appear to ease the access to hospital care for many workers living in rural areas. In certain places, it does not appear to reduce horizontal inequalities in the quality of care. Social insurance appears to deliver small pension income or no income at all to many workers who currently reach retirement age with short contributory periods or who have had contributions paid on under-reported wages. Since more than two-thirds of employment is in the informal sector, so even in case of mandatory participation, enforcing participation and reaching universal coverage will likely be difficult if many workers are not willing to join.

In both cases formalization and higher participation of the workers in the informal sector do not require major structural changes but rather reforms that aim at coordinating the action of several stakeholders, the state, Vietnam Social Security (VSS, health insurance, and social insurance), as well as the networks of health care providers, enterprises, and workers in the informal sector.

In the sector of health insurance, the introduction of performance based arrangements under which providers are rewarded for meeting pre-established targets for delivery of health care services to under-served groups (poor, population in rural areas, etc.) could help improve the quality of care to those groups and improve public perception in rural areas of the usefulness of health insurance. In the sector of social insurance, eliminating the practice of under-reporting wages would likely require coordinated actions between the state and enterprises to implement a transition period over which the share of contributions paid on wages could increase without creating downward pressures on wages, or increasing the recruiting problems of enterprises. Larger coverage of the existing elderly population and a better cooperation between VSS, enterprises associations, and staff unions would likely increase the visibility of the system and increase the willingness to participate and comply.

The state or VSS could also, during a transition period, subsidize pension income in order to offer the opportunity to the people who have contributed to social insurance but currently reach retirement without being entitled to a pension or with too little entitlement to become pensioners or to obtain higher pension income. Subsidizing pension income is likely a better approach than non-contributory pensions or the reduction of the vesting period for pension rights because the latter might stimulate free-riding behaviors. In principle, non-contributory pensions are of very small amounts like poverty alleviation benefits and, in case of short contributory periods, the resulting accumulation of low contribution amounts at retirement should simply entitle the recipient to very low pension incomes. However, because providing very low pensions to the elderly is perceived to be socially unacceptable, there are risks that the pension system or the state budget is forced, after some time, to top up these "too low pensions" to a socially acceptable minimum. These transfers would benefit the poor who anyway could not have been able to contribute or to contribute higher amounts but also free-riders who would obtain a pension higher than they should obtain on fair terms. Free-riding behaviors and the resulting excessive levels of subsidies can significantly undermine the financial sustainability of a pension system.[2]

For these reasons policies based on commercial principles that encourage participation and increase the number of elderly receiving pension income are, likely, more effective in supporting the development of financially sustainable systems. An innovative approach in Chengdu, China (O'Keefe and Wang, 2010) using "family binding" relationship is of interest in that respect. In Chengdu, the persons reaching retirement age without pension rights can receive a basic pension provided their children are contributing.

Overall, the coordinated participation of stakeholders like health care providers, enterprises and worker associations, and family networks in the design, the implementation, and the monitoring of innovative policies is necessary to help reduce the current misunderstanding of the general public about the role and capacities of social security to prevent shocks in social matters and increase the capacity of the systems to attract and serve a larger share of the population.

## Notes

1 Interviewers were given tables that indicated based on a respondent's age, gender, years of participation, and amount of savings the levels of the pension or the lump sum amounts this participant could obtain in both systems.
2 Such reason pushed many of the pension reforms in the 1980s and the 1990s to eliminate any redistributive elements of the pension system.

# References

Bales, S. and Castel, P. (2005) Survey on Voluntary Social Insurance for the Informal Sector in Vietnam (VSIIS): Policy Implications. Report ASEM-II trust fund Project Development of Social Insurance Law in Vietnam, Ministry of Labor Invalids and Social Affairs of Vietnam (unpublished).

Barr, A. and Packard, T. (2003) Preferences, Constraints and Alternative to Coverage under Peru's Pension System. Background paper for the Regional Study on Social Security Reform, World Bank.

Berheim, B.D. and Rangel, A. (2005) Behavioral Public Economics: Welfare and Policy Analysis with Non-standard Decision Makers. NBER Working Paper series 11518.

Castel, P. (2005) Financial Sustainability of the Nghe An Voluntary Pension Fund. Ministry of Labor Invalids and Social Affairs of Vietnam (unpublished).

Castel, P. (2007) Nghe An Voluntary Pension Fund: Transition to the National Scheme: Policy Options. Ministry of Labor Invalids and Social Affairs of Vietnam (unpublished).

Castel, P. (2008) Voluntary Defined Benefit Pension System Willingness to Participate the Case of Vietnam. Asian Social Policy in Comparative Perspective: Conference Proceedings. Online, available at: www.welfareacademy.org/pubs/international/policy_exchanges/asp_papers/index1.shtml.

Castel, P. (2009) Vietnam Health Insurance: Use of Health Care Services by the Poor; Efficiency and Equity Issues in the Province of Kon Tum. Poverty Assessment, Social Protection Chapter Background Paper 5, Hanoi: Vietnamese Academy of Social Sciences/CentEr for Analysis and Forecasting.

Castel, P. and To, T.-T. (2012) Informal Employment in the Formal Sector: Wages and Social Security Tax Evasion in Vietnam. *Journal of the Asia Pacific Economy (JAPE)*, Volume 17, issue 4, 626–31, Special Issue: The Informal Economy in Asia, October.

Castel, P., Tran Mai Oanh, Tran Ngo Thi Minh Tam, and Vu Hoang Dat (2011) Health Insurance in Viet Nam towards Universal Coverage: The Case of the Workers of the Informal Sector. Policy Research Study, Hanoi: UNDP.

Cling, J.-P., Lê, V.-D., Merceron, S., Nguyen, Thi Thu Huyen, Nguyen, Huu Chi, Phan, T. Ngoc Trâm, Razafindrakoto, M., Roubaud, F., and Constance. T. (2010) The Informal Sector in Vietnam: A Focus on Hanoi and Ho Chi Minh City. ISS-GSO/DIAL-IRD.

Cling, J.-P., Razafindrakoto, M., and Roubaud, F. (2011) The Informal Economy in Vietnam. Study for the ILO. Online, available at: www.ilo.org/wcmsp5/groups/public/asia/ro-bangkok/ilo-hanoi/documents/publication/wcms_171370.pdf.

Da Costa, R., de Laiglesia, J.R., Martinez, E., and Melguizo, A. (2011) The Economy of the Possible: Pensions and Informality in Latin America. Working paper No. 295, Paris: OECD Development Centre.

Forteza, A., Lucchetti, L., and Montserrat, Pallares-Miralles (2009) Measuring the Coverage Gap. In Robert Holzmann, David A. Robalino, and Noriyuki Takayama, eds: *Closing the Coverage Gap: The Role of Social Pensions and Other Retirement Income Transfers*, World Bank.

IFC (2011) Vietnam. Enterprise Surveys Country Note Series. Online, available at: www.enterprisesurveys.org/~/media/FPDKM/EnterpriseSurveys/Documents/Country%20Notes/Vietnam-2011.pdf.

ILSSA (2010) Social Protection Strategy Period 2011–2020 (7th draft). Institute for Labour Science and Social Affairs – Ministry of Labour, Invalids, and Social Affairs (MOLISA) of Vietnam (unpublished).

Kugler, A. and Kugler, M. (2003) The Labor Market Effects of Payroll Taxes in a Middle-income Country: Evidence from Colombia. IZA Discussion paper, No. 852.

Nguyen, Thi Thu Phuong and Castel, P. (2009) Voluntary Pension System in Vietnam: Challenge of Expanding Coverage. Working Paper Vietnamese Academy of Social Sciences Poverty Assessment, Center for Analysis and Forecasting. Online, available at: www-wds.worldbank.org/external/default/main?pagePK=64193027&piPK=641879 37&theSitePK=523679&menuPK=64187510&searchMenuPK=64187283&theSitePK =523679&entityID=000356161_20110825032343&searchMenuPK=64187283&the SitePK=523679.

O'Keefe, P. and Wang, D. (2010) Closing the Coverage Gap: Evolution and Issues for Rural Pensions in China. Presentation at the Conference: Ageing in Asia, Beijing, Chengdu, December.

Packard, T. (2002) Pooling, Savings and Prevention: Mitigating the Risk of Old Age Poverty in Chile. Background Paper for Regional Study on Social Security Reform, Office of the Chief Economist, Latin America and Caribbean Regional Office, Washington DC: World Bank.

Palacios, R. and Pallares, M. (2000) International Patterns of Pension Provision. Social Protection Discussion Paper Series 9, World Bank.

Rofman, R. and Oliveri, M.-L. eds (2011) La Cobertura de los Sistemas Previsionales en América Latina: Conceptos e Indicadores. Social Protection Discussion Paper Series No. 7, World Bank.

Von Hauff, M. and Knop, M.R. (2004) Social Security for the Poor. Ministry of Labor Invalids and Social Affairs of Vietnam – GTZ (unpublished).

VDR (2006) Vietnam Development Report: Business 2006. Joint Donor Report to the Vietnam Consultative Group Meeting Hanoi. Online, available at: http://siteresources. worldbank.org/INTVIETNAM/Resources/vdr_2006_english.pdf.

# Part II
# Economic, institutional and social constraints

# 6 Efficiency of informal production units and its determinants

## Applying the quantile regression method in the case of Antananarivo

*Faly Hery Rakotomanana*

The efficiency of a production unit plays an important role in the development of a country, as much in the creation of new wealth as in the management of resources and factors of production. As well as reducing to a minimum the waste of factors of production, an improvement in efficiency can break the vicious circle which links the access to resources to the dynamic of an activity insofar as the inefficiency of a production unit leads to a rise in production costs, reduces profitability and competitiveness and limits the growth of the activities and the profits linked to returns to scale; which reduces the chance of obtaining capital or financing.

In developing countries like Madagascar, the study of the efficiency of small- and medium-sized enterprises becomes especially important particularly in the framework of policies aiming to reduce poverty. First, the success of policies aiming to promote income-generating activities – among which the development of microfinance – depends inevitably on the efficiency of production units in this sector. Second, this type of activity has a relatively high economic influence and affects the majority of the population, especially the poor.[1] The improvement in the quality of these activities has a positive effect on the living conditions of households without going through the mechanisms of income redistribution. On the one hand, the more efficient a production unit is, the more the managing households benefit from its direct financial benefits. On the other hand, consumers benefit from potential price cuts due to the fall in production costs or the rise in supply resulting from the improvement of the production system's efficiency.

This study proposes to analyse the technical efficiency of informal production units in Antananarivo and is the first of its kind concerning Madagascar. First, the analysis especially concerns the evaluation of the level of technical efficiency according to the different categories of activity. The objective is to assess the disparities which exist between informal production units and to pinpoint the weak links of the informal sector in terms of inefficiency in order to target more precisely possible interventions and support policies. Second, the analysis leads to the identification of the determining factors of the technical efficiency of production units. This should allow us to isolate the principal levers which might be pulled and, in particular, outline the role that microfinance might play in the improvement of informal activities.

The study is limited to the notion of technical efficiency, which refers to the capacity of the unit of production to minimize the quantities of inputs used in order to produce a given quantity of output considering a given production technique. In other terms, a production unit is considered to be technically efficient, if its level of effective production is situated on the frontier of production possibilities. From this viewpoint, the degree of technical inefficiency of a production unit is defined by the ratio between the level of production effectively carried out and that which is potentially feasible. Consequently, this study cannot define allocative efficiency (Farrell, 1957), the other component of efficiency which indicates the capacity of a production unit to combine inputs in optimal proportions considering their relative prices and the production techniques used in order to attain a given level of production.

The quantile regression method (Koenker and Bassett, 1978; Koenker and Hallock, 2001) has been retained in order to evaluate the technical capacity of informal production units. This method consists in measuring the inefficiency of a production unit according to the ratio between the observed performances and those estimated for sufficiently high quantiles (higher than 0.8 or 0.9) with identical characteristics thus considered as being potentially realizable performances. This method, which is part of the recent progress in techniques for measuring efficiency, attempts to work around the problems which arise when using more habitual methods such as the Stochastic Frontier Analysis (SFA)[2] and the Data Envelopment Analysis (DEA).[3] Nevertheless, in order to assess the accuracy of the method, given that it is the first study in this domain, the results are compared with those obtained using traditional methods.

This chapter is composed of five sections. After the introduction, the second section is devoted to concepts and methodology. The databases and the variables used will be presented in the third section. The results of the estimations will be revealed in the fourth section. Finally, the last section will deal with the conclusions.

## Concepts and methodology

### Concept of the efficiency of a production unit

The notion of efficiency for a production unit appeared subsequent to the development of theories about the function of production frontiers. The production frontier is the maximum level of production attainable by a production unit adopting a given production technique and using a given level of inputs. For various reasons, production units are unable to efficiently attain their production frontier.

The concept of production efficiency has evolved over the years. According to Koopmans (1951), a production process is technically efficient, if, and only if, increasing the level of a given output or decreasing the level of a given input is possible only by decreasing the level of certain other outputs or by increasing the levels of certain other inputs. Classical economic theory has formalized

Koopmans' concept by referring to Pareto's notion of the optimum: a production technique is not at Pareto's optimum if there still exists a possibility of increasing the level of outputs and decreasing the level of inputs.

The formal definition is given as follows:

- a production unit adopting the production technique $(X, Y) \in T$ is efficient if there exists no other production technique $(X', Y') \in T$ such as $(X', Y') \neq (X, Y)$ with $(X' \leq X$ and $Y' \geq Y)$, where T stands for the whole of possible productions, X the vector of inputs and Y the output.

Farrell (1957) built on the work of Koopmans and Debreu by introducing another dimension of efficiency relating to the optimal composition of inputs and the minimizing of costs by considering the relative prices of outputs and inputs.

Thus, a production unit's efficiency can be defined as its ability to mobilize a minimum of costs or minimize waste in order to attain a maximal level of production or profit, considering that the best available techniques of production are used. This concept of efficiency can be broken down into constituents: allocative efficiency and technical efficiency (Farrell, 1957). Technical efficiency refers to a production unit's ability to either attain the maximal level of production situated on the production frontier after having chosen a production technique considering the levels of inputs or factors of production mobilized, or to use the minimum possible number of resources to produce a fixed level taking into account the different types of possible production techniques. Allocative efficiency concerns a production unit's ability to adjust to optimal proportions the levels of inputs used taking into account their relative price. A production process is "allocatively" efficient if the marginal rate of substitution between each pair of inputs is equal to the ratio of the corresponding prices.

In order to measure a production unit's efficiency, the indicators used are functions of the ratio between the level of production actually observed and the maximal level which could have been attained by the same production unit if it had operated with perfect efficiency.

### The different stages of analysis

The methodology used follows the following stages. The first stage consists in evaluating the degree of efficiency by applying the quantile regression method using the following procedure. First, with the help of the quantile regression method, the production functions are estimated according to the different quantiles of economic performance. Once these estimations have been made, variability is analysed by quantile regarding the coefficients relative to the different factors of production (principally capital and labour) indicating their marginal productivity. Next, in order to construct a reference measure of performance for the production frontier (that is to say when the production unit is operating with perfect efficiency), performance levels are predicted with the help of the estimated production function for a sufficiently high quantile. Given that the number of observations of our sample is not high enough to obtain reference perform-ance levels, we have chosen the quantile level 0.9 instead of 0.95 which is usually used in studies. Finally, for each production unit, the degree of efficiency is calculated by dividing the performance level actually attained or observed by the predicted reference performance level.

In the second stage, in order to highlight the importance of the contribution made by the quantile regression method in the estimation of the degree of effi-ciency of a production unit, different types of analysis have been carried out. Descriptive analyses are carried out on the previously constructed variable indi-cating the degree of efficiency in order to verify work hypotheses and isolate a rough draft of discriminating factors. Other analyses, in the form of robustness tests, consist in studying the correlations between the variable obtained indicat-ing the degree of efficiency and those resulting from the SFA method which are usually used. At this level, two other degree of efficiency variables are gener-ated: one resulting from SFA with the "half-normal" efficiency distribution law and the other resulting from SFA with the "exponential" efficiency distribution law.

The last stage consists in identifying the determinants of efficiency with the help of simple linear regression models. The considered variables are variables which have not yet been introduced into the estimation model of production functions and which are linked to the individual characteristics of the manager of the production unit, to the economic characteristics of the unit as well as its environment.

### The models

The Cobb–Douglas function has been retained for the production functions since it is relatively simple, easy to manipulate and has been unanimously adopted by other authors writing about this subject thus making the comparative analyses of the results easier (Piesse and Thirtle, 2000; Movshuk, 2004; Behr, 2010). In order to simplify the analyses, the production function is a function with only one output and several inputs.

$$y_i = a_0 \prod_{j=1}^{k} x_{ji}^{a_j} \tag{6.1}$$

where $i$ is the number of observed production units and $x_{ji}$ with $j=1$ to $k$ are the $k$ inputs used for the production of the output $y_i$.

In order to identify the determinants of the degree of efficiency, models of linear regression have been retained. In order to consider sectional heterogen-eity, three different models which correspond to "manufacturing", "trade" and "services" are formulated.

*The principal advantages of the methodology*

The use of quantile regression presents several advantages. First of all, the heterogeneity of the informal sector – in which this study is particularly interested – in terms of economic performance (turnover, profit, productivity of factors) is so important that to confine oneself to a single average (provided by a simple OLS) in order to estimate the production function is not sufficient enough.[4] Error distribution stemming from estimations can vary according to not only characteristics (explanatory variables), but also to the economic performances of the production units (dependent variable). By way of an illustration, the dispersion of production level or of value added tends to diminish as the size of production units gets bigger: the coefficient variation of value added went from 1.8 for one man units to about 1.0 for units with three or more employees.

This method better meets the needs of our objective which is to propose political economic recommendations and better targeted actions in favour of the informal sector, particularly microfinance. Indeed, in reality the productivity of factors of production is not the same depending on whether an IPU has a relatively small, medium or big scale of activity. The application of quantile regression allows us to provide a more complete analysis by estimating production functions with differentiated coefficients for each production quantile: which allows us to obtain quantified and detailed information about the expected impact on the performances of interventions in the different segments of the informal sector.

On a technical scale, quantile regression has several advantages: unlike other methods such as the DEA method, it is less sensitive to outliers, it is not reliant on hypotheses about the choice of distribution laws of inefficiency and noise like the SFA method (half-normal, or exponential), and it minimizes bias in cases of heteroscedasticity problems. Contrary to the SFA method, the use of the quantile regression method allows us to avoid making relatively excessive hypotheses about the independence of inefficiency variables (the second constituent of errors).

## The databases and the variables

The data used in this study results from a series of surveys into the informal sector entitled "1-2-3 surveys" initiated by DIAL/IRD and carried out in Antananarivo, the capital of Madagascar in 2001 and 2004 (Rakotomanana, 2004). It is a mixed type study carried out in several phases. The first phase is a labour force survey with a sample of 3,000 households. The objectives of this phase were to first understand the labour conditions and how the labour market functions and then to identify the individuals managing a production unit in the informal sector. The second phase is a survey of 1,000 informal production units among those identified during the first phase of the study. This survey deals comprehensively with the characteristics and performances of a production unit as well as its economic environment. The databases allow us to draw up the different accounts of a production unit and to isolate the principal indicators of economic performance such as value added and gross profits.

The dependent variable chosen for the production function is the monthly value added instead of production or profit. As for the explanatory variables introduced into the production function, three sorts of input are considered: capital, labour and human capital.

*Capital.* This variable is approximated by using the total estimated value of the physical value of the production unit. It considers, among other things, the estimated replacement cost of the premises, the land, the machines, the cars and big and smalls tools.

*Labour.* This variable includes the total number of hours actually worked by all the employees in the production unit (manager or head of production unit, wage-workers, family workers, partners, etc.).

*Human capital.* Several variables have been introduced into the model in order to measure it. The characteristics of the manager of the production unit are distinguished from those of the dependent workers. The productivity of these two types of work is deemed to be very different given the large part played by non-remunerated work, particularly family worker among dependent workers and the high implication of the manager in all tasks throughout the production process.

- The average number of years dependent workers have attended school. The average is better adapted than the total sum of all of the number of school years given that there is no real specialization of tasks within small production units. Every employee often participates in all the tasks and this versatility results in a permanent exchange of experience and know-how between employees.[5]
- The average number of years of experience of the dependent workers.
- The number of years the manager of the production unit spent at school.
- The number of years of experience of the manager of the production unit.

As for identifying efficiency determinants, the following variables have been retained in the regression models:

*Characteristics of the production unit*
- the ratio capital/number of hours worked measuring intensity of capital;
- dummy variable indicating whether or not there are wage-workers operating in the production unit;
- dummy variable indicating whether or not the production unit is registered on the administrative lists;
- dummy variables indicating whether or not the unit has experienced demand side problems, credit access problems, problems concerning the working premises or any other type of problem;
- production unit's age and its square.

*Characteristics of the manager of the production unit*

- dummy variable indicating whether or not the manager of the production unit has already studied for a professional course corresponding to his/her job;
- dummy variable indicating whether or not the manager is male;
- manager's age and its square;
- dummy variables indicating whether or not the manager has media access or is well perceived by the administration;
- dummy variable indicating if the observation was made in 2004.

## Estimation of the degree of efficiency

### Some descriptive statistics

The production units in the informal sector in the agglomeration of Antananarivo are characterized by managers who have acquired a relatively long number of years of experience (more than ten years of professional experience) but who rarely have professional qualifications (less than 2 per cent of them), dependent workers who have attended school for very short periods (less than two years), very low rates of salaried workers (less than 16 per cent of production units employ salaried workers), very low rate of credit access for financing capital (scarcely 4 per cent) and a very high rate of access to information (more than 87 per cent).

However, more detailed analysis highlights that these production units are very heterogeneous (Table 6.A.1 in the chapter Appendix). The size of production units varies considerably with relatively high standard deviations, both in terms of economic performance levels (output) and of levels of factors of production (inputs). Even within the principal branches of activity (manufacturing, trade and services), there remain big disparities. Generally, "services" production units are a lot more competitive. They create an average value added of about 15 per cent more than the "trade" and "manufacturing" branches. The influence of capital might play a role in this. Indeed, in the "services" branch the estimated average level of physical capital is almost triple that used in the units of the "trade" and "manufacturing" branches. This might compensate for the low number of years of professional experience of dependent workers in the "services" branch. Furthermore, production units in the "manufacturing" branch are distinguished by the relatively high level of professional experience of their managers. Production units in the "trade" branch have access less frequently to basic public services in their workplace compared to those in the two other branches.

When the relationships between the factors of production and the value added are analysed, two points can be emphasized (see Figures 6.A.1 and 6.A.2 in the Appendix). First, the influence of the labour factor linked to the first variable is, generally, a lot greater than that of the capital factor linked to the second variable. Second, these situations have more or less remained unchanged between 2001 and 2004. However surprising this absence of temporal effect may appear given the radical change of economic circumstances, it is proof of the quality and robustness of the data.

### *Results of estimations of production functions using the quantile regression method*

Tables 6.1 and 6.2 show the results of the estimations of production functions using the quantile regression method and considering the ten deciles 0.1 to 0.9. In the first column, a simple ordinary linear model (OLS) in Cobb–Douglas form is estimated with the aim of not only identifying, with the help of the significance of the parameters, the relevant variables but, also, and above all, demonstrating the relevance of carrying out the quantile regression which allows the variability of the parameters along the distribution of informal production units, which a simple linear model cannot take into account.

The estimation of the simple linear model (OLS) justifies the choice of the factors introduced into the production function if the average performance of informal production units is considered. Generally, the coefficients relative to labour, physical capital and human capital are statistically significant with the expected signs, all acting positively on the value added. The variable which indicates the average number of years of experience of dependent workers is the only one which is not significant in the creation of value added. The results confirm the fact previously observed during the descriptive analysis, that is to say, the influence of the labour factor is a lot greater than that of physical capital. However, the latter's contribution is far from negligible. Indeed, the coefficients are 0.54 and 0.11 respectively for the "number of hours worked" and "total amount of physical capital" variables. As far as human capital is concerned, three interesting points can be remarked. First, its effects are significant but relatively weak with coefficients of less than 0.09. Second, the quality of the manager of the production unit is more crucial compared to that of the dependent workers. Finally, professional experience and practice are more important than academic studies.

The results of the estimations by quantile regression highlight the relatively high variability of the coefficients for the different categories of production unit depending on their level of value added. The parameters are very different between different categories of production unit depending on their actual performance level. This proves the handicap of the methods of analysis based on models which concentrate only on the average production unit such as the simple linear model or "Stochastic Frontier Analysis". It can be observed that there is a relatively big drop in the elasticity of the number of hours worked as the production units in the highest value added deciles are considered. It thus ranges from more than 0.7 in the 0.1 decile to less than 0.4 in the 0.9 decile. The coefficient values are even situated outside the confidence range (95 per cent) of the coefficient resulting from the simple linear model for the extreme deciles. On the other

Table 6.1 Estimations by quantile regression of the production function in 2004

| Variables | OLS | Decile | | | | | | | | | |
|---|---|---|---|---|---|---|---|---|---|---|---|
| | | 0.1 | 0.2 | 0.3 | 0.4 | 0.5 | 0.6 | 0.7 | 0.8 | 0.9 | |
| *Labour* | | | | | | | | | | | |
| Hours worked (log) | 0.539*** | 0.717*** | 0.740*** | 0.716*** | 0.669*** | 0.617*** | 0.589*** | 0.453*** | 0.447*** | 0.378*** | |
| *Physical capital* | | | | | | | | | | | |
| Capital (log) | 0.105*** | 0.071*** | 0.084*** | 0.108*** | 0.112*** | 0.111*** | 0.110*** | 0.129*** | 0.135*** | 0.123*** | |
| *Human capital* | | | | | | | | | | | |
| Average time in studies dependent workers (log) | 0.048** | 0.020 | 0.044 | 0.037 | 0.045* | 0.045*** | 0.050** | 0.046** | 0.028 | 0.032 | |
| Head's studies (log) | 0.090*** | 0.150*** | 0.090** | 0.051* | 0.059* | 0.058*** | 0.057* | 0.058* | 0.039 | 0.085* | |
| Average experience dependent workers (log) | 0.009 | 0.040 | −0.011 | 0.003 | −0.002 | 0.001 | −0.009 | 0.006 | 0.030 | 0.057* | |
| Head's experience (log) | 0.056*** | 0.077*** | 0.097*** | 0.067*** | 0.058*** | 0.047*** | 0.056*** | 0.038** | 0.030* | 0.037 | |
| *Branch of activity* | | | | | | | | | | | |
| Manufacturing | −0.130 | −0.460*** | −0.246* | −0.141 | −0.083 | −0.102 | −0.046 | 0.006 | 0.031 | −0.058 | |
| Trade | −0.236** | −1.103*** | −0.588*** | −0.428*** | −0.297** | −0.214*** | −0.170 | 0.060 | 0.073 | 0.114 | |
| Cons. | 2.612*** | 0.665 | 0.729 | 1.136*** | 1.640*** | 2.179*** | 2.514*** | 3.475*** | 3.835*** | 4.840*** | |
| No. obs | 1,048 | 1,048 | 1,048 | 1,048 | 1,048 | 1,048 | 1,048 | 1,048 | 1,048 | 1,048 | |

Source: INSTAT-IRD/DSM/EE2004, author's calculations.

Notes
Significance: *** at 1%, ** at 5% and * at 10%.

Table 6.2 Estimations by quantile regression of the production function in 2001

| Variables | OLS | Decile | | | | | | | | |
|---|---|---|---|---|---|---|---|---|---|---|
| | | 0.1 | 0.2 | 0.3 | 0.4 | 0.5 | 0.6 | 0.7 | 0.8 | 0.9 |
| *Labour* | | | | | | | | | | |
| Hours worked (log) | 0.378*** | 0.619*** | 0.579*** | 0.534*** | 0.540*** | 0.501*** | 0.497*** | 0.450*** | 0.321*** | 0.221*** |
| *Physical capital* | | | | | | | | | | |
| Capital (log) | 0.135*** | 0.158*** | 0.115*** | 0.116*** | 0.112*** | 0.119*** | 0.116*** | 0.115*** | 0.139*** | 0.153*** |
| *Human capital* | | | | | | | | | | |
| Average study time dependent workers (log) | 0.052** | 0.061* | 0.054* | 0.080*** | 0.070*** | 0.051** | 0.045** | 0.026 | 0.048 | 0.029 |
| Head's studies (log) | 0.073** | 0.046 | 0.030 | 0.041 | 0.069** | 0.051 | 0.076** | 0.102*** | 0.075 | 0.115* |
| Average experience dependent workers (log) | 0.014 | −0.031 | −0.000 | −0.035 | −0.029 | 0.003 | 0.007 | 0.035 | 0.039 | 0.081** |
| Head's experience (log) | 0.059*** | 0.102*** | 0.044 | 0.060*** | 0.059*** | 0.051*** | 0.052*** | 0.039** | 0.051* | 0.050** |
| *Branch of activity* | | | | | | | | | | |
| Manufacturing | −0.188** | −0.418*** | −0.209 | −0.204* | −0.157 | −0.147 | −0.136 | −0.134 | −0.043 | −0.174 |
| Trade | 0.097 | −0.302* | −0.218 | −0.151 | −0.070 | 0.026 | 0.156 | 0.135 | 0.447*** | 0.677*** |
| Cons. | 3.111*** | 0.384 | 1.479*** | 1.916*** | 2.061*** | 2.547*** | 2.722*** | 3.274*** | 4.230*** | 5.214*** |
| No. obs | 907 | 907 | 907 | 907 | 907 | 907 | 907 | 907 | 907 | 907 |

Source: INSTAT-IRD/DSM/EE2001, author's calculations.

Notes
Significance: *** at 1%, ** at 5% and * at 10%.

hand, for physical capital, elasticity grows in the upper deciles but the trend is less accentuated (from 0.07 for the 0.1 decile to 0.12 for the 0.9 decile) and the coefficient values stay within the confidence range resulting from the simple linear model. The other coefficient which undergoes variations but whose size is relatively low in relation to those relative to labour and physical capital is the one which is relative to the number of years the production unit manager spent at school. This coefficient follows a downward trend if we go from the lowest to the highest decile. Nevertheless, the estimated values of the parameter are always found within the confidence range of the value obtained by the simple linear model. As far as the other human capital variables are concerned, the coefficients remain practically constant for every decile and remain within the confidence range of the coefficients of the simple linear model.

### *Description of the degree of efficiency of production units*

The degree of efficiency of a production unit is defined as the relationship between the total amount of value added really observed and the amount predicted using the model obtained for the 0.9 decile which is considered the reference value at which maximum efficiency is attained for a production unit sharing the same characteristics.

Figure 6.1 presents the distribution of the degree of efficiency of informal production units. This is stacked to the left and resembles the form of the gamma law. The results show that the informal production units are quite largely inefficient. The average degree of efficiency is only 33 per cent. This figure signifies that, on average, informal production units produce only a little more than 33 per cent of their potential production level, given the levels of factors of production mobilized. In other terms, the current value added could be improved by 66 per cent by adopting more efficient production techniques. Less than one production unit out of four is reaching a degree of efficiency of over 50 per cent. The majority of informal production units reached less than 25 per cent of their potential production level.

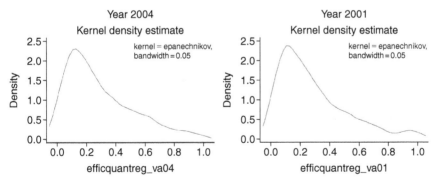

*Figure 6.1* Distribution of the degree of inefficiency of production units in 2004 and 2001 (source: INSTAT-IRD/DSM/EE2001–2004, author's calculations).

No progress has been observed concerning the short-term efficiency of informal production units. The results obtained in 2001 and 2004 show a great stability of the situation during that period. On the one hand, in absolute level terms, the degree of efficiency was 33.5 per cent in 2004 and 33.8 per cent in 2001. Even the levels obtained in each category of production unit have not registered significant variations during this period (Table 6.4, below). On the other hand, in distribution terms, the two curves of degree of efficiency have almost the same form with practically identical parameters: skewness 0.91 in 2004 and 0.98 in 2001, Kurtosis 2.64 in 2004 and 2.75 in 2001. This stability confirms the quality of the databases used. Indeed, in principle, efficiency must not undergo any big short-term changes since it is heavily dependent on the production technique and on the behaviour of the workforce and of the particular manager.

The descriptive analysis of the degree of efficiency (Table 6.3) demonstrates a few powerful discriminating factors. First, there is a high correlation between the degree of efficiency and the real level of performance of a production unit. The more the production unit belongs to the upper fringe, the more efficient it is. The degree of efficiency rises from 11 per cent among the units in the first quartile (in value added terms) to more than 70 per cent among the units of the fourth quartile. Depending on their branch of activity, production units in the "trade" branch are, on average, less efficient than those in "manufacturing" or "services" branches. Indeed, if the average degree of efficiency is around 34 per cent in the two latter categories, it scarcely reaches 30 per cent in the "trade" branch. The existence of a salaried worker within a production unit has a positive effect on its degree of efficiency: there is a gap of ten points between the average degree of efficiency of a production unit with salaried workers and one without. The fact that the manager of a production unit has undergone formal professional training for his job results in a higher degree of efficiency: a rise of 10 per cent in the average degree of efficiency. Appearing on administrative registers is another factor which influences a unit's degree of efficiency: 35 per cent for registered units and 30 per cent for those not registered. Having problems obtaining credit or finding premises corresponds to a drop in efficiency. However, problems linked to demand or to the customer do not show up on the degree of technical efficiency of the production units. Finally, production units managed by a woman are, on average, a lot less efficient than those managed by a man.

### Comparison with the results from the SFA method

Comparing the results with those obtained using the SFA method highlights several phenomena. First, the SFA method tends to overestimate the efficiency degree. Indeed, the average degrees of efficiency resulting from the SFA method, depending on whether the half-normal or exponential distribution law is retained for inefficiency, are respectively 47 and 60 per cent. Furthermore, these figures also show the sensitivity of the SFA results according to the distribution of inefficiency law. Nevertheless, the level of correlation between the inefficiency variable resulting from the quantile regression method and those resulting from

*Table 6.3* Description of the degree of efficiency of informal production units in 2004

| | Average degree of efficiency (%) | |
|---|---|---|
| | *2004* | *2001* |
| *Activity branch* | | |
| Manufacturing | 35.9 | 37.5 |
| Trade | 29.5 | 27.0 |
| Services | 34.9 | 38.2 |
| *Registering* | | |
| No | 30.5 | 31.0 |
| Yes | 35.1 | 35.6 |
| *Operating in Antananarivo* | | |
| No | 34.2 | 35.1 |
| Yes | 33.4 | 33.6 |
| *Unit with salaried worker* | | |
| No | 32.6 | 33.4 |
| Yes | 42.1 | 37.0 |
| *Manager having undergone professional training* | | |
| No | 32.5 | 33.4 |
| Yes | 41.2 | 37.7 |
| *Manager's gender* | | |
| Female | 26.4 | 26.9 |
| Male | 41.2 | 39.8 |
| *Having experienced demand problems* | | |
| No | 33.5 | 34.1 |
| Yes | 33.5 | 33.6 |
| *Having experienced credit problems* | | |
| No | 34.4 | 34.1 |
| Yes | 30.4 | 32.6 |
| *Having experienced problems with premises* | | |
| No | 34.8 | 34.6 |
| Yes | 29.7 | 31.2 |
| *Quartile of value added* | | |
| Quartile 1 | 11.3 | 12.6 |
| Quartile 2 | 26.4 | 24.5 |
| Quartile 3 | 43.2 | 41.5 |
| Quartile 4 | 70.6 | 62.5 |
| Total | 33.5 | 33.8 |

Source: INSTAT-IRD/DSM/EE2001–2004, author's calculations.

the SFA method is relatively high: 0.85 with the SFA half-normal and 0.76 with the SFA exponential. Figure 6.2 shows the correlation curves which generally follow logarithmic trends. The degree of efficiency by quantile regression is greatly inferior to that obtained using the SFA method especially among the least efficient production units.

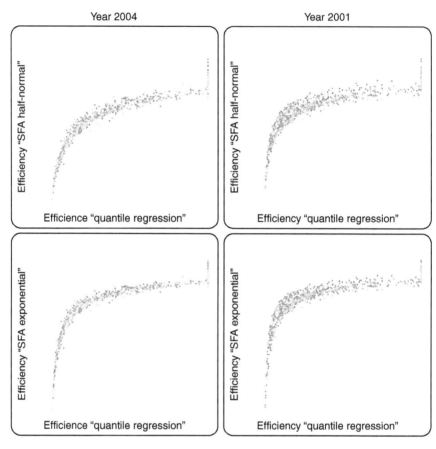

*Figure 6.2* Correlation curves between the inefficiency variable resulting from the quantile regression method and those resulting from the SFA method in 2004 and 2001 (source: INSTAT-IRD/DSM/EE2001–2004, author's calculations).

## Informal production unit efficiency determinants

In order to identify factors determining efficiency in informal production units, simple linear regression models have been estimated. They allow us to isolate easily the relationships with the characteristics of the households. The model does not claim to identify the sense of the causality which potentially exists between efficiency and certain explanatory variables. Indeed, signing the administrative register or gaining credit access can improve a production unit's efficiency. Inversely, the more efficient a production unit is, the more probable it is that the unit will have access to credit and appear on administrative registers. The results are presented in Table 6.4. A first model includes all observations, while the three other models examine separately

Table 6.4 Simple linear regression of the degree of efficiency of informal production units

| Variable | Total | Manufacturing | Trade | Services |
|---|---|---|---|---|
| *Branch of activity* | | | | |
| Manufacturing | −0.004 | — | — | — |
| Trade | −0.061*** | — | — | — |
| *Characteristics of production unit* | | | | |
| Capital/hours (log) | −0.014*** | −0.022*** | −0.023*** | −0.006 |
| Existence of salaried workers (dummy) | 0.064*** | 0.049* | 0.021 | 0.076*** |
| Being registered (dummy) | 0.042*** | 0.027 | 0.044 | 0.047* |
| Having demand problems (dummy) | 0.013 | 0.011 | 0.004 | 0.011 |
| Having credit access problems (dummy) | −0.037** | 0.001 | −0.033 | −0.083*** |
| Having problems with premises (dummy) | −0.052*** | −0.021 | −0.024 | −0.097*** |
| Having other types of problems (dummy) | 0.050*** | 0.105*** | −0.021 | 0.029 |
| Age of unit (log) | 0.012 | 0.010 | 0.025 | −0.014 |
| Square of unit's age (log) | −0.001 | 0.001 | −0.004 | 0.005 |
| Head having undergone training (dummy) | 0.037* | 0.051* | −0.055 | 0.014 |
| *Characteristics of the manager* | | | | |
| Male manager (dummy) | 0.105*** | 0.115*** | 0.073** | 0.111*** |
| Age of manager (log) | 0.295*** | 0.311** | 1.868** | 1.238** |
| Square of the manager's age (log) | −0.048*** | −0.059*** | −0.270** | −0.173** |
| Having media access (dummy) | 0.034* | 0.034 | 0.032 | 0.016 |
| Well perceived by the administration (dummy) | 0.005 | −0.007 | 0.035 | 0.003 |
| Year 2004 (ref: 2001) | −0.003 | −0.033 | 0.037 | −0.003 |
| Constant | −0.215 | −0.145 | −3.029** | −1.923** |
| Pseudo_R$^2$ | 0.08 | 0.10 | 0.04 | 0.08 |
| N | 1,821 | 701 | 407 | 713 |

Source: INSTAT-IRD/DSM/EE2001–2004, author's calculations.

Notes
Significance: *** at 1%, ** at 5% and * at 10%.

the production units belonging to the "manufacturing", "trade" and "services" branches in order to monitor the inter-sectional differences. The likelihood-ratio test rejects the stability of the coefficients in the separated models. The McFadden $R^2$ level is relatively low which is inherent to the use of transversal data.

The coefficients estimated in the efficiency models generally conform to the expected signs and to the results provided by the preceding descriptive analyses. Differences are observed in terms of the efficiency levels between the units of production according to the branch of activity. By taking the "service" branch as reference, the coefficients relating to the dummy variables "manufacturing" and "trade" are all negative, but significant at the 1 per cent level for "trade" only. The interpretation of these results is that the "trade" production units are less efficient than the "service" ones, all other things being equal.

The effects on efficiency of the constraints and problems that the heads of the informal production units said they had experienced are examined. Constraints linked to supply rather than demand affect the efficiency of activities in the informal sector; indeed, the coefficients relative to the variables which respectively indicate credit access problems and problems linked to the premises of the production units are negative, even though they are only significant in the "services" branch. On the other hand, the estimated coefficient for the variable indicating demand problems is not significant. There are two possible explanations for these results. On the one hand, credit access and work premises are real obstacles which limit the efficiency of the informal sector and prevent its development. And as the problem was evoked by the production unit heads themselves, the demands relating to these services really exist and satisfying these demands will certainly result in the improvement of activity performance. On the other hand, in small production units, the production techniques used are relatively flexible and make it easier to adjust the level of mobilized inputs, notably labour in relation to received demand. This phenomenon results in demand-side problems having repercussions on the quantity of inputs and not on the degree of efficiency.

The (capital)/(number of hours worked) ratio has a significant negative relationship with an informal production unit's degree of efficiency. The more capital intense the activity is in relation to labour, the less efficient it is. If, in the formal sector, this result appears to be the opposite of what intuition tells us, several explanations are possible for the informal sector. First, this result shows the determining role played by the labour factor in the production process in the informal sector. Because of the inadequacies in technical know-how of the workforce and the lack of professional qualifications of small, informal operators, the more sophisticated and expensive their equipment is, the more this equipment is under-used. Furthermore, given the small size of the market share because of low purchasing power, of the rarity of big orders or subcontracting, of free entry into a sector and of high competition, certain sectors are saturated. In this case, there is a low rate of the use of capital and the total amount of capital appears to be overvalued in relation to what is actually used and only the number of hours worked can be reduced. Because of the nature of the products ordered, especially craftwork, the activity in certain sectors is characterized by manual work. In the craftwork sectors, the "hand-made" label is a sign of the good quality of the products such as for sculpture and embroidery, and machines cannot take the place of manual work in order to preserve the quality of these products.

Regarding the other characteristics of production units, the coefficient related to "registering" is positive and significant both for the whole model and for "services". Being registered is the sign of a more rigorous management and more developed technologies within the production unit. What is more, the additional costs imposed by administrative control and insertion into the formal circuit incite management to be more efficient with their resources. Likewise, the "existence of salaried workers" variable is associated with positive and significant coefficients for all the models except in the case of "trade". The recruitment of salaried workers is the sign of a certain degree of professionalism both on an activity organization level of the production unit and at the level of tasks attributed to each employee. The obligation to produce results principle is probably bigger for a salaried worker than for a family worker or an apprentice. The coefficients linked respectively to the age of the informal production unit and its square are not significant. Thus, experience acquired within the production unit has no significant effect on the production unit's efficiency.

As far as the head of the production unit's characteristics are concerned, the coefficient linked to the "having undergone professional training" variable is positive but only at 10 per cent in the "manufacturing" branch. The activities in this branch require relatively more technical and technological skills than the other types of activities. The demographic characteristics of the production unit manager have a strong influence on efficiency: being managed by a relatively old male has a positive effect with significant negative second-order effects for age. Linking this with the results from the previous paragraph, two interpretations are possible to explain this phenomenon. On the one hand, the efficiency of an informal production unit depends on how it was initially endowed, notably the head of production's experience before he/she arrived in the unit, rather than on know-how acquired during activity. On the other hand, the natural qualities of the head of the production unit (such as physical strength and maturity) are more important for efficiency than his/her professional qualities. Furthermore, the low efficiency of female managed units may be due to their very aim in carrying out the activity, which is considered as a simple source of extra household income and is done at the same time as household chores. On the other hand, activities managed by men often constitute the principal household income so more profitability and rigor is demanded.

## Conclusion

Given the importance of the role played by these income generating activities in the socio-economic development and in the struggle against poverty in Madagascar, the improvement of their efficiency must constitute one of the pillars of development policy. The aim of this study is to analyse the degree of technical efficiency of informal production units and its determining factors in the case of the agglomeration of Antananarivo in Madagascar. The quantile regression method has been used in the models in order to consider the big disparities between units in performance terms. Given these disparities, analyses obtained using methods based on the average individual characteristics such as Statistical Frontier Analysis (SFA) are not relevant.

The results show that the degree of efficiency of informal production units is very low and that no significant improvement has been observed during the period 2001–2004. By mobilizing the same resources it would be possible to reach a production level three times superior to the one currently attained. Fewer than one out of four production units attains more than half the production level it could achieve, if it was working in perfect efficiency. The situation is different depending on the branch of activity: the degree of efficiency is lower in the "trade" branch.

Several factors have an influence on a production unit's efficiency, but these factors differ according to the branch of activity. Contrary to demand-side constraints which have no significant effect on efficiency, supply-side constraints, such as problems linked to credit access and premises, have a negative effect, particularly in "services" activities. In "manufacturing" and "trade", the negative relationship between efficiency and the ratio capital/hours worked shows the determining role of the labour factor which cannot be replaced by the capital factor as the lack of technical skills of the workforce results in a less and less optimal use of more and more complex and expensive equipment. The efficiency of an informal production unit depends on how it is initially endowed, for example, the experience acquired by the manager before becoming head of the unit, rather than know-how acquired during the exercise of his/her activity. Indeed, experience acquired through practice harnessed to the age of the informal production unit and its square has no significant impact. Moreover, the impact of the head of production's professional studies is only positively significant in the "manufacturing" branch. On the other hand, the demographic characteristics of the head of the production unit have the same effect whatever branch of activity is considered. The older the head of production is, the higher his/her degree of efficiency. Besides, units managed by men are more efficient than female managed ones, which might be explained by the fact that the aim of the activity for a woman is to generate extra family income while also doing domestic chores. The more rigorous management of activities and the professionalism generated by the "existence of a salaried worker" and the official "registering" of the production unit favours efficiency, particularly in the "services" branch.

These results allow us to propose a few ideas for an economic policy which could be implemented to promote microenterprises. In the case of service activities, priority action plans must focus on the improvement of supply conditions: easier credit access, support for the recruitment of salaried workers and the improvement of working premises. In the "manufacturing" branch, strategies must especially focus on the improvement of human capital such as professional training about production techniques. As far as commercial activities are concerned, the improvement of the relationship with the administration, training in administrative management and in prospecting for new market techniques is indispensable. Furthermore, global policy for the whole of the informal sector must focus in particular on the professionalization of the trade and the promotion of entrepreneurial spirit, especially for woman at the head of production units.

**Appendix**

Table 6.A.1 Characteristics and economic performances of production units in Antananarivo in 2001 and 2004

| Branch | Variables | Year | | | | |
| --- | --- | --- | --- | --- | --- | --- |
| | | 2004 | | 2001 | | |
| | | Average | Standard deviation | Average | Standard deviation | |
| Manufacturing | Monthly value added (1,000 Ariary) | 1,065 | 2,705.57 | 759 | 1,541.40 | |
| (No. obs | Number of hours worked monthly | 304 | 332.56 | 296 | 258.19 | |
| 2004: 426 | Capital (1,000 Ariary) | 2,958 | 10,375.96 | 2,166 | 3,827.58 | |
| 2001: 315) | Average no. of years at school of employees | 1.7 | 2.96 | 2.7 | 3.87 | |
| | Average experience of employees (years) | 1.2 | 2.77 | 1.4 | 3.39 | |
| | Years spent in education of head | 7.1 | 3.44 | 7.6 | 3.74 | |
| | Experience of head (years) | 11.3 | 9.58 | 9.5 | 8.69 | |
| | Professional training of head | 0.18 | 0.39 | 0.17 | 0.38 | |
| | Existence of salaried workers | 0.18 | 0.38 | 0.23 | 0.42 | |
| | Access to public services | 0.45 | 0.50 | 0.57 | 0.50 | |
| | Access to capital credits | 0.05 | 0.22 | 0.13 | 0.33 | |
| | Access to information | 0.88 | 0.32 | 0.82 | 0.38 | |
| | Victim of corruption | 0.03 | 0.18 | 0.07 | 0.25 | |

| Trade | | | | |
|---|---|---|---|---|
| (No. obs | | | | |
| 2004: 210 | | | | |
| 2001: 248) | | | | |
| Monthly value added (1,000 Ariary) | 2,012.61 | 902 | 2,931.35 | 1,038 |
| Number of hours worked monthly | 216.37 | 310 | 199.62 | 286 |
| Capital (1,000 Ariary) | 8,530.81 | 2,406 | 6,149.40 | 2,957 |
| Average no. of years at school of employees | 3.72 | 2.6 | 3.14 | 1.9 |
| Average experience of employees (years) | 3.05 | 1.5 | 4.55 | 1.6 |
| Years spent in education of head | 3.54 | 7.0 | 4.14 | 7.5 |
| Experience of head (years) | 6.20 | 5.7 | 9.58 | 7.7 |
| Professional training of head | 0.09 | 0.01 | 0.18 | 0.03 |
| Existence of salaried workers | 0.32 | 0.11 | 0.34 | 0.13 |
| Access to public services | 0.46 | 0.30 | 0.45 | 0.27 |
| Access to capital credits | 0.37 | 0.16 | 0.14 | 0.02 |
| Access to information | 0.44 | 0.74 | 0.36 | 0.85 |
| Victim of corruption | 0.19 | 0.04 | 0.21 | 0.05 |
| Services | | | | |
| (No. obs | | | | |
| 2004: 418 | | | | |
| 2001: 361) | | | | |
| Monthly value added (1,000 Ariary) | 2,608.33 | 965 | 2,740.99 | 1,204 |
| Number of hours worked monthly | 335.17 | 302 | 349.57 | 291 |
| Capital (1,000 Ariary) | 20,820.98 | 8,881 | 18,861.87 | 8,252 |
| Average no. of years at school of employees | 3.61 | 2.1 | 3.41 | 1.7 |
| Average experience of employees | 2.31 | 0.9 | 2.11 | 0.8 |
| Years spent in education of head | 3.85 | 7.7 | 4.30 | 7.7 |
| No. of years experience of head | 8.46 | 8.1 | 8.60 | 8.8 |
| Professional training of head | 0.38 | 0.18 | 0.40 | 0.19 |
| Existence of salaried workers | 0.41 | 0.21 | 0.38 | 0.17 |
| Access to public services | 0.50 | 0.46 | 0.49 | 0.40 |
| Access to capital credits | 0.38 | 0.18 | 0.21 | 0.05 |
| Access to information | 0.40 | 0.80 | 0.32 | 0.88 |
| Victim of corruption | 0.20 | 0.04 | 0.19 | 0.04 |
| Total | | | | |
| Monthly value added (1,000 Ariary) | 2,133.94 | 878 | 2,764.15 | 1,115 |

Source: INSTAT – IRD/DSM/EE2001–2004, author's calculations.

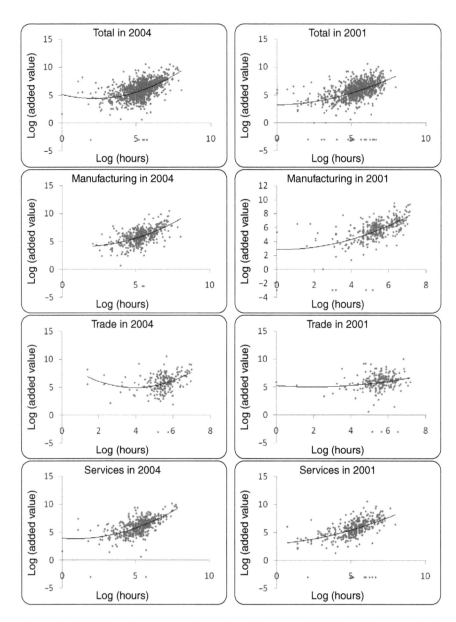

*Figure 6.A.1* Relationships between the number of hours worked (log) and the value added (log) (source: INSTAT-IRD/DSM/EE2001–2004, author's calculations).

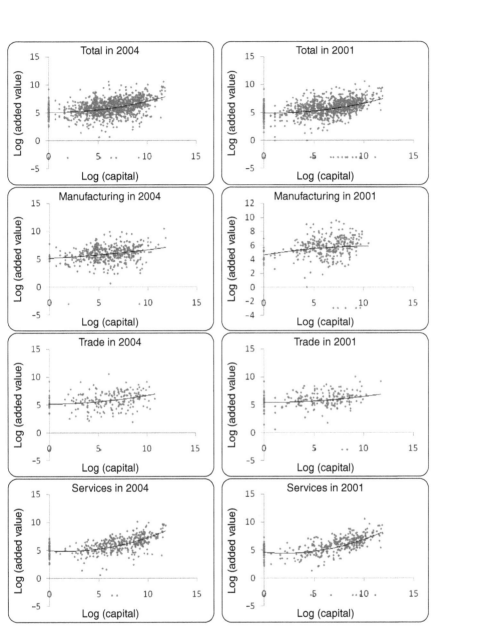

*Figure 6.A.2* Relationships between the value of physical capital (log) and value added (log).

## Notes

1  In 2004, this sector represents more than 17 per cent of the official GNP and 25 per cent of non-agricultural trade in Madagascar. More than 58 per cent of the active workforce in Antananarivo was working in this sector and more than two-thirds of households were managing at least one non-agricultural production unit (Rakotomanana, 2004).
2  Method initiated by Meeusen and van den Broeke (1977), Aigner *et al.* (1977), Battese and Coelli (1988, 1992, 1993). See also Chapelle and Plane (2005).
3  Method initiated by Farrell (1957). See also Charnes *et al.* (1978), Fare *et al.* (1985).
4  Masakure *et al.* (2008) demonstrate the relevance of a quantile regression approach in order to uncover the heterogeneous nature of microenterprise performance in Ghana.
5  The average rather than the sum of the number of years spent studying is taken into account in certain other studies such as Söderbom and Teal (2001).

## References

Aigner D., Lovell C., Schmidt P. (1977) "Formulation and estimation of stochastic frontier production function models", *Journal of Econometrics*, 6: 21–37.
Battese G.E., Coelli T.J. (1992) "Frontier production functions, technical efficiency and panel data: with application to paddy farmers in India", *Journal of Productivity Analysis*, 3: 159–169.
Battese G.E., Coelli T.J. (1988) "Prediction of firm-level technical efficiencies with a generalized frontier production function and panel data", *Journal of Econometrics*, 38: 387–399.
Battese G.E., Coelli T.J. (1993) "A stochastic frontier production function incorporating a model of technical inefficiency effects", Working Papers in Econometrics and Applied Statistics, vol. 69. Department of Econometrics, University of New England, Armidale, Australia.
Behr A. (2010) "Quantile regression for robust bank efficiency score estimation", *European Journal of Operational Research*, 200(2): 568–581.
Chapelle K., Plane P. (2005) "Technical efficiency measurement within the manufacturing sector in Côte d'Ivoire: a stochastic frontier approach", *Journal of Development Studies*, 41(7): 1303–1324.
Charnes A., Cooper W.W., Rhodes E. (1978) "Measuring the efficiency of decision making units", *European Journal of Operational Research*, 2: 429–444.
Coelli, T.J., Battese G.E. (1996) "Identification of factors with influence the technical efficiency of Indian farmers", *Australian Journal of Agricultural Economics*, 40(2): 19–44.
Fare R., Grosskopf S., Lovell C.A.K. (1985) *The Measurement of Efficiency of Production*, Kluwer Academic Publishers, Boston, MA.
Farrell M.J. (1957) "The measurement of productive efficiency", *Journal of the Royal Statistical Society Series*, 120: 253–281.
Koenker R., Hallock K.F. (2001) "Quantile regression", *Journal of Economic Perspectives*, 15(4): 143–156.
Koenker R., Bassett G. (1978) "Regression quantiles", *Econometrica*, 46(1): 33–50.
Koopmans T.C. (1951) "An analysis of production as an efficient combination of activities", Activity analysis of production and allocation, Cowles Commission for Research in Economics, Monograph No. 13, New York.
Masakure O., Cranfield J., Henson S. (2008) "The financial performance of non-farm microenterprises in Ghana", *World Development*, 36(12): 2733–2762.

Meeusen W., Van den Broek J. (1977) "Efficiency estimation from Cobb–Douglas production functions with composite errors", *International Economic Review*, 18: 435–444.

Movshuk O. (2004) "Restructuring, productivity and technical efficiency in China's iron and steel industry, 1988–2000", *Journal of Asian Economics*, 15(2004): 135–151.

Piesse J., Thirtle C. (2000) "A stochastic frontier approach to firm level efficiency, technological change, and productivity during the early transition in Hungary", *Journal of Comparative Economics*, 28: 473–501.

Rakotomanana F. (2004) "Le secteur informel à Antananarivo, phase 2 de l'enquête 1-2-3", Projet Madio – INSTAT/IRD.

Söderbom M., Teal F. (2001) "Firm size and human capital as determinants of productivity and earnings", CSAE Working Paper WPS 2001.9, Centre for the Study of African Economies, Department of Economics, University of Oxford, England.

# 7 Estimating the returns to education in Cameroon informal sector[1]

*Pierre Nguetse Tegoum*

Cameroon experienced a serious economic slump from 1984–1993 resulting from a fall in oil prices and the principal cash products (cocoa, coffee). The financial tensions forced the government to proceed with liquidation and restructuring of many public and parastatals companies and to downsize the civil service. These measures have contributed to a deterioration in the labour market and the living conditions of people. Growth recovered in 1994, consecutive to the devaluation of the CFA franc and the initiative for heavily indebted poor countries failed to raise the standard of living of Cameroonians. Indeed, data from the second Cameroon Households survey (ECAM 2) situated poverty rate at 40 per cent (INS, 2002). The results of the survey on Employment and the Informal Sector (EESI), realized in 2005, indicate a situation of under-employment and widespread informal activities (75.8 per cent and 90.4 per cent respectively, INS, 2005a). Because work is the main source of income of Cameroonians, employment issues should be taken into account in strategies aiming to fight against poverty. This is why in 2009, the government developed the Growth and Employment Strategy Paper in replacement for the Poverty Reduction Strategy elaborated in 2003, which did not sufficiently take into account the concerns related to the labour market.

In this perspective, the question of the benefits of schooling is essential: education significantly influences the income of workers which, in turn, determines the state of poverty of households. In fact, education influences the hourly earnings of workers of all the institutional sectors (public, private, formal, non-agricultural informal and agricultural informal). For example, in the agricultural sector, the average hourly income in the main activity increased from 80 CFA francs for non-school workers to 223 CFA francs for up-graduated workers (INS, 2005a). Furthermore, the educational level of the head of household significantly influences the likelihood for a household to be poor (INS, 2002). In addition, schooling plays an important role on the mode of insertion of individuals into Cameroon's labour market. For example, the unemployment rate or the duration of unemployment increases with the level of education (INS, 2005a).

The main objective of this study is to evaluate the benefits of a worker of the informal sector in terms of income, having completed primary education successfully; that is, obtaining at least the First School Leaving Certificate (FSLC) or an equivalent certificate. It also seeks to estimate the benefits of the first cycle of secondary education (obtaining the General Certificate of Education Ordinary Level; GCE-OL).

For a long time, as noted by Bennell (1996), many studies on returns to schooling in developing countries were limited to workers of the formal sector while ignoring the informal sector where the benefits of education were supposed to be very low. Then the role of primary education in the informal sector income was recognized with sometimes the reluctance that primary education had an impact on informal sector income only if the primary education was completed (three years of schooling not worth more than no years, what mattered was the completion of this cycle). These findings have prompted international organizations to advocate for the completion of primary education at the expense of advocacy of school attendance. Today, the role of secondary education on informal sector income is beginning to be revealed (Kuepie *et al.*, 2009).

In practice, there are two types of methods for assessing the impact: experimental methods and quasi-experimental or non-experimental methods. For both methods, there are two groups: the treated group made up of individuals who have received treatment (here, having obtained FSLC) and the non-treated group (control group) comprising individuals who have not received treatment (here, not having obtained the FSLC).

When exposure to treatment is random (case of experimental methods), then, the analysis of the impact of a policy can be measured simply by comparing the average score of the two groups (here, the average income of both groups). If the treatment is not random, as is the case here because the right to obtain the FSLC is not random, this simple comparison is biased. That is why the ordinary least squares method (OLS) proposed by Mincer (1962), naively used, leads to non-convergent estimators because of the endogeneity of education (Heckman *et al.*, 1998; Blundell *et al.*, 2001; Sianesi, 2002). Indeed, there are variables affecting both the fact of obtaining the FSLC and the level of income. It is then necessary to use impact evaluation methods that take into account the differences *ex ante* of the variable of interest between individuals of the treated group and individuals of the control group; it is the selection to treatment. These methods are: the matching method, the instrumental variables method, selection models and the double differences method.

The advantage of the matching method is that it is non-parametric, therefore does not conjecture on income and residuals distribution. However, it is based on the assumption that the selection is based on observable variables. This is to say that, what distinguishes a person with the FSLC from an individual not having it can be observed. But this assumption is very strong. There may be unobservable variables affecting the school courses and earnings (for example the intellectual quotient). The verification of this hypothesis requires a lot of variables describing the status of the individual before treatment and predicting the likelihood of obtaining the FSLC.

Accepting this methodological option obviously solves the problem of endogeneity of the model. Thus, it is not necessary to have an instrument as it is the case in the instrumental variables method (IVM),[2] which requires having at least one instrument that affects education, but that does not affect income other than through education. The matching method does not require instrumentals variables. The matching on propensity score summarizes the information contained in a large number of variables explaining exposure to treatment into a probability to be treated (Rosenbaum and Rubin, 1983).

However, matching has certain limits. Because obtaining the status of independence that allows the identification of parameters may require the introduction of too many conditional variables; those variables are not always accessible. The relevance of the analysis is also reducing, because the possibilities of matching an individual to another are reduced, when we better explain exposure to treatment. In addition, matching on observable is mechanical process only based on statistical properties, which in practice is difficult to justify from the behaviour of agents (Crépon, 2005). It may be preferable to model jointly the potential earnings of workers and schooling. This yields to the selection on unobservable model which is a parametric model.

The first section of this chapter presents the models used for estimating the impact of education on the income of informal sector workers. The following section describes the dataset used and the characteristics of informal sector workers. Then, estimation results are provided and discussed in the third section. The last section concludes and formulates recommendations.

## Econometric models

The model considered for the evaluation of the impact of the possession of the FSLC on the earnings of informal sector workers is the causal model of Rubin (1977). The workers who possess the FLSC are the treated group. The causal effect of the possession of FSLC ($T$ the treatment variable) on incomes ($Y$ the outcome) represents the difference between what would be the situation if the individual was treated and what it would be if he was not.

If the outcome variables are independent of the treatment variable, the causal effect may simply be estimated as the difference of the average incomes observed in the group of workers having the FSLC and the group of workers who do not have it. If the independence assumption is no longer satisfied, the difference in average incomes is affected by a selection bias.

Indeed,

$$
\begin{aligned}
E(Y \mid T = 1) - E(Y \mid T = 0) &= E(Y_1 \mid T = 1) - E(Y_0 \mid T = 0) \\
&= E(Y_1 \mid T = 1) - E(Y_0 \mid T = 1) + E(Y_0 \mid T = 1) - E(Y_0 \mid T = 0) \quad (7.1) \\
&= \Delta^{TT} + B^{TT}
\end{aligned}
$$

where $B^{TT} = (E(Y_0 \mid T = 1) - E(Y_0 \mid T = 0))$.

This term is the selection bias. This bias would have been zero if the average income of educated individuals was, in absence of treatment, equal to the one of non-educated workers. In other words, if educated and non-educated workers were similar before treatment. The full independence between the potential outcomes $(Y_0, Y_1)$ and obtaining the FSLC is a highly improbable scenario.

## Matching on observable characteristics

The alternative to solve the problem of independence is to find a set of observable variables $X$ with which the conditional independence between the potential results and obtaining the FSLC is verified. Each educated individual is associated to a non-educated person called counterfactual, with identical or very close $X$ characteristics. The counterfactual individual represents what would have been the situation of the treated individual if it had not been treated. $\Delta^{TT}$ can therefore be estimated by the difference between the average income of the group of educated workers and the counterfactual group.

The matching method originally proposed by Rubin (1977) is to match every educated worker $i$ to a non-educated person, noted $ĩ(i)$, with the same observable characteristics $X$. For some treated individuals, we cannot find an individual having exactly the same characteristics. The estimator proposed by Rubin consists of choosing a non-treated individual as close as possible to the treated individual.

## Matching methods on the propensity score

The conditional independence property generally requires taking into account a significant number of conditional variables. Rosenbaum and Rubin (1983) show that it is therefore sufficient to match individuals on the propensity score $P(X)$ which is a one-dimension vector summarizing the vector $X$ of observables. But once the score $P(X)$ is estimated, it must verify the balance property, that is to say that individuals with the same propensity scores have the same distribution of observable variables irrespective of the status of treatment. We will test the balance property with the algorithm developed by Ichino and Becker (2002).

Among the matching methods used, the more common is the one-to-one matching with replacement. But we will also implement the Epanechnikov kernel matching which Heckman *et al.* (1998) have shown its convergence and asymptotic normality under certain assumptions of regularity. This method consists of associating an educated individual with a fictional non-educated person, an average person. All non-educated individuals quite close to the educated individual $i$ participate in the construction of counterfactual income, with an importance that varies depending on the distance between their score and that of the educated worker $i$. The counterfactual is done with all individuals who are within a given bandwidth $h$. We have tested the sensitivity of results to multiple values of this parameter.

Observable variables on which the matching will be carried out are first of all variables related to the worker's father when the worker was 15 years old. They are a proxy of the situation of the worker before treatment. It is about the social professional category of the father (high rank officer; employee; *independent in reference*), the sector of activity of the father (formal private sector or not), the branch of activity of the father (commerce/industry; services; *agriculture/fisheries/breeding in reference*) and the level of education (secondary and higher; primary; *no education in reference*). On the other hand, individual characteristics which are beyond or independent of his current situation will be introduced in the model. But, finally, we will only keep those of the variables permitting to get a score verifying the balance property.

### Selection on unobservable model

The matching methods are based on the assumption that everything that differentiates educated individuals from non-educated individuals is observable. It is possible that unobservable variables (or variables not available in the database) affect both the likelihood of obtaining the FSLC and the level of income. Thus, we will use the selection on unobservable model, which is another alternative for solving the problem of selectivity. This model has the advantage of modelling simultaneously the potential earnings and the likelihood of obtaining the FSLC. We have implemented the following selection model (Heckman, 1979):

$$
\begin{cases}
Y_i = \beta'Z_i + \Delta T_i + u_i \\
\begin{cases}
T_i = 1 & \text{if } \gamma'X_i + e_i > 0 \\
T_i = 0 & \text{otherwise}
\end{cases}
\end{cases}
\tag{7.2}
$$

$u_i$ and $e_i$ follow a bivariate with mean zero and a correlation coefficient $\rho$.

We will estimate equation (7.2) in two stages. We will first estimate the probit model to get a value of the inverse Mills ratio (*lambda*); then, this variable will be included as an independent in the earnings equation in the second stage.

### Determinants of sectoral allocation and selection test at entry into the informal sector

Labour markets in developing countries are segmented, with each having its own specificities as regards to the level of demand, the job quality, the structure and the level of wages (Adams, 1991; Schultz, 2004). The labour market segmentation in Cameroon can be defined by four sectors: the public sector, the private formal sector, the non-agricultural sector and the agricultural sector. A person in age to work may be in one of the following situations: be inactive; active and be unemployed; work in one of the four sectors. The determinants of this "choice" can be estimated using a multinomial logistic model.

But, paid workers of the informal sector are not chosen randomly in the working age population. The restriction of earnings equation on these workers is therefore potentially biased by a selection at the entry into the informal sector. In this case where the selection variable has several modalities, Lee's model

(1983),[3] which is an extension of the Heckman method, helps to estimate the earnings equations while testing the hypothesis of selection at the entry into the labour market segments.

## The data and some descriptive statistics

### *The survey and the data*

The data used are those of the Survey on Employment and the Informal Sector (EESI) conducted in 2005 by the National Institute of Statistics of Cameroon (INS, 2005b). This is a nationwide operation with two phases. During the first phase, the socio-demographic and employment data on a representative sample of 8,540 households was collected. The second phase is a survey on non-agricultural informal production units identified during the first phase. The methodology of the survey EESI is actually that of phases 1 and 2 of a *1-2-3 survey*; meaning that phase 3 on household consumption was not done. Only data from the first phase are used in analyses.

The working age population is, in accordance with international recommendations, all individuals aged 15 years and above. The concept of informal sector chosen for the EESI survey is the one adopted by the 1993 System of National Accounts (set of international standards to establish a framework for the production of national accounts statistics). The distinction between sectors is made at the enterprise level, on the basis of administrative record and the fact of keeping formal accounts. The informal enterprises (or informal production units (IPU)) are those that do not have a taxpayer number and/or do not keep formal accounts. Informal sector workers are persons exercising their main job in informal establishments.

The informal sector can be divided into two segments: the agricultural sector and non-agricultural sector. The agricultural informal sector includes workers of informal production units whose main activities are: agriculture, livestock (including poultry) and the manufacture of products of animal origin, hunting, fishery and pisciculture.

The variable of income used in the estimations is the logarithm of hourly income based on the declared monthly income and the number of hours worked. Income includes salary, end of the year bonuses, profit sharing, paid leaves, benefits in kind. For self-employed, it refers to the profit or the mixed income of their production unit. For dependent employees (apprentices and family-aids), the earning[4] is the sum of bonuses in cash or in kind they received if these elements have a regular character.

### *Descriptive statistics*

Cameroon informal sector employs 89.4 per cent of workers aged 15 and above (Table 7.1). Workers of this sector are younger than those working in the formal sector. The average age is 32.6 years in the non-agricultural informal sector and

*Table 7.1* Workers' characteristics and job characteristics according to the institutional sector (15 years old and above)

| Variables | | Institutional sector | | |
|---|---|---|---|---|
| | | *Formal* | *Non-agricultural informal* | *Agricultural informal* |
| Percentage of persons working in the sector (%) | | 10.7 | 37.1 | 52.2 |
| Average age | | 37.8 | 32.6 | 37.2 |
| Proportion of women (%) | | 24.4 | 49.4 | 53.9 |
| Average number of school years completed | | 10.9 | 5.9 | 3.4 |
| Level of education | No education | 1.1 | 19.4 | 35.8 |
| | Primary | 17.8 | 40.0 | 46.8 |
| | Secondary 1st cycle | 23.9 | 28.0 | 14.4 |
| | Secondary 2nd cycle and + | 57.3 | 12.6 | 2.9 |
| | Total | 100.0 | 100.0 | 100.0 |
| Highest certificate | No certificate | 6.9 | 43.8 | 73.8 |
| | FSLC | 29.3 | 40.4 | 22.5 |
| | GCE-OL/PROBATOIRE | 25.0 | 11.4 | 2.9 |
| | GCE-AL and + | 38.9 | 4.4 | 0.8 |
| | Total | 100.0 | 100.0 | 100.0 |
| Number of hours worked per week | No certificate | 50.9 | 41.7 | 39.1 |
| | FSLC and more | 44.2 | 45.0 | 32.1 |
| | Total | 44.6 | 43.6 | 37.1 |
| Average monthly income (average hourly income) in CFAF | No certificate | 51,659 (249) | 22,902 (162) | 11,485 (86) |
| | FSLC and more | 118,433 (713) | 32,150 (224) | 15,942 (154) |
| | Total | 113,847 (682) | 28,263 (198) | 12,771 (105) |

Source: EESI (2005), Phase 1; author's calculations; weighted data.

37.2 years in the agricultural sector against 37.8 years in the formal sector. Women constitute the main workforce of the informal sector. They represent half the workforce of non-agricultural informal enterprises and 53.9 per cent of the workforce of the traditional primary sector. Conversely, in the formal sector, only one worker out of four is a woman (24.4 per cent).

Workers of the formal sector are more educated and more skilled than those of the informal sector. However, the workforce of the non-agricultural sector is relatively qualified as 56 per cent of the workers of this informal sector have completed primary education and 4.4 per cent of them have obtained the GCE-OL, degree or a higher education certificate. But in the agricultural sector, workers are generally less educated because almost three-quarters of them have not obtained the FSLC.

The number of hours worked per week is higher in the non-agricultural sector than in the agricultural sector, due to the fact that agricultural activities are more constrained by the length of the day. Moreover, the effect of the possession of FSLC is different in the two sectors since it increases the weekly working time in non-agricultural activities and decreases it in agricultural activities. The formal sector workers work on average more than those of the informal sector.

The average income (monthly or hourly) in the non-agricultural sector is more than twice that of the agricultural sector. Possession of the FSLC increases the average hourly income of 38 per cent in the non-agricultural sector. This increment is about 79 per cent in the informal agricultural sector; a worker of the informal agricultural sector earns more if he has graduated, but he also works longer. Incomes in the formal sector are very high compared to those of the informal sector; in fact, a worker of the formal sector averagely earns 3.9 times more than one exercising in non-agricultural sector and 8.8 times more than a worker of the rural sector.

## Results

The results are based on the sample of informal sector workers that are paid, whose fathers were alive when they were 15 years and who have briefed the question of the level of the father.

### *Naive estimate of the effect of FSLC on earnings in the informal sector*

The OLS regressions carried out indicate that whatever the segment, the model is globally significant at 1 per cent. The variable FSLC is also significant at 1 per cent (Table 7.2). But all the variables are not significant in both models. We noted that several other factors (such as the characteristics of production units) may also explain the income of workers in the informal sector in Cameroon, since each model explains less than 13 per cent of income dispersion.

The results show that the effect of FSLC on workers of the informal sector is quite important, particularly in the agricultural segment where it reached 38 per

*Table 7.2* Naive estimation of returns to education in the informal sector: OLS

| Variables | Non-agricultural | | Agricultural | |
|---|---|---|---|---|
| | Coefficient | Standard error | Coefficient | Standard error |
| FSLC | 0.30*** | 0.04 | 0.38*** | 0.05 |
| Potential experience | 0.01*** | 0.01 | 0.01 | 0.01 |
| (Potential experience)^2/100 | −0.01 | 0.01 | −0.01 | 0.01 |
| More than 32 years old | 0.18*** | 0.04 | 0.21*** | 0.06 |
| Female | −0.30*** | 0.03 | −0.45*** | 0.05 |
| Union (married or free union) | 0.06** | 0.03 | 0.08* | 0.05 |
| Christian | 0.05 | 0.07 | 0.20** | 0.08 |
| Muslim | 0.01 | 0.07 | 0.11 | 0.10 |
| Migrant | 0.07** | 0.03 | 0.08** | 0.05 |
| Urban milieu | 0.12*** | 0.03 | 0.27*** | 0.06 |
| Constant | 4.52*** | 0.08 | 3.92*** | 0.10 |
| *Statistics of the model* | | | | |
| Adjusted R² (%) | 11.3 | | 12.8 | |
| Observations | 2,391 | | 1,571 | |

Source: EESI (2005), Phase 1; author's calculations.

Notes
*    significant at 10%.
**   significant at 5%.
***  significant at 1%.

cent against 30 per cent in the non-agricultural segment. But these estimates are biased because the possession of FSLC is not randomly distributed, it depends on certain factors that can be observed or not. We will therefore proceed to a selectivity bias correction on observable variables then a correction on unobservable variables.

### Correction of treatment selectivity based on observable variables: matching

#### Estimating the probability of obtaining FSLC

Table 7.3 summarizes the results on the estimation of the determinants of possession of FSLC. Whatever the segment, statistics on the quality of the model are satisfactory. In the non-agricultural sector, 44 per cent of the variability is explained by the model against 27 per cent in the agricultural sector. In addition, the model is able to allocate at least 83 per cent of individuals in their observed categories.

The main characteristic of the worker's father that explains the school course of a worker of the informal sector in Cameroon is the level of education. Indeed, a child whose father had a level of primary education had four times more chances to obtain the FSLC compared with a child whose father had not been to

*Table 7.3* Estimated propensity for workers of the informal sector to obtain the FSLC

| | | Non-agricultural | | Agricultural | |
|---|---|---|---|---|---|
| | | Odds-ratio | SE | Odds-ratio | SE |
| *Variables related to the father* | | | | | |
| CSP (ref.: self-employed worked) | High rank officer | 1.38 | 0.38 | 0.74 | 0.27 |
| | Employee | 1.00 | 0.26 | 0.53** | 0.17 |
| Sector of activity (ref: formal) | Informal | 1.50 | 0.38 | 2.16*** | 0.70 |
| Branch of activity (ref.: agriculture, fishery, hearing) | Commerce/industry | 1.85*** | 0.32 | 1.46* | 0.34 |
| | Services | 1.61*** | 0.31 | 1.54* | 0.41 |
| Level of education (ref.: no education) | Primary | 4.91*** | 0.71 | 4.27*** | 0.63 |
| | Secondary and + | 11.34*** | 2.86 | 7.52*** | 2.56 |
| *Variables related to the worker* | | | | | |
| Age | – | 1.34*** | 0.04 | 1.14*** | 0.03 |
| Age squared | – | 1.00*** | 0.00 | 1.00*** | 0.00 |
| Female | – | 0.31*** | 0.04 | 0.41*** | 0.05 |
| Religion (ref.: other/no religion) | Christian | 2.37*** | 0.60 | 2.53*** | 0.65 |
| | Muslim | 0.15*** | 0.04 | 0.18*** | 0.07 |
| Place of birth (ref.: village) | Headquarter of division/subdivision | 1.90*** | 0.26 | 2.00*** | 0.30 |
| | Headquarter of province | 1.98*** | 0.37 | 0.62 | 0.22 |
| *Statistics of the model* | | | | | |
| Pseudo R$^2$ (in %) | | 44.0 | | 27.0 | |
| Area Under Roc Curve (AURC) in % | | 90.7 | | 83.1 | |
| Observations | | 2,382 | | 1,581 | |

Source: EESI (2005), Phase 1; author's calculations.

Notes
*   significant at 10%.
**  significant at 5%.
*** significant at 1%.

school. This odds ratio is more than seven if this individual is compared to a worker whose father had reached the secondary education. For workers of the non-agricultural informal sector, the institutional sector and the branch of activity of the father have also influenced their school attendance. Because their parents were mostly working in the informal sector, they were paid less than those working in the formal sector. Therefore, they did not have enough financial resources to enrol their children at school.

Individual characteristics (age, sex, religion, place of birth) have also influenced the likelihood of obtaining FSLC. Persons born in rural areas were less likely to get the FSLC than those born in urban areas (province, division or subdivision headquarters); they were generally used as labour force in farm activities. Thus the negative impact of child labour on child education can be noticed. Finally, men have got at least two times more chances to get the FSLC than women, because of gender discrimination and certain traditions/customs that still hamper the education of Cameroonian young girls.

*Distribution of the propensity score and analysis of the common support*

With the variables used to model the likelihood to obtain FSLC we have implemented the algorithm of Ichino and Becker (2002) to identify variables permitting to have a score verifying the balance propriety. Results show that, whatever the segment, all the initially selected variables are balanced at the threshold 0.1 per cent, thus these variables were retained in the computation of the propensity score.

The propensity score is simply the predicted probability of obtaining the FSLC derived from the logit equation modelling the likelihood of obtaining the FSLC. Individuals are matched with respect to the segment to which they belong: non-agricultural workers on one side and agricultural workers on the other side. Before performing the matching, it is necessary to analyse the spectrum of the score distributions in both groups (treated and non-treated) to identify individuals who fall within the common support.

The common support has been determined using the rule of min–max. This rule compares the minimum and maximum score in both groups (treated and non-treated). Individuals who are on the common support are those whose score is equal or greater than the maximum of the minimum values and less or equal to the minimum of maximum values. The application of this rule shows that whatever the institutional sector, more than 95 per cent of individuals are on the common support. Therefore, individuals from both groups have close characteristics regardless to observable variables.

*Matching*

We tested two matching methods: one-to-one matching with replacement and Epanechnikov kernel matching. Both methods have been restricted to the common support because the inclusion of individuals who are out of this region may bias the estimates. The two techniques effectively permit the reduction of the differences between the average characteristics of the treatment and the control groups. But kernel methods are more efficient since they better bring closer the two groups in terms of average characteristics (Tables 7.A.1 and 7.A.2 in the chapter Appendix). No average characteristic is significantly different between the two groups using the kernel Epanechnikov matching. Moreover, whatever the segment, there is no significant difference of the average effect of education on the treated when the bandwidth varies between 0.04 and 0.08. We finally adopted the bandwidth $h=0.06$; this value was also used by Blundell *et al.* (2001).

Table 7.4 presents the average treatment effects after matching. It shows that the returns to primary education for workers of the informal sector in Cameroon are considerable and significant at the threshold 1 per cent. These benefits are lower than those obtained with the OLS method which is biased.

In the non-agricultural segment, the returns of FSLC on the hourly earnings of workers who have this certificate are estimated to 20 per cent. In other words, if these workers had not successfully completed primary education, their incomes would have been 20 per cent less than what they have now. Furthermore, if workers of this labour market segment not having the FSLC had got it, their income would improve by 23 per cent. So, if workers not having the FSLC return to school and get the certificate, the impact on their income would be at least equal to the initial training received by workers currently graduated, assuming that the age at which the certificate is obtained does not affect the treatment returns. The average benefit of basic education on the workers of the non-agricultural informal sector is an increase of their earnings by 21 per cent.

In the agricultural segment, the returns from schooling are even greater. Indeed, returns of primary education on the income of workers holding the FSLC are about 28 per cent. While, non-graduated workers would have earned 25 per cent more if they had graduated. The average benefits of FSLC on the income of agricultural workers are estimated to 26 per cent. In summary, basic education plays an important role on the income of Cameroon informal sector workers.

*Table 7.4* Returns to basic education in the informal sector: matching method

| *Returns of FSLC* | *Non-agricultural* | | *Agricultural* | |
|---|---|---|---|---|
| | *Estimation* | *SE* | *Estimation* | *SE* |
| On the income of workers holding the FSLC: $\Delta^{TT}$ | 20.0*** | 4.9 | 27.6*** | 6.1 |
| On the income of workers not having the FSLC: $\Delta^{TNT}$ | 22.7*** | 7.2 | 25.1*** | 7.4 |
| On the income of workers: $\Delta^{ATE}$ | 21.0*** | 5.5 | 26.0*** | 5.9 |

Source: EESI (2005), Phase 1; author's calculations.

Notes
Bootstrapped standard errors (200 replications).
* significant at 10%.
** significant at 5%.
*** significant at 1%.

*Correction of treatment selectivity based on unobservable variables*

The model reveals two important results. First, there is a bias induced by unobservable; because, whatever the segment, the variable *lambda* that captures the action of unobservable variables is significant at 1 per cent (Table 7.5). But its negative sign indicates a negative influence of these unobservable on the income of workers. Second, basic education significantly influences (at the threshold 1 per cent) the income of workers of the informal sector. The average treatment effect of the FSLC is estimated at 22 per cent in the non-agricultural segment and it is around 28 per cent in the agricultural segment. These effects are similar to those obtained with the matching model but are significantly lower than the values obtained with the naive model which overstates parameters.

*Returns to the first cycle of secondary education on informal sector workers*

With the same methodology, we now analyse the effect of obtaining the GCE-OL on informal sector workers. Here the treatment group is made of workers exercising in the informal sector who have the GCE-OL or a certificate that is superior and the control group consists of workers who have just had the

*Table 7.5* Returns to basic education in the informal sector: selection on unobservable model

| Variables | Non-agricultural | | Agricultural | |
|---|---|---|---|---|
| | Coefficient | Standard error | Coefficient | Standard error |
| FSLC | 0.22*** | 0.04 | 0.28*** | 0.05 |
| Potential experience | 0.01** | 0.01 | 0.00 | 0.01 |
| (Potential experience)^2/100 | 0.01 | 0.01 | 0.01 | 0.01 |
| More than 32 years old | 0.22*** | 0.04 | 0.29*** | 0.06 |
| Female | −0.26*** | 0.03 | −0.36*** | 0.05 |
| Union (married or free union) | 0.08** | 0.03 | 0.11** | 0.05 |
| Christian | −0.02 | 0.07 | 0.05 | 0.08 |
| Muslim | 0.18** | 0.07 | 0.21** | 0.10 |
| Migrant | 0.08** | 0.03 | 0.08* | 0.05 |
| Urban milieu | 0.08*** | 0.03 | 0.23*** | 0.06 |
| Lambda | −0.29*** | 0.04 | −0.40*** | 0.06 |
| Constant | 4.75*** | 0.08 | 4.39*** | 0.12 |
| *Statistics of the model* | | | | |
| Adjusted R² (%) | 13.0 | | 15.1 | |
| Observations | 2,532 | | 1,659 | |

Source: EESI (2005), Phase 1; author's calculations.

Notes
*    significant at 10%.
**   significant at 5%.
***  significant at 1%.

FSLC. This allows us to assess the net impact of the first cycle of secondary education on the incomes of workers. We have applied the kernel Epanechnikov matching (taking the bandwidth $h=0.06$) and we also implement the selection on unobservable model.

*Selection on observable*

Observable variables that we consider in the computation of the propensity score are the same we have used in estimating the probability of obtaining FSLC. This score assesses the likelihood of obtaining the GCE-OL conditionally to the possession of the FSLC. The examination of spectra of scores shows that in the non-agricultural segment 99.6 per cent of observations fall within the common support against 96.5 per cent in the agricultural segment (Figures 7.A.1 and 7.A.2 in the Appendix).

The matching method shows that the returns to GCE-OL on the income of workers of the non-agricultural sector who have this certificate are estimated to 33 per cent (Table 7.6). On the other hand, if workers who have FSLC return to school and obtain the GCE-OL, this will increase their income by 30 per cent assuming that the age at which the certificate is obtained does not affect the benefits it provides. The average effect of the first cycle of secondary education on workers of the non-agricultural sector having the FSLC is estimated at 31 per cent. In contrary, in the agricultural segment the average effect of GCE-OL on the income of workers may be very low, quite zero; in fact, none of the three parameters is significant.

*Selection on unobservable*

The model selection on unobservable is justified in both segment, since the inverse Mills ratio (*lambda*) is significant at 1 per cent threshold, which confirms the existence of unobservable variables affecting both the possession of GCE-OL

*Table 7.6* Returns to the secondary education first cycle in the informal sector: matching method

| Returns to GCE-OL | Non-agricultural | | Agricultural | |
|---|---|---|---|---|
| | *Estimation* | *SE* | *Estimation* | *SE* |
| On the income of workers holding the GCE-OL: $\Delta^{TT}$ | 33.0*** | 4.9 | 12.9 | 12.3 |
| On the income of workers not having the GCE-OL but holders of the FSLC: $\Delta^{TNT}$ | 29.9*** | 5.4 | 21.6 | 13.9 |
| On the income of workers having the FSLC: $\Delta^{ATE}$ | 31.0*** | 5.1 | 20.2 | 12.7 |

Source: EESI (2005), Phase 1; author's calculations.

Notes
Bootstrapped standard errors (200 replications).
* significant at 10%.
** significant at 5%.
*** significant at 1%.

and income (Table 7.7). Several control variables related to the potential experience, religion and marital status are not significant. But excluding these variables does not significantly affect the other coefficients.

In the non-agricultural sector, the variable GCE-OL reflecting the possession or not of the GCE-OL is significant at threshold of 1 per cent and it indicates that the average benefits of this certificate on the income of workers of the non-agricultural informal sector are around 31 per cent. In opposite, in the agricultural sector this variable is not significant. So the possession of GCE-OL would have no impact on the income of workers exercising in agricultural activities. The results obtained with the selection on unobservable model thus converge with those of the matching method.

### Selection at the entry into the informal sector

We are now testing the selection at the entry into the informal sector. In fact, the previous earnings equations have been restricted, ignoring the existence of the formal sector; they can therefore be biased. Then, we are going to find out the determinants of sectoral allocation. The sample set used is that of potential active persons (aged 15 years and above) interviewed during the survey EESI.

*Table 7.7* Returns to the secondary education first cycle in the informal sector: selection on unobservable model

| Variables | Non-agricultural | | Agricultural | |
|---|---|---|---|---|
| | Coefficient | Standard error | Coefficient | Standard error |
| GCE-OL | 0.31*** | 0.04 | 0.11 | 0.11 |
| Potential experience | 0.02* | 0.01 | 0.02 | 0.01 |
| (Potential experience)^2/100 | −0.04 | 0.05 | −0.03 | 0.03 |
| More than 32 years old | 0.09* | 0.05 | 0.27*** | 0.08 |
| Female | −0.18*** | 0.04 | 0.41** | 0.18 |
| Union (married or free union) | 0.06 | 0.04 | −0.03 | 0.08 |
| Christian | −0.09 | 0.09 | 0.22 | 0.18 |
| Muslim | 0.00 | 0.10 | −0.01 | 0.23 |
| Migrant | 0.14*** | 0.04 | −0.04 | 0.07 |
| Urban milieu | 0.05 | 0.04 | 0.06 | 0.09 |
| Lambda | −0.35*** | 0.06 | −1.02*** | 0.23 |
| Constant | 5.19*** | 0.13 | 5.67*** | 0.31 |
| *Statistics of the model* | | | | |
| Adjusted R$^2$ (%) | 14.9 | | 11.1 | |
| Observations | 1,471 | | 574 | |

Source: EESI (2005), Phase 1; author's calculations.

Notes
*   significant at 10%.
**  significant at 5%.
*** significant at 1%.

The results of the selection test show that the inverse Mills ratio (*lambda*)[5] is significant and positive in the equations of formal sector segments (public and private) and it is negative in the informal sector equations (Table 7.8). But in the non-agricultural sector, this variable is not significant, even at the threshold 10 per cent. So in formal sectors (public or private), the unobserved characteristics affecting the sectoral "choice" of an individual also affect his wage once he gets in this segment of the labour market. In the agricultural sector, these unobserved characteristics play harmfully on the potential earnings of workers and in the non-agricultural segment they have no impact. Thus, Cameroonian workers exercising in the informal sector have not made their choice so as to maximize their potential earnings as it should have been the case in a competitive market. They therefore found themselves there against their aspiration; because they were unable to enter into the formal sector.

Since the estimation of a sectoral allocation model shows that education plays a fundamental role on the occupational status of people, the analysis clearly confirm the positive impact of education.[6] The probability of being unemployed increases with the level of education; qualified people preferring to remain unemployed rather than engaging themselves into the informal sector characterized by precarious jobs and low incomes. Moreover, the probability of entering formal segments increases sharply with the level of education. But it is the opposite effect in the informal segments where the entry probability is decreasing with the level of education.

*Table 7.8* Selectivity test at the entry into the labour market segments

| Variables | Public | Private formal | Non-agricultural informal | Agricultural informal |
|---|---|---|---|---|
| FSLC | 0.45*** | 0.22** | 0.32*** | 0.36*** |
| Potential experience | 0.03*** | 0.03*** | 0.02*** | 0.00 |
| (Potential experience)^2/100 | −0.05* | −0.04 | −0.05*** | 0.00 |
| More than 32 years old | 0.18*** | 0.27*** | 0.20*** | 0.24*** |
| Female | −0.13*** | 0.37*** | −0.34*** | −0.36*** |
| Union (married or free union) | 0.00 | 0.15*** | 0.09*** | 0.04 |
| Christian | 0.05 | 0.02 | 0.19* | 0.28*** |
| Muslim | −0.12 | 0.00 | 0.10*** | 0.30*** |
| Migrant | 0.14*** | 0.06 | 0.07*** | 0.08** |
| Urban milieu | 0.28*** | 0.17*** | 0.17*** | 0.22*** |
| Constant | 6.10*** | 6.09*** | 4.31*** | 3.74*** |
| Lambda *(selectivity test)* | 0.51*** | 0.71*** | −0.04 | −0.15*** |
| *Statistics of the model* | | | | |
| Adjusted R$^2$ (%) | 30.4 | 29.2 | 10.5 | 9.5 |
| Observations | 1,204 | 1,160 | 6,572 | 3,540 |

Source: EESI (2005), Phase 1; author's calculations.

Notes
* significant at 10%.
** significant at 5%.
*** significant at 1%.

## Conclusion and policy implications

The study aimed to analyse the returns to schooling on workers of the Cameroonian informal sector. We have implemented matching on observables methods and selection on unobservables models to assess the effects of basic education on the income of people working in the informal sector (non-agricultural and agricultural). The study has also analysed the benefits of the first cycle of secondary education on these workers.

The results obtained with both methods are converging and confirm the positive impact of education on the incomes of informal sector workers. The benefits brought by the completion of basic education (possession of the FSLC) are estimated to 20 per cent in the non-agricultural sector and to 28 per cent in the rural sector. But, if non-educated workers now return to school and obtain the FSLC (or an equivalent certificate), this will increase their income by 22 to 25 per cent, assuming that the age at which the certificate is obtained does not affect the potential benefits it provides.

The effects of the completion of the first cycle of secondary education on the incomes of the workers of non-agricultural sector are even more important. The possession of GCE-OL helps to increase by 33 per cent the income of those who have this certificate, while the loss of workers who have stopped at the FSLC is about 30 per cent. The average treatment effect of GCE-OL on the income of the non-agricultural sector workers is estimated at 31 per cent. But, in the agricultural segment, the returns of this qualification would be quite zero. However, this result should be confirmed by other studies.

In addition, the selection test at the entry into the informal sector has revealed the existence of a selectivity bias affecting the results of the agricultural sector. However, the results of the non-agricultural sector are not affected by this bias. This test also showed that Cameroonian workers exercising in the informal sector have not made their choice so as to maximize their potential earnings as it should have been the case in a competitive market. They therefore found themselves there because they were unable to enter into the formal sector. Then the significant effect of the level of education in the sectoral allocation model confirms more broadly the importance of returns to education.

In summary, the study puts the spotlight on the role of basic education and the first cycle of secondary education in Cameroon informal sector. Lessons learned will therefore appeal for greater accessibility to education at least until the first cycle of secondary education. The Cameroonian government should intervene to improve the access to education and its quality. Because even if primary education was declared free of charge in Cameroon since 2000, we must acknowledge that the results of this action are not very suitable. Indeed, education supply is still very low since there is a lack of school infrastructure in many rural areas. There is also an overcrowding of pupils, a lack of teachers, a lack of equipment etc. The consequences are high repetition rates and high dropout rates.

The Cameroonian government should recruit more teachers, build and equip schools, strengthen vocational training and also develop and implement a national social education policy to help poor parents who have no means to buy school materials for their children. In the medium term, free schooling could be extended to the first cycle of secondary education. Furthermore, the government could regulate the informal sector actors; introduce incentive programmes to encourage young graduates to enter the informal sector (for example, granting of credits, tax exemption for a number of years). The central administration may also organize free of charge vocational training (train rural farmers with new agricultural technologies with high efficiency) and implement policies for the follow-up of efficient informal production units in order to facilitate their transition into the formal sector.

# Appendix

Table 7.A.1 Average characteristics of workers of the non-agricultural sector before and after matching methods

| Characteristics | Before matching | | After matching | | | | |
|---|---|---|---|---|---|---|---|
| | TG | Difference (TG-CG) | TG | One-to-one Difference (TG-CG) | bandwidth h = 0.04 Difference (TG-CG) | bandwidth h = 0.06 Difference (TG-CG) | bandwidth h = 0.08 Difference (TG-CG) |
| **Log of the hourly income** | **4.723** | **0.305***** | **5.007** | **0.167***** | **0.199***** | **0.200***** | **0.201***** |
| *Individual characteristics* | | | | | | | |
| Age | 36.084 | -5.704*** | 30.407 | -0.257 | 0.318 | 0.332 | 0.322 |
| Female | 0.468 | -0.061*** | 0.432 | 0.067*** | 0.059*** | 0.057*** | 0.053*** |
| Christian | 0.436 | 0.388*** | 0.814 | -0.035** | -0.008 | -0.008 | -0.008 |
| Muslim | 0.514 | -0.389*** | 0.133 | 0.025** | -0.001 | -0.001 | -0.002 |
| Province | 0.141 | 0.146*** | 0.272 | 0.051*** | 0.053*** | 0.056*** | 0.059*** |
| Division | 0.427 | 0.040* | 0.467 | -0.018 | -0.023 | -0.025 | -0.023 |
| *Father's characteristics* | | | | | | | |
| Primary | 0.215 | 0.232*** | 0.475 | -0.061*** | -0.046** | -0.047** | -0.047** |
| Secondary and + | 0.063 | 0.239*** | 0.260 | 0.073*** | 0.043*** | 0.045*** | 0.046*** |
| High rank officer | 0.065 | 0.117*** | 0.154 | 0.004 | 0.017 | 0.018 | 0.018 |
| Employee | 0.148 | 0.172*** | 0.319 | -0.016 | -0.027 | -0.026 | -0.025 |
| Commerce/industry | 0.179 | 0.029* | 0.211 | 0.021 | -0.003 | -0.002 | -0.001 |
| Services | 0.199 | 0.225*** | 0.398 | 0.015 | 0.007 | 0.008 | 0.011 |
| Informal sector | 0.146 | 0.283*** | 0.396 | -0.003 | 0.008 | 0.010 | 0.014 |

Source: EESI (2005), Phase 1; author's calculations.

Notes
* significant at 10%.
** significant at 5%.
*** significant at 1%.
TG: treated group; CG: control group.

Table 7.A.2 Average characteristics of workers of the agricultural sector before and after matching methods

| Characteristics | Before matching | | After matching | | | | |
| | TG | Difference (TG-CG) | TG | One-to-one Difference (TG-CG) | bandwidth h = 0.04 Difference (TG-CG) | bandwidth h = 0.06 Difference (TG-CG) | bandwidth h = 0.08 Difference (TG-CG) |
|---|---|---|---|---|---|---|---|
| **Log of the hourly income** | *4.598* | *0.371\*\*\** | *4.594* | *0.226\*\*\** | *0.272\*\*\** | *0.276\*\*\** | *0.279\*\*\** |
| *Individual characteristics* | | | | | | | |
| Age | 36.760 | −7.883\*\*\* | 36.784 | 0.339 | 0.389 | 0.301 | 0.252 |
| Female | 0.451 | −0.103\*\*\* | 0.453 | −0.005 | 0.004 | −0.001 | −0.002 |
| Christian | 0.894 | 0.213\*\*\* | 0.894 | −0.032\* | −0.020 | −0.017 | −0.016 |
| Muslim | 0.055 | −0.166\*\*\* | 0.055 | 0.008 | 0.016 | 0.015 | 0.015 |
| Province | 0.043 | 0.014\* | 0.043 | 0.010 | 0.001 | 0.000 | −0.001 |
| Division | 0.349 | 0.155\*\*\* | 0.346 | 0.017 | 0.013 | 0.010 | 0.012 |
| *Father's characteristics* | | | | | | | |
| Primary | 0.474 | 0.305\*\*\* | 0.477 | −0.013 | 0.029 | 0.032 | 0.032 |
| Secondary and + | 0.099 | 0.078\*\*\* | 0.095 | 0.000 | −0.003 | −0.006 | −0.004 |
| High rank officer | 0.063 | 0.027\*\*\* | 0.058 | 0.030\*\* | 0.014 | 0.014 | 0.014 |
| Employee | 0.197 | 0.116\*\*\* | 0.198 | −0.033 | −0.011 | −0.006 | −0.001 |
| Commerce/industry | 0.109 | 0.036\* | 0.110 | 0.038\*\* | 0.017 | 0.015 | 0.015 |
| Services | 0.203 | 0.126\*\*\* | 0.199 | −0.002 | 0.005 | 0.012 | 0.018 |
| Informal sector | 0.213 | 0.149\*\*\* | 0.209 | −0.008 | 0.000 | 0.004 | 0.009 |

Source: EESI (2005), Phase 1; author's calculations.

Notes
* significant at 10%.
** significant at 5%.
*** significant at 1%.
TG: treated group; CG: control group.

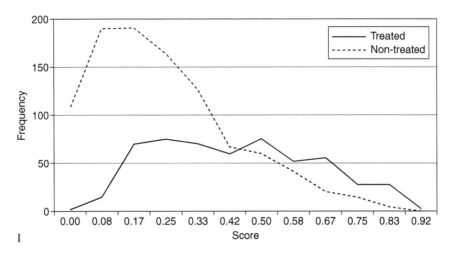

I

*Figure 7.A.1* Distribution of the propensity score for non-agricultural sector workers having the FSLC (source: EESI (2005), Phase 1; author's calculations).

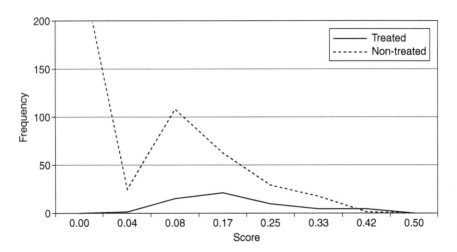

*Figure 7.A.2* Distribution of the propensity score for agricultural sector workers having the FSLC (source: EESI (2005), Phase 1; author's calculations).

# Notes

1 This chapter received the First Prize of the Jan Tinbergen 2009 Competition for best papers prepared by young statisticians from developing countries. The competition is organized by the International Statistical Institute (ISI): http://isi.cbs.nl/awards-prizes. htm. Research assistance was provided by the Observatoire Economique et Statistique d'Afrique Subsaharienne (AFRISTAT). I would like to acknowledge helpful comments from Siriki Coulibaly, Aude Vescovo and Christophe Nordman.
2 See Altonji and Dunn (1996) or Behrman and Stacey (1997) for applications of instrumental variables methods in the estimation of returns to education.
3 This model does not pose a problem even when Assumption IIA (Independence of Irrelevant Alternatives) is not verified.
4 Undeclared incomes were estimated by INS with technical assistance of DIAL and AFRISTAT.
5 A multinomial selection model which considers the place of residence, the level of education, the family environment has permitted to obtain the parameter *lambda*. For a detailed presentation, see Nguetse Tegoum (2010).
6 See Nguetse Tegoum (2010).

# References

Adams, J. (1991) "The Rural Labour Market in Zimbabwe", *Development and Change*, 22 (2), pp. 297–320.
Altonji, J. and T. Dunn (1996) "Using Siblings to Estimate the Effect of Schooling Quality on Wages", *Review of Economics and Statistics*, 78 (4), pp. 665–671.
Behrman, J.-R. and N. Stacey, eds (1997) *The Social Benefits of Education*, University of Michigan Press, Ann Arbor.
Bennell, P. (1996) "Rates of Return on Education: Does the Conventional Pattern Prevail in Sub-Saharan Africa?" *World Development*, 24 (1), pp. 183–199.
Blundell, R., L. Dearden and B. Sianesi (2001) "Estimating the Returns to Education: Models, Methods and Results", *Economic Journal*, CEE, London School of Economics, London.
Crépon, B. (2005) "Econométrie Linéaire", INSEE France (www.ensae.fr/paristech/ SE2C2/Cours_2005_06.pdf).
Heckman, J. (1979) "Sample Selection Bias as a Specification Error", *Econometrica*, 47 (1), p. 153.
Heckman, J., H. Ichimura and P. Todd (1998) "Matching as an Econometric Evaluation Estimator", *Review of Economic Studies*, 65, pp. 261–294.
Ichino, A. and S. Becker (2002) "Estimation of Average Treatment Effects Based on Propensity Score", Laboratorio R. Revelli, Centre for Employment Studies, Moncalieri.
INS (2002) "Conditions de vie des populations et profil de pauvreté au Cameroun en 2001", Deuxième enquête camerounaise auprès des ménages, Yaoundé.
INS (2005a) "Phase 1: enquête employ", Enquête sur l'emploi et le secteur informel, Yaoundé.
INS (2005b) "Document de méthodologie", Enquête sur l'emploi et le secteur informel, Yaoundé.
Kuepie, M., C. Nordman and F. Roubaud (2009) "Education and Earnings in Urban West Africa", *Journal of Comparative Economics*, 37 (3), pp. 491–515.
Lee, L.-F. (1983) "Generalized Econometric Models with Selectivity", *Econometrica*, 51 (2), pp. 507–512.

Mincer, J. (1962) "On-the-Job Training: Costs, Returns and Some Implications", *Journal of Political Economy*, Supplement 1962, Vol. 70.

Nguetse Tegoum, P. (2010) "Estimating Education Returns within the Informal Sector in Cameroon", Paper presented at the international conference on "The Informal Sector and Informal Employment" held in Hanoi, Vietnam, 6–7 May 2010.

Rosenbaum, P. and D.B. Rubin (1983) "Constructing a Control Group Using Multivariate Matched Sampling Methods that Incorporate the Propensity Score", *American Statistician*, 39 (1), pp. 33–38.

Rubin, D.B. (1977) "Estimating Causal Effects of Treatments in Randomized and Non-randomized Studies", *Journal of Educational Psychology*, 66 (5), pp. 688–701.

Schultz, T.P. (2004) "Evidence of Returns to Schooling in Africa from Household Surveys: Monitoring and Restructuring the Market for Education", *Journal of African Economies*, 13, AERC Supplement, pp. ii95–ii148.

Sianesi, B. (2002) "Estimating the Returns to Education", IFAU-Institute For Labor Market Policy Evaluation.

# 8 Does corruption matter for informal sector economic performance?
## Microdata evidence from Sub-Saharan Africa

*Emmanuelle Lavallée and François Roubaud*

In Sub-Saharan Africa (SSA) the informal sector represents a huge share of the economy. In spite of its intrinsic measurement difficulties, there is a large consensus about this key stylized feature. The size of the sector is estimated to account on average for 38 percent of GDP in Africa in 2005 (Buehn and Schneider, 2012). According to the International Labor Office (ILO), the share of informal sector employment varies from nearly 18 percent in South Africa to over 71 percent in Mali (ILO, 2012). Another distinctive feature of SSA is the high incidence of corruption. The 2009 Transparency International (TI) Corruption Perception Index indicates that corruption is a major issue in SSA countries (TI, 2013a). Of SSA countries ranked, 90 percent register a score below 50 (on a scale from 1 to 100), indicating that corruption is perceived as rampant. In comparison, this proportion is about 66 percent in the Americas, and 64 percent in the Asian Pacific region. The Global Corruption Barometer, which reports the experience of petty corruption in more than 100 countries over the world, shows that 51 percent of African citizens had to pay bribes in 2013 in order to obtain a public service, a much higher rate than in any other region (around 27 percent on average; TI, 2013b).

Burdensome regulations, red-tape, high taxation are often presented as the main causes of large informal sector in developing countries (see, for instance, de Soto, 1989; Djankov, 2008). To the best of our knowledge, the peculiar institutional constraints faced by the informal entrepreneurs in developing countries have not yet been explored. Indeed, most of the empirical work done on institutional constraints use surveys carried out mainly on registered firms and then miss a large part of the economy in countries where operating in the informal sector is rather the rule than the exception. In others words, little is known about how informal enterprises – which are also called informal production units (IPUs) – are using public goods and services and what they spend on it or about the intensity of corruption and its consequences in the informal economy.

This chapter intends to fill this gap using a unique data set, called the *1-2-3 Survey*, collected in seven capital cities in countries of the West-African Monetary and Economic Union (WAEMU) in the early 2000s. It is worth mentioning that, as the data collected in the phase 2 of the survey cover only the informal enterprises, we won't be able to assess the role played by institutional constraints in firms' decisions to operate in the informal sector.

As a first step, we will analyze the interactions between informal enterprises and the state. More precisely, we will examine how informal enterprises are (already) using public services and what they spend on it (expenditures for water, energy, electricity, telecommunication, tax payments). Given that the need for such services increases the "exposure" to public bureaucrats we then shift our attention to corruption. We will, then, explore the causes and the consequences of corruption in the informal sector, for several reasons. First, it appears quite interesting to analyze whether they differ from the formal sector in this respect. Second, we think our data are particularly suited to do so. Most of the existing empirical literature on bribes either uses cross-country data (thus ignoring the heterogeneity in the behavior and the exposure of firms within countries) or single-country data, which prevents accounting for cultural differences in norms and values related to corruption. The *1-2-3 Surveys* allow for both, accounting for within and between-country heterogeneity in SSA. Furthermore, our survey captures the experience of corruption, rather than the perception of corruption. Thus, it avoids the bias inherent to many perception surveys widely used in the literature (Razafindrakoto and Roubaud, 2010).

The chapter is structured as follows. In the next section, we briefly review the literature on the causes and consequences of corruption focusing on firms. The third section describes our data. The fourth section provides descriptive statistics on the scope and characteristics of the informal sector in WAEMU capital cities, and its relationship with state agencies. In the following section, we analyze what drives informal payments in the informal sector. Then, we study the effects of corruption on IPU's performance. The last section presents our concluding comments.

## A brief review of literature on firms and corruption

Despite corruption being widely seen today as a threat to economic development, the mechanisms at its origin are still not well identified. If the theoretical literature allows understanding specific corruptive situations (public procurement contract, etc.), the empirical literature is incomplete. Indeed, with few exceptions, the existing literature on the causes of corruption focuses mainly on national-level determinants using cross-country databases. The general picture that emerges from this literature is that common law legal system, Protestant traditions and British colonial rule (Treisman, 2000), fiscal decentralization (Fisman and Gatti, 2002), higher relative civil service pay (van Rijckeghem and Weder, 2001) and the absence of an industrial policy (Ades and Di Tella, 1997) are associated with lower corruption. But most of these studies are plagued by methodological issues, such as reverse causation, and fail to provide clear guidance for policy design. Another strand of the existing literature explores the determinants of corruption at the individual level. The growing availability of micro-level data on corruption enables understanding of the individual or firm characteristics associated with the probability of being a victim of corruption or on the proneness to tolerate corruption (Swamy *et al.*, 2001; Svensson, 2003; Hunt, 2004, 2006; Lavallée, 2007; Lavallée *et al.*, 2010; Rose, 2013).

However, micro-level studies dealing with the determinants of bribes payments across firms are quite rare, especially in Africa despite the fact that corruption is widespread in this area of the world. To the best of our knowledge, the only exception is the study by Svensson (2003) that analyzes the incidence and magnitude of graft across 250 Ugandan formal firms. As regards the incidence of bribery, Svensson shows that firms using public services, firms engaged in trade and firms paying more types of taxes face a higher probability of having to pay bribes; but that the firm profitability and size have no significant impact on the probability to pay bribes. As far as the amount of bribes paid is concerned, the basic findings are the following: the more a firm can pay, i.e., the higher are its current and expected future profits, the more it must pay.

Corruption is generally considered as detrimental to both economic performances and development outcomes at the macro-level (for empirical evidence, see Mauro, 1995; Méon and Sekkat, 2005). Such conclusions contrast sharply with an earlier body of political science and economic literature on corruption. "Efficient grease" and "second-best" theories long prevailed in the political science and economic analysis of corruption. They argue that bribery is an efficient way to reduce effective red tape in an environment of heavy bureaucratic burden and long delays, and therefore that corruption can boost economic development (Leff, 1964; Huntington, 1968). The central assumption of efficient grease theory that corruption can speed up an otherwise sluggish bureaucracy can be overturned. For instance, Myrdal (1968) argues that corrupt civil servants can cause delays that would not otherwise occur just to give themselves an opportunity to extract a bribe; then, rather than improving efficiency, corruption may add distortions and increase overall costs. Whereas this question is still a hot debate in the macro-econometric literature (see, for instance, Méon and Weill, 2010), to the best of our knowledge, few studies analyze the impact of corruption at the firm level.

More recently, Fisman and Svensson (2007) examined the relationship between bribe payments and firm growth using the same data on mostly formal Ugandan firms than Svensson (2003).[1] They find bribe payment to have a negative impact on firm growth and to be more harmful than taxation. A one percentage point increase in the bribery rate is associated with a reduction in firm growth of three percentage points, an effect about three times greater than of taxation.

Using unique panel data of formal Indonesian manufacturing firms (20 or more employees), Vial and Hanoteau (2010) find a positive relation between corruption and firm output and labor productivity. More precisely, using plant-level panel data estimations and controlling for the potential endogeneity of bribe payments through their industry-location average and a proxy for infrastructure quality, they find that plants displaying a higher bribe-to-value added ratio enjoy significantly higher output and productivity growth. The effect of the ratio of indirect taxes to value added, another proxy for corruption, is similar in the scope and significance of its effect on labor productivity growth, but it is less dramatic in its scope for output growth. Their results support the efficient grease hypothesis, from the perspective of individual plants. Indonesian firms that pay bribes are better able to overcome red tape and barriers to doing business.

## Data description

### *The* 1-2-3 Surveys

Our data are taken from an original series of urban household surveys in West Africa, the *1-2-3 Surveys* conducted by the National Statistical Offices with the assistance of the authors in seven major cities (Abidjan, Bamako, Cotonou, Dakar, Lomé, Niamey and Ouagadougou) from 2001 to 2002. As suggested by its name, the *1-2-3 Survey* is a three-phase survey, the basic rationale of this tool is the following. The first phase is an augmented labor force survey (LFS) on employment, unemployment and working conditions of households and individuals. It allows documentation and analysis of labor market functioning and is used as a filter for the second phase, where a representative sample of IPUs is surveyed.[2] Thus, in the second phase of the survey a sample of the heads of the IPUs identified in the first phase are interviewed: it aims at measuring principal economic and productive characteristics of the production units (production, value added, investment, financing), the major difficulties encountered in developing the business activity and the demands for public support by the informal entrepreneurs. Finally in the third phase, a sub-sample of households, selected from phase 1, is administrated a specific income/expenditure survey, designed to estimate the weights of the formal and informal sectors in households' consumption.

### *Corruption measurement*

In addition to the fact we use a cross-national representative survey of informal enterprises, further points dealing with corruption measurement set apart our work from other studies done in this area of research.

Each survey respondent was asked if he or she had personally been affected by corruption in the year preceding the survey and, if so, on what occasion (type of transaction and service concerned) and the total sum paid out on corruption over the year. More precisely, the survey asks the following series of questions: "In the past year, did you get into trouble with public official for exercising your activity?"; "How did the dispute settle: by the payment of a fine, of a 'gift', or by other means?"; "In the past year, in total for your establishment, how much had you got to pay to government officials in forms of 'gifts' or 'fines'?" Special care was taken to guarantee the quality of the information collected.

We then measure specifically the experience with one of the possible forms of corruption – petty administrative corruption – which occurs when the population enters into contact with the public administration. In this point, our study differs from Vial and Hanoteau (2010) which rather deals with grand corruption that is to say "bribes to top level officials in exchange of favours".

Focusing on experience with corruption distinguishes our survey from the ones generally used in the literature. Indeed, questions about corruption are generally phrased indirectly and turn to ask the respondent about his/her perception of corruption rather than his/her experience with corruption. For instance, in the Ugandan enterprise survey used by Svensson (2003) the key question on bribes payments was the following:

> Many business people have told us that firms are often required to make informal payments to public official to deal with customs, taxes, licenses, regulations, services etc. Can you estimate what a firm in your line of business and of similar size and characteristics typically pays each year?

However, Razafindrakoto and Roubaud (2010) show that measurements of corruption based on perception do not provide a good gauge of the real level of corruption, and systematically overestimate the frequency of corruption.[3]

Finally, we have taken into account the fact that a certain number of constituents did not get into trouble with public officials. This aspect is particularly important in that the frequency of interactions with the administration varies from one activity to the next and that certain entrepreneurs might steer clear of public officials precisely because they are afraid of being confronted with corruption. This means that not controlling for actual contact with public officials may lead to an underestimation of the real risks of corruption.

## Informal enterprises, relation with the state and corruption: a descriptive analysis

This section presents the first general lessons that can be drawn from these surveys concerning the relationships between the informal sector and the state.[4] Phase 2 data covers in detail only informal enterprises, but contains questions dealing with registration in administrative records, use of public services or tax payments that allow us to assess further the degree of informality and the heterogeneity of IPUs.

In all WAEMU capital cities, in addition to the administrative or fiscal registration number there is at least three records with which a law enforcing firm should register: license, trade register and social security (for IPUs with employees). Less than 20 percent of the IPUs record to at least one of these registers. The most extreme cases are Dakar and Lomé where this rate is less than 10 percent. In almost 60 percent of cases, the non-registration is due to ignorance of the law: 39 percent of the IPUs think that registrations are not compulsory and 21 percent don't know if they are required.

Regarding the relationship between the informal sector and public agents, the survey's results suggest that there is no will of the state to force IPUs to comply with the law. In the seven capital cities, only 6 percent of the heads of IPUs say they got into trouble with public agents the year before the survey; this proportion ranges from 4 percent in Bamako to 9 percent in Dakar (Table 8.1). This proportion is particularly high (30 percent) in the transport sector. This result illustrates the real harassment of police forces toward taxi drivers, moto-taxi and so on, even if in some cases some of them may not fully comply with the regulations.

As a consequence, only a minority of IPUs (4.2 percent) declare they had to pay bribes the year before the survey (Figure 8.1). Nevertheless, if we take into account only IPUs that had contact with the state that year before the survey, this proportion rises to 37 percent which makes bribery a significant mean of settling disputes with public agents. The incidence of corruption varies dramatically from one city to another; it is particularly high in Lomé (47 percent), Abidjan (45 percent) and Bamako (40 percent).

*Table 8.1* Proportion of IPU that got into trouble with public agents during the past year

|  | Cotonou | Ouagadougou | Abidjan | Bamako | Niamey | Dakar | Lomé | Total |
|---|---|---|---|---|---|---|---|---|
| Manufacturing | 5.8 | 5.9 | 7.5 | 3.0 | 3.7 | 2.9 | 3.3 | 5.2 |
| Trade | 4.8 | 3.9 | 4.8 | 3.2 | 8.5 | 9.5 | 5.0 | 5.4 |
| Services | 3.5 | 6.4 | 9.3 | 5.2 | 7.2 | 14.5 | 10.6 | 8.7 |
| Total | 4.7 | 5.0 | 7.0 | 3.5 | 6.2 | 8.5 | 6.2 | 6.2 |

Source: *1-2-3 Surveys*, phase 2, 2001–2003, NSOs, AFRISTAT, DIAL; authors' calculations.

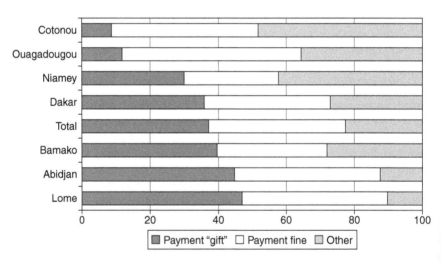

*Figure 8.1* Settlement of disputes with public agents (source: *1-2-3 Surveys*, phase 2, 2001–2002, NSOs, AFRISTAT, DIAL; authors' calculation).

# What drives corruption in the informal sector?

## *Empirical strategy*

In this section, we propose first to extend Svensson's (2003) analysis of the incidence of graft to firms operating in the informal sector. The novelty of our approach is not only its extension to the informal economy (to the best of our knowledge, on a representative basis for the first time ever) but also its cross-country dimension. Indeed, our data were collected through questionnaires that were perfectly harmonized, which guarantee comparability across countries. However, one should acknowledge here that given the low incidence of corruption and the limited number of countries under review, our cross-country comparisons should be taken as a first exploration.

We study the propensity of a firm to bribe, when the firm vulnerability or propensity to corruption is unobservable. This vulnerability or propensity to corruption is supposed to be linked to characteristics of IPUs. We explain the probability of having paid a bribe by three sets of independent variables. The first one refers to an IPU's characteristics: the size of the IPU (in terms of employees and value added), its age, the amount of taxes paid as well as industries. We argue that larger firms and firms with capital are more likely to be harassed by rent seeking officials. Moreover, older firms may have a lower probability to pay bribes because they benefit from experience and social networks, and from repeated interactions with public officials. Lastly, descriptive statistics suggest that some industries are particularly prone to corruption, especially transport. This fact could be explained by the huge impact of discretionary police control on the business operations in this sector.

The second set of independent variables deals with the personal characteristics of the head of IPUs. We use gender as an independent variable because some studies show that women are less tolerant and less victim of corruption than men (Dollar *et al.*, 2001; Gatti *et al.*, 2003; Swamy *et al.*, 2001; Lavallée *et al.*, 2010). Ultimately, we introduce a dummy variable denoting that the head of IPU is born in town as proxy for social integration. The third one is city fixed effects which aim at capturing cities' heterogeneity and unobservable characteristics.

To analyze properly what drives corruption in the informal sector, we have to circumvent two potential problems: selection bias and the fact that bribe payment and firm value added may be determined simultaneously.

## *Correcting for a selection bias*

As regards the selection bias, the issue is that only the IPUs that get into trouble with public agents are exposed to bribery. However, several theoretical arguments suggest the absence of trouble with public agents is potentially a consequence of corruption. For instance, corruption is often presented as reducing the quantity (Shleifer and Vishny, 1993) and the quality (Bearse *et al.*, 2000) of publicly provided goods and then corruption could reduce the administrative controls over firms and particularly the IPUs. Furthermore, some firms may avoid using public facilities precisely because they do not want to be confronted with corruption. Therefore, an analysis conducted exclusively on a sample of IPUs that got into trouble with public agents could be biased by under-estimating potential bribe payments. To properly analyze the determinants of bribe payments we test the existence of such a selection bias and, eventually, correct it by estimating probit model with sample selection (van de Ven and van Pragg, 1981).

For the model to be well identified, the selection equation should have at least one variable that is not in the first equation. Otherwise the model is identified only by functional form, and the estimated coefficient has no structural interpretation. We therefore computed a dummy variable taking the value of one if IPU's premises are favorable to control and zero otherwise. More precisely, we consider that IPUs whose activities take place on highways, public markets or permanent premises are particularly exposed to control by public agents.

Our results are depicted in Table 8.2. We estimate two sets of equations, the second set including individual characteristics of the head of the IPUs. In both cases, the likelihood-ratio test of independent equations indicates that ignoring the selection would not render the estimates of a probit on the incidence of corruption biased and inconsistent.

The selection equation shows that, as expected, the probability of having troubles with public officials is higher for the bigger enterprises and the most visible ones. Women heads are less prone to solicit public agencies (or to be controlled by them). Transportation IPUs are, *ceteris paribus*, more often in contact with public agents. Finally, the country effects are in the majority of the cases non-significant, suggesting a common pattern in the relationship between the state and the informal sector.

Let us now turn to the corruption equation. Some findings are in keeping with our expectations. Whereas workforce size does not have a significant impact on the probability to have trouble with public agents, larger output and amounts of taxes paid increase the probability of getting trouble with public agents. Marginal effects computed at mean provide some quantitative insight. The fact that an IPU is managed by a woman reduces the probability of corruption by 4 percent. Our results also confirm that transport is the area of activities where the probability of control is the greatest. For instance, doing in-shop retail and wholesale rather than transport decreases the probability of getting into trouble with public agents by 3.8 percent. Here, again, the country fixed effects are low and generally non-significant, except for Cotonou and Ouagadougou which seem to be less corrupt than other cities.

*Correcting for an endogeneity bias*

The second estimation issue is the potential simultaneity in the determination of output and bribe payment. Indeed, optimal harassment theories (Myrdal, 1968; Kaufmann and Wei, 1999) suggest that the ability to bribe varies greatly from

*Table 8.2* Probit model with sample selection on the incidence of corruption

|  | *Probit* | *Selection* | *Probit* | *Selection* |
|---|---|---|---|---|
|  | *Corruption* | *Contact* | *Corruption* | *Contact* |
| Premise prone to control | – | 0.14*** | – | 0.12** |
|  |  | (0.05) |  | (0.05) |
| Value added in log | 0.06** | 0.00 | 0.05* | −0.02 |
|  | (0.03) | (0.02) | (0.03) | (0.02) |
| Workforce size in log | −0.01 | 0.25*** | 0.04 | 0.26*** |
|  | (0.13) | (0.05) | (0.09) | (0.05) |
| Capital in log | 0.09*** | 0.08*** | 0.08*** | 0.07*** |
|  | (0.03) | (0.01) | (0.02) | (0.01) |
| Age of IPU | 0.00 | −0.00 | 0.00 | −0.00 |
|  | (0.01) | (0.00) | (0.01) | (0.00) |
| Age of IPU squared | −0.00 | 0.00 | −0.00 | 0.00 |
|  | (0.00) | (0.00) | (0.00) | (0.00) |
| Tax paid in log | 0.12** | 0.15*** | 0.10** | 0.14*** |
|  | (0.05) | (0.03) | (0.05) | (0.03) |
| Woman | – | – | −0.42*** | −0.30*** |
|  |  |  | (0.15) | (0.07) |
| Born in town | – | – | −0.07 | −0.02 |
|  |  |  | (0.09) | (0.06) |
| Clothing, leather, shoe industry | −0.65*** | −0.76*** | −0.62*** | −0.73*** |
|  | (0.24) | (0.12) | (0.22) | (0.13) |
| Other industries, agribusiness | −0.84*** | −0.75*** | −0.79*** | −0.69*** |
|  | (0.16) | (0.11) | (0.16) | (0.12) |
| Building and civil engineering | −1.04*** | −1.12*** | −1.13*** | −1.16*** |
|  | (0.33) | (0.16) | (0.30) | (0.17) |
| In-shop retail and wholesale | −0.52** | −0.57*** | −0.45** | −0.56*** |
|  | (0.23) | (0.12) | (0.23) | (0.12) |
| Out of shop retail sale | −0.55*** | −0.57*** | −0.40* | −0.48*** |
|  | (0.21) | (0.11) | (0.21) | (0.12) |
| Catering | −0.94*** | −0.87*** | −0.68** | −0.67*** |
|  | (0.24) | (0.14) | (0.27) | (0.15) |
| Repair | −0.57*** | −0.59*** | −0.70*** | −0.67*** |
|  | (0.18) | (0.13) | (0.19) | (0.14) |
| Other services | −1.17*** | −0.85*** | −1.14*** | −0.86*** |
|  | (0.22) | (0.13) | (0.22) | (0.14) |
| Constant | −1.98*** | −1.38*** | −1.77*** | −1.12*** |
|  | (0.25) | (0.15) | (0.26) | (0.17) |
| Country control | Yes | Yes | Yes | Yes |
| Wald test of indep. equations | chi2(1)=0.66 |  | chi2(1)=0.98 |  |
|  | Prob>chi=0.42 |  | Prob>chi= 0.32 |  |
| Uncensored observations | 421 | 421 | 397 | 397 |
| Observations | 6,400 | 6,400 | 5,971 | 5,971 |

Source: *1-2-3 Surveys*, phase 2, 2001–2002, NSOs, AFRISTAT, DIAL; authors' calculations.

Notes

Robust standard errors in parentheses.

*** $p<0.01$.

** $p<0.05$.

* $p<0.1$.

one firm to another. Rent seeking officials manipulate regulation, tax, bureaucratic red tape and their discretionary enforcement according to the firm's "ability to pay" in order to induce the firm to pay, and to pay the maximum amount of bribe it is willing to tolerate. Then, we expect that public officials demand more often bribes from the better performing firms. Moreover, as pointed out by Shleifer (2004), and Fisman and Svensson (2007), corruption can be used by some entrepreneurs as a strategy to develop their business. Indeed, it is possible that the IPUs choose to devote resources on bribery. For instance, one could imagine that, in case of control, a taxi driver systematically chooses to bribe the policeman in order to lose the minimum of time and/or money.

This endogeneity issue can be mitigated by instrumenting for the output. We use average turnover by industry and location as an instrument for value added. In our point of view, this measure is a good proxy for the costs of entry in a particular industry in a particular location. It should also be a good proxy for the intensity of demand. Both should influence a firm's value added but not its experience with corruption.

Columns 1, 2, 3 and 4 of Table 8.3 report our OLS estimations on the incidence of corruption when we increase progressively the number of independent variables. As regards firm characteristics, the level of value added has a positive and significant influence on the incidence of bribery, and the value of capital increases the probability to pay a bribe. In the same line as Svensson, higher capital can be viewed as reducing IPUs' outside option and then refusal power. Estimation results also indicate that neither the number of employee, nor the age, nor the fact that the informal enterprise is involved directly in international trade have a significant impact on the incidence of corruption. Moreover, they suggest that the IPUs paying more taxes are more likely to bribe. This result may be apparently paradoxical, as one could have expected a trade-off between bribing and complying with the tax regulations. In fact, in SSA, tax regulation is a gray zone where the rule of the game is never clear cut. Dealing with tax agent often means embarking in a negotiation process, which can be cleared by paying both tax and bribe. Belonging to a business organization is also associated with higher corruption. The direction of causality is not obvious. On the one hand, the IPUs which have been affected by corruption may join a producer's association to protect them. On the other hand, members of business associations may be targeted by corrupted public agents, as a form of retaliation.

As far as the heads of IPUs are concerned, only gender and a secondary educational level have a significant impact on the probability to pay a bribe. Indeed, the fact that an IPU is run by a woman decreases the probability to have to pay bribe. On the contrary, the fact that the head of IPU has a secondary educational level (rather than no education) increases the probability of corruption. It is worth noting that no other personal characteristics of the head of the IPU, such as the level of wealth, the place of birth or ethnicity, have a significant influence on the incidence of bribery.

In column 5 of Table 8.3, we control for the potential endogeneity bias. The Wald test of exogeneity confirms the simultaneity in the determination of output and bribe payment. The coefficients estimated by the probit model and the instrumental variable probit model differ for several independent variables. The logarithm of capital, dummy variables denoting that the head of IPU belongs to a business organization, is a woman or has a secondary educational level become non-significant. On the contrary, workforce size, IPU's age and the dummy variable indicating that the head of the IPU has a university educational level turn out to be significant in instrumental variable probit estimations. Their estimated signs are in line with our expectations. They indicate that smaller, younger informal enterprises and IPUs whose head has a university educational level are less likely to pay a bribe. Lastly, the coefficient of the endogenous regressor, value added, is still positive and significant, so that an increase in the IPU value added is estimated to increase the probability of having to pay a bribe. The average marginal effect of the logarithm of value added on the probability of corruption is 0.55. This figure may appear dramatically high, but one should remember that the probability of having to pay a bribe is very low.

## Do bribe payments reduce economic performance?

Our empirical question is whether a link can be found between experience with corruption and IPUs' performances. To assess this, we consider the following production function:

$$y_{i,j,k} = \alpha + \beta_1 k_{i,j,k} + \beta_2 l_{i,j,k} + \sum \gamma_n X_{i,j,k} + \varepsilon_{i,j,k}$$

where $y_{i,j,k}$ is the log of value added of firm $i$ of sector $j$ in city $k$, $k_{i,j,k}$ is the log of capital input, $l_{i,j,k}$ is the log of labor input, $X_{i,j,k}$ is a vector of $n$ characteristics of the IPU and $\varepsilon_{i,j,k}$ an error term.

One obvious concern with this approach is the possible endogeneity between corruption and firm performance as already discussed in the previous section. Then, studying empirically the impact of corruption on firm performance requires circumventing the problem posed by the potential simultaneous determination of performance and bribes. In this section, we proceed as Fisman and Svensson (2007) and Vial and Hanoteau (2010) by instrumenting bribe payments by industry-location specific variables. Fisman and Svensson's argument is that the part of bribe payment related to that particular industry-location is a function of the underlying characteristics inherent to that particular industry-location, such as the possibility of bureaucrats to extract bribes, and this component should be exogenous to the firm.

Table 8.4 displays our set of results. The two first columns exhibit the coefficients of the estimated production function through OLS. In column 1, independent variables only focus on firms' characteristics, whereas in column 2 we introduce independent variables characterizing the head of IPUs. All models include country fixed effects.

With regard to firms' characteristics, at first glance, the estimated production functions are stable across estimations. All control variables are either intuitively

Table 8.3 Probit models on the incidence of corruption

| | 1 | 2 | 3 | 4 | 5 |
|---|---|---|---|---|---|
| | OLS | OLS | OLS | OLS | IV |
| Output in log | 0.06** | 0.05* | 0.05* | 0.05* | 0.55*** |
| | (0.03) | (0.03) | (0.03) | (0.03) | (0.09) |
| Capital in log | 0.09*** | 0.08*** | 0.08*** | 0.08*** | 0.00 |
| | (0.02) | (0.02) | (0.02) | (0.02) | (0.03) |
| Workforce size in log | -0.02 | 0.02 | 0.03 | 0.03 | -0.33*** |
| | (0.08) | (0.08) | (0.08) | (0.08) | (0.10) |
| Tax paid in log | 0.11*** | 0.09** | 0.09** | 0.09** | -0.11* |
| | (0.04) | (0.04) | (0.04) | (0.04) | (0.06) |
| IPU age | -0.00 | -0.00 | -0.00 | -0.00 | -0.01** |
| | (0.01) | (0.01) | (0.01) | (0.01) | (0.00) |
| IPU age squared | -0.00 | -0.00 | -0.00 | -0.00 | 0.00** |
| | (0.00) | (0.00) | (0.00) | (0.00) | (0.00) |
| Belong to a business organization | 0.30** | 0.28** | 0.28** | 0.28** | 0.03 |
| | (0.13) | (0.14) | (0.14) | (0.14) | (0.14) |
| Export or import | 0.13 | 0.03 | 0.03 | 0.03 | -0.16* |
| | (0.12) | (0.13) | (0.13) | (0.13) | (0.09) |
| Woman | – | -0.39*** | -0.38*** | -0.37*** | 0.04 |
| | | (0.11) | (0.12) | (0.11) | (0.15) |
| Born in town | – | -0.10 | -0.09 | -0.09 | -0.09 |
| | | (0.09) | (0.09) | (0.09) | (0.06) |
| Primary education | – | -0.09 | -0.08 | -0.08 | -0.08 |
| | | (0.11) | (0.11) | (0.11) | (0.07) |
| Secondary education | – | 0.19* | 0.20** | 0.21** | 0.04 |
| | | (0.10) | (0.10) | (0.10) | (0.09) |
| University education | – | -0.34 | -0.31 | -0.31 | -0.42** |
| | | (0.26) | (0.27) | (0.26) | (0.17) |

| | | | | | |
|---|---|---|---|---|---|
| Belong to the 1st quintile of wealth | — | — | -0.01<br>(0.16) | -0.01<br>(0.16) | -0.09<br>(0.10) |
| Belong to the 2nd quintile of wealth | — | — | 0.07<br>(0.14) | 0.07<br>(0.14) | -0.03<br>(0.10) |
| Belong to the 3rd quintile of wealth | — | — | -0.01<br>(0.16) | -0.01<br>(0.16) | -0.06<br>(0.10) |
| Belong to the 4th quintile of wealth | — | — | 0.22<br>(0.14) | 0.21<br>(0.14) | 0.06<br>(0.11) |
| Belong to the city main ethnic group | — | — | — | -0.06<br>(0.09) | -0.00<br>(0.06) |
| Constant | -2.03***<br>(0.21) | -1.83***<br>(0.24) | -1.94***<br>(0.26) | -1.92***<br>(0.26) | -3.65***<br>(0.17) |
| Sector control | Yes | Yes | Yes | Yes | Yes |
| Country control | Yes | Yes | Yes | Yes | Yes |
| Pseudo $R^2$ | 0.16 | 0.19 | 0.19 | 0.19 | |
| Athrho | — | — | — | — | -1.14**<br>(0.50) |
| Wald test of exogeneity | — | — | — | — | chi2(1)=5.27<br>Prob>chi2=0.02 |
| 1st-stage partial $R^2$/Shea's partial $R^2$ for logy | — | — | — | — | 0.00 |
| 1st-stage F statistic/Shea's partial $R^2$ for bribes | — | — | — | — | 16.29 |
| Observations | 6,371 | 5,943 | 5,941 | 5,941 | 5,941 |

Source: *1-2-3 Surveys*, phase 2, 2001–2002, NSOs, AFRISTAT, DIAL; authors' calculations.

Notes

Robust standard errors in parentheses.

*** $p < 0.01$.

** $p < 0.05$.

* $p < 0.1$.

Table 8.4 Effect of bribery and taxation on firm performance

| | 1 | 2 | 3[a] | 4[b] |
|---|---|---|---|---|
| | OLS | OLS | IV | IV |
| Had to pay a bribe | 0.20 | 0.14 | −3.00** | −4.49** |
| | (0.12) | (0.12) | (1.72) | (1.99) |
| Taxes paid in log | 0.31*** | 0.30*** | 0.33*** | 0.61** |
| | (0.03) | (0.03) | (0.03) | (0.26) |
| Capital in log | 0.14*** | 0.10*** | 0.12*** | 0.10*** |
| | (0.01) | (0.02) | (0.02) | (0.02) |
| IPU without capital | 0.23*** | 0.08 | 0.09 | 0.06 |
| | (0.07) | (0.08) | (0.08) | (0.08) |
| Workforce size in log | 0.69*** | 0.68*** | 0.68*** | 0.61*** |
| | (0.05) | (0.05) | (0.05) | (0.08) |
| Age of IPU | 0.02*** | 0.02*** | 0.02*** | 0.02*** |
| | (0.00) | (0.00) | (0.00) | (0.00) |
| Age of IPU squared | −0.00*** | −0.00*** | −0.00*** | −0.00*** |
| | (0.00) | (0.00) | (0.00) | (0.00) |
| Index of use of public services | 0.01 | −0.00 | −0.01 | −0.02 |
| | (0.04) | (0.04) | (0.04) | (0.04) |
| Export or import | 0.47*** | 0.36*** | 0.36*** | 0.32*** |
| | (0.07) | (0.07) | (0.08) | (0.09) |
| Primary activity | – | 0.25 | 0.27 | 0.23 |
| | | (0.16) | (0.17) | (0.18) |
| Woman | – | −0.48*** | −0.53*** | −0.51*** |
| | | (0.05) | (0.06) | (0.07) |
| Born in town | – | 0.08* | 0.06 | 0.06 |
| | | (0.04) | (0.05) | (0.05) |
| Primary education | – | 0.07 | 0.05 | 0.06 |
| | | (0.05) | (0.05) | (0.06) |
| Secondary education | – | 0.16*** | 0.19*** | 0.21*** |
| | | (0.06) | (0.06) | (0.07) |
| University education | – | 0.54*** | 0.50*** | 0.51*** |
| | | (0.14) | (0.15) | (0.15) |
| Belong to the two first quintile of wealth | – | 0.06 | 0.05 | 0.05 |
| | | (0.05) | (0.05) | (0.05) |
| Constant | 4.70*** | 4.57*** | 5.06*** | 5.04*** |
| | (0.12) | (0.21) | (0.32) | (0.33) |
| Sector control | Yes | Yes | Yes | Yes |
| Country coutrol | Yes | Yes | Yes | Yes |
| Durbin (score) chi$^2$(2) | – | – | 6.64 ($p=0.01$) | 8.18 ($p=0.02$) |
| Wu-Hausman F(2,5143) | – | – | 6.62 ($p=0.01$) | 4.08 ($p=0.02$) |
| Shea's partial $R^2$ for bribery | – | – | 0.01 | 0.01 |
| Shea's partial $R^2$ for taxes | – | – | – | 0.02 |
| 1st-stage F statistic for bribery | – | – | 11.92 | 12.49 |
| 1st-stage F statistic for taxes | – | – | – | 27.79 |
| Observations | 6,344 | 5,916 | 5,916 | 5,916 |
| R-squared | 0.28 | 0.30 | 0.21 | 0.16 |

Source: 1-2-3 Surveys, phase 2, 2001–2002, NSOs, AFRISTAT, DIAL; authors' calculations.

Notes

Robust standard errors in parentheses.

*** $p<0.01$. ** $p<0.05$. * $p<0.1$.

a: corruption instrumented by industry-location corruption incidence and amount of tax paid; b: corruption and tax paid instrumented by the same variables.

signed or insignificant. The significant positive sign of the openness dummy suggests that greater openness tends to be associated with better performances. As expected, value added *ceteris paribus* grows as inputs used increase (capital and labor) and the firm gets older (along with its head's social networks).

With regard to the variables specific to the head of IPUs, results are consistent with our expectations. IPUs run by women are less successful, probably because they have more diversified objectives than just maximizing their business benefit. Moreover, our results suggest that informal enterprises' performance rise with the educational level of its head.

However, our regressions yield two striking results. First, the coefficient of the experience with corruption is not significant at the 10 percent level, indicating that there is no association between corruption and firm output. It is worth noting that Fisman and Svensson (2007) also find a weak association between rates of bribery and firm performances, measured by growth in firm sales, in their OLS regressions. Second, paying more taxes appears to be positively correlated with firms' performance which is contradictory with the basic intuition and conclusions of previous studies, among which Fisman and Svensson (2007).

Nevertheless, the oddness of such a result can be mitigated by the kind of taxes paid by IPUs. Indeed, half of the value of taxes paid by informal enterprises is, in fact, local taxes such as the fees for a spot in a public market. Obviously, if these local taxes represent costs for IPUs, they may also dramatically ease their activities by giving them access to infrastructure services by improving their exposure to customers and then increase their performance. This point is supported by evidence about the advantage of formalization (Rand and Torm, 2012).

Again to address endogeneity issues, we now present the results of IV regression where experience with corruption is instrumented by the industry-location-specific percentage of firms declaring they had to pay a bribe, and mean by industry and location of taxes paid. The results from IV estimation, listed in column 3, provide support for the hypothesis that bribery decreases firm performance; and confirm that, in the informal sector, the more enterprises pay taxes the better they perform.

To test further the robustness of our results we also run IV regression on firms' performance where the experience with corruption and the logarithm of taxes paid are instrumented by the industry-location percentage of firms declaring they had to pay a bribe, and mean amount of taxes paid by industry and location. The estimated effect of bribery rises, as well as the one of taxes. The estimated effects of bribery are dramatically high and cast doubt on the relevance of our instruments. Unfortunately, we have no better instruments to test and we cannot compare our results with previous one. Indeed Svensson (2003) and Vial and Hanoteau (2010) use the indicators of firms' growth rather than the level of performance as dependent variables.

## Conclusion

This chapter investigates the relationships between the informal sector and the state. It analyses especially the intensity of corruption and its consequences in the informal economy. It is worth noting it is the first time ever the issue of corruption, measured by experience rather than perception, in the informal sector is extensively analyzed. Our study provides several new insights.

Above all and contrary to the common belief, our data show that in West African capital cities, IPUs are not massively victims of corruption by public officials. Indeed, only 4.2 percent of IPUs declare they had to pay bribes the year before the survey. Such a figure does not mean that corruption is an anecdotal phenomenon. If experience with bribery was unevenly and independently distributed in the population, in less than 12 years half of the IPUs would experience it.

Moreover, if we take into account only IPUs that had contact with the state the year before the survey, this proportion rises to 37 percent which makes bribery a significant mean of settling disputes with public agents. Our analysis of the determinants of corruption among IPUs shows that the mechanisms are not different from those prevailing in the formal sector. The larger firms, firms operating in transport are more likely to face predatory behavior by government officials. Moreover, our findings strongly suggest that experience with corruption drastically reduces firms' performances.

Then, policies designed to fight against corruption are needed; they do not need to be targeted on the informal sector. Although corruption doesn't seem to be widespread in the informal sector, the fight against corruption seems to be a key element of the success of policies aiming at increasing formalization.

Our study provides also sobering results concerning non-registration. Phase 2 data indicate that non-registration is rather an issue of weak law enforcement than of corruption, or in other words of a will to avoid predatory behavior by government officials seeking bribes from anyone with officially registered activities. Of the IPUs, 39 percent think that registrations are not compulsory and 21 percent don't know if they are required. Moreover the survey's results suggest that there is no will of the state to force IPUs to comply with the law. In the seven capital cities, only 6.2 percent of the heads of IPUs say they got into trouble with public agents the year before the survey.

## Notes

1  Fisman and Svensson's data come from an industrial survey, which implies that these firms are likely to be registered with the tax administration.
2  The IPUs are defined as firms with no fiscal register or not keeping formal book accounts.
3  This may partly explain the huge difference in the incidence of corruption between Svensson's study and ours (81 vs 4 percent).
4  For a description of the general characteristics of the informal sector in the WAEMU capital cities, see Brilleau et al. (2005).

# References

Ades, Alberto and Di Tella, Rafael (1997) "National Champions and Corruption: Some Unpleasant Interventionist Arithmetic", *Economic Journal, Royal Economic Society* 107(443): 1023–1042.

Ades, A. and Di Tella, R. (1999) "Rents, Competition, and Corruption", *American Economic Review* 89(4): 982–993.

Bearse, P., Glomm, G. and Janeba, E. (2000) "Why Poor Countries Rely Mostly on Redistribution in Kind", *Journal of Public Economics* 75(3): 463–481.

Brilleau, A., Ouedraogo, E. and Roubaud, F. (2005) "L'*enquête 1-2-3* dans les pays de l'UEMOA: la consolidation d'une méthode", *Statéco* 99: 15–170.

Buehn, A. and Schneider, F. (2012) "Shadow Economies Around the World: Novel Insights, Accepted Knowledge, and New Estimates", *International Tax Public Finance* 19(1): 139–171

de Soto, H. (1989) *The Other Path*. New York: Harper and Row.

Djankov, S. (2008) "A Response to 'Is Doing Business Damaging Business?'" *Journal of Comparative Economics*.

Dollar, D., Fisman, R. and Gatti, R. (2001) "Are Women Really the 'Fairer' Sex? Corruption and Women in Government", *Journal of Economic Behaviour and Organization* 46(4): 423–429.

Fisman, R. and Gatti, R. (2002) "Decentralization and Corruption: Evidence across Countries", *Journal of Public Economics* 83(3): 325–345.

Fisman, R. and Svensson, J. (2007) "Are Corruption and Taxation Really Harmful to Growth? Firm Level Evidence", *Journal of Development Economics* 83(1): 63–75.

Gatti, R., Paternostro, S. and Rigolini, J. (2003) "Individual Attitudes toward Corruption: Do Social Effects Matter?" Policy Research Working Paper Series 3122, Washington, DC: World Bank.

Hunt, J. (2004) "Trust and Bribery: The Role of the Quid Pro Quo and the Link with Crime", NBER Working Papers 10510, NBER.

Hunt, J. (2006) "How Corruption hits People When They are Down", NBER Working Papers 12490, NBER.

Hunt, J. and Laszlo, S. (2005) "Bribery: Who Pays, Who Refuses, What are the Payoffs?" NBER Working Papers 11635, NBER.

Huntington, S. (1968) *Political Order in Changing Societies*. New Haven, CT: Yale University Press.

ILO (2012) *Statistical Update on Employment in the Informal Economy*. Geneva: ILO.

Kaufmann, D. and Wei, S.-J. (1999) "Does 'Grease Money'Speed up the Wheels of Commerce?" NBER Working Paper 7093, NBER.

Lavallée, E. (2007) "Corruption, concurrence et développement: Une analyse économétrique à l'échelle des entreprises", *European Journal of Development Research* 19(2): 274–304.

Lavallée, E., Razafindrakoto, M. and Roubaud, F. (2010) "Ce qui engendre la corruption: Une analyse microéconomique sur données africaines", *Revue d'Economie du Développement* 3: 5–47.

Leff, N. (1964) "Economic Development through Bureaucratic Corruption", *American Behavioural Scientist* 8(2): 8–14.

Mauro, P. (1995) "Corruption and Growth", *Quarterly Journal of Economics* 60(3): 681–712.

Méon, P.-G. and Sekkat, K. (2005) "Does Corruption Grease or Sand the Wheels of Growth?" *Public Choice* 122(1–2): 69–97.

Méon, P.-G. and Weill, L. (2010) "Is Corruption an Efficient Grease?" *World Development* 38(3): 244–259.

Myrdal, G. (1968) *Asian Drama: An Inquiry into Poverty of Nations*. New York: Pantheon Books.

Rand, J. and Torm, N. (2012) "The Benefits of Formalization: Evidence from Vietnamese SMEs", *World Development* 40(5): 983–998.

Razafindrakoto, M. and Roubaud, F. (2010) "Are International Databases on Corruption Reliable? A Comparison of Expert Opinions Surveys and Household Surveys in Sub-Saharan Africa", *World Development* 38(8): 1057–1069.

Rose, R. (2013) "Why do Africans differs in Paying Bribes?" Working Paper 502, University of Strathclyde Glasgow.

Shleifer, A. (2004) "Does Competition destroy Ethical Behaviour?" *AEA Papers and Proceedings* 94(2): 414–418.

Shleifer, A. and Vishny, R. (1993) "Corruption", *Quarterly Journal of Economics* 108(3): 599–617.

Svensson, J. (2003) "Who must Pay Bribes and How Much? Evidence from a Cross-Section of Firms", *Quarterly Journal of Economics* 118(1): 207–230.

Swamy, A., Knack, S. and Azfar, O. (2001) "Gender and Corruption", *Journal of Development Economics* 64(1): 25–55.

Transparency International (2013a) *Corruption Perceptions Index 2013*. Berlin: TI.

Transparency International (2013b) *The Global Corruption Barometer 2013*. Berlin: TI.

Treisman, D. (2000) "The Causes of Corruption: A Cross-national Study", *Journal of Public Economics* 76(3): 399–457.

Van de Ven, W. and Van Praag, B. (1981) "The Demand for Deductibles in Private Health Insurance: A Probit Model with Sample Selection", *Journal of Econometrics* 17(2): 229–252.

Van Rijckeghem, C. and Weder, B. (1997) "Corruption and the Role of Temptation: Do Low Wages in Civil Service Cause Corruption?" IMF Working Paper, WP/97/73, Washington, DC.

Van Rijckeghem, Caroline and Weder, Beatrice (2001) "Bureaucratic Corruption and the Rate of Temptation: Do Wages in the Civil Service affect Corruption, and by How Much?" *Journal of Development Economics* 65(2): 307–331.

Vial, V. and Hanoteau, J. (2010) "Corruption, Manufacturing Plant Growth, and the Asian Paradox: Indonesian Evidence", *World Development* 38(5): 693–705.

# 9 Does forced solidarity hamper entrepreneurial activity?

## Evidence from seven West-African countries[1]

*Michael Grimm, Flore Gubert, Ousman Koriko, Jann Lay and Christophe J. Nordman*

In many parts of Sub-Saharan Africa a large share of informal firms does not grow over time, either in terms of employment, or in terms of invested physical capital. Reinvestment rates of profits seem to be generally low. The question is why this is the case? Many reasons might be evoked, ranging from capital market constraints, possibly in conjunction with non-convex production functions, to risk aversion and a lack of skills and business attitude. Some researchers think the cause is rooted in the family and kin of the entrepreneur. Potentially successful entrepreneurs would have problems to save, because they are exposed to high consumption demands by their family and kin, or at least that incentives to invest would be low, because the entrepreneur would anticipate that a large share of benefits will have to be shared with others. In the sociological literature this is often denoted as 'forced solidarity' or the 'dark side of social capital' (Portes and Sensenbrenner, 1993).

The idea that family and kinship ties may also imply adverse incentive effects is often mentioned in the anthropological literature (see, e.g. Barth, 1967) and was emphasized by modernization theorists but with very different nuances and clearly distinguished conclusions (see, e.g. Lewis, 1955; Meier and Baldwin, 1957; Bauer and Yamey, 1957; Hirschman, 1958). It is also discussed in the field of economic sociology as the downside of strong ties, which are also often referred to as 'bonding ties' (Granovetter, 1973, 1983, 1985; Barr, 2002). More recently the aspect has been taken up again by a few economists (see, e.g. Platteau, 2000; Hoff and Sen, 2006). Although acknowledging that family and kinship ties can be a vehicle for social contracts of mutual insurance in a context where markets for these goods and services do not exist, these authors argue that family and kinship ties may become an important obstacle in the process of transition. Opting out of such kin systems and refusing to comply with these obligations may be possible, but may result in strong sanctions and high psychological costs. If forced redistribution of this type is widespread it may partly explain the failure of many African micro and small enterprises to grow. As pointed out by Platteau (2000), it might also explain why minority entrepreneurs like the Indians in East Africa and the Lebanese and Syrians in West Africa are often so successful. These minorities are not directly exposed to requests of relatives and stand outside the complex web of social obligations.

To date, there is very little empirical backup for the existence of negative effects of social networks on entrepreneurial activities. Some related evidence however indicates that the composition and structure of the households matter for capital accumulation, for example that larger polygamous households find it more difficult to save and accumulate (Morrisson, 2006). Di Falco and Bulte (2009) find some evidence that kinship size is associated with higher budget shares for non-sharable goods. They also find evidence that compulsory sharing leads to free riding and attenuates incentives for self-protection against shocks (Di Falco and Bulte, 2010). Baland *et al.* (2007) analyse borrowing behaviour and find that some people take up credits even without a liquidity constraint – just to signal to their kin that they are unable to provide financial assistance. Anderson and Baland (2002) provide some evidence that women in Kenya participate in ROSCA (Rotating Savings and Credit Association) to protect savings against consumption claims from their husbands. Fafchamps (2002) finds a negative association between perceived 'fear of predation by relatives' and value added among agricultural traders in Madagascar; however, this is not the focus of his paper and he does not further discuss this result. Lastly, Jakiela and Ozier (2010) studied the problem of forced solidarity by conducting lab experiments in rural Kenyan villages. In these experiments, they randomly vary the observability of investment returns to test whether subjects reduce their income in order to keep it hidden. They find that participants who know that the outcome of their investment will be made public, choose decisions that are less profitable in expectation. They conclude that the risk pooling arrangements operating in the village and family are inefficient.

In this chapter, we explore the 'forced solidarity hypothesis' using a large sample of informal entrepreneurs covering seven economic capitals in West Africa. We distinguish between 'family and kinship ties', on the one hand, and 'social network capital', on the other. There is large consensus in the literature that the latter provides a wide range of benefits by reducing transaction costs, facilitating the access to information, helping to overcome the dilemmas of collective action, generating learning spin-offs and providing informal insurance (see e.g. Coleman, 1990; Fafchamps, 1996, 2001, 2002; Kranton, 1996; Woolcock, 2001; Minten and Fafchamps, 1999; Platteau, 2000; Knorringa and van Staveren, 2006). In line with La Ferrara (2007), we use family and kinship ties to refer to any form of blood relationship. The main difference of family and kinship ties, on the one hand, and a generic set of interacting individuals, on the other, is that family and kinship ties can be seen as largely exogenous and cannot be freely changed or only at a high psychological cost (La Ferrara, 2007).

The remainder of this chapter is organized as follows. The next section briefly describes our theoretical framework mainly explaining how sharing obligations may adversely affect the allocation of resources to the household business. We abstract from other constraints that have been shown to be relevant such as capital market imperfections or poor quality of public services. The third section presents the data. The fourth section explains how we measure the intensity of family and kinship ties. Then the main results are discussed in the following section before the conclusion.

## Theoretical framework

For the moment we focus on the potential adverse incentive effects of family and kinship ties, hence ignoring possible positive effects. We assume that urban households can potentially engage in a number of activities, among them the production and sale of goods and services and dependent wage work in someone else's firm. Moreover, we assume that value added generated in own productive activities is subject to a 'solidarity tax' imposed by the family and kin. Failing to pay this tax implies prohibitive social sanctions, for instance the denial of a burial in the home village. The share of the generated value added that is transferred to the family is assumed to depend on egalitarian norms prevailing among the entrepreneur's kin, on the size of the kin and on the costs of the family to observe the entrepreneur's business activity and value added. Wage income is not subject to such a tax (or significantly less). Our idea is that the kin can more easily observe the firm's value added than labour income from the market. This should in particular be true if firms exceed a certain size, operate from a fixed location, exceed a certain level of capital stock and employ non-family labour.

We assume that informal firms operate under a neoclassical production technology with constant returns to scale, using capital and labour subject to diminishing returns. In this case the solidarity tax will reduce the factor returns and hence entrepreneurs will allocate less capital and labour to their production activity and reallocate resources to alternative activities. Put differently, the solidarity tax on value added drives a wedge between the marginal factor products and real factor prices. *Ceteris paribus*, households allocate the less labour and capital to production the higher the tax rate. In the case of labour, this implies that with a higher tax less labour is hired or more family labour is supplied in dependent wage work outside the household. This hypothesis is tested in the empirical part of our chapter, i.e. we test the link between the intensity of family and kinship ties and the use of capital and labour in informal production.

However, family and kinship ties may also have positive effects on the business activity. We assume that these positive effects exist in particular in the presence of imperfect capital and labour markets. Such imperfections may arise if, for instance, access to capital is limited, if there is a shortage of labour with certain skills or if moral hazard problems arise because of high supervision costs. Hence, such positive effects could affect the use of capital and labour at least through three different channels: (i) family and kinship ties may act as insurance against the effects of shocks that could diminish the stock of physical capital and labour; (ii) family and kinship ties may help entrepreneurs to obtain information about investment opportunities and where to hire reliable labour; and (iii) within families and kin groups both factors, capital and labour, may be rotated according to individual needs. If these effects exist they may partly or even fully offset the adverse effects that arise from the solidarity tax.

## Data

We use a set of surveys called 1-2-3 surveys or in its French synonym 'Enquêtes 1-2-3' covering seven economic capitals of the West-African Economic and Monetary Union (WAEMU) in the early 2000s.[2] A 1-2-3 survey is a multi-layer survey organized in three phases and specially designed to study the informal sector (Brilleau *et al.*, 2005). Phase 1 is a representative labour force survey collecting detailed information about individual socio-demographic characteristics and employment. Phase 2 is a survey which interviews a sub-sample of informal production units identified in Phase 1. The focus of this phase is on the characteristics of the entrepreneurs and their production unit, including the characteristics of employed workers. Firms are defined as informal if (a) they do not have written formal accounts and/or (b) are not registered with the tax administration. Phase 3 is a household expenditure survey interviewing (again) a representative sub-sample of Phase 1 and hence part of the Phase 2 households. Hence, for a (representative) sub-sample of informal entrepreneurs we have information from Phase 1 and Phase 2 ($n=6{,}580$) and, again for a sub-sample, information from all three phases ($n=1{,}511$). Phase 3 is not available for Abidjan.

In our empirical analysis we focus on internal migrants, i.e. entrepreneurs who migrated from rural areas or secondary cities to the economic capital and started an informal business. Analysing urban migrants has the advantage of looking at entrepreneurs who usually have two different types of family and kinship ties; ties located at their destination and ties leading to their point of departure. We assume that the latter are heavily shaped by traditional norms. Comparing the role of both will provide interesting insights.

In line with our theoretical model, we use the household as the observation unit. Hence, we aggregate all enterprises in a given household into one single enterprise. This aggregation is done as follows: we define the main firm in the household as the firm that generates the highest value added. Then we sum up within each household total labour, total capital and total value added. Regarding all other characteristics, such as the sector of the firm and characteristics of the owner, we keep the values from the main firm. There may be various reasons why a household owns several enterprises. Diversifying entrepreneurial activities may represent an optimal portfolio choice in the presence of activities with different expected returns and associated risks. Enterprises may also belong to different household members that do not necessarily pool their resources. Finally, splitting activities may serve as a strategy to reduce the 'solidarity tax', because it is easier to hide several smaller enterprises than one large enterprise.

Table 9.1 presents descriptive statistics of the migrant entrepreneurs, their enterprises and the households they belong to. We see that about half of all entrepreneurs in our sample are men, they are on average 38 years old, about 43 per cent of them speak French and 72 per cent do not have any diploma. We also coded a variable for ethnicity. In ethnic group '1' are those entrepreneurs who belong to the largest ethnic group in their country. Ethnic group '2' are those who

*Table 9.1* Descriptive statistics

|  | Mean | SD |
|---|---|---|
| *Owner characteristics* | | |
| Male (=1) | 0.509 | – |
| Age owner | 38.4 | 11.4 |
| Speaks French (=1) | 0.434 | – |
| No diploma | 0.718 | – |
| Primary completed | 0.179 | – |
| Some secondary | 0.048 | – |
| Other post primary | 0.055 | – |
| Ethnic group 1 | 0.420 | – |
| Ethnic group 2 | 0.184 | – |
| Ethnic group 3 | 0.195 | – |
| *Household characteristics* | | |
| Household size | 6.3 | 4.2 |
| Only informal firm | 0.795 | – |
| Public wage earner | 0.097 | – |
| Private formal wage earner | 0.100 | – |
| Other combination | 0.008 | – |
| *Firm characteristics* | | |
| Age of firm | 8.6 | 8.6 |
| Clothing and apparel | 0.096 | – |
| Other manufact. and food | 0.143 | – |
| Construction | 0.087 | – |
| Wholesale/retail shops | 0.114 | – |
| Petty trading | 0.272 | – |
| Hotels and restaurants | 0.073 | – |
| Repair services | 0.053 | – |
| Transport | 0.052 | – |
| Other services | 0.110 | – |
| Ann. VA in intl. $ PPP | 5,556 | 28,459 |
| Monthly hours owner | 225 | 127 |
| Total monthly hours | 381 | 379 |
| Total staff incl. owner | 1.9 | 1.6 |
| Hired paid staff | 0.2 | 0.9 |
| No physical capital (=1) | 0.126 | – |
| Physical. cap. in intl. $ PPP | 1,029 | 3,647 |
| Physical cap. (lowest 33%) | 11 | 12 |
| Physical cap. (middle 33%) | 127 | 75 |
| Physical cap. (highest 33%) | 2,953 | 5,865 |
| No. of firms | 1.3 | 0.6 |
| *Country* | | |
| Benin | 0.159 | – |
| Burkina Faso | 0.141 | – |
| Côte d'Ivoire | 0.162 | – |
| Mali | 0.178 | – |
| Niger | 0.062 | – |
| Senegal | 0.128 | – |
| Togo | 0.169 | – |
| N | 2,369 | – |

Source: *1-2-3 Surveys*, WAEMU 2001/02; own computations.

belong to the second largest group and so on. One can see that about 80 per cent of all entrepreneurs fall into one of the three largest groups in their country.

The next block in Table 9.1 reports the activity portfolio of the entrepreneur's household. These portfolios consider all primary and secondary activities of all household members. About 79.5 per cent of all entrepreneurs live in households that rely only on informal firms. In some of these households, one or several household members are additionally engaged in some dependent informal wage work. Only 19.8 per cent of all entrepreneurs live in households that have in addition to their enterprise at least one wage worker in the public sector (9.7 per cent) or in the formal private sector (10 per cent). The activity portfolio is a potentially important factor of firm performance, as it may influence the capacity to save, to take a loan and to invest in a context of incomplete capital markets. It may also determine the business' network size and shape the relation to the public sector and hence affect access to public services and exposure to corruption.

The mean age of these enterprises is about 8.6 years. The largest sector is 'petty trading'. The smallest sectors are 'transport' and 'repair services', which are both rather capital intensive. The average annual value added is about 5,600 Intl. 2005 $ PPP. Entrepreneurs work on average 225 hours per month in their firm. In total, they use about 381 hours of labour per month. Mean employment is about 1.9 including the owner and, on average, only one out of four enterprises hires a paid employee. Of all enterprises, 12.6 per cent do not report any invested physical capital. Hence, it is not surprising to see that the mean capital stock for the lower third in the distribution of capital is just about 10 Intl. 2005 $ PPP. On average, the households in the sample have 1.3 enterprises.

## Measuring the potential intensity of family and kinship ties

From our data set, we have derived the following proxies of the potential intensity of family and kinship ties, which in turn should determine the size of the solidarity tax, but also the possible positive network effects in case of imperfect capital and labour markets. First, the share of the population from the same ethnic group in the cluster in which a household resides. This share is computed from Phase 1. Clusters correspond to neighbourhoods in each of the agglomerations represented in our sample. There are about 125 per country (city) and they cover a population from about 300 up to 35,000. This measure of ethnic concentration is an obvious measure of the potential intensity of family and kinship ties. The higher the concentration of the own kin group in the neighbourhood, the higher the pressure to share earnings. However, a higher concentration of the own kin group may also mean more support for *own* entrepreneurial activities. Hence, it is an empirical question whether positive or negative effects dominate. Both effects might be at work, probably off-setting each other to some extent. This would imply in turn that we will assess the 'net effect' of family and kinship ties in our empirical analysis. We also have to be aware of the fact that this first social network proxy cannot be considered as fully exogenous given that location is a choice. Our second proxy for the potential intensity of family and kinship ties is the share of the population in a cluster that grew up in the same area as the enterprise owner – i.e. in the same region or district of the country. Again we assume that the higher the share, the higher the potential pressure for redistribution. But here again, the measure will capture both the potential negative and positive effects of these ties. Third, we use the geographical distance to the entrepreneur's region or district of origin. We assume that a longer distance makes it more difficult and costly to observe the entrepreneur's activities and productivity and hence redistributive pressure should decline with distance. Moreover, the costs of making transfers may also increase with distance in the absence of a formal banking system. However, this should not affect the amount that is transferred but rather the decision to transfer and the frequency of transfers. Fourth, we use the number of years the migrant has been living in the capital. The idea behind this is that family and kinship ties may not only erode with distance but also with time – an 'out of sight, out of mind' effect. Table 9.2 shows the descriptive statistics for these variables.

## Redistributive pressure, capital accumulation, labour demand and the owner's effort level

### Specification and general results

We now examine whether the potential (not actual) intensity of family and kinship ties has any adverse incentive effects. We focus on three different production inputs of the (informal) household firm: physical capital, $K$, total number of employed working hours (including those provided by the owner), $L_i^T$, and working hours provided by the owner alone, $L_i^O$. It has been tested that all these factors are indeed positively related to value added, i.e. they are relevant production inputs in our context (see Grimm *et al.*, 2011). Hence, we run the following three regressions:

$$\log K_i = \beta_{K_0} + \beta_{K_1} P_i + X'_{ji}\beta_{K_2} + Z'_i\beta_{K_3} + S'_i\beta_{K_4} + C'_i\beta_{K_5} + \vartheta_{K_i} \qquad (9.1)$$

$$\log L_i^T = \beta_{L_0^T} + \beta_{L_1^T} P_i + \beta_{L_2^T} \log K_i + X'_{ji}\beta_{L_3^T} + Z'_i\beta_{L_4^T} + S'_i\beta_{L_5^T} + C'_i\beta_{L_6^T} + \vartheta_{L_i^T} \quad (9.2)$$

$$\log L_i^O = \beta_{L_0^O} + \beta_{L_1^O} P_i + \beta_{L_2^O} \log K_i + X'_{ji}\beta_{L_3^O} + Z'_i\beta_{L_4^O} + S'_i\beta_{L_5^O} + C'_i\beta_{L_6^O} + \vartheta_{L_i^O} \quad (9.3)$$

*Table 9.2* Proxies of the potential intensity of family and kinship ties

|  | Mean | SD |
|---|---|---|
| Share same ethnic group | 0.373 | 0.266 |
| Share same origin | 0.038 | 0.043 |
| Distance to origin | 188.5 | 169.4 |
| Time since migration | 17.7 | 11.7 |
| N |  | 2,369 |

Source: *1-2-3 Surveys*, WAEMU 2001/02; own computations.

where $P_i$ is the vector of variables used to measure the potential intensity of family and kinship ties faced by household $i$. $X_{ji}$ is a vector of characteristics specific to the entrepreneur $j$ residing in household $i$, such as age, gender, education and migrant status. $Z_i$ is a vector of household characteristics such as ethnicity and the activity portfolio of the household. The vectors $S_i$ and $C_i$ control for sector and country effects respectively. Controlling for sector effects is important here, since production technologies are likely to differ between sectors. For instance, petty trade is less capital intensive than most transport services. Moreover, sector choice may, in turn, be correlated with (perceived) redistributive pressure. The terms $\vartheta$ are the respective error terms.[3]

In what follows, we discuss the results of each regression starting with the model that looks at the association between family and kinship ties and the total stock of physical capital used. Given that entrepreneurs may accumulate physical capital in particular in the beginning of their activity, we estimate the model for those migrants who are in the economic capital for less than five years (columns (1) and (2)) and less than 15 years, respectively (columns (3) and (4)). This sample reduction should lessen the problem of measurement error and increase the homogeneity of the sampled migrants. The results are shown in Table 9.3. The first specification uses a simple linear regression model (columns (1) and (3)). The second specification uses a tobit model (columns (2) and (4)) to account for the fact that 13.6 per cent of all entrepreneurs do not use any physical capital.

The proxies for family and kinship ties – our main variables of interest – are partly significant in the smaller sample of recent migrants. In this sample, the effects associated with distance (columns (1) and (2)), turn out significant. In contrast, we cannot detect any significant effects of local family ties, i.e. kinship density in the neighbourhood. The positive coefficient of the distance variable is consistent with the idea that redistributive pressure and the related adverse incentive effects get diluted with distance. The further away an entrepreneur is from the family, the higher the investment in the household firm. The estimates in columns (1) and (2) suggest that an increase of the distance from 100 km to 200 km implies an increase in the size of capital stock by about 30 per cent, which is an economically important effect. In columns (3) and (4), i.e. using the sample that also includes those migrants who have been living in the city for a longer period, we find a positive effect of 'years since migration' on capital use. This is consistent with the view that family ties may become weaker over time and hence increase the incentives to invest.

These findings are in line with those by Beegle *et al.* (2008). The authors find for Tanzania a positive effect of distance on consumption growth, i.e. migrants that are further away from their village of origin experienced higher long-term consumption growth than those that stay closer. They interpret this effect as the result of a positive correlation between favourable work and business opportunities and distance, i.e. the larger the migration radius the higher the potential returns from migration. They also show that migrants share less than their non-migrant counterparts, controlling for household fixed effects, i.e. migrants

*Table 9.3* Family and kinship ties and household firm's use of physical capital

| | (1) | (2) | (3) | (4) |
|---|---|---|---|---|
| | Migrants, 5 years and less in the capital | | Migrants, 15 years and less in the capital | |
| | OLS | Tobit | OLS | Tobit |
| Share same ethnic group | 0.310 | 0.291 | 0.158 | 0.170 |
| | (0.549) | (0.581) | (0.347) | (0.359) |
| Share same origin | 0.464 | 0.370 | 0.271 | 0.062 |
| | (3.105) | (3.085) | (1.972) | (1.803) |
| Ln distance to origin | 0.263* | 0.316* | 0.002 | 0.009 |
| | (0.152) | (0.161) | (0.089) | (0.098) |
| Years since migration | 0.032 | 0.042 | 0.033** | 0.036** |
| | (0.067) | (0.083) | (0.016) | (0.017) |
| Male (=1) | 1.061*** | 1.118*** | 0.878*** | 0.917*** |
| | (0.316) | (0.337) | (0.178) | (0.197) |
| Age owner | 0.041*** | 0.047*** | 0.032*** | 0.036*** |
| | (0.014) | (0.015) | (0.008) | (0.010) |
| Speaks French (=1) | 0.297 | 0.384 | 0.341* | 0.364* |
| | (0.345) | (0.388) | (0.182) | (0.219) |
| No diploma | (Ref.) | (Ref.) | (Ref.) | (Ref.) |
| Primary completed | −0.529 | −0.753* | −0.212 | −0.300 |
| | (0.391) | (0.443) | (0.220) | (0.241) |
| Some secondary | −0.218 | −0.355 | −0.282 | −0.357 |
| | (0.743) | (0.770) | (0.347) | (0.383) |
| Other post primary | −0.718 | −1.051 | −0.328 | −0.485 |
| | (0.710) | (0.678) | (0.369) | (0.377) |
| Ethnic group 1 | (Ref.) | (Ref.) | (Ref.) | (Ref.) |
| Ethnic group 2 | −0.700* | −0.868* | −0.524** | −0.586** |
| | (0.399) | (0.503) | (0.215) | (0.249) |
| Ethnic group 3 | 0.030 | 0.068 | −0.084 | −0.086 |
| | (0.311) | (0.353) | (0.180) | (0.211) |
| Age of firm | −0.011 | −0.019 | 0.001 | 0.001 |
| | (0.023) | (0.027) | (0.013) | (0.016) |
| *Only informal firm* | | | | |
| Public wage earner | 0.416 | 0.489 | 0.345 | 0.397 |
| | (0.438) | (0.489) | (0.235) | (0.268) |
| Private formal wage earner | 0.550 | 0.556 | 0.222 | 0.252 |
| | (0.400) | (0.439) | (0.235) | (0.264) |
| Other combination | −0.849 | −1.093 | −0.972 | −1.158 |
| | (1.515) | (1.353) | (0.891) | (0.788) |
| Sector effects | Yes | Yes | Yes | Yes |
| Country effects | Yes | Yes | Yes | Yes |
| Constant | 1.972* | 1.592 | 3.714*** | 3.512*** |
| | (1.034) | (1.140) | (0.589) | (0.664) |
| R-squared | 0.215 | | 0.185 | |
| N | 370 | 370 | 1,117 | 1,117 |

Source: *1-2-3 Surveys*, WAEMU 2001/02; own estimations.

Notes
Robust standard errors in parentheses (clustered at the neighbourhood level).
* $p<0.10$. ** $p<0.05$. *** $p<0.01$.

transfer less than their brothers who stayed at home. This finding would also be consistent with a situation in which the perceived obligation to remit declines with distance helping to protect savings for profitable investments. In our case, we consider only migrants who went to the economic capital, so the potential pool of business opportunities is constant for a given country and only distance varies across migrants. What could however drive our results is that distance may be correlated with unobserved characteristics of entrepreneurs, in a sense that high ability entrepreneurs are willing to migrate further. If these (unobserved) abilities also drive investment in physical capital, then the positive effect of distance may just pick up this ability effect. In addition, distance might be correlated with household wealth, because richer households can more easily bear the costs of migration over longer distances. However, these differences in the fixed costs of migration are likely to be very small in the sample of countries we consider, in particular in relation to annual earnings of a migrant. Below we present some robustness checks in order to rule out these potential biases.

With respect to the control variables, we find that the total capital stock is higher for enterprises owned by men than for women and that it increases with age. Education is not significant in most cases. Knowledge of French enters significantly only in the larger sample. There are no significant effects associated with other activities in the household, i.e. the capital stock is not significantly higher in households that also have earnings from wage work in the public or private formal sector. This may be unexpected, but in these households the informal firm is very frequently just a secondary activity of the household and is often managed by the spouse of the household head or one of his children. Investment is then probably kept at a relatively low level. Sector and country effects are highly significant (coefficients not reported).

Next, we turn to the regressions that explore the effects of redistributive pressure on labour input into the household firm (Table 9.4). Again, we use two different samples. A sample that is limited to entrepreneurs who have spent less than 15 years in the capital (columns (1) and (3)) and a sample with all migrant entrepreneurs (columns (2) and (4)). Given that we now look at a flow and not a stock measure, recall bias (regarding the assessment of the replacement value of assets that were bought a long time ago) is not a problem anymore and hence there is no need to limit the sample to very recent migrants. We first examine the total amount of working hours employed in the enterprise (columns (1) and (2)). There are again interesting effects associated with the four measures of the potential intensity of family and kinship ties. The share of people in the neighbourhood that belongs to the same ethnic group as the entrepreneur has a significant positive effect. Likewise has the share of the population in the neighbourhood that grew up in the same area of origin. However, being closer to the area of origin has a significant negative effect, i.e. the coefficient associated with distance is again positive. Finally, the number of years since migration is positively correlated with the use of total labour hours. The effects do not differ much between the two samples. An increase by ten percentage points in the share of people in the neighbourhood belonging to the same ethnic group

*Table 9.4* Family and kinship ties and household firm's use of labour (OLS)

| | (1) | (2) | (3) | (4) |
|---|---|---|---|---|
| | *Ln total labour hours* | | *Ln total labour hours owner* | |
| | *Migrants, 15 years and less in the capital* | *All migrants* | *Migrants, 15 years and less in the capital* | *All migrants* |
| Share same ethnic group | 0.281** | 0.248*** | 0.217** | 0.117 |
| | (0.132) | (0.096) | (0.097) | (0.072) |
| Share same origin | 1.340** | 1.356*** | 0.781* | 0.643* |
| | (0.532) | (0.444) | (0.428) | (0.361) |
| Ln distance to origin | 0.087*** | 0.057** | 0.048* | 0.032* |
| | (0.033) | (0.024) | (0.026) | (0.019) |
| Years since migration | 0.012* | 0.005** | 0.005 | 0.000 |
| | (0.006) | (0.002) | (0.005) | (0.002) |
| Ln physical capital | 0.176*** | 0.169*** | 0.069*** | 0.059*** |
| | (0.019) | (0.013) | (0.014) | (0.010) |
| No capital | 0.402*** | 0.367*** | 0.118 | 0.058 |
| | (0.124) | (0.092) | (0.097) | (0.069) |
| Male (=1) | 0.334*** | 0.298*** | 0.359*** | 0.284*** |
| | (0.073) | (0.054) | (0.054) | (0.039) |
| Age owner | −0.002 | −0.000 | −0.003 | −0.000 |
| | (0.005) | (0.003) | (0.003) | (0.002) |
| Speaks French (=1) | −0.003 | 0.044 | −0.018 | −0.010 |
| | (0.078) | (0.056) | (0.058) | (0.042) |
| No diploma | (Ref.) | (Ref.) | (Ref.) | (Ref.) |
| Primary completed | −0.062 | −0.024 | −0.058 | −0.008 |
| | (0.091) | (0.066) | (0.065) | (0.047) |
| Some secondary | 0.119 | 0.147 | −0.056 | 0.005 |
| | (0.144) | (0.097) | (0.105) | (0.070) |
| Other post primary | −0.194 | −0.147 | −0.418*** | −0.280*** |
| | (0.150) | (0.119) | (0.121) | (0.094) |
| Ethnic group 1 | (Ref.) | (Ref.) | (Ref.) | (Ref.) |
| Ethnic group 2 | −0.208 | −0.162** | −0.139 | −0.104* |
| | (0.130) | (0.079) | (0.092) | (0.058) |
| Ethnic group 3 | 0.076 | 0.120** | 0.028 | 0.052 |
| | (0.073) | (0.051) | (0.057) | (0.038) |
| Age of firm | 0.005 | 0.004 | 0.003 | −0.000 |
| | (0.006) | (0.003) | (0.004) | (0.002) |
| Only informal firm | (Ref.) | (Ref.) | (Ref.) | (Ref.) |
| Public wage earner | −0.101 | −0.094 | 0.074 | −0.088 |
| | (0.114) | (0.071) | (0.082) | (0.060) |
| Private formal wage earner | −0.105 | −0.047 | −0.033 | −0.015 |
| | (0.100) | (0.064) | (0.080) | (0.054) |
| Other combination | −0.321 | −0.567* | −0.347** | −0.403** |
| | (0.244) | (0.307) | (0.175) | (0.184) |
| Sector effects | Yes | Yes | Yes | Yes |
| Country effects | Yes | Yes | Yes | Yes |

*continued*

*Table 9.4* Continued

|  | (1) | (2) | (3) | (4) |
|---|---|---|---|---|
|  | Ln total labour hours | | Ln total labour hours owner | |
|  | Migrants, 15 years and less in the capital | All migrants | Migrants, 15 years and less in the capital | All migrants |
| Constant | 3.865*** | 3.934*** | 4.309*** | 4.428*** |
|  | (0.289) | (0.200) | (0.218) | (0.147) |
| R-squared | 0.208 | 0.206 | 0.136 | 0.116 |
| N | 1,116 | 2,288 | 1,116 | 2,288 |

Source: *1-2-3 Surveys*, WAEMU 2001/02; own estimations.

Notes

Robust standard errors in parentheses (clustered at the neighbourhood level).

\* $p<0.10$.

\*\* $p<0.05$.

\*\*\* $p<0.01$.

Ln = (Natural) logarithm.

increases the amount of labour hours used by 2.8 per cent. Evaluated at the sample mean this implies approximately 10.7 hours per month. If the proportion of people who share the same origin is increased by one percentage point (sample mean is about 3.8 per cent) labour hours employed increase by 1.4 per cent. An increase of distance by 100 per cent is associated with an increase of employed labour hours by about 6 to 9 per cent. Hence, the results suggest that ties linked to the city – or local ties – are associated with positive effects whereas ties to the village have negative effects. With respect to the control variables, we find that firms owned by men employ more labour and that the use of labour increases with the size of the capital stock. Age, knowledge of French, education and the household's activity portfolio are not significant.

Finally, we explore the effects of family and kinship ties on working hours provided by the owner alone (columns (3) and (4)). Again we find that local ties within the city are positively correlated with working hours. For instance, an increase by ten percentage points in the share of people in the neighbourhood belonging to the same ethnic group increases the owner's labour hours by about 1 to 2 per cent, which corresponds at the sample mean to about three to 5.5 hours per month. Similarly, if the share of the population from the same area of origin increases by one percentage point, working hours increase by about 0.7 per cent or about two hours at the sample mean. We also find positive effects of the distance to the area of origin, but not for years since migration. More distant migrant entrepreneurs use more of their time for their production activity. Here, a decrease in the distance by 100 per cent, decreases labour hours provided by the owner by about 4 per cent or 11.5 hours at the sample mean. As the estimated coefficients for total labour are higher than those for the owner's labour alone, adverse incentives affect both own and hired labour.

### Results disaggregated by gender

The results above have shown that – controlling for sector effects – firms managed by men employ systematically more labour and physical capital than enterprises managed by women. We now test whether our proxies for redistributive pressure have a different effect if we estimate equations (9.1) to (9.3) separately for men and women. In our sample 50 per cent of all firms are managed by women.[4] One may expect that women are more likely than men to spend on household public goods and children's health and education. The potential pressure to spend each additional dollar earned on these goods may discourage women from expanding their businesses.

Regarding the use of physical capital, we find that the positive local effects of family and kin ties associated with the share of people of the same village of origin and the same ethnic group are more pronounced for men than for women. The effect of distance to the village of origin on capital use is insignificant for both, men and women, but has at least the same sign as in the joint sample. With respect to the use of labour, men seem to rely more on persons from the same village of origin, whereas women rely more on persons from the same ethnic group. The distance effect on labour is also larger for women and is highly significant. This might be the case because women who are closer to their village of origin have closer links with the family there and thus are involved more intensively in activities unrelated to their business (including more frequent visits to the family). These results are presented in full detail in Grimm *et al.* (2011). There the interested reader can also find an analysis by country and sector. However, the limited sample size leads to rather fragile results when we disaggregate along these two dimensions.

### Robustness checks

To rule out the possibility that a correlation between distance and unobserved characteristics of entrepreneurs biases our results, we re-estimate equations (9.1) to (9.3) for various sub-samples that are limited to entrepreneurs that migrated *at least* a certain distance away from their area of origin. The idea is that a migrant who stays relatively close to his origin, say 5 km, may indeed differ substantially in observable and unobservable characteristics from someone who has migrated over considerably larger distances, say 100 km. In contrast, the latter migrant may not be very different from a migrant who moved 150 km. In other words, the relationship between distance and unobserved characteristics is likely to be non-linear. It turned out that the estimated effects are very robust, hence we are confident that distance does not just capture systematic differences in effort-related unobservables between internal migrants with different distance to their area of origin. The details of this robustness check are again shown in Grimm *et al.* (2011). Another aspect should be kept in mind. We only consider migrants who decided to migrate to the economic capital of their country. We may assume that this decision is often taken whatever the distance to the capital is. In other words, migrants do not so much choose between places of different distance to their home, but rather whether they migrate to one of the secondary cities or to the economic capital. In particular in our sample of West-African countries, most of which have one major large urban centre and only smaller secondary cities and towns, the differences between both types of destinations are quite pronounced. Hence, we may argue that all those who opted for the economic capital share similar unobservable characteristics implying a relatively small potential bias associated with our distance measure.

To provide further support for our findings and to examine specifically the role of 'forced remittances', we compute an alternative measure of redistributive pressure using the information on actual transfers. More precisely, we regress 'transfers given' on total household consumption expenditures. The residual of this regression can be interpreted as an indicator for whether a household pays more or less transfers than the average household conditional on its consumption level. In this regression we control for age, gender and education of the household head as well as the activity portfolio of the household and country effects. The consumption aggregate also includes self-consumption and received transfers and is thus an adequate measure of the resources available in the household. The residual that we label 'excess transfers' is then used as a regressor in our equations of physical capital, employed total hours of labour and supplied labour hours by the owner of the firm. Again the details of this exercise are presented in Grimm *et al.* (2011). We find that predicted excess transfers are significantly negatively associated with the amount of physical capital used. A 10 per cent increase in excess transfers reduces the amount of physical capital used by about 0.5 per cent. The effects associated with labour input are also negative, but only borderline significant. However, actual transfers are only available for a small – though representative – sub-sample of households, which makes it somewhat more difficult to obtain precise estimates.

## Conclusion

On the one hand our findings confirm the positive aspects that are often associated with social capital in particular in contexts where market mechanisms fail. Local family and kinship ties within the city enhance the use of labour inputs. This may happen because local ties help to overcome labour market imperfections. However, we also find some support for the hypothesis that redistributive pressure tied to the village leads to adverse incentive effects and that these adverse incentive effects seem to get diluted with distance. We find that looser ties are correlated with a higher capital and labour inputs, in particular for women. Greater distance from home may hence make it easier to protect savings from abusive demands. We can rule out that this result is driven by unobservables that would determine both the willingness and ability to migrate far and the ability to run an enterprise. We also find weak evidence that the migration duration – controlling for the enterprise age – is positively correlated with the use of capital and labour. We also show that migrants with several enterprises transfer less to their families than those with only one firm. This is consistent with the hypothesis that some entrepreneurs prefer to invest in several small activities instead of expanding an existing firm; an expansion that would probably send a signal of entrepreneurial success to the entrepreneur's kin. Such behaviour would also partly explain why we see so many micro firms.

Our analysis takes a relatively static perspective and ignores that remittances from urban migrants to the village may be part of the migration contract and serve to pay back the costs of migration. This limitation, however, should not invalidate our conclusions. Even with such a contract, we would expect migrants to just maximize their profits, i.e. use their resources optimally, and then redistribute part of their profits to the family. If such a contract implied adverse incentive effects on entrepreneurial activities, the contract would be inefficient.

We think this chapter sheds new light on the debate about the 'dark side of social capital'. However, the intention is definitely not to deny the substantial evidence for all the positive aspects associated with social capital in particular in contexts in which market mechanisms fail. However, social capital can take many forms and its accumulation can only partly be controlled by the entrepreneur. As we argued in this chapter, family ties as one special form of social capital are at least to some extent exogenous and may imply conflicting interests. How can policy take this into account? We think two dimensions of sharing have to be distinguished: sharing that is mainly motivated by insurance considerations and sharing that is mainly motivated by egalitarian norms. Sharing that serves as an insurance device and which sends out adverse incentives because it is excessive or at least not 'fair', can be addressed through the provision of formal insurance. One of the most important types of shocks rural households are exposed to is a health shock, both in terms of frequency and financial burden. Hence, if for example health insurance becomes available the need for informal insurance may decline. This is thus a further argument for the roll out of social health insurance with which some African countries have recently started to experiment (e.g. Ghana, Rwanda, Ethiopia). Obviously, implementing insurance comes with its own problems, but these problems need to be solved anyway if health insurance is the primary objective. Further benefits might be achieved to offer in addition other types of insurance together with health insurance as well as credit and savings devices as then several often interdependent constraints can be addressed simultaneously.

Sharing that is based on pure egalitarian norms is more difficult to tackle. It would neither be desirable nor possible to change norms by force, i.e. without changing the environment that conditions the same. However, as with many other traditions it is quite likely that such norms change as an economy develops. The strong positive effects related to family and kinship ties in the city we find suggest that such ties have the potential to enhance entrepreneurial activity. They are also an indication of factor market failures that policies may be able to address, possibly by mimicking such support networks.

More generally, we have shown elsewhere (Grimm *et al.*, 2012), that in the sector of small and micro enterprises there is a substantial share of firms that have the potential to grow if constraining factors are removed. This study points to one particular constraint which so far has received a lot of attention in the anthropological literature but only little in private sector development approaches.

## Notes

1 This research is part of a project entitled 'Unlocking Potential: Tackling Economic, Institutional and Social Constraints of Informal Entrepreneurship in Sub-Saharan Africa' (www.iss.nl/informality) funded by the Austrian, German, Norwegian and Korean governments through the World Bank's Multi Donor Trust Fund Project: 'Labor Markets, Job Creation, and Economic Growth, Scaling up Research, Capacity Building, and Action on the Ground'. The financial support is gratefully acknowledged. We also thank participants at conferences and workshops in Cape Town (IZA/World Bank), Hanoi (DIAL/VASS), Paris (PSE) and The Hague (ISS) for useful comments and suggestions.

2 These urban centres are Abidjan, Bamako, Cotonou, Dakar, Niamey, Lomé and Oua-gadougou. The surveys have been carried out by AFRISTAT and the National Statistical Institutes (INS) with the support of DIAL as part of the Regional Programme of Statistical Support for Multilateral Surveillance (PARSTAT) between 2001 and 2003. For a more detailed description of the data see Brilleau *et al.* (2005).

3 To reduce a bias due to measurement and reporting errors, we trim the data and drop influential outliers from our sample that we identify by the DFITS-statistic (see Belsley *et al.*, 1980). Depending on the estimation, this procedure removes between 25 and 100 observations from our sample.

4 Note that this share is higher, if individual firms are considered, i.e. if firms are not aggregated at the household level and coded as being managed by the manager of the largest firm in the households (in terms of value added).

## References

Anderson, S. and Baland, J.-M. (2002) The Economics of Roscas and Intrahousehold Resource Allocation. *Quarterly Journal of Economics*, 117 (3): 963–995.

Baland, J.-M., Guirkinger, C. and Mali, C. (2007) Pretending to be Poor: Borrowing to Escape Forced Solidarity in Cameroon. Mimeo.

Barr, A.M. (2002) The Functional Diversity and Spillover Effects of Social Capital. *Journal of African Economies*, 11 (1): 90–113.

Barth, F. (1967) On the Study of Social Change. *American Anthropologist* (new series), 69 (6): 661–669.

Bauer P.T. and Yamey, B.S. (1957) *The Economics of Under-developed Countries*. Cambridge University Press, Cambridge.

Beegle, K., De Weerdt, J. and Dercon, S. (2008) Migration and Economic Mobility in Tanzania: Evidence from a Tracking Survey. World Bank Policy Research Working Paper 4798, World Bank, Washington DC.

Belsley, D.A., Kuh, E. and Welsch, R.E. (1980) *Regression Diagnostics: Identifying Influential Data and Sources of Collinearity*. John Wiley, New York.

Brilleau, A., Ouedraogo, E. and Roubaud, F. (2005) L'Enquête 1-2-3 dans les Principales Agglomérations de l'UEMOA: la Consolidation d'une Méthode. *Stateco*, 99, 15–19.

Coleman, J. (1990) *Foundations of Social Theory*. Harvard University Press, Cambridge MA.

Di Falco, S. and Bulte, E. (2009) The Dark Side of Social Capital: Kinship, Consumption, and Investment. Mimeo, LSE and Wageningen University.

Di Falco, S. and Bulte, E. (2010) Social Capital and Weather Shocks in Ethiopia: Climate Change and Culturally-induced Poverty Traps. Mimeo, LSE and Wageningen University.

Fafchamps, F. (1996) The Enforcement of Commercial Contracts in Ghana. *World Development*, 24 (3): 427–448.

Fafchamps, F. (2001) Networks, Communities, and Markets in Sub-Saharan Africa: Implications for Firm Growth and Investment. *Journal of African Economies*, 10: 119–142.

Fafchamps, F. (2002) Returns to Social Network Capital among Traders. *Oxford Economic Papers*, 54 (2): 173–206.

Fafchamps, M., McKenzie, D., Quinn, S. and Woodruff, C. (2011) When is Capital enough to get Female Microenterprises Growing? Evidence from a Randomized Experiment in Ghana. Mimeo, University of Oxford.

Granovetter, M. (1973) The Strength of Weak Ties. *American Journal of Sociology*, 78: 1360–1380.

Granovetter, M. (1983) The Strength of Weak Ties: A Network Theory Revisited. *Sociological Theory*, 1: 201–233.

Granovetter, M. (1985) Economic Action and Social Structure: The Problem of Embeddedness. *American Journal of Sociology*, 91 (3): 481–510.

Grimm, M., Gubert, F., Koriko, O., Lay, J. and Nordman, C.J. (2011) Kinship-Ties and Entrepreneurship in Western Africa. Mimeo, International Institute of Social Studies, Erasmus University Rotterdam.

Grimm, M., Knorringa, P. and Lay, J. (2012) Informal Entrepreneurs in Western Africa: Constrained Gazelles in the Lower Tier. *World Development*, 40 (7): 1352–1368.

Hirschman, A.O. (1958) *The Strategy of Economic Development*. Yale University Press, New Haven, CT and London.

Hoff, K. and Sen, A. (2006) The Kin as a Poverty Trap. In Bowles, S., Durlauf, S.N. and Hoff, K. (eds), *Poverty Traps*. Princeton University Press, New York.

Jakiela, P. and Ozier, O. (2010) *Does Africa Need a Rotten Kid Theorem?* Mimeo, Washington University.

Knorringa, P. and van Staveren, I. (2006) *Social Capital for Industrial Development: Operationalizing the Concept*. UNIDO, Vienna.

Kranton, R.E. (1996) Reciprocal Exchange: A Self-sustaining System. *American Economic Review*, 86 (4): 830–851.

La Ferrara, E. (2007) Family and Kinship ties in Development: An Economist's Perspective. Paper presented at the 5th AFD-EUDN Conference, Paris, December (www.afd.fr/jahia/webdav/users/administrateur/public/eudn2007/laferrara.pdf).

Lewis, W.A. (1955) *The Theory of Economic Growth*. Richard D. Irwin, Homewood IL.

Meier, G.M. and Baldwin, R.E. (1957) *Economic Development: Theory, History, Policy*. John Wiley & Sons, New York.

Minten, B. and Fafchamps, F. (1999) Relationships and Traders in Madagascar. *Journal of Development Studies*, 35 (6): 1–35.

Morrisson, C. (2006) Structures familiales, transferts et épargne. Document de travail No. 255, OECD Development Centre, Paris.

Platteau, J.-P. (2000) *Institutions, Social Norms and Economic Development*. Harwood Academic Publishers, Amsterdam.

Portes, A. and Sensenbrenner, J. (1993) Embeddedness and Immigration: Notes on the Social Determinants of Economic Action. *American Journal of Sociology*, 98 (6), 1320–1350.

Woolcock, M. (2001) Microenterprise and Social Capital: A Framework for Theory, Research, and Policy. *Journal of Socio-Economics*, 30 (2): 193–198.

# 10 The political economy of micro entrepreneurship

## Why does microcredit fail to promote self-employment in rural South India?

*Isabelle Guérin*

Since the second half of the twentieth century, the debate on informal labour, self-employment, poverty and development has swung back and forth like a pendulum. Researchers and policy makers discovered in the early 1970s the importance of small enterprises in creating local economies, but at the same time realized that these local economies being built are typically 'informal', beyond any regulation and have a hard time growing into profitable businesses. The 'informal nature' of self-employment was supposed to disappear with the modernization and the formalization of local economies. From the 1990s onwards, however, social scientists and development planners realized that the removal of the informal economy was complex, and that informal sector development could facilitate agrarian transitions and industrialization. In the face of structural economic adjustments where jobs could not be provided anymore by the state, self-employment was promoted as an individual safety net as well as an accelerating mechanism to spur local development.

The first decade of the twenty-first century has probably been the peak of this praise of self-employment and the great success of microcredit is an illustration of this. The year 2005 was declared the International Year of Microcredit, with the purpose of 'building inclusive financial sectors and strengthening the powerful, but often untapped, entrepreneurial spirit existing in communities around the world'.[1] When Muhammad Yunus and the Grameen Bank were awarded the Nobel peace prize in 2006, the Nobel Committee affirmed that 'Across cultures and civilisations, Yunus and Grameen Bank have shown that the poor can work to bring about their own development [...]. Microcredit promotes entrepreneurship, and puts each individual poor person, especially women, in the driving-seat in their own lives.'[2] While the Grameen Bank is increasingly criticized,[3] Yunus is still highly supported by a wide range of personalities. Hillary and Bill Clinton have always shown continuous support. As early as 2002, Bill Clinton declared publicly that Yunus was deserving the Nobel prize.[4] Among many honours and awards, Yunus received from Barak Obama the two most prestigious distinctions awarded by the United States government: the Congress gold medal (in 2010) and the presidential medal for freedom (in 2012). In March 2012, the magazine *Fortune* listed him among the 12 most innovative entrepreneurs of the year.

Microcredit has also attracted many academics, intellectuals, senior executives of international organizations, businessmen and businesswomen, philanthropists. In his book *The End of Poverty*, Jeffrey Sachs, one of the leading economists in the aid development world, describes his fascination for women borrowing groups in Bangladesh. In a conference in 2003, James Wolfensohn, then president of the World Bank, said that 'microfinance has a demonstrated, powerful impact in improving the livelihood of the poor, and a crucial role in reducing poverty'. He also said that the poor's ability to access financial services 'is a critical condition for the attainment of the Millennium Development Goals'.[5] Jacques Attali, economist, writer, honorary state counsellor in France founded the group PlaNet Finance in 1998, with a mission of 'enabling those in poverty to access financial services in order to bring about sustained improvements to their living standards'. It is also stated in its website that 'With a presence in 88 countries, the PlaNet Finance Group is now acknowledged as a major player in the war on poverty through the development of entrepreneurship'.[6] In a paper written in 2006, Attali was claiming that 'poverty could be eradicated globally with a professional development of microfinance' (Attali 2006: 115).

Today, however, the enthusiasm for self-employment and related policies are increasingly questioned. Several years ago a number of in-depth studies already pointed out the difficulty for microcredit to transform the poor into entrepreneurs (Servet 2006). This was shown for instance in Senegal (Perry 2002), in Egypt (Elyachar 2006) and in Bangladesh (Rahman 1999). In the 1980s in Bangladesh, a few studies warned against the illusions of microcredit as a tool for boosting local economies, showing that new micro-entrepreneurs acted only as substitute for others and/or led to a drastic diminution of margins (Osmani 1989). But these studies were regarded as exceptions.

We had to wait for tragic events – in various parts of the world microfinance borrowers are now over-indebted and unable to repay, sometimes victims to considerable pressure which include the extreme of suicide (Guérin *et al.* 2013b) – and to randomized control trial studies to cast doubts about the effective potential of microcredit. Indeed, one of the main conclusions of recent experimental studies, considered presently as the most rigorous way of assessing the impact of development programmes despite their numerous weaknesses (Bédécarrats *et al.* 2013), is to observe very limited effects of microcredit in terms of job creation. In their book *Poor Economics*, Banerjee and Duflo, who are among the most prominent scholars in this new branch of development economics, devote a specific chapter to employment and explain why microcredit impacts are not as high as expected. They find that many poor are their own bosses, but scopes for improvement are limited as most of these businesses are small and unprofitable. Marginal returns may be high, but overall returns are often very low, they argue. Scopes for expansion and creation of new businesses are equally limited as the poor are often reluctant to engage in self-employment. Entrepreneurship, they say, 'is too hard' (Banerjee and Duflo 2011: 223).

There is no doubt that entrepreneurship is 'hard' and can work only for a few. The reasons for this, however, remain unclear in Banerjee and Duflo's analysis.

Insofar as they restrict themselves to the micro scale, they can hardly provide answers. The very low profitability of businesses is only the tip of the iceberg. A complete picture requires other methods of investigation and a different episte-mological position. A political economy approach – by this we mean an approach which focuses on the structural dialectics producing political and eco-nomic differentiation within and between societies and which combines various scales of analysis, both macro, micro and meso (Harriss-White and Heyer 2011) – gives a rather different explanation: microcredit fails not because the poor are risk adverse or lack skills – though this is partly true – but mainly because local demand is missing and because existing markets are highly hierarchical and socially regulated along lines that reinforce pre-existing inequalities.

This is partly what Bateman does in his book *Why doesn't Microfinance Work?* extending an argument already made by authors like Servet (2006, 2010), Davis (2006), Chang (2007) or Karnani (2011). The biggest mistake of micro-credit promoters, Bateman argues, is their ignorance of composition effects and their naive adherence to a certain interpretation of the law of Say, according to which the supply would create its own demand. Very often local markets are already saturated. New and expanded microcredit-induced microenterprises do not increase local demand but merely redistribute it, with many displacement effects (a new enterprise replaces old ones) and typically reduced profitability.

Beyond the size of local markets, the way markets are structured, organized and regulated is also a key explanatory factor. This issue has been largely unex-plored, while I believe it largely explains the numerous barriers outsiders face when they try to enter a market. This chapter is an attempt to fulfil this gap. Drawing on field work done over the last ten years in rural Tamil Nadu, South India, this chapter focuses on the role of social institutions to explain why micro-credit fails in promoting employment. Far beyond household surveys and case studies – which are certainly useful but capture only one part of the story – a detailed analysis of how markets operate – who are the producers, the traders, the buyers and how do they interact – sheds light on the *social regulation* of markets (Harriss-White 2003). By this we mean that markets do not emerge mechanically from the confrontation of supply and demand. Scarcity is not just a matter of the availability of resources. Markets, as scarcity, are institutionalized processes that are historically and socially produced. Social institutions, in par-ticular those of gender, religious plurality, caste, space, classes and the state, shape property rights and property transfers, production processes and labour management (who is recruited and how). They also regulate relationships between enterprises, cooperation and competition. They also shape access to markets, information, credit and state support. The fundamental role of institu-tions explains the intensity of the segmentation of labour markets and of value chains, the existence of oligopolistic and collusive markets, the concentration of capital and the collusion between capital and the state, etc.

The results presented in this chapter are part of a long-term research pro-gramme located at the French Institute of Pondicherry and looking at labour and finance in various districts of north and coastal rural Tamil Nadu. This research programme started in 2003 and still continues today. It brings together research-ers from various origins and backgrounds, some of which live on site. It relies on a wide range of methods, including semi-directive interviews, case studies, detailed analysis of villages, value chains and markets and household surveys. Some of us spent considerable time in the villages and in the markets, observing transactions, discussing informally with vendors, buyers, wholesalers and financ-ers. Field work was also done in various sectors such as transport, tailoring and food retail, which are the most commonly found crafts among local entrepren-eurs. We did specific case studies with around 40 entrepreneurs with businesses of varying size and from different sectors and backgrounds. Through repeated interviews and informal discussions, the main objective was to understand their trajectories, how their business works and their positioning within the value chain. We also spent time in strategic locations, such as tea stalls highly fre-quented by local entrepreneurs and where many transactions and discussions take place. The plurality of methods of data collection and analysis allows for a comprehensive analysis of how markets operate, and why microcredit fails in creating jobs.

The chapter starts by locating self-employment into the broader labour land-scape, first at the Indian level and then in the region under study. It then details the multiple barriers that micro-entrepreneurs may face in starting a business, by shedding light on the very unequal structure of power that underlies markets and the key role of social institutions such as caste and gender.

## The Indian labour landscape

India illustrates the contradictions of current globalized and neo-liberal eco-nomies well. India has experienced sustained economic growth over the last two decades, and yet the quality of employment in the non-agricultural sectors con-tinues to deteriorate. While informality has always been a dominant feature of the Indian labour landscape, survey data and case studies have shown a con-tinued expansion of its informal economy over the last decades. According to the latest detailed survey results available (2009–10), 93 per cent of the work-force belongs to the informal economy (Government of India 2012). Further-more, as suggested by Ravi Srivastava, 'the formal is becoming informal in a variety of ways' (2012: 64). The current labour landscape in the Indian economy highlights three major features.

### *Informalization*

First, there is an informalization of what would have been regular employment in non-agricultural employment in an earlier context and this suggests that boundaries between formal and informal are increasingly blurred (Srivastava 2012; Lerche *et al.* 2012). While the formal sector of the economy and the ser-vices sector in particular have grown rapidly, employment relations have become more vulnerable and flexible, including those which were usually considered as secure. Between 1999–2000 and 2004–05 for instance, the total workforce grew by around 15 per cent, but this was entirely due to the rise of informal employment. This was observed in agriculture, industry and services (Srivastava 2012). Between 2004–05 and 2009–10, not only did the total workforce barely increase (0.3 per cent), but labour conditions have deteriorated: indicators such as the number of written contracts, long-term positions, paid leave and social benefits are on the decline (Government of India 2012: 63–64).

## The importance of self-employment

Like many southern countries, the share of self-employment (which is mostly informal) is quite high. Following a decline in the 1990s, the share of self-employment grew in the first half of the last decade (representing 56.4 per cent of the total workforce in 2004–2005). This was observed in agriculture but above all in services and manufacturing, both for men and women and in rural and urban areas. The highest increase in share was observed for rural self-employed women. In manufacturing, the rise of self-employment probably reflected an increase in sub-contracting in own account units, with women representing the greater number (Srivastava 2012). The feminization and casualization of the manufacturing workforce, observed as early as the 1960s in different parts of the world and drawing on the 'comparative advantages' of a female workforce – namely its cheapness and docility (see for instance Elson and Pearson 1981; Standing 1999) – continue today. Between 2004–05 and 2009–10, however, self-employment was on the decline (50.7 per cent of the total workforce) while casual labour was on the rise. The decline of agriculture and also of manufacturing, and the rise in construction (which is currently nearly the only job-creating sector and relies mostly on casual labour) probably explain these trends (Government of India 2012).

## Non-farm sector

Although the working conditions of this 'self-employment' category are highly heterogeneous, vulnerability is more the rule than the exception (National Commission for Enterprises in the Unorganised Sector 2007: 52 seq.). Most self-employed workers are tiny units: 37 per cent of them have a fixed capital lower than INR5,000 (around US$82),[7] whilst 8 per cent have a capital higher than 100,000 INR. Of these activities, 40 per cent are carried out at home (46 per cent in rural areas). A total of 12 per cent do not have a stable place of work and 7 per cent of the work is by nature itinerant. Close to 64 per cent of self-employed workers consider that their units are stagnating with very little prospects for expansion (18 per cent feel that their units are expanding and 10 per cent that they are contracting). Looking at added-value creation, the majority are in survival rather than accumulation mode, particularly as regards women, scheduled castes (ex untouchables, also called Dalits) and scheduled tribes, as well as those in rural areas. A total of 83 per cent of the self-employed units led by women

(89 per cent in rural areas) have an added-value lower than the minimum wage (41 per cent for men). As far as women are concerned, 36 per cent work at home (as opposed to 4 per cent of men), mainly in the manufacturing sector, along with situations of subcontracting and often exclusive dependence on a contractor, as indicated above. Autonomous activity is concentrated in two primarily home-based branches of industry, namely craft (spinning, weaving and sewing) and livestock (in rural areas).

## Social regulation

The third feature of the Indian labour landscape is its social regulation (Harriss-White 2003, 2010; Harriss-White and Gooptu 2001). There is now a wide consensus that informal does not mean unstructured and this is particularly true in India. Formal mechanisms such as labour contracts are absent, but employers, recruiters and workers use a wide range of arrangements to secure their relationships. This includes the personalization of relations within known circles such as kinship, caste and village-based networks. This also includes debt-based labour relations, which act as a guarantee both for employers and workers. Social institutions such as caste, class and gender shape both the access to and the conditions of employment. Not only do practices of social discrimination persist, they also structure and feed accumulation processes, leading to a 'growth-discrimination nexus' (Ghosh 2011). Capital accumulation is both shaped by and constitutive of social and geographical discrimination. Social regulation does not mean that labour follows a pre-determined path, nor is it unchanging over time. Social interactions and processes shaping labour relations tend to evolve highly irregularly, depending on local circumstances and specific periods in history (Harriss-White 2003). The nature of social regulation varies greatly from one sector to another and from one region to another, relating both to strategies of capital and of labour. Employers are showing an extraordinary ability to use the social structure in ways that suit the organization of their production (Lerche *et al.* 2012).

## The labour landscape in rural Tamil Nadu

We shall now turn to our own data, drawing on several micro-studies carried out in around 20 villages in various districts of north and coastal Tamil Nadu (Tiruvallur, Villupuram, Cudalore and Vellore). The 20 villages we studied have variable physiognomies. Agriculture has been in crisis and declining to differing extents in the villages, depending on agro-ecological conditions and the extent of real-estate speculation. The villages also differ according to their proximity to the city and their inclusion into the wider economy. This in turn affects levels of social stratification, which serves to shape identities, the intensity of dependency ties, and the extent to which caste and class overlap. Our sample is not at all representative of the whole of rural Tamil Nadu, let alone of all rural India. It does however present some degree of diversity, allowing us to go beyond the specificities of a village monograph.

As elsewhere, most rural households have a diversified livelihood portfolio, both in terms of the family members who earn money, and their activities. Approximate figures are provided below as to workers' occupation, given that many of them juggle with various sources of income. The diversity of figures depends upon the type of village – more or less agrarian, semi-urbanized or specialized in migration.

Daily agricultural waged work (as an *agricultural coolie*) continues to be the most common source of labour (30 to 60 per cent), especially for Dalits, and especially for women. Its importance varies according to agro-climatic conditions, such as dry as opposed to irrigated areas, and the labour intensity level of a given crop. A total of 5 to 25 per cent of households cultivate their own land, mostly over a small area of less than 5 acres, which is owned or leased (often through sharecropping) or 'borrowed' from unused public land. Women might be involved, but mostly as unpaid family labour. A total of 10 to 25 per cent of households raise livestock, usually along the lines of rearing one or two cows, or a few goats. This is a typical occupation of women.

It is worth noting that small farmers' agricultural incomes remain very low and that they most frequently carry out non-agricultural labour alongside this work. Cultivating the land is often a way to fill time between other periods of employment, as well as maintaining dignity given that working one's 'own' land, regardless of profitability, is considered to be much more honourable than working for others. Cultivating the most profitable crops such as sugar cane or horticulture necessitates specific agricultural conditions that are often unaffordable for many households, including access to water, a minimum area of cultivable land and direct access to markets, namely those related to the agro-business industry. This in turn demands access to specific information and to other networks. As far as sharecroppers are concerned, contracts are very often disadvantageous to tenants, who are only able to make small profits. Similarly, small-scale livestock rearing can bring in only a very modest supplementary income (Roesch 2010).

As in other rural areas, non-agricultural labour is currently expanding (Lerche 2010). Yet it mainly takes the form of casual work and it is mainly a male preserve. Casual labour in the non-agricultural sector amounts to 10 to 30 per cent of labour sources and mainly involves manual and unskilled work in the construction industry at building sites or brick kilns, service work as a security guard, driver or in domestic employment, and work at markets in loading and unloading. Much of this work is done away from the village via seasonal migration over several months a year, or by commuting with a regular return to the village. Migration is certainly motivated by making a living, but also by the desire to loosen local ties of dependence and domination. Some occupations are carried out on subcontract from home and are particularly relevant to women, for instance incense stick rolling, assembling manufactured goods, working in the garment industry and groundnut or cashew nut dehusking. Women are the main users of the '100 Days Public Programme' – the flagship employment programme of the Indian government since 2005 and which promises 100 days of work at the minimum wage for every 'poor' rural household. In the region covered here, about one-third of households have access to it, with no significant differences between castes. Annual earnings represent only a meagre share of family income (around 5 per cent on average), but a higher part of women's income (20 per cent on average) (Guérin *et al*. forthcoming).

In all villages, permanent employment continues to be a highly unusual scenario, seldom accounting for more than a few per cent of employment sources, and limited to public sector jobs such as teaching, nursing, office clerk work, railroad or postal service work, and military posts. In some areas, the delocalization of industrial zones provides regular contracts for educated youths. Young women find jobs in the garment industry, while young men are more specialized in electronic assembling and automotive engineering.

Last, but not least, non-agricultural self-employment consistently amounts to barely over 20 per cent of labour sources across the villages studied. The most frequent activities undertaken include running small businesses such as home-based small grocery shops, varieties of street vending catering in vegetables, fish, flowers, etc., restaurants that often amount to tiny stalls, the production of processed foods such as pickles and snacks, handicraft and, finally, the provision of various services such as bicycle repair, farm equipment for hiring or audio material for ceremonies and in particular marriages, as well as printing and reproduction services, for which there is high demand for social and religious rituals. There is also a wide variety of local illegal trafficking. This includes informal lending, land sale brokerage, ration card black marketing (giving access to subsidized goods), black marketing in subsidized goods and natural resource black marketing, for instance in sand, which is highly coveted by construction entrepreneurs for brick production. It also includes local alcohol production, and brokerage for access to governmental programmes. Whatever they might be, the most sustainable and profitable businesses need to meet various conditions, in the context of which finance plays only a minor role as we shall see below.

## Why microcredit fails?

We shall start with a first observation. According to various surveys that I have conducted with my colleagues over the last ten years, the percentage of microcredits that are used for generating direct income represents a minor part of microcredit uses and ranges from almost zero to a quarter of usage at most, depending on location and the profile of microfinance organizations. Microcredit is primarily used for consumer purposes: food security, health, ceremonies, paying off past debts and investments in statutory expenses such as ceremonies. Owing to the fungibility of monetary flows and the fact that loans are used for a variety of purposes, it is limiting to stick to this type of indicator. What is clear however is that the direct impact on job creation is marginal (Guérin *et al*. 2013a). Far beyond the Indian case, the fact that a large part of microcredits are used for purposes which do not generate income is now widely acknowledged (Morduch 2013). Why is it so? The poor are not all entrepreneurs, explain Banerjee and Duflo in *Poor Economics*. When it is the case, it is most often because they lack alternatives, with poor benefits and few prospects of growth. There is nothing really new in this. It is well known that micro-entrepreneurs in southern countries are closer to the model of self-exploitation described by Chayanov than that of the Schumpeterian entrepreneur.

### *Self-employment or self-exploitation?*

The self-employment category is an official category recorded in many national and international statistical systems. But it is also a 'catch-all' category, with fundamental differences between those who have (economic, social or human) capital and those who do not, those who are really independent and those who depend entirely on suppliers or clients and whose employment can be compared to disguised waged labour (Heuzé 1992). The label 'self-employed' includes both small and medium-sized entrepreneurs, but also a hyper-educated section of Indian middle class professionals, working independently as doctors, lawyers, architects and accountants, etc. The label 'self-employed' also includes a mass of destitute people who have no other choice than creating their own activity to be saved from begging. Here we find multiple survival micro-activities such as street vendors, hawkers, bicycle-rickshaw drivers, shoe polishers, waste collectors, small brokers. We also find those who work at piece-rate or on a commission basis in an endless list of occupations including motor-rickshaw drivers, brick moulders, rice driers, *beedie* rollers. The latter category escapes official classifications and its importance is therefore difficult to estimate, but their number is probably considerable (Breman 2007). Considered as 'independent' workers because they are at least in theory 'free' to fix their own rate of production, these workers are usually classified as 'self-employed', even though their degree of dependence on contractors is total.

Far beyond the risk aversion highlighted by Banerjee and Duflo, the magnitude of conditions that are necessary for exerting an independent income generating activity considerably limits the potential of microcredit. Surprisingly, and despite a very abundant literature specifically devoted to microcredit, very few studies have analysed in detail the conditions for sustainable small enterprises. A first crucial issue has to do with the demand and with local markets. What should we sell, where and to whom? These are the questions repeatedly asked by microcredit borrowers.

A second fundamental issue has to do with the social regulation of markets. To start a business, even on a very small scale and even in the informal economy, demands specific skills, for instance the capacity to assess and manage risk, to access and process information, to discuss, argue and negotiate, and this with a wide range of stakeholders. To start a business also demands social networks and the ability to activate them. Networks with suppliers are needed in order to access cheap and good quality raw materials, at the right time and possibly with credit, but without too much overhead. Links to public authorities and political parties are also key to avoid or limit irritating red tape, to circumvent or reduce the cost of electricity, registration, and licences and taxes if required. For illegal businesses, allegiance to local political parties or gangs is unavoidable. Relying on networks of clients also allows to ensure local outlets, but also to avoid long-term payments, an ongoing source of fragility for small businesses. Last, and not least, networks with peers are also fundamental to fix prices, defend the interests of the industry and support each other through mutual help.

### The social regulation of markets

Neither skills nor networks are purely individual resources: they are in large part inherited and strengthened through close circles of belonging. This is not a matter of being determinist or fatalist, but of recognizing the fact that markets are fundamentally unequal and socially regulated. Markets, and the social networks which constitute the framework of markets, tend to concentrate access to information, to goods and technologies in the hands of a few (Harriss 2006). In many contexts and sectors, the organization of value chains is both hierarchical and quasi-monopolistic, in the sense that a very limited number of actors control the extraction of the added value while the others share the crumbs of retail sale. Institutions such as gender and caste are a dominant factor in determining the networks that distribute the necessary skills, resources and markets for running the business. For instance, gender and caste are determining factors for getting accurate market information, getting orders and supplies, fulfilling credit needs, as well as arranging labour supplies. This goes for both new and existing businesses. Second, caste and gender do not only determine the functionality of the network (the 'social capital' explanation), but also influence existing social norms and ideology, which in turn are fundamental drivers for the functioning of the local markets. In a companion paper I have shown that statistically, and 'all things being equal', gender and caste significantly influence the chance of being self-employed as well as the nature of self-employment (Guérin *et al.* 2013a).

### Gender

For women, restrictions on their physical mobility and contact with strangers are a major obstacle. In a context where social norms relegate women to a status of dependence, female entrepreneurship goes against existing standards. Patriarchal norms considerably restrict women's labour. These are related to the control of their body – a woman who moves loses her reputation and her honour, especially among higher castes – and to domestic obligations, as women still bear most of them. Among Dalits, norms restricting women's mobility are more flexible, but they have as many domestic obligations while facing additional barriers related to their Dalit status. Women may be involved in a business managed by a male relative as unpaid workers. But very few of them run businesses on their own, and when they do so it is in specific segments of the market. In the retail trade, for example, women are typically found in the sale of products of low value, intended primarily or exclusively for women and located in the villages: food, saris, imitation jewellery, cosmetics, etc. They sell from home or door-to-door.

Sometimes men (husband, son, brother or father) are involved in the supply, thus allowing women to stay at home and respect social norms. Some women take care of the supply themselves, but this means they are allowed to move around. Among middle and upper castes, this is more often the case for older women or widows. Dalit women have fewer restrictions, but their freedom remains very relative. Moreover, women don't escape the rules of untouchability: it is rare for Dalit women to sell to non-Dalit women.

## *Caste*

Dalits can hardly engage in sectors that relate to food and clothing, two types of goods with high symbolic connotation. When they start out in these sectors, it is necessarily for a very restricted clientele within their own caste. With some exceptions, self-employed Dalits deal with non-Dalit customers only when it comes to activities which are traditional caste based or in continuity, and which are socially degrading and/or demanding physical work.

A very frequent business targeted by microcredit providers is small grocery shops. At a first glance it seems easy. The investment in fixed assets is negligible. Sales take place at home or in a small metal or wooden stall, and equipment is limited to a measuring scale, sometimes a radio for attracting clients, exceptionally a fridge and a telephone. Looking at the working of the grocery products markets gives a more complicated picture. This sector is highly monopolized by non-Dalits, for several reasons. Food trade was traditionally restricted to castes of merchants such as Chettiars and Nadars. Even today they control a large part of the business, and this is a matter of ideology (untouchability), reputation and networks. They still exert a quasi monopoly on highly symbolic products such as oil. Among Vanniars, for instance, one of the dominant castes in the region, many have small grocery stores, but very few sell oil. Intouchability prevents Dalits from selling food to non-Dalits. We observed a few cases in small towns, but in the villages this is hardly thinkable. Moreover, for food products with high symbolic value, such as oil, milk or rice, many Dalits prefer to buy from non-Dalits. Reputation is probably critical here. Many products are sold by weight and are not pre-packaged. A shopkeeper is therefore valued in large part according to his/her honesty. Chettiars and Nadars enjoy a solid reputation of reliability. Dalits often accuse their caste-fellows of cheating on weight, which would be the only way for them to have margins, as we have been told several times. In one of the villages studied, a Dalit woman started selling oil, but quickly closed, apparently for this reason. Caste as an access to networks and resources also plays an important role. Chettiars, Nadars and to some extent Vanniars, control the entire value chain, from wholesalers to retailers. The latter therefore have a privileged access to quality products at preferential rates and often at credit without additional cost. Repayments are very flexible and often based on sales rather than on pre-fixed instalments. Shops are frequently part of a family network, with regular transfers of goods, which avoids stock shortages. In case of high competition, retailers can afford to adopt lower prices as it is the profitability of the entire chain which matters. Sale on credit is a basic rule for competitiveness and client loyalty, but this requires a sound financial base. For individual retailers, selling on credit is an ongoing source of fragility. In villages one may find few grocery shops run by Dalits, and probably much more than before. But they are necessarily confined to the Dalits' settlements and sell only to Dalits, with very little stocks on display, and probably a lower profitability. And many have had to shut down because of too many default payments, too few clients or owing to purchases on credit which put a strain on the profitability of the activity. I came across a number of cases of grocery stores started thanks to microcredit, and many of them failed. Two main problems arise. Sale on credit is a basic rule for competitiveness and client loyalty, but is an ongoing source of financial fragility. Several small retailers have had to shut up shop because of too many insolvent clients, or owing to purchases on credit which put a strain on the profitability of the activity. Second, market saturation and displacement effects are very common. With more than two or three shops per neighbourhood (depending on the size), the market is completely saturated. Apart from daily consumer goods and repair services, local markets are very limited, probably increasingly so. On the one hand, people increasingly travel to the city and take the opportunity to make purchases there. It is not always easy to return to the village, even after very short-term migrations, without something 'to show'. Meanwhile more tradesmen visit villages offering door-to-door sales, often on credit. An increasing choice of daily consumer goods and hardware is now available on the doorstep such as crockery, clothing and, more recently, televisions, refrigerators, CD or DVD players.

Tailoring is another very common sector targeted by microcredit providers. Tailors suffer from strong competition from manufactured products. Even the poor amongst local populations want to buy 'modern' clothing. Women want nylon saris bought in Chennai and not cotton blouses produced locally. Young men no longer want dhotis, but blue jeans. At the same time the demand for custom-made clothes for special occasions increases. On the one hand children are more likely to go to school and, in the early years until the end of secondary school, students wear a costume that is often custom-made. On the other hand, religious festivals and family celebrations are expanding and represent a large market for tailors, whether for gifts or clothing to wear on the day of the event. Tailors are also frequently approached to recycle old clothes. Here, too, the market is highly segmented. Non-Dalits refuse to touch clothes handled by the lowest castes. Moreover, experience is a key element of quality. Most tailors have first worked as an apprentice or employee. Dalits, as they lack networks and contacts, don't have access to this opportunity. Some NGOs provide training, but these are not long enough to provide participants with real knowledge and know-how. Some try to help women accessing markets, but all the cases we met have failed. There is therefore virtually no tailor among Dalits.

It is much more profitable for women, whatever their caste, and provided they are allowed to move out from the house, to do so in the textile company subcontracting workshops that are established in some decentralized industrial parks. Some NGOs have tried to help create local garment production units by offering training, machinery loans and contacts with contractors. All of the cases we came across had failed, and always for the same reasons: the poor quality of the products produced, which probably meant that training had been insufficient and also that close supervision was lacking; discontinuity of orders; discontinuity of the electricity supply, as the workshops are located in poorly serviced areas; obligatory registration and hence taxation (whereas the majority of the textile units are not registered but benefited from 'contacts' enabling them to circumvent the rules).

### The modernity of social regulation

The social regulation of markets is not a reminiscence of the past that would gradually disappear with 'modernisation' (Harriss-White 2003). Transport services give a good illustration of the persistence of caste segmentation. Both Dalits and non-Dalits are involved. But looking at who transports whom clearly shows a strong segmentation. Non-Dalits transport passengers, while Dalits transport goods. The former requires personal links, the latter requires physical strength. Traditionally, Dalits were involved in transporting goods (mostly agricultural products) with bullock carts. These tend to disappear and are replaced by small motor vehicles. Many financial companies sell them on credit to Dalits through leasing contracts, which prevent any risk, both for creditors and debtors. Dalits' transport activities remain limited to small quantities and small distance, however. The vehicles they can afford to buy have limited capacity and cannot drive on highways. Long-distance transport, which is a very profitable business, is monopolized by middle and upper castes. Dalits are involved, but as daily labourers, in charge of the very physical work of loading and unloading.

Networks not only facilitate access to providers or clients. They may also defend collective interests and privileges and organize markets. Here, too, the example of the transport industry is a good example. The strong segmentation – Dalits specialized in small distance and non-Dalits in long distance – is closely linked to non-Dalit corporatism, which plays a key role in lobbying, monitoring and controlling access to markets. Through strong alliances with the public administration, in which they are also over-represented, non-Dalits manage licensing and procurement. They spend a great deal of time in places (tea shops, their own shops) where flows of information circulate. They conspire together on price fixing: the market structure here is much closer to collusion than competition. They lend to each other (bank loans represent only a meagre share of debt). They help each other, for example when one of them is unable to respond to an order on their own. Dalits by contrast are typically poorly organized. Most bought their vehicle on credit from a financial company and have a strong pressure for repayment. The market for short distance transport is over-crowded and therefore highly competitive. Small transporters may help each other occasionally but they don't engage in any collective action and have very little control over pricing. They don't need a licence, but they are often harassed by public officials to pay taxes, while the great majority of big transporters operates without any legal and fiscal constraint.

## Conclusion

Drawing on the rural South Indian case, the main purpose of this chapter was to show the weight of social institutions in shaping and regulating markets and, as a consequence, in explaining why microcredit fails to promote successful and sustainable self-employment. The success of microcredit as a development tool derives from the fundamental assumption that the poor are no longer seen as passive victims but as capable and creative entrepreneurs who are able to take care of their own destiny. The idea is appealing insofar as it breaks from down-trodden visions of poverty, but it is however both naive and dangerous. As Aneel Karnani (2011) argues, such a romanticized vision of the poor is far from viable and harms rather than helps them. It is naive because it neglects structural barriers to successful self-employment. Entrepreneurship is often seen only as a matter of access to resources and to credit in particular, initiated by individuals in isolation. To consider the poor as creative entrepreneurs is also very dangerous because it shifts the responsibility of under-employment to the poor themselves and downplays the critical role and responsibility of the state (Fernando 2006; Fouillet *et al.* 2007; Karnani 2011; Servet 2006).

Randomized studies have helped break the myth of microcredit as an efficient tool for job creation. However by restricting their analysis to a micro scale, they miss the point. Their conception of the economy and of poverty is cut off from issues of social relations and structural constraints. But a real understanding of employment – employment in general and self-employment in particular – should look at the larger political economy. Entrepreneurship requires access to a broad range of resources, of which credit is just one factor among many. It above all requires markets and the access to markets. Not only the local demand may be very limited or even missing, but it is often monopolized by social groups and corporations who fix the rules and give no space to outsiders. Though mostly informal, in the sense they are not registered and regulated by the state, entrepreneurs' behaviour, constraints and opportunities are both shaped by and constitutive of a wide range of social networks. These networks are not only individual resources: they also act as powerful institutions that structure and regulate markets and this structuring effect should be looked at if we really want to understand how markets operate. Diversity in self-employment, most often located in individual or household characteristics, should rather be understood in terms of unequal relations in the larger political economy. The most vulnerable groups – in the region studied here these are mostly women and Dalits – are actually the least likely to successfully start-up a business, because of the existence of these persistent social regulations that shape local markets. The norms underlying social regulations are not fixed over time and are permanently reworked, as we have seen for instance with caste, but they still restrict considerably opportunities for the marginalized categories.

# Notes

1  This is stated on the first page of their website (www.yearofmicrocredit.org/).
2  See www.nobelprize.org/nobel_prizes/peace/laureates/2006/presentation-speech.html.
3  Several very critical documentaries have been produced over the last few years. *Over-indebted in microcredit* (*Les surendettés du microcredit*), by the French channel France 24 in 2008; *Caught in microdebt* (*Fanget I Mikrogjeld*), by a Danish independent journalist, Tom Heinemann, in 2010 (2011 for the English version).
4  In a conference delivered at University of California, Berkeley, in 2002 and in his autobiography (Clinton 2004).
5  Quoted by Daley-Harriss (2005: 5).
6  www.planetfinancegroup.org/en.
7  In December 2013, US$1 was worth about INR61.

# References

Attali J. (2006) La microfinance aujourd'hui *in Rapport moral sur l'argent dans le monde 2006*. Finance et lutte contre la pauvreté dans le monde, Paris: Association d'économie financière, pp. 325–346.

Banerjee A.V. and Duflo E. (2011) *Poor economics: a radical rethinking of the way to fight global poverty*. New York: Public Affairs.

Bateman M. (2011) *Why doesn't microfinance work: the destructive rise of local neoliberalism*. New York: Zed Books.

Bédécarrats F., Guérin I. and Roubaud F. (2013) "L'étalon-or des évaluations randomisées: du discours de la méthode à l'économie politique", *Sociologies Pratiques*, 27: 56–72.

Breman J. (2007) *Labour bondage in West India: from past to present*. Oxford: Oxford University Press.

Chang H.-J. (2007) *Bad samaritans: rich nations, poor policies and the threat to the developing world*. London: Random House.

Clinton B. (2004) *My life*. New York: Knopf Publishing Group (Random House).

Daley-Harris S. (2005) *State of the microcredit summit campaign: report 2005*. Washington, DC: Microcredit Summit Campaign.

Davis M. (2006) *Planet of slums*. London: Verso.

Elson D. and Pearson P. (1981) 'Nimble fingers make cheap workers: an analysis of women's employment in third world export manufacturing', *Feminist Review*, 7: 87–107.

Elyachar J. (2006) *Markets of dispossession: NGOs, economic development and the state in Cairo*. Durham, NC: Duke University Press.

Fernando J. (ed.) (2006) *Microfinance: perils and prospects*. London and New York: Routledge.

Fouillet C., Guérin I., Morvant S., Roesch M. and Servet J.-M. (2007) 'Le microcrédit au péril du néolibéralisme et de marchands d'illusions. Manifeste pour une inclusion financière socialement responsable', *Revue du Mauss*, 29: 248–268.

Ghosh J. (2011) 'The growth–discrimination nexus', MacroScan. www.macroscan.org/cur/apr11/cur130411Growth_Discrimination.htm.

Government of India (2012) *Informal sector and conditions of employment in India, NSS 66th round (July 2009 – June 2010)*, New-Delhi: National Sample Survey Office National Statistical Organisation Ministry of Statistics and Programme Implementation Government of India.

Guérin I., d'Espallier B. and Venkatasubramanian G. (2013a) 'Why does microfinance fail in rural south-India? The social regulation of self-employment', CEB Working Paper No. 13/034.

Guérin I., Morvant-Roux S. and Villarreal M. (eds) (2013b) *Microfinance, debt and over-indebtedness: juggling with money.* London: Routledge.

Guérin I., Venkatasubramanian G. and Michiels S. (forthcoming) 'Labour in contemporary South India', in J. Heyer and B. Harriss-White (eds) *Capitalism in rural India.* London: Routledge.

Harriss J. (2006) *Power matters: essays on institutions, politics and society in India.* New Delhi: Oxford University Press.

Harriss-White B. (2003) *India working: essays on society and economy.* Cambridge: Cambridge University Press.

Harriss-White B. (2010) 'Stigma and regions of accumulation: mapping Dalit and Adivasi capital in the 1990s', in B. Harriss-White and J. Heyer (eds) *The political economy of development: Africa and South Asia compared.* London: Routledge, pp. 291–316.

Harriss-White B. and Gooptu N. (2001) 'Mapping India's world of unorganised labour', *Socialist Register* (Working Classes: Global Realities), 37: 89–118.

Harriss-White B. and Heyer J. (eds) *The political economy of development: Africa and South Asia compared.* London: Routledge.

Heuzé G. (1992) *Pour une nouvelle compréhension des faits et des hommes du secteur non structuré.* Paris: Orstom.

Karnani A. (2011) *Fighting poverty together: rethinking strategies for business, governments, and civil society to reduce poverty.* New York: Palgrave Macmillan.

Lerche J. (2010) 'From "rural labour" to "classes of labour": class fragmentation, caste and caste struggle at the bottom of the Indian labour hierarchy', in B. Harriss-White and J. Heyer (eds) *The comparative political economy of development: Africa and South Asia.* London: Routledge, pp. 64–85.

Lerche J., Guérin I. and Srivastava R. (eds) 'Labour regulations and labour standards in India', Special issue of *Global Labour Journal.*

Morduch J. (2013) 'How microfinance really works? (What new research tells us about)', *CERMi's 5th Birthday Celebration,* Brussels, 18 March.

National Commission for Enterprises in the Unorganised Sector (2007) *Report on conditions of work and promotion of livelihoods in the unorganised sector.* New Delhi: NCEUS.

Osmani S.R. (1989) 'Limits to the alleviation of poverty through non farm credit', *Bangladesh Development Studies,* 17(4): 1–18.

Perry D. (2002) 'Microcredit and women moneylenders: the shifting terrain of credit in rural Senegal', *Human Organization,* 61(1): 30–40.

Rahman A. (1999) *Women and microcredit in rural Bangladesh: an anthropological study of Grameen bank lending.* Boulder, CO: Westview Press.

Roesch M. (2010) 'Un microcrédit pour acheter une vache … et le miracle n'aura pas lieu. Histoire d'une innovation en Inde du Sud', in *Innovation and Sustainable Development in Agriculture and Food – ISDA 2010.* Montpellier: France (http://hal.archives-ouvertes.fr/hal-00529062).

Servet J.-M. (2006) *Banquiers aux pieds nus: la microfinance.* Paris: Odile Jacob.

Servet J.-M. (2010) 'Microcredit', in H. Keith, J.-L. Laville, A.D. Cattani (eds) *The human economy.* Boston, MA/Cambridge/Oxford: Polity Press, pp. 130–141.

Srivastava R.S. (2012) 'Changing employment conditions of the Indian workforce and implications for decent work', *Global Labour Journal,* 3(1): 118–142.

Standing G. (1999) 'Global feminisation through flexible labour: a theme revisited', *World Development,* 27(3): 583–602.

# Part III

# Micro macro dynamics and poverty

# 11 Micro analysis of formal–informal nexus in Madagascar

## Job transitions and earnings dynamics

*Christophe J. Nordman, Faly Hery Rakotomanana, François Roubaud*

Little is known about the informal sector's income structure vis-à-vis the formal sector, despite its predominant economic weight in developing countries. Some works have been carried out in this field, but they only consider some emerging Latin American countries (Argentina, Brazil, Colombia and Mexico; Gong *et al.*, 2004; Perry *et al.*, 2007) and more recently South Africa, Ghana and Tanzania for Africa (Bargain and Kwenda, 2011; Falco *et al.*, 2010) and Vietnam for Asia (Nguyen *et al.*, 2013). It is then hazardous to generalize these results (sometimes diverging) to other parts of the developing world, in particular in very poor countries in Sub-Saharan Africa where the informal sector is the most widespread.

Empirical evidence shows that the existence of informality in poor countries can be understood by a mix of two traditional assumptions (Maloney, 1999; Perry *et al.*, 2007): the exclusion and the exit hypotheses, following Hirschman's seminal work. The first hypothesis, also called the "dualist approach", considers a dual labour market model where the informal sector is viewed as a residual component of this market and is totally unrelated to the formal economy. It is a subsistence economy that only exists because the formal economy is incapable of providing enough jobs, and is condemned to disappear with the development process. Informal workers, suffering from poor labour conditions, are queuing for better jobs in the formal sector. The second assumption, also known as the "legalist approach", considers that the informal sector is made up of micro-entrepreneurs who prefer to operate informally to evade the economic regulations (de Soto, 1989); this conservative school of thought is in sharp contrast to the former in that the choice of informality is voluntary due to the exorbitant legalization costs associated with formal status and registration. Then, confirming Fields' stylized assessment (1990), a few studies stress the huge heterogeneity among informal jobs, which combine two main components: a lower-tier segment, where occupying an informal job is a constraint choice ("exclusion hypothesis"); an upper-tier segment, in which informal jobs are chosen for better earnings and non-pecuniary benefits ("exit hypothesis"). Usually, the former segment is assimilated to the informal wage jobs, while the latter is associated with the self-employed jobs. Therefore, whether one segment is predominant over the other remains an empirical question, depending on local circumstances.

To test these alternative views, one major strand of literature focuses on the estimation of earning gaps. Embedded in revealed preferences principle, and considering income as a proxy of individual utility, the approach assumes that if informal workers earn more than their formal counterparts all else being equal, one could presume that they have deliberately chosen the informal sector. This may not be true for all informal sector workers. Thus, the challenge is to identify segments of jobs or position in the income distribution where informal sector workers get a higher pay.

In this chapter, this is the method we follow in the case of Madagascar. We take advantage of the rich *1-2-3 Surveys* dataset for Antananarivo, specifically designed to capture the informal sector, and in particular its four-wave panel data (2000–2001–2002–2004), to ask the following question: is there an informal sector job earnings penalty? Do some informal sector jobs provide pecuniary premiums and which ones? Do possible gaps vary along the earnings distribution?

While most of the papers on this topic are drawn from (emerging) Latin American, Asian or some African countries, Madagascar represents an interesting case. It experienced an exceptional period of economic expansion between 1995 and 2001. Growth appeared to be associated with a decline in the share of the informal sector in urban employment (see Vaillant *et al.*, 2014). But, in 2002, a major political crisis following presidential elections reversed this trend. This crisis had disastrous effects on the economy: exports and foreign direct investments fell sharply, GDP declined by about 13 per cent and inflation was close to 16 per cent in 2002 (Cling *et al.*, 2005). The share of employment in the informal sector grew again, as workers were laid off from the private sector, in particular in the Export Processing Zones (EPZs). Despite the severity of the economic downturn, recovery was quick, with a GDP growth of about 10 per cent in 2003 and around 5 per cent in the two following years, the period covered by our panel dataset. The country remains today however one of the poorest countries in the world.

Our empirical analysis consists of assessing the magnitude of different types of informal–formal earnings gaps using fixed effects OLS and quantile regressions. While many pieces of work rely on proxy variables to identify the informal sector, we use the official international definition of the informal sector elaborated by the ILO (1993), including all non-registered non-farm unincorporated enterprises (household businesses). Standard earnings equations are estimated at the mean and at various conditional quantiles of the earnings distribution. In particular, we estimate fixed effects quantile regressions to control for unobserved individual characteristics, focusing particularly on heterogeneity within both the formal and informal employment categories. Our purpose is to address the important issue of heterogeneity at three levels: the worker level, taking into account individual unobserved characteristics; the job level, comparing wage workers with self-employed workers; and the earnings distribution.

The remainder of this chapter is organized as follows. The next section presents the context, the data and some descriptive elements of income dynamics in the recent period, while the third section focuses on the econometric approach to assess formal–informal earnings gaps. Empirical results are discussed in the fourth section, and the fifth section concludes.

## Context, labour market dynamics and data

### Context

After a long period of economic recession which started with the country's independence in 1960 and interrupted only by very short periods of growth, Madagascar experienced an exceptional period of economic expansion between 1997 and 2001. The presidential elections of December 2001 triggered a serious political crisis that lasted six months and had catastrophic economic effects (Razafindrakoto and Roubaud, 2002). GDP collapsed by 12.7 per cent and inflation was close to 16 per cent in 2002 (Gubert and Robilliard, 2010). Exports and foreign direct investments fell sharply, unemployment rose by 71 per cent between mid-2001 and the end of 2002 (Cling *et al.*, 2005). Between 2003 and 2009, the political stability boosted economic growth. Unfortunately, a second political turmoil occurred in 2009, which, combined with the international financial crisis, resulted in a new drastic shock.

These macroeconomic turbulences had a direct impact on the labour market dynamics and household living conditions. Between 1997 and 2001, the growth process translated into a significant decline in the informal sector and vice versa in the following period (Table 11.1). At the macro level, this contra-cyclical evolution of the informal sector employment, taken as a whole, seems to confirm the dualistic hypothesis discussed in the introduction.

### Data description

The data used in this chapter are drawn from the *1-2-3 Surveys* conducted in the capital city, Antananarivo, since 1995 by the National Statistics Institute, with the assistance of the authors (Rakotomanana *et al.*, 2003). The first phase of the

*Table 11.1* Share of employment by institutional sector in Antananarivo, 1995–2010 (%)

|  | 1995 | 1996 | 1997 | 1998 | 1999 | 2000 | 2001 | 2002 | 2004 | 2006 | 2010 |
|---|---|---|---|---|---|---|---|---|---|---|---|
| Public sector | 14.2 | 14.3 | 13.0 | 13.2 | 13.1 | 10.6 | 10.7 | 11.2 | 10.4 | 8.8 | 7.8 |
| Private formal sector | 25.1 | 22.6 | 22.9 | 24.6 | 24.2 | 25.3 | 25.9 | 24.9 | 22.2 | 25.2 | 22.4 |
| EPZs | 3.1 | 4.4 | 4.6 | 5.5 | 6.7 | 8.9 | 10.2 | 4.1 | 8.9 | 8.0 | 4.8 |
| Informal sector | 57.6 | 58.8 | 59.6 | 56.7 | 56.0 | 55.3 | 53.1 | 59.9 | 58.4 | 58.0 | 65.1 |
| Total | 100 | 100 | 100 | 100 | 100 | 100 | 100 | 100 | 100 | 100 | 100 |

Source: *1-2-3 Surveys*, phases 1, 1995–2010, MADIO, DIAL and INSTAT; authors' calculations.

Note
Private formal sector figures do not include EPZs.

*1-2-3 Surveys* consists of an augmented labour force survey, providing two main advantages: it is specifically designed at capturing the informal sector in all its dimensions (Razafindrakoto *et al.*, 2009); between 2000 and 2004, the four rounds of survey include a unique panel component.

The structure of the panel, summing 23,926 observations (individual * year) is described in Table 11.2. Among the 7,544 individuals in the working age population, 3,503 are observed for the four years (balanced panel), that is nearly half of our sample (47 per cent); 24 per cent are present thrice and 29 per cent twice. Comparisons of means and distribution of earnings and observables between the cross-section samples and the panel sub-sample suggest that selective attrition is not an issue (Nordman *et al.*, 2012).

In Madagascar, the *informal sector* is defined as all private unincorporated enterprises that produce at least some of their goods and services for sale or barter, are not registered (*statistics* licence, supposed to be compulsory for all kinds of businesses) or do not keep book accounts. To our knowledge, the database used in this chapter is one of the largest and highest quality labour market panels in Sub-Saharan Africa (apart from being one of the few ones available).

## Econometric approach to measuring informal–formal earnings gaps

The econometric analysis consists of assessing the magnitude of different types of informal–formal earnings gaps using OLS and quantile regressions with log hourly earnings as dependent variable. Standard earnings equations are thus estimated at the mean and at various conditional quantiles of the earnings

*Table 11.2* The panel structure of the *1-2-3 Surveys* 2000, 2001, 2002 and 2004

|  | 2000 | 2001 | 2002 | 2004 |
|---|---|---|---|---|
| Cross section sample (household) | 2,999 | 3,020 | 3,019 | 3,020 |
| Cross section sample (individual 18 years and over) | 9,537 | 9,459 | 9,409 | 9,658 |
| Cross section sample (occupied workers) | 5,685 | 5,499 | 5,196 | 5,272 |
| Panel (household) | 2,999 | 2,559 | 2,607 | 2,396 |
| Panel (individual 18 years and over) | 5,823 | 6,771 | 6,381 | 4,951 |
| Observed 2 years | 1,163 | 1,436 | 1,046 | 773 |
| Observed 3 years | 1,157 | 1,832 | 1,832 | 675 |
| Observed 4 years (balanced panel) | 3,503 | 3,503 | 3,503 | 3,503 |
| Panel (individual 18 years and over holding a job) | 4,161 | 4,863 | 4,472 | 3,637 |
| Observed 2 years | 803 | 995 | 705 | 551 |
| Observed 3 years | 771 | 1,265 | 1,245 | 484 |
| Observed 4 years (balanced panel) | 2,587 | 2,603 | 2,522 | 2,602 |

Source: *1-2-3 Surveys*, phases 1, 2000–2004, DIAL/INSTAT; authors' calculations.

Note
In Madagascar the working age population is defined as all individuals aged 10 years and over. The number of observations of the balanced panel for occupied workers changes a little bit as some individuals enter and exit the labour force.

distribution. The models are regressed on a pooled sample of workers over years employed formally and informally. The different covariates introduced into the regressions are the completed years of education, the years of potential experience (with quadratic profiles for these two regressors), a dummy for being married, a dummy for being a woman, ten dummy variables of industries to account for technological differences between branches of activity, ten area dummies to capture labour market local specificities and four time dummies to control for macroeconomic trend effects on earnings.

To account for informal–formal differences in earnings at the mean earnings level, we rely on pooled OLS regressions across years and fixed effects OLS regressions (FEOLS), the latter accounting for time-invariant unobserved heterogeneity. The FE model can be written as:

$$y_{it} = x'_{it}\beta + \gamma I_{it} + \alpha_i + \varepsilon_{it} \tag{11.1}$$

where $x_{it}$ denotes the vector of characteristics of individual $i$ observed at time $t$ (which includes a constant term), $I_{it}$ represents a dummy taking value one if person $i$ observed at time $t$ is an informal sector worker, $\alpha_i$ is the time-invariant individual heterogeneity (or the individual fixed effect) and $\varepsilon_{it}$ is an i.i.d. normally distributed stochastic term absorbing measurement error.

The estimated coefficient $\hat{\gamma}$ is interpreted as a measure of the conditional earnings premium/penalty experienced by workers who change status between informal sector jobs to formal sector employment (or the reversal). However, as mentioned previously, informal employment sector is extremely heterogeneous and a finer job divide should be considered. We then define four categories of workers split by job status (wage workers vs self-employed workers) and institutional sector (formal vs informal) and create four dummies taking value one if the individual $i$ at time $t$ is an informal wage worker ($IW_{it}$), a formal wage worker ($FW_{it}$), an informal self-employed worker ($IS_{it}$) and a formal self-employed worker ($FS_{it}$). Taking the formal wage workers as the reference category, the model we estimate can be written as:

$$y_{it} = x'_{it}\beta + \delta IW_{it} + \theta IS_{it} + \lambda FS_{it} + \alpha_i + \varepsilon_{it} \tag{11.2}$$

Finally, to allow the earnings gaps between job statuses to differ along the earnings distribution, we rely on quantile regressions (QR). Quantile earnings regressions consider specific parts of the conditional distribution of the hourly earnings and indicate the influence of the different explanatory variables on conditional earnings respectively at the bottom, at the median and at the top of the distribution. Using our previous notation, the model that we seek to estimate is

$$q_\varrho(y_{it}) = x'_{it}\beta(\varrho) + \delta(\varrho)IW_{it} + \theta(\varrho)IS_{it} + \lambda(\varrho)FS_{it} + \alpha_i, \forall \varrho \in [0, 1] \tag{11.3}$$

where $q_\varrho(y_{it})$ is the $\varrho$th conditional quantile of the log hourly earnings. The set of coefficients $\beta(\varrho)$ provide the estimated rates of return to the different covariates at the $\varrho$th quantile of the log earnings distribution and the coefficients $\delta(\varrho)$, $\theta(\varrho)$ and $\lambda(\varrho)$ measure the parts of the earnings differentials that are due to informal–formal job differences at the various quantiles.

We then turn to fixed effects quantile regressions (FEQR). The extension of the standard QR model to longitudinal data has been originally developed by Koenker (2004). More recently, Canay (2011) proposed an alternative and simpler approach which assumes that the unobserved heterogeneity terms have a pure location shift effect on the conditional quantiles of the dependent variable. In other words, they are assumed to affect all quantiles in the same way. It follows that these unobserved terms can be estimated in a first step by traditional mean estimations (for instance by FE). Then, the predicted $\hat{\alpha}_i$ are used to correct earnings, such as $\hat{y}_i = y_i - \hat{\alpha}_i$, which are regressed on the other regressors by traditional QR. When running the regressions (11.2) and (11.3), we always provide robust standard errors using bootstrap replications.

## Descriptive statistics and validity checks

Table 11.3 presents some basic summary statistics of the main characteristics of the panel data used in our analysis. These descriptive statistics are reported for the sub-samples of wage/self-employed workers, broken down by formal and informal sector jobs.

The results obtained for average earnings are in line with common findings in the literature. Workers holding formal sector jobs earn more on average than those engaged in informal sector jobs. Among each group of formal and informal sector workers, self-employed workers are those with higher earnings in comparison with wage earners. If the average age of the labour force is the same between the two sectors, informal sector wage workers tend to be younger than their formal worker counterparts. Self-employed workers exhibit on average longer potential experience in the labour market (which is calculated as age minus years of reported schooling minus five). As expected, workers having a higher level of education are less likely to be engaged in the informal sector and vice versa. The gender ratio varies significantly between formal and informal sector jobs. Female workers have more opportunity to get informal sector jobs; female participation is at its highest in informal self-employment and at its lowest in formal one.

Finally, formal and informal sector workers are differently allocated across industries. Specifically, informal sector employment is found more in trade, restaurants and construction, while formal sector jobs are more concentrated in clothing and services (in particular public administration). Interestingly, the share of manufacture is identical between informal sector jobs and formal ones (31 per cent in both cases). Within institutional sectors, the distribution is even more unbalanced: informal sector wage workers are stubbornly engaged in services to the person (51 per cent), whereas informal self-employed workers hold trade jobs (36 per cent). Formal sector wage workers are engaged prominently in services (63 per cent), while formal self-employed job's structure looks like the informal self-employed one. In terms of firm size, formal sector wage workers are as expected over-represented in large enterprises, while the three other groups are quasi exclusively engaged in micro-enterprises (informal self-employed workers operating the smallest ones). These significant differences in the distribution of job structure underline the importance of controlling for industries and size in our earnings estimations.

Table 11.4 reports the job transition matrices by institutional sector and status in employment between 2000 and 2004. All individuals aged 18 years and over are included and split into four groups: formal sector wage workers, informal sector wage workers, self-employed workers and non-working individuals. To save space and given the small number of observations, formal self-employed workers have been aggregated with informal ones (we will distinguish them in our estimations; see next section). Inactive and unemployed are also aggregated into one broad category (not working). First, the proportion of movers (from one category to another) is far from negligible and is quite stable over time. From one year to the next, movers represent around one-third of the three samples (from a minimum of 31 per cent between 2000 and 2001 to a maximum of 36 per cent between 2002 and 2004). If we consider only those holding a job, the target of our earnings gap estimations, the rate of movers is reduced to one-quarter (22 to 26 per cent respectively for the same periods). Formal sector wage jobs are the most stable, followed by the self-employed ones. Informal sector wage workers are the most mobile: only 30 per cent keep their status from one year to the other. The flows between sectors follow a consistent pattern. Informal sector wage worker movers mainly get formal sector wage and (informal) self-employed jobs, equally distributed. Formal sector wage worker movers privilege self-employment, but substantial flows go to informal wage jobs. Conversely, self-employed workers change more often for formal sector wage jobs than for informal jobs, withdrawing from work being their first option (retirement). On the methodological side, the substantial numbers of movers, in both directions, and for all types of jobs, is key for our estimation strategy.

Another striking finding is the surprising weak impact of the macroeconomic context on transition flows. Changes in year-to-year transition flows (direction and intensity) are limited, stressing a robust structural pattern. This assessment is confirmed by the long run transition matrix, as shown in the low right panel of Table 11.4. The 2000–2004 matrix is very similar to the short run matrices. At our four states level, 61 per cent of the sample are stayers, compared to 64–69 per cent in the year to year matrices (73 and 74–79 per cent respectively for those who kept a job). For each of the four initial positions, the distribution of movers between categories is surprisingly close to the year-to-year one. However, at the margins, the crisis spell (between 2001 and 2002) shows a significantly lower rate of formal sector wage worker stayers, while the transitions from the informal sector jobs to formal sector ones decline. Bad conditions on the labour markets affect transitions between working and non-working positions: in time of crisis, all kind of workers more often become unemployed or inactive than during the growth periods.

Table 11.3 Summary statistics of the variables used in the regressions (pooled rounds 2000–2001–2002–2004)

| | Formal sector workers | | | | | | Informal sector workers | | | | | |
|---|---|---|---|---|---|---|---|---|---|---|---|---|
| | Wage workers | | Self-employed | | Total | | Wage workers | | Self-employed | | Total | |
| | Mean | Std dev. | Mean | Std dev. | Mean | Std dev. | Mean | Std dev. | Mean | Std dev. | Mean | Std dev. |
| Hourly earnings (in CPI deflated Ariary) | 0.025 | 0.031 | 0.055 | 0.117 | 0.027 | 0.041 | 0.011 | 0.012 | 0.019 | 0.041 | 0.017 | 0.037 |
| Years of completed schooling | 10.3 | 4.1 | 11.3 | 4.1 | 10.3 | 4.1 | 6.7 | 3.4 | 7.4 | 3.7 | 7.3 | 3.7 |
| Potential experience | 22.8 | 11.2 | 25.3 | 11.9 | 23.0 | 11.2 | 24.1 | 12.5 | 26.8 | 12.8 | 26.2 | 12.8 |
| Age | 38.1 | 11.02 | 41.6 | 11.0 | 38.3 | 11.0 | 35.9 | 11.8 | 39.2 | 11.9 | 38.5 | 12.0 |
| Female | 0.408 | 0.491 | 0.299 | 0.459 | 0.402 | 0.490 | 0.476 | 0.500 | 0.503 | 0.500 | 0.497 | 0.500 |
| Married | 0.689 | 0.463 | 0.768 | 0.423 | 0.693 | 0.461 | 0.554 | 0.497 | 0.712 | 0.453 | 0.678 | 0.467 |
| *Industries* | | | | | | | | | | | | |
| Agriculture | 0.007 | 0.081 | 0.013 | 0.115 | 0.007 | 0.083 | 0.013 | 0.113 | 0.075 | 0.263 | 0.062 | 0.240 |
| Food processing | 0.025 | 0.156 | 0.005 | 0.073 | 0.024 | 0.153 | 0.021 | 0.145 | 0.024 | 0.152 | 0.023 | 0.150 |
| Clothing | 0.193 | 0.395 | 0.027 | 0.162 | 0.185 | 0.388 | 0.081 | 0.273 | 0.139 | 0.346 | 0.126 | 0.332 |
| Machinery | 0.013 | 0.112 | 0.003 | 0.052 | 0.012 | 0.110 | 0.000 | 0.000 | 0.000 | 0.013 | 0.000 | 0.011 |
| Other manufacturing | 0.093 | 0.290 | 0.116 | 0.321 | 0.094 | 0.292 | 0.098 | 0.298 | 0.098 | 0.298 | 0.098 | 0.298 |
| Construction | 0.036 | 0.187 | 0.081 | 0.273 | 0.038 | 0.192 | 0.102 | 0.303 | 0.066 | 0.249 | 0.074 | 0.262 |
| Transportation | 0.075 | 0.263 | 0.124 | 0.330 | 0.077 | 0.267 | 0.062 | 0.241 | 0.049 | 0.216 | 0.052 | 0.221 |
| Trade | 0.089 | 0.285 | 0.394 | 0.489 | 0.105 | 0.306 | 0.112 | 0.316 | 0.356 | 0.479 | 0.303 | 0.460 |
| Public administration | 0.151 | 0.358 | 0.000 | 0.000 | 0.143 | 0.351 | 0.001 | 0.034 | 0.000 | 0.018 | 0.000 | 0.022 |
| Other services | 0.318 | 0.466 | 0.237 | 0.426 | 0.314 | 0.464 | 0.509 | 0.500 | 0.192 | 0.394 | 0.261 | 0.439 |

| | | | | | | | | | | | | |
|---|---|---|---|---|---|---|---|---|---|---|---|---|
| *Size of the firm* | | | | | | | | | | | | |
| 1 to 10 | 0.158 | 0.365 | 0.876 | 0.330 | 0.194 | 0.396 | 0.859 | 0.348 | 0.993 | 0.083 | 0.964 | 0.186 |
| 11 to 100 | 0.306 | 0.461 | 0.124 | 0.330 | 0.297 | 0.457 | 0.141 | 0.348 | 0.007 | 0.083 | 0.036 | 0.186 |
| 101 to 500 | 0.155 | 0.362 | 0.000 | 0.000 | 0.147 | 0.354 | 0.000 | 0.000 | 0.000 | 0.000 | 0.000 | 0.000 |
| More than 500 | 0.380 | 0.485 | 0.000 | 0.000 | 0.361 | 0.480 | 0.000 | 0.000 | 0.000 | 0.000 | 0.000 | 0.000 |
| *Year dummies* | | | | | | | | | | | | |
| 2000 | 0.250 | 0.433 | 0.186 | 0.390 | 0.246 | 0.431 | 0.235 | 0.424 | 0.237 | 0.426 | 0.237 | 0.425 |
| 2001 | 0.303 | 0.460 | 0.235 | 0.424 | 0.300 | 0.458 | 0.277 | 0.448 | 0.267 | 0.442 | 0.269 | 0.444 |
| 2002 | 0.237 | 0.426 | 0.399 | 0.490 | 0.246 | 0.430 | 0.283 | 0.451 | 0.268 | 0.443 | 0.272 | 0.445 |
| 2004 | 0.210 | 0.407 | 0.181 | 0.385 | 0.208 | 0.406 | 0.204 | 0.403 | 0.227 | 0.419 | 0.222 | 0.416 |
| *Observations* | 7,007 | | 371 | | 7,378 | | 1,781 | | 6,397 | | 8,178 | |

Source: *1-2-3 Surveys*, phases 1, 2000–2004, DIAL/INSTAT; authors' calculations.

Table 11.4 Transition matrices of employment status between 2000 and 2004 (%)

| 2000 | 2001 | | | | |
|---|---|---|---|---|---|
| | Not working | Formal wage workers | Informal wage workers | Self-employed | Total |
| Not working | 72.2 | 9.6 | 4.6 | 13.6 | 100.00 |
| Formal wage | 8.6 | 79.0 | 5.4 | 7.0 | 100.00 |
| Informal wage | 15.1 | 26.0 | 30.2 | 28.7 | 100.00 |
| Self-employed | 16.6 | 10.0 | 7.7 | 65.7 | 100.00 |
| Total | 32.9 | 32.1 | 7.6 | 27.4 | 100.00 |
| Observations | 5,883 | | | | |

| 2001 | 2002 | | | | |
|---|---|---|---|---|---|
| | Not working | Formal wage workers | Informal wage workers | Self-employed | Total |
| Not working | 71.2 | 8.5 | 3.5 | 16.8 | 100.00 |
| Formal wage | 14.7 | 65.0 | 7.3 | 13.0 | 100.00 |
| Informal wage | 18.5 | 18.8 | 33.8 | 28.9 | 100.00 |
| Self-employed | 19.7 | 7.1 | 7.0 | 66.2 | 100.00 |
| Total | 35.2 | 26.5 | 7.9 | 30.4 | 100.00 |
| Observations | 5,608 | | | | |

| 2002 | 2004 | | | | |
|---|---|---|---|---|---|
| | Not working | Formal wage workers | Informal wage workers | Self-employed | Total |
| Not working | 64.4 | 14.3 | 3.6 | 17.7 | 100.00 |
| Formal wage | 9.4 | 73.9 | 6.5 | 10.2 | 100.00 |
| Informal wage | 16.9 | 24.6 | 30.0 | 28.5 | 100.00 |
| Self-employed | 16.0 | 11.4 | 7.5 | 65.1 | 100.00 |
| Total | 30.9 | 29.8 | 7.8 | 31.5 | 100.00 |
| Observations | 4,951 | | | | |

| 2000 | 2004 | | | | |
|---|---|---|---|---|---|
| | Not working | Formal wage workers | Informal wage workers | Self-employed | Total |
| Not working | 60.1 | 13.9 | 4.9 | 21.2 | 100.00 |
| Formal wage | 13.2 | 67.2 | 6.7 | 12.9 | 100.00 |
| Informal wage | 17.5 | 21.3 | 27.6 | 33.6 | 100.00 |
| Self-employed | 18.2 | 11.1 | 6.8 | 63.9 | 100.00 |
| Total | 29.7 | 29.7 | 7.6 | 33.0 | 100.00 |
| Observations | 3,503 | | | | |

Source: 1-2-3 Surveys, phases 1, 2000–2004, DIAL/INSTAT; authors' calculations.

To end this descriptive analysis, we turn to the earnings dynamics by institutional sector and status in employment. Compared to Table 11.4, the panel sample is restricted to the individuals holding a job and having positive earnings in both periods. Consequently, those who are not working or unpaid family workers are excluded. The number of observations is around 3,000 for year-to-year matrices and 2,000 for the 2000–2004 matrix.

Consistently with Table 11.4, informal sector wage workers get the lowest pay, followed by informal self-employed, formal sector wage workers and the formal self-employed workers at the highest end of the earnings ladder. If we now take into account transition status, informal sector wage worker stayers systematically perceive less than those who changed to self-employment or formal sector wage jobs. Symmetrically, self-employed stayers get a better remuneration than those who move to formal or informal sector wage jobs, with the exception of the 2001–2002 period. Such exception can be due to a crisis effect (shrink in demand and increased competition), while formal sector wages are more rigid. Finally, formal sector wage worker stayers, as primary labour market insiders, are by far the best compensated workers (compared with the other eight transition statuses); the only exceptions are formal self-employed workers. This result suggests that, on average, creating an informal firm from a formal sector wage job induces a decline in earnings. Two potential reasons may be invocated: some have been constrained to settle an informal business because of a lay-off in a formal activity or other institutional factors (like retirement age); non-pecuniary considerations may be at stake, but a lower pay than those who obtained a formal sector wage job.

These unconditional earnings in the end year do not tell much on earning dynamics, initial conditions being only taken into account through the labour status in the base year. Considering growth rates is a first step to control for initial earnings. Moving to informal sector wage jobs is associated with the lowest increase in earnings over all periods, whereas being able to change to a formal self-employed job is associated with the highest earnings growth. Moving out of informal sector wage job ensures higher earnings growth rates, while abandoning self-employment for wage jobs, or formal to informal wage jobs provides lower growth rates. In terms of earnings growth, the picture for those who quit a formal sector wage job to create an informal business is mixed: in two cases out of four they perform better than their stayers counterparts (2000–2001 and 2001–2002), but do worse in the two other cases (2002–2004 and 2000–2004). This suggests a potential trade-off between these two kinds of jobs, a stylized feature underlined in the literature.

Of course, these unconditional averages should be controlled for observed and unobserved characteristics, which is the purpose of the following section. Finally, our analysis shows that earnings levels and changes are highly dependent on transitions. Transition and earnings matrices are very consistent, confirming the high quality of our data, a feature already stressed in previous methodological papers (Rakotomanana, 2011).

*Earnings gaps analysis*

In this section we discuss the earnings gaps between formal and informal sector jobs at the aggregate level, estimated using the four estimations procedures presented in the third section of this chapter. In the following discussion, we compare the three other work statuses with formal sector wage workers, as our benchmark.

*Formal vs informal sector workers*

At the aggregate level, not considering firm size, the OLS estimate of the informal sector earnings gap is a rather huge –20 per cent. Taking into account the (time invariant) unobserved individual characteristics (UICs) through fixed effect OLS estimation (FEOLS) reduces the earnings penalty significantly, down to –10 per cent. Thus, nearly half of the gap can be explained by unobserved characteristics, the most productive workers privileging the formal sector. As always, this standard feature does not tell us much about what specific factors are really at play. On the one hand, the innate ability or the "talent parabola" is commonly stressed in the literature. On the other hand, many other explanations can be put forward. For instance, UICs may have to do with more efficient social networks to get a formal sector job. However, the remaining –10 per cent gap, once we control for UICs, highlights that formal sector jobs provide higher earnings per se. Here again, this result can be due to various factors which end up, at the firm level, to a higher productivity or market power, and/or, at the worker level, to a stronger bargaining power of formal workers to negotiate higher earnings.

To go beyond average, we ran quantile regressions. While informal sector workers suffer earnings penalties at almost all levels of the conditional distribution, the gap is sharply decreasing from the bottom to the upper part. Beginning with a huge –38 per cent (quantile 0.10), the gap continuously shrinks to become insignificant around quantile 0.80. From then, it even reverts to reach +7 per cent at the upper-tier of the distribution (quantile 0.90). The FEQR gap not only confirms both the key role of UICs in reducing the "true" gap but also the pattern along the earnings distribution: from –28 per cent for the bottom quantile (quantile 0.10) to 14 per cent for the upper one (quantile 0.90).

However, once we control for the size of the enterprises, the average earnings gap nearly disappears. The OLS gap is only –6.3 per cent (Figure 11.1), while the FEOLS gap is slightly negative but non-significant. Interestingly, the profiles of the earnings gap along the distribution remain unchanged, with a systematic penalty decline for informal sector workers from the lower to the upper tier (QR, Figure 11.1). The QR estimates range from a –23 per cent penalty for informal sector workers at the bottom (quantile 10) to a 11 per cent bonus at the top (quantile 90), while the respective numbers are –13 per cent and 10 per cent for FEQR, the turning point (from penalty to premium) being around the third quartile in both cases.

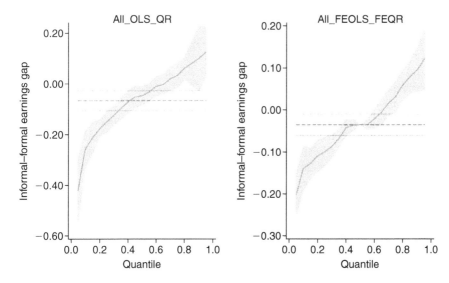

*Figure 11.1* Informal sector worker–formal sector worker earnings gap (source: *1-2-3 Surveys*, phases 1, 2000–2004, DIAL/INSTAT; authors' calculations).

Note
Fixed effects (FE) Ordinary Least Square (OLS) are denoted by FEOLS, and Fixed Effects Quantile Regressions (QR) by FEQR. Bootstrapped 95% confidence intervals are represented by the grey surface for QR and by dashed lines for the OLS.

The interpretation of the size effect is not straightforward in our informal vs formal perspective. First, conditional earnings grow with the size of the enterprise. This result is robust to any of our specification and consistent with the literature in this respect. Second, as the informal sector is often defined as enterprises under a certain size threshold (minus five or ten workers), introducing the size in our estimation as an independent variable tends to absorb the impact of informality on earnings. This is all the more the case that the two criteria used to identify the informal sector (size and registration) are highly correlated. In the remainder of this chapter we still decide to comment on the earnings gaps based on the regression including the size as an independent variable. As a consequence, two important points should be kept in mind: our results focus on the impact of non-registration on earnings, net from the size effect; the exhibited gaps should be interpreted as the most conservative estimates, which are systematically higher without control for the firm size.

Finally, whatever the earnings specification (with or without firm size), the huge gap variations along the distribution point to the intrinsic informal sector heterogeneity. This result is mainly due to the fact that the "dualistic assumption" is too rough, gathering together very diverse categories of workers within each sector, which we investigate below in more details.

*Formal vs informal wage workers*

As expected, within wage workers, those employed in the informal sector are on average worse-off than their formal sector counterparts (Figure 11.2). The OLS gap (–18 per cent) is significantly reduced to –9 per cent when individual fixed effects are introduced, suggesting that informal wage workers may have a disadvantage in terms of their unobserved productive attributes. Taking or not taking into account the fixed effects, the gap is continuously decreasing (Figure 11.2): from –30 per cent (quantile 0.10) to –5 per cent (quantile 0.90; nonsignificant) for the latter, and from –16 to 1 per cent (non-significant) respectively controlling for UICs. In both cases, formal sector wage workers conserve an earnings advantage at any position in the pay ladder. Even if we cannot exclude that non-pecuniary disadvantages of formal wage jobs may be compensated by earnings (such as poor working conditions), these results could be taken as an acceptable validation of the *exclusion hypothesis* (for this category of workers), according to which informal wage workers are constrained in their job choice, and are probably queuing for formal jobs.

*Formal wage vs informal self-employed workers*

For the bulk of the labour force, this alternative choice is probably the main trade-off, and also the most discussed in the literature. At odds with the previous

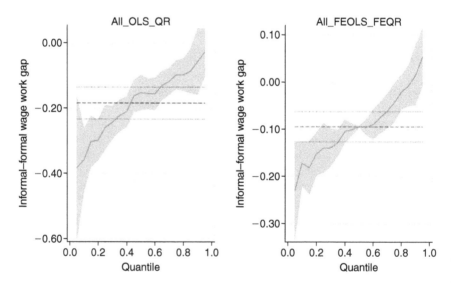

*Figure 11.2* Informal sector wage worker–formal sector wage worker earnings gap (source: *1-2-3 Surveys*, phases 1, 2000–2004, DIAL/INSTAT; authors' calculations).

Note
Fixed effects (FE) Ordinary Least Square (OLS) are denoted by FEOLS, and Fixed Effects Quantile Regressions (QR) by FEQR. Bootstrapped 95% confidence intervals are represented by the grey surface for QR and by dashed lines for the OLS.

case considered and more generally the dualistic approach, the conditional OLS gap is positive, with a significant premium of +18 per cent for the informal self-employed (Figure 11.3). Furthermore, the FEOLS models still shows a premium at +12 per cent. Again, this would mean that informal self-employed workers have an advantage in terms of their unobserved productive characteristics (probably in terms of their entrepreneurial skills), which produces an overestimation of the premium associated with being an informal self-employed worker compared to exerting as a formal wage worker if this individual heterogeneity is not accounted for. We nevertheless should be cautious before claiming that the *exit option* may be at stake, as the self-employed earnings may be overestimated for at least two reasons: first, the measure of earnings we computed remunerates both labour and capital factors (mixed income), the latter being far from negligible in the informal sector (Vaillant *et al.*, 2014); second, the self-employed earnings include the share which should be attributed to the productive contribution of unpaid family workers. As we do not have any order of magnitude of these two phenomena, it is difficult to exclude the possibility that the premium we obtain may not turn into a penalty, once these two factors are taken into account.

When turning to quantile regressions (Figure 11.3), the distributional profile of the gap presents the same now clear pattern, as in the two previous cases. The gap steeply increases with earnings level, and is in favour of the informal

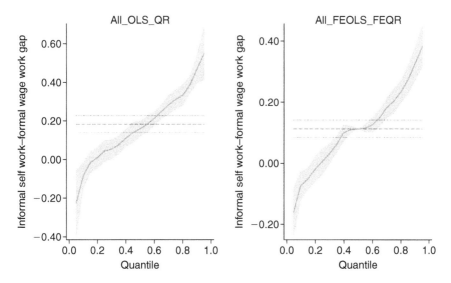

*Figure 11.3* Informal self-employed worker–formal sector wage worker earnings gap (source: *1-2-3 Surveys*, phases 1, 2000–2004, DIAL/INSTAT; authors' calculations).

Note
Fixed effects (FE) Ordinary Least Square (OLS) are denoted by FEOLS, and Fixed Effects Quantile Regressions (QR) by FEQR. Bootstrapped 95% confidence intervals are represented by the grey surface for QR and by dashed lines for the OLS.

self-employed workers. In absolute terms, informal self-employed labourers suffer a penalty only at the lowest end of the conditional distribution (up to about the first quartile where the gap is not significant). Afterwards, the gap is reversed into a significant premium, growing continuously up to 60 per cent for the richest decile (quantile 0.90), crossing the OLS estimate at the median point of the earnings distribution. FEQR confirm this trend, the only difference being that the range of variation of the gap along the distribution is attenuated. Once the UICs are controlled for, informal self-employed workers are better off at all points of the pay scale above the first quartile up to 39 per cent at quantile 0.90. All in all, and given the size of the premium, we can confidently conclude that informal self-employment may be more lucrative than formal wage alternatives, especially for the richest workers. As a matter of consequence, we have good presumptions to assert that, in Madagascar, a substantial part of the labour force has deliberately chosen to work in the informal sector as non-wage workers, for pecuniary reasons.

*Formal wage vs formal self-employed workers*

The earnings comparison of formal wage workers and formal self-employed workers is clearly in favour of the latter, whatever the model chosen (Figure 11.4). The OLS estimate presents a +93 per cent premium, just slightly reduced

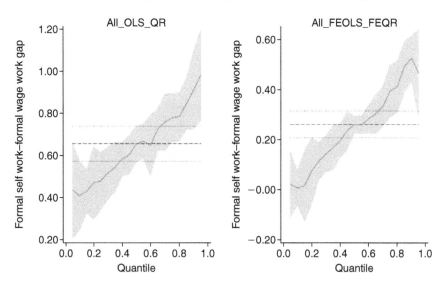

*Figure 11.4* Formal self-employed worker–formal sector wage worker earnings gap (source: *1-2-3 Surveys*, phases 1, 2000–2004, DIAL/INSTAT; authors' calculations).

Note
Fixed effects (FE) Ordinary Least Square (OLS) are denoted by FEOLS, and Fixed Effects Quantile Regressions (QR) by FEQR. Bootstrapped 95% confidence intervals are represented by the grey surface for QR and by dashed lines for the OLS.

with fixed effects (+30 per cent). As with the informal self-employed workers, their unobserved productive attributes may be better than those of the formal wage workers. As in the case of informal self-employed workers, the premium is continuously increasing with earnings levels, but is translated upwards, a pattern in line with the empirical results obtained in the literature for developed countries. Controlling for UICs or not, formal self-employed workers are always better off in terms of earnings than formal sector wage workers, the premium culminating at +149 per cent (QR) and +69 per cent (FEQR). Overall, it seems that the Malagasy labour market functions under a regime of wage repression. Whatever the reasons – macro pressures of international integration, deliberate policies to control inflation or weak bargaining power of the wage workers; the latter being the most plausible – it seems globally preferable to work as an independent (even in the informal sector) than as a wage worker (at least in non-farm activities).

*Formal vs informal self-employed workers*

Lastly, we turn to the comparison between the two types of self-employed workers: formal and informal. Formal self-employed workers are rarely considered in the literature on LDCs, maybe because they are too few in the countries considered. But there are many reasons to focus on this category of workers: first, to compare our results with those obtained in developed countries on salaried vs non-salaried workers' earnings gap, as in these countries self-employed workers are quasi-exclusively formal; second, because it allows us to establish the link with the existing formal/informal sector literature from a business perspective (not job). Finally, the comparison appears more legitimate as the nature of incomes and unobservables potentially at play are in both cases equivalent (which is not true concerning wage workers).

Formal self-employed workers are systematically in a better position than their informal counterparts, all along the pay scale (Figure 11.5; the reference group is now informal self-employed workers). Returns to firm's formalization is always positive and increasing with the net earnings, even when controlling for entrepreneurial skills and other unobserved characteristics, the most favoured in this respect choosing disproportionately the formal sector. This advantage of formal household businesses may be due to higher initial level of physical capital or more productive combination of factors (our models do not provide elements on this point), but it is compatible with the potential causal benefits of getting formal (access to credit and markets) as found in the literature.

## Conclusion

In this chapter, we study which of the exclusion or the exit hypothesis regarding informality is best suited to the urban Malagasy labour market. To this end, we focus on the earnings gaps between formal and informal workers. Assuming that individual earnings are proxies of individual utilities, our approach considers

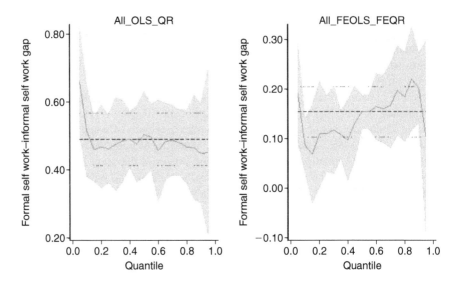

*Figure 11.5* Formal self-employed worker–informal self-employed worker earnings gap (source: *1-2-3 Surveys*, phases 1, 2000–2004, DIAL/INSTAT; authors' calculations).

Note
Fixed effects (FE) Ordinary Least Square (OLS) are denoted by FEOLS, and Fixed Effects Quantile Regressions (QR) by FEQR. Bootstrapped 95% confidence intervals are represented by the grey surface for QR and by dashed lines for the OLS.

that if informal workers earn more than their formal counterparts, this reflects a deliberate choice of the former to be informal workers. Taking advantage of the rich *1-2-3 Surveys* for Madagascar, the four wave panel data (2000–2001–2002–2004) give us the unique opportunity to control for time-invariant unobserved individual characteristics. Using both standard and fixed effects earnings equations estimated at the mean and at various conditional quantiles of the earnings distribution, we address the key issue of heterogeneity, at three different levels: the worker level, taking into account individual unobserved characteristics; the job level, comparing wage workers with self-employed workers; the distributional level. To our knowledge, this approach is applied for the first time ever in Madagascar, and rarely for Sub-Saharan Africa.

Our results suggest that the informal earnings gap highly depends on the workers' job status (wage employment vs self-employment) and on their relative position in the earnings distribution. Our main conclusions are often at odds with the exclusion hypothesis and what would show the observed raw earnings gaps: in many cases, informal jobs are more rewarding (self-employment) or as rewarding (male wage workers) as formal wage jobs. This feature is due to the relatively low wages of formal wage jobs. The reason for such a specificity should be investigated further (international competition pressure? wage repression policy?). Second, Madagascar's labour market seems more integrated than its development level would have predicted. The earnings gaps look more like those observed in emerging countries, characterized by a weak segmentation between formal and informal jobs, than the standard dualistic Sub-Saharan labour markets. Third, the systematic premium at all points of the distribution of formal self-employed workers over their informal counterparts suggests that formalization of non-farm household businesses seems to be beneficial. Policies aiming at easing administrative procedures to register informal firms should be encouraged

Our chapter raises further promising prospects, and could be extended in various directions. A first extension would be to better control for individual unobserved characteristics, by purging our earning estimations of differences in the amount of physical capital (for self-employed workers) and social networks. A firm based panel approach may be an interesting alternative entry in this respect. Another potential extension would be to exploit further the nature of our data (four point panel) by estimating dynamic earnings equations. Lastly, our work could be usefully complemented by investigating the determinants of job satisfaction, to enlarge the perspective which relies exclusively on earnings outputs and to check the robustness of our conclusions in this regard.

## References

Bargain, O., Kwenda, P. (2011) "Earnings Structures, Informal Employment, and Self-Employment: New Evidence from Brazil, Mexico, and South Africa", *Review of Income and Wealth*, 57: S100–S122.

Canay, I.A. (2011) "A Simple Approach to Quantile Regression for Panel Data", *Econometrics Journal*, 14(3): 368–386.

Cling, J.P., Razafindrakoto, M., Roubaud, F. (2005) "Export Processing Zones in Madagascar: A Success Story under Threat?" *World Development*, 33(5): 785–803.

De Soto, H. (1989) *The Other Path: The Invisible Revolution in the Third World*, New York: Harper & Row.

Falco, P., Kerr, A., Rankin, N., Sandefur, J., Teal, F. (2010) "The Returns to Formality and Informality in Urban Africa", *CSAE WPS.2010–03*, Oxford.

Fields, G.S. (1990) "Labor Market Modeling and the Urban Informal Sector: Theory and Evidence", in David Turnham, Bernard Salomé and Antoine Schwarz, eds, *The Informal Sector Revisited*, Paris: OECD.

Gong, X., Van Soest, A., Villagomez, E. (2004) "Mobility in the Urban Labor Market: A Panel Data Analysis for Mexico", *Economic Development and Cultural Change*, 53(1): 1–36.

Gubert, F., Robilliard, A.-S. (2010) "Croissance et pauvreté à Madagascar: un aperçu de la dernière décennie (1997–2007)", in B. Gastineau, F. Gubert, A.-S. Robilliard and F. Roubaud eds, *Madagascar face au défi des Objectifs du millénaire pour le développement*, Marseille: IRD.

ILO (1993) "Resolution Concerning Statistics of Employment in the Informal Sector", Fifteenth International Conference of Labour Statisticians, Geneva: ILO.

Koenker, R. (2004) "Quantile Regression for Longitudinal Data", *Journal of Multivariate Analysis*, 91(1): 74–89.

Maloney, W. (1999) "Does Informality imply Segmentation in Urban Labor Markets? Evidence from Sectoral Transitions in Mexico", *World Bank Economic Review*, 13(2): 275–302.

Nordman, C.J., Rakotomanana, F., Roubaud, F. (2012) "Informal versus Formal: A Panel Data Analysis of Earnings Gaps in Madagascar", Working Paper 2012-12, DIAL, Paris (www.dial.prd.fr/dial_publications/PDF/Doc_travail/2012-12.pdf).

Nguyen, H.C., Nordman, C.J., Roubaud, F. (2013) "Who Suffers the Penalty? A Panel Data Analysis of Earnings Gaps in Vietnam", *Journal of Development Studies*, 49(12): 1694–1710.

Perry, G.E., Maloney, W.F., Arias, O.S., Fajnzylber, P., Mason, A.D., Saavedra-Chanduvi, J. (2007) *Informality: Exit and Exclusion*, Washington DC: World Bank, World Bank Latin American and Caribbean Studies.

Rakotomanana, F. (2011) "Secteur informel urbain, marché du travail et pauvreté: essais d'analyse sur le cas de Madagascar", PhD dissertation, Bordeaux IV University, December.

Rakotomanana, F., Ramilison, E., Roubaud, F. (2003) "The Creation of an Annual Labour Force Survey in Madagascar: An Example for Sub-saharan Africa", *InterStat*, (27): 35–58.

Razafindrakoto, M., Roubaud, F. (2002) "Madagascar à la croisée des chemins: la croissance durable est-elle possible?" *Afrique contemporaine*, 75–92.

Razafindrakoto, M., Roubaud, F., Torelli, C. (2009) "Measuring the Informal Sector and Informal Employment: The Experience drawn from 1-2-3 Surveys in African Countries", *African Statistical Journal*, 9 (Special Issue): 88–147.

Vaillant, J., Grimm, M., Lay, J., Roubaud, F. (2014), "Informal Sector Dynamics in Times of Fragile Growth: The Case of Madagascar", in *Understanding the Links between Labour and Development*, R. Dimova and C.J. Nordman (eds), *The European Journal of Development*, Special Issue (forthcoming).

# 12 Do limits exist to informality growth in South America?

## A preliminary exploration

*Francisco Verdera*[1]

The purpose of this chapter is to explore whether there are limits, ceilings, to the growth of urban informal employment in South America (SA). To do this, we need to describe and analyse the factors that determined the evolution of employment in the urban informal sector (UIS) in the region. The period of analysis goes from 1970, when the UIS was defined and measured for the first time, until the 2008–2009 crisis. The detection of the pattern of UIS employment growth and the factors that contributed to it require a long-term analysis. Once this is done we can evaluate its limits.

Informality in this chapter is conceived as a massive and long-lasting urban phenomenon. Understanding and facing the challenge of UIS means not just to consider small variations in its magnitude, as it represents an enormous proportion of the urban employment. UIS is a result of a structural problem that can only be explained with a long-term structural analysis. The diagnosis, measurement and proposed solutions for the formalization of UIS workers cannot be confined to short-term aspects, such as the low labour formalization of independent workers and those of micro enterprises (MSEs), or to regulatory issues such as high non-wage labour costs – or fringe benefits – that companies have to cover.

The need for a long period of time to analyse the behaviour and persistence of UIS, as opposed to the usual short-term analysis, have two main interests: studying the relationship between the UIS and economic growth; evaluating the impact of external shocks on labour informality.

On the relationship between the UIS evolution and economic growth, Bourguignon (in this book) argues that growth has been insufficient to reduce informality. As in recent years economic growth resumed in the region, we will have look at the UIS dynamics. On the other hand, the evaluation of the impact of external shocks on informality in a long-term perspective can be seen as a declination in SA of the long-standing debate on unemployment in developed countries. The argument posed by Boeri and van Ours (2008) while comparing the US and Europe unemployment rates, is that the latter starts rising above the former because of the prolonged effect of the oil crisis of the 1970s and the level and structure of costs, and not because of the usually criticized employment protection regime, allegedly more rigid. The same applies with the UIS dynamics in

SA, as discussed below. The impact of the external debt crisis marked the turning point, and not social protection regimes which were identified as the main factor culprit for the rise in informality.

The operational definition of informality, which allows us to build series from 1970 to date, is the employment in the UIS, originated in the PREALC–ILO programme. The same definition has been estimated and published by ILO (1990–2006). The magnitude of the UIS is the result of adding employees and employers in small businesses up to five workers, plus workers self-employed (non-professionals or technicians), unpaid family workers and domestic workers.

This chapter covers ten SA countries, for which it has been possible to get more or less continuous information about their active age population (AAP), the economically active population (EAP) and urban employment, including the UIS, for a period of 38 years. These countries are Argentina, Bolivia, Brazil, Colombia, Chile, Ecuador, Paraguay, Peru (Metropolitan Lima only), Uruguay and Venezuela. We have built an annual data base for these ten countries from 1970 to 2008.

## Employment growth in the urban informal sector, 1970–2008

In the ten countries, the UIS employment growth during the whole period 1970–2008 has witnessed a high rate (4.4 per cent, in weighted average).[2] The share of UIS employment on the whole has incremented from 34.9 per cent in 1970 to 47.8 per cent in 2008, an increase of 12.9 in percentage points in 38 years. The higher growth rate occurred between 1991 and 2003, as the effect of the structural adjustment that followed the 1982 external debt crisis.

### Stages of UIS development in the region

The evolution of employment in the UIS (changes in size and features) runs through at least five stages (Figure 12.1). The first phase (1970–1974), corresponds to the discovery of the UIS and of the recognition of its early growth, from a relatively low level. In this first phase, it increased from 34.9 per cent of urban employment to 40.6 per cent. The second phase (1975–1979) resulted in a temporary stabilization in about 40 per cent of urban employment, with a slight initial decline, followed by a rapid increase. The third phase (1980–1991), was one of new stabilizing after strong fluctuations of up to five percentage points in the second half of the decade to 1980, from 37.7 to 43.6 per cent as the result of external debt crisis in the region. The fourth stage (1992–2003) showed a strong and sustained growth of the UIS, from 40.7 per cent to the peak of 52.6 per cent in 2003. This phase covers the period of the structural adjustment and the promotion of growth through primary export. Finally, the fifth and most recent stage (2004–2008) showed for the first time a significant reduction in the share of the UIS, from 52.6 to 47.8 per cent. This decrease was the result of GDP high growth, based on a very strong recovery of primary exports prices. Nevertheless,

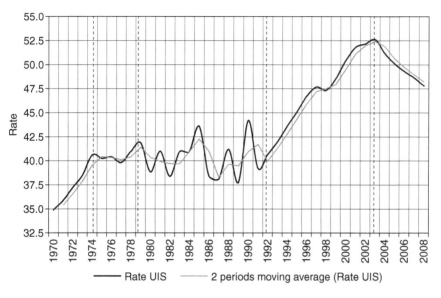

*Figure 12.1* South America: UIS growth, 1970–2008 (source: ECLAC and ILO, author's calculations).

the impact of the global crisis of 2008 in the region stopped the reduction of the UIS.

In summary, we can establish two major periods. The first one, from 1970 to 1991, is driven mainly by demographic factors (increase in the urban EAP). The second, from 1992 to 2008, is driven by economic factors, such as the external debt crisis, the structural adjustment and the significant growth spell between 2003 and 2008, before the recent crisis. It should be noted that in terms of absolute size, the magnitude of the employment in the UIS never fell, even in the 2003–2008 period in which the rate decreased.

### UIS employment level and growth rate by groups of countries

The evolution of the UIS employment in SA for the entire period 1970–2008 can be classified into three groups of countries (Table 12.1). Countries with relatively low UIS rates (less than 40 per cent): Uruguay and Chile. Countries with intermediate levels of UIS rates, between 40 and 50 per cent: Argentina, Brazil and Venezuela, and where its percentage is rising. And finally countries with high UIS rates (more than 50 per cent): Paraguay, Bolivia, Peru, Ecuador and Colombia. The first two countries reached the highest levels of informality, with UIS rates over 60 per cent of urban jobs.

What are the factors behind these ranges and persistence, showing either relatively low or very high levels of informality, differing a lot between groups of countries? At this stage, a first response, yet descriptive, is that most of the

*Table 12.1* Evolution of the UIS size by countries and periods, 1970–2008

| Years | ≤30% | >30% and ≤ 40% | 40% and ≤50% | >50% and ≤60% | >60% |
|---|---|---|---|---|---|
| 1970 | Uruguay (20.7%)<br>Brazil (30.3%) | Argentina (37.6%)<br>Chile (39.9%)<br>Peru (33.1%) | Colombia (43.4%)<br>Ecuador (45.4%)<br>Venezuela (44.0%) | Bolivia (56.0%)<br>Paraguay (57.0%) | – |
| 1980 | Chile (25.9%)<br>Uruguay (27.0%)<br>Venezuela (29.3%) | Brazil (38.0%)<br>Colombia (34.4%) | Argentina (48.4%) | Bolivia (53.7%)<br>Ecuador (53.0%)<br>Paraguay (57.0%)<br>Peru (52.0%) | – |
| 1990 | Uruguay (30.7%) | Chile (37.8%)<br>Venezuela (33.0%)<br>Colombia (40.0%) | Argentina (44.6%)<br>Brazil (46.0%)<br>Ecuador (49.6%)<br>Paraguay (48.2%) | Peru (50.8%) | Bolivia (64.0%) |
| 2000 | | Chile (38.9%)<br>Uruguay (40.4%) | Brazil (48.9)<br>Venezuela (47.5)<br>Argentina (49.9%) | Colombia (55.6%)<br>Ecuador (57.2)<br>Peru (58.8%) | Bolivia (63.7%)<br>Paraguay (60.9%) |

Sources: ECLAC and ILO.

countries had very high growth rates of their UIS, above the average of SA of 4.4 per cent for the whole period. If not considered the reduction of UIS in 2003–2008, the average growth rate would be even higher.

## Determinants of growth of labour informality

Current consensus is that there are two main views on labour informality (see the introduction of the book). On the one hand, informality is a consequence of low productivity from small units of production and independent workers (ILO, 1972). On the other hand, informality is due to employers finding it impossible to comply with excessive legal regulations, which would be too costly to implement (Loayza and Rigolini, 2006; Perry *et al.*, 2007; Galli and Kucera, 2008). These two views have a short-term focus. They do not take into account that informal employment is a persistent and massive phenomenon, and that it shows an upward trend in the long run. Therefore, to have an understanding of informality and its evolution we need a long-term approach. Thus, appropriate policies to respond to the challenge of reducing informality should also have a long-term horizon.

Given growth in informality over a long period of time, and taking into account the different UIS growth levels by groups of countries, we can make several hypotheses about the factors that have caused the emergence, growth and permanence of urban informal employment in South America. We can separate these factors into three groups: demographic, economic (macro and structural) and labour market functionings.

The central argument of this chapter is that the rise – and the large size – in urban informal employment in SA was caused by two main factors. On the one hand, a sustained increase of the urban labour force, driven by the increase of urban population. This was a consequence of the effects of the successive stages of demographic transition, by groups of countries. On the other hand, the relative stagnation of economic activity limited the absorption of large increases in the EAP as formal wage employment, a phenomenon accentuated by the impact of the crisis of external debt of 1982. The structural adjustment that followed the crisis and the consequent reduction in the size of the state were needed to be able to comply with the payment of external debt service.

As for the argument of the structural view and the question of whether the UIS will gradually disappear when a country becomes developed, Bourguignon (in this book) responds with an argument similar to the proposed scheme. He argues:

> What we expect, ideally, is of course *that economic growth will progressively eliminate the informal sector*. This is more or less what we observed in today's developed countries.... Why is the case that apparently in many developing countries there is some growth yet the informal remains in relative terms more or less constant? At the same time, the urban population is growing.... One explanation is to say that at the same time that growth is taking place, there is technical change ... which means that the formal sector is growing in output but with much less and less employment content.

By analogy with the argument posed by Boeri and van Ours (2008), we can state that it is not possible to understand the UIS growth in the 1980s if the impact of external debt crisis and the consequent recession of urban formal employment is not taken into account. The argument can be developed in two ways. First, we can compare the pattern of evolution and the levels of the UIS, on average for the region and for groups of countries, highlighting their differences. The evolution of demographic, economic and productive factors will determine the rate of urban informality, as the role of the public sector. The role of these factors becomes evident when comparing the different sizes of the UIS by groups of countries and their different evolution patterns.

The evolution of the economic factors by groups of countries is determined by their respective GDP structure and their sectoral productivity. These factors were affected by successive crises. Among the causes of the stagnation in the GDP and the average productivity of labour, three key characteristics should be underlined: the net transfer of resources abroad for external debt service; the insufficient gross fix capital accumulation; the decreasing role of the state, expressed in the decline in spending and in public employment. The very low share of public spending in the public labour administration is one additional aspect to consider.

Second, we can evaluate the factors that determine growth in urban informal employment in the long term. These factors will serve to establish the limits of possible growth. We propose the following determining factors in UIS growth (see Figure 12.2):

- the increase in labour supply (EAP) in the long term, due to the growth of urban population, and to the increase of the AAP and of the female activity rate (FAR);

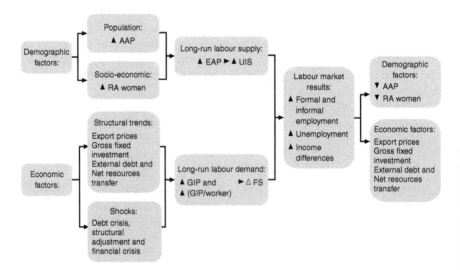

*Figure 12.2* Relationships in determining UIS size and evolution (source: author).

- the structural economic factors that led to the decline in GDP growth and to the increase in labour productivity in the formal sector, i.e. the components of the formal labour demand in the long term. It is assumed that only the modern sector is responsible for the growth of GDP and of the labour productivity;
- the relative stability of the urban unemployment rate and the lack of employment absorption by the formal sector (FS), i.e. jobless growth (as a trend), resulting in the large increase in UIS employment.

After evaluating the relevance of these factors in explaining the growth of UIS employment, we will assess whether these same factors could limit the expansion of the UIS. First, the growth of the EAP will slow down because the increase of the AAP and the FAR will become smaller, which will consolidate a demographic transition, as in the cases of Uruguay and Argentina. Second, the growth of non-agricultural (urban) GDP, being greater than the productivity of labour in the FS will further increase formal employment, with greater absorption of the EAP. Finally, the excess in labour supply will be reduced if the FS continues growing. Thus the UIS employment will decrease.

## The importance of demographic trends

The huge increase in the UIS would not have been possible without the enormous growth of the urban workforce in SA in the long term. This growth, in turn, was a consequence at least of the following processes: the passage from the initial phase of demographic transition to the next phases; the large increase in urban population and the consequent increase of the AAP; the increase in the urban labour force, almost entirely due to increased urban AAP and also, to a lesser extent, to the increment in FAR.

### *Countries according to their stage of demographic transition*

The large increase in the UIS employment occurred when most SA countries were passing from the early stage to the moderate stage of their demographic transition. Table 12.2 shows the ten countries grouped according to their stage of transition in the first part of the decades 1960, 1980 and 2000.

Countries with the highest rates of informality (Bolivia, Colombia, Ecuador, Paraguay and Peru) remained until the period 1980–1985 in the moderate stage of transition, with high birth rates, between 32 and 42 per 1,000 inhabitants. By contrast, countries with lower rates of informality were in the same five years in full transition with lower birth rates, and lower natural growth, as in the cases of Argentina, Chile and Uruguay and, up to some point, Brazil.

The high population growth in 1960 and 1980 contributed to higher levels of informality in some countries (Table 12.2). Conversely, informality decreases when these countries engage in the process of demographic transition. A lower pressure of population growth in countries that have already achieved the

*Table 12.2* Demographic transition phases by countries

| Demographic transition stages | | | |
|---|---|---|---|
| *Incipient* | *Moderate* | *Advanced* | *Full* |
| *BR: ≥42 per thousand* | *BR: between 32 and 42 per thousand* | *BR: between 22 and 32 per thousand* | *BR: ≤22 per thousand* |
| *1960–1965*<br>Bolivia (2.2)<br>Brazil (3.0)<br>Colombia (3.0)<br>Ecuador (2.9)<br>Peru (2.9)<br>Venezuela (3.6) | Chile (2.5)<br>Paraguay (2.7) | Argentina (1.6) | Uruguay (1.2) |
| *1980–1985*<br>– | Bolivia (2.1)<br>Ecuador (2.7)<br>Paraguay (2.9)<br>Peru (2.4) | Argentina (1.5)<br>Brazil (2.3)<br>Chile (1.6)<br>Colombia (2.2)<br>Venezuela (2.8) | Uruguay (0.6) |
| *2000–2005*<br>– | – | Bolivia (2.0)<br>Colombia (1.6)<br>Ecuador (1.2)<br>Paraguay (2.0)<br>Peru (1.4)<br>Venezuela (1.8) | Argentina (1.0)<br>Brazil (1.3)<br>Chile (1.1)<br>Uruguay (0.04) |

Source: CEPAL, *Statistical Yearbook*, 2009.

Note
Values for each country correspond to the average annual growth rate of the population for each spell of 5 years (in %). BR: birth rate (1,000).

advanced stage should reduce urban informality. The increased urbanization in the region means less informality. The countries where the rural population and rural–urban migration are still significant displayed higher rates of informality. The UIS will continue to increase according to AAP natural growth and internal migration.

## Composition of the urban labour force growth

The two sources of the growth of EAP have been the increases of the AAP and of the rate of activity. The main source that explains the large increase in the urban labour force in the countries of the region between 1980 and 2008 was the AAP, which represents almost all the increase in EAP in the period: 2.9 per cent of 3.0 per cent of the increase in EAP (annual averages for both rates, Table 12.3).

*Table 12.3* Sources of urban labour force growth by sex, 1980–2008

|  | Total | Men | Women |
|---|---|---|---|
| Urban labour force (EAP) | 3.0 | 2.9 | 4.3 |
| Urban active age population (AAP) | 2.9 | 2.9 | 2.9 |
| Urban activity rate: |  |  |  |
| • Growth rate | 0.1 | −0.1 | 1.3 |
| • Difference in % points | 1.8 | −1.3 | 15.4 |

Source: ECLAC, author's calculations.

Note
Rates are calculated from the beginning to the end of period. Moving averages give similar results.

The contribution of the growth of the urban activity rate, the second source of growth in the EAP, was only significant for women. Still, the increased rate of activity represents 30 per cent of the total increase in female urban EAP between 1980 and 2008. The rate rose by 15.4 percentage points. In contrast, male AR decreased by 1.3 percentage points. The group of countries with the lowest rates of urban EAP growth – below the regional average – can be associated with those with lower rates of urban informality, and countries with fastest EAP growing led to higher informality rates.

Therefore, it is reasonable to establish a direct relationship between population growth, the AAP and the UIS employment growth in all countries (on average) and by groups of countries. It must be emphasized that the increase in urban female EAP was due to the substantial increase in AR, and its increased presence in informal sector employment. In short, the increase of urban AAP led to a very significant growth of the UIS.

## Macroeconomic context and UIS dynamics

### Major stages of macroeconomic evolution

Until the end of the 1970s, Latin America benefitted from an outstanding economic growth. Between 1950 and 1979, the average annual growth was about 6 per cent, with a total of 11 years with average rates above that level, and none were negative. In the mid 1970s there was a fall in GDP growth compared to the early years of this decade, but always with positive and high rates, the lowest being near 3 per cent, in 1974 and 1977 (Figure 12.3).

By contrast, from 1980 to 1982, 1988, 1989, 1998 and 2001 there were sharp growth falls. The first fall was caused by the impact of the external debt crisis. The second and the third were due to the international financial crisis, which included the effect of a severe credit contraction and banking crisis, in most countries. Between 1980 and 2002, the GDP growth rate fluctuated around 3 per cent, being negative seven years, until the recent phase of growth led by primary export, from 2003 to 2008. The annual growth rate returned to oscillate around 6 per cent, with only two years above that level.

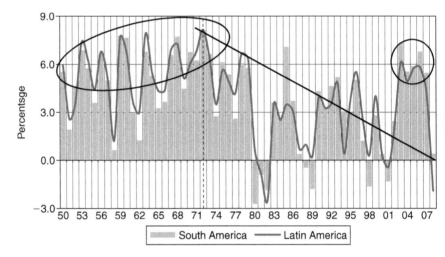

*Figure 12.3* GDP growth, 1950–2009 (source: ECLAC, author's calculations).

Summing up, the trigger for the fall in the average growth rate from 6 to 3 per cent was the external debt crisis at the beginning of the decade of 1980. The first shock was accompanied by a second impact linked with structural adjustment and liberal structural reforms in the early 1990s in most countries. Finally, the third impact came from the international financial crisis as well as the national banking systems of many countries in 1998.

### Relationship between the GDP and the UIS

If we relate GDP growth with the evolution of UIS employment in SA, an inverse relation can be found. Growth decreased from its high level in the early 1970s, while the UIS grew continuously. The conjunction of these two dynamics allows us identify different phases:

- In the first half of 1970s GDP growth was high until 1974 and, yet, the UIS increased by five percentage points. Apparently this initial expansion of the UIS was due to a significant growth in urban population.
- From 1975 to 1979, GDP growth remained high, except in 1977, and the size of UIS stabilized at 40 per cent of urban employment. It rose again only in 1979 (42.5 per cent). The large increase in labour supply was partly absorbed by formal wage employment, in parallel with unemployment or emigration to other neighbour countries, like Venezuela, or outside the region.
- Between 1980 and 1985, with the external debt crisis, GDP growth became negative for the first time since 1950. The UIS employment share rose to 43.5 per cent.

- From 1986 to 1990 GDP growth decreased, becoming negative in 1988 and 1989. This led to an increase in UIS up to nearly 45 per cent of urban employment. A temporary recovery in 1990 diminished the rate of informality to less than 40 per cent.
- From 1991 to 2003, despite GDP going from moderate to high rates of growth until 1995, the UIS employment grew from about 40 to 47.5 per cent in 1997. The structural adjustment in the early 1990s, which led to the loss of manufacturing jobs and public employment, prompted this leap. Negative GDP growth in 1998 and 2001 meant a new impulse to the UIS (from 47.5 per cent in 1998 to 52.5 per cent in 2003).
- Finally, with the strong growth from 2003 to 2007, UIS employment share was reduced by five percentage points from 52.5 to 47.5 per cent, returning to its level of 1998, but still far above its 44 per cent peak in 1990.

To sum up, between 1980 and 1990 the growing share of UIS employment was due to the 1982 crisis. GDP contraction between 1990 and 2003 tended to consolidate the upward trend of UIS employment, which rose 12.5 percentage points in 13 years. All in all, there is an inverse relationship between GDP and UIS employment share, of about one percentage point per year on average.

### The impact of the external debt crisis of 1982

The crisis of the foreign debt in 1982 doubled the average ratio of debt to the GDP of the region (Figure 12.4). Between 1980 and 1985 this ratio climbed from 24 to 50 per cent, and then declined to 30 per cent in 1995–1997. With the financial crisis in emerging countries – initiated with the Asian crisis – at the end of the 1990s, the ratio of external debt reached a peak of 55 per cent in 2002–2003. Finally, the recent expansion of GDP based on the exports allowed this ratio to drop below 30 per cent in 2005 and to 20 per cent in 2008, at the beginning of the current international financial crisis.

The outbreak of the financial crisis in emerging countries in 1998 resulted in a huge transfer of resources from 1999 to 2007, due to the remittances of the higher profits. The external debt service augmented – by the increased capacity of countries to pay for the primary export prices boom – and countries achieved a significant debt reduction in 2005–2007. Finally, the returns on short-term capital were important and very profitable for the financial markets.

### Stagnation of labour productivity and its impact on the UIS

The consequences of this evolution were the exit and loss of the limited natural resources and a low ratio of investment to GDP. GDP per capita and per worker (a proxy for labour productivity) remained stagnant from 1980 to 2003, in sharp contrast with the period previous to the debt crisis (1982), where both indicators showed an upward trend. Figure 12.5 shows the evolution of GDP per capita and per worker from 1950 to 2007 in constant US$ (left axis), in

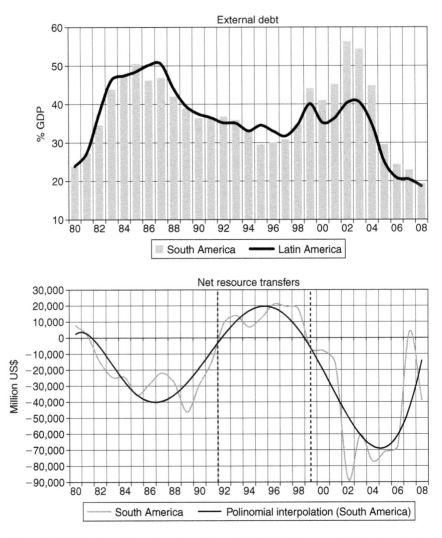

*Figure 12.4* Latin America external position, 1980–2008 (sources: ECLAC; author's calculation).

comparison with the evolution of the rate of UIS (right axis). Between 1950 and 1980 there was a remarkable increase in the GDP per worker. However, between 1974 and 1980 the GDP growth rate was greater than the GDP per worker growth rate, the gap allowing absorption of more jobs and slowing of the increase in the UIS, which shows an inverse relation with labour productivity. The decline in the GDP per worker as a result of the crisis of 1982 and its downward trend until 2003 corresponded to a stagnation of informality until 1991 (with liberal adjustment), followed by a continuous increase until 2003.

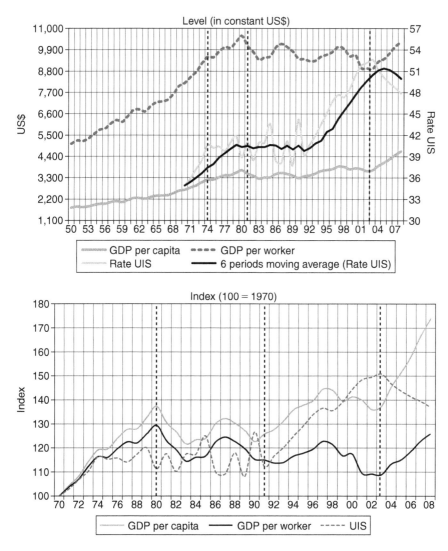

*Figure 12.5* GDP per worker and per capita, and the UIS, 1970–2008 (source: ECLAC and ILO, author's calculations).

From 2003 to 2008, an expansion phase based on the primary export boom, informality decreased.

In Figure 12.5 we can observe also that GDP per capita and GDP per worker indices follow the same trend, the former at a higher level, especially after 1990. This may be due to the type of growth derived from the structural adjustment, which has put the emphasis on raw exports and the expansion of urban public services with high technology. The result was a large increase in GDP per capita, and greater inequality, while formal employment in high productivity sectors increased slightly.

The low level of GDP per worker compared to the GDP per capita, and its tendency to fall over time is linked to increased informality. The low profitability of MSEs with limited or absence of capacity to invest was compensated by a huge absorption of low-wage UIS employment.

## Urban labour market trends in the long run

So far we have been concerned with the major macro trends that determine the aggregate labour supply (AAP, AR and EAP) and aggregate demand (product and labour productivity) in the long term. Now we need to consider these trends in relation with the UIS. This means, for the supply side, comparing the evolution of the AR and the UIS and, on the demand side or the employment absorption, analysing the evolution of the UIS in relation to the unemployment rate (UR).

### Relationship between the activity rate and the UIS

As shown above, the growth of the EAP can be explained by a large increase in the AAP and, to a lesser extent, of the AR. These changes were concomitant to a higher proportion of female employment in the UIS, which should be analysed. What is the relationship between AR, especially of women, and the rate of UIS in the region? We can identify two successive phases (Figure 12.6). From 1970 to 1990, both rates increased. They both gained five percentage points between 1975/1976 and 1990. This period is characterized by a relative absorption of EAP growth by formal employment and also by an increase in the UR, especially between 1977 and 1983.

However, the slight upward trend in the level of UIS was also accompanied with a sharp increase of the urban FAR during the whole decade of the 1980s. Again, the rise in female labour supply was partly absorbed by formal employment, and partly by unemployment. Since 1990, the urban AR stabilized at about 60 per cent while the rate of UIS went up by about 13 percentage points. This is mainly due to increased AAP as already indicated. But it is also caused by a significant increase in urban FAR. The urban FAR and the rate of UIS have increased substantially and in parallel until 2003.

### Relationship between of unemployment and the UIS

The central question in the relationship between the UR and the UIS is why the large labour supply excess, in the long term, remains unemployed if job seekers have the option to be hired or to work in the UIS (Solimano, 1988). There would be an inverse relationship between the two, corresponding to the short-term vision of the UIS when it emerged as a concept. The role of the UIS was supposed to be counter-cyclical, serving as a buffer which helps to contain the

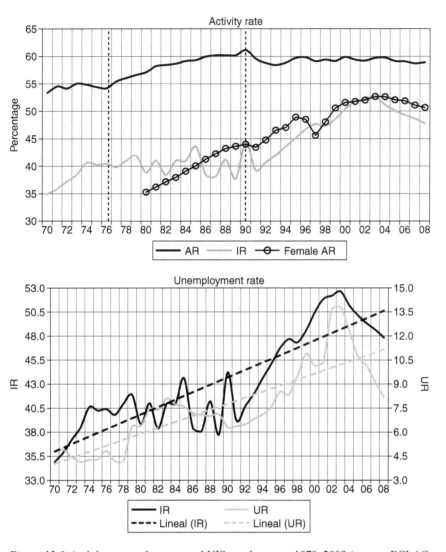

*Figure 12.6* Activity, unemployment and UIS employment, 1970–2008 (source: ECLAC and ILO, author's calculations).

Note
No information for activity rate by sex before 1980.

increase in cyclical unemployment. Solimano inferred from this that if there is unemployment and UIS at the same time, the former would be voluntary.

Globally Figure 12.6 shows that the unemployment rate and the UIS employment share go together for the entire period 1970–2008. This positive correlation is even clearer between 1990 and 2002 when the UR went up from 6 to 13.5 per cent and the UIS employment share rose from 39 to 53 per cent on average for the ten countries. Decomposing the period prior to 1990 in two phases, one can distinguish a first phase (1970–1978), in which the rate of the UIS increased, but not the UR. In the second phase (1980–1990), it seems that the UIS fulfilled its role of buffer: while UIS employment went up – with marked fluctuations – the UR decreased from 8 to 6.5 per cent, approximately.[3]

## Panel estimation of the determinants of the growth of the UIS

The argument of this chapter is that in SA, between 1970 and 2008, there was a positive association between the growth of the urban EAP and the growth of urban informal sector employment. This result is a consequence of the increasing AAP and AR, as well as of the growth of the urban (or non-agricultural) GDP. As for the relationship between the UIS and labour productivity a distinction is needed. On the one hand, the level of *total* labour productivity is inversely related to the UIS, both to the magnitude of informal sector employment as well as to its low contribution to GDP growth.

The limited increase of labour productivity in the urban formal sector compared with (non-farm) GDP growth led to a reduction of formal employment (Figure 12.2). Given the steady growth of EAP, the effect was an increase of employment in the UIS. To test the significance and the magnitude of these effects, some econometric estimations were carried out to explain the UIS employment share in the long term. For this purpose, a panel database was constructed, with 380 observations (ten countries for the period 1970–2008). The independent variables, expressed in annual percentage changes, are:

- *Total urban active age population* (app_t). The expected coefficient should be positive. With greater AAP, the EAP will increase and therefore the employment in the UIS will increase.
- *Total urban activity rate* (ar). The expected coefficient should be positive: if the supply of labour is greater, labour informality will increase.
- *(Non-primary sector) GDP* (gipnoagri). The expected coefficient should be negative: a higher GDP growth will lead to higher formal employment and therefore less informality.
- *Labour productivity in the formal sector* (gipnasf), used a proxy of the (non-primary) GDP over the EAP in the formal sector. The expected coefficient should be positive: the greater the productivity of formal employment, the more the workers will be displaced to the UIS or to a lesser extent to unemployment.

Estimations were run with country fixed effects and random effects, and also with a lag in the dependent variable (using Arellano–Bond dynamic panel estimation procedure). The estimated coefficients are all significant, with the expected signs and high values (Table 12.4). The results suggest that the annual percentage changes in the UIS is positively determined by annual percentage

*Table 12.4* Panel estimates of urban informal sector growth rate

| Estimation | FE | RE | LM |
|---|---|---|---|
| UIS$_{t-1}$ | – | – | **-0.081** |
| | | | [0.0290] |
| gipnafs | 0.995 | 0.997 | 0.992 |
| | [0.0342] | [0.0337] | [0.0348] |
| ar | **0.874** | **0.872** | **0.852** |
| | [0.0748] | [0.0739] | [0.0773] |
| aap_t | **0.822** | **0.750** | **0.887** |
| | [0.1709] | [0.1214] | [0.1880] |
| gip_no_agri | **-0.802** | **-0.808** | **-0.801** |
| | [0.0433] | [0.0426] | [0.0457] |
| _cons | 0.132 | 0.387 | -0.038 |
| | [0.6057] | [0.4461] | [0.6645] |
| sigma_u | 0.3570 | 0.0000 | – |
| sigma_e | 3.4812 | 3.4812 | – |
| Rho | 0.0104 | 0.0000 | – |
| Observations | 380 | 380 | 360 |
| Countries | 10 | 10 | 10 |
| Observations per group | 38 | 38 | 36 |
| Number of instruments | – | – | 320 |
| Period | 1971–2008 | 1971–2008 | 1971–2008 |
| R-square | 0.7023 | 0.7026 | – |
| Corr (u_i, xb) | 0.0143 | – | – |
| Corr (u_i, x) | – | 0.0000 | – |
| F (4,366) | 216.4400 | – | – |
| Prob>F | 0.0000 | – | – |
| Wald chi$^2$(4), (5) | – | 885.9800 | 848.6700 |
| Prob>chi$^2$ | – | 0.0000 | 0.0000 |

Source: author's calculations.

Note
Fixed effects (FE), random effects (RE) and lag model (LM). Standard errors are reported in brackets below each coefficient.

changes in the labour productivity in the formal sector, the AR and the AAP, and negatively by the percentage changes in the non-primary sector GDP. The coefficient of the first lag of the dependent variable (UIS$_{t-1}$) is very low.

## Conclusions: the limits to UIS growth

The first conclusion of this study is that the urban informal sector employment is a phenomenon that has reached huge proportions in all countries of South America. The UIS not only persists in time, its participation in urban employment has grown over its 38 years of existence, up to 2008, either measured as a proportion of urban employment or as a proportion of the total AAP.

Second, evidence gathered suggest that the large increase in UIS was due to the continuous increase, in the long term, of labour supply, primarily because of the urban population and activity rate growth. Non-farm GDP growth could not overcome the effects of the determinants of the labour supply side. The increased labour productivity of the formal sector also contributed to UIS growth. Not only did the labour productivity increase in the formal sector not absorb enough workers but it also displaced them to the UIS.

Third, evidence has been presented for these relationships, both on average for the ten countries of SA, as well as by groups of countries. These comparisons allow us to observe how the different stages of demographic transition directly determine the various levels of UIS. Fourth, the successive shocks, like the external debt crisis of 1982, and consecutively the structural adjustment reduced GDP growth and accentuated the growth of the UIS. Fifth, the impact of the debt crisis and the structural adjustment meant a severe reduction of public expenditure and employment. These processes contributed to an increase in the UIS, directly, by the downsizing of the state and, indirectly, by the weakening of the state's capacity to reduce tax evasion and to enforce social protection and labour laws.

Sixth, the relationship between the long-term increase of the activity rate and the growth of the UIS confirms the direct influence of the EAP on the UIS size. The relationship between the unemployment and the UIS in the long run is positive, given the large increase in the EAP. In the short run, given the size of the EAP, the correlation is negative, and the UIS is a buffer to absorb part of the unemployed during recession spells.

Finally, in seventh place, the relationship between percentage changes in the UIS and its determinants in the long term has been estimated. The results are as expected, with the expected signs of the coefficients. UIS growth depends positively on AAP growth, the AR and the labour productivity in the formal sector, and inversely on the increase of the non-agricultural GDP.

To conclude let us turn back to our initial question: are there limits to the growth of informality? According to our results, the answer is definitively yes. We can look at it in three different ways.

As the average of aggregate trends (for the urban areas) we found that the increase in UIS should decelerate if the rate of increase of the AAP, the AR and particularly the AR of women diminish. If the non-primary GDP increases above the growth of labour productivity, given the EAP, formal employment will increase and thus the UIS will tend to decrease. If there is an increase in average labour productivity, which means also some increase of the productivity of the UIS, the investment capacity of the UIS would increase, as well as the employment in the formal sector at the expense of the UIS. If the increase in labour productivity of the formal sector declines, workers would not move to the UIS. If public spending increases and the role of the government including that of the ministries of labour are strengthened, the tax coverage and the enforcement of labour regulations, including social protection, could improve. If this is not accompanied by the above-mentioned structural trends, the increased presence of state will be very limited in reducing the size of the UIS.

By groups of countries, the progress in the demographic transition in countries with high rates of UIS will slow down the growth of its urban population and AAP. These countries will converge towards those with lower UIS. The latter countries become the model to be reached by countries with high levels of UIS, with relatively low GDP and low labour productivity. If similar levels of GDP and national labour productivity growth were achieved to those of the countries with lower UIS, firms and workers would be more likely to be formalized. If countries with higher UIS increase the capacity of their states, similar to countries with lower UIS, the size of their UIS should be reduced.

Finally, we computed projections, based on the estimates of average variables. We estimated an ARMA model of the UIS for the whole region (weighted averages for the ten countries) with the same independent variables used in the panel regression with one lag of the dependent variable. On the basis of the coefficients obtained – to explain the average growth of the UIS – we derived the projected average growth trends to observe their possible evolution in the long-term.

Some of the results are shown in Figure 12.A.1 (in Annex). The values of the adjusted variables appear first, as a trend until 2008, and then as a projection up to 2028. We can infer that the upward trend of AAP will slow down. With family planning policies for informed decisions this trend can be accentuated. On the other hand, the non-primary GDP growth would increase formal employment and would reduce the tendency of the UIS to grow. Policies to ensure sustained high growth of non-primary GDP will be required. The sum of both effects, and of other variables (not reported in the figure), should lead the UIS to decrease.

In light of these results, the discussions to increase the formalization of firms or of workers, or to reduce the UIS size, whether through greater effectiveness of tax or labour legislation, or by launching programmes to support or promote informal MSEs, will have poor results. A phenomenon with the characteristics of the urban labour informality must be addressed as a long-term challenge, with policies designed to change the structural behavioural patterns of demographics, economics and the role of the state of the countries in the region.

# Annex

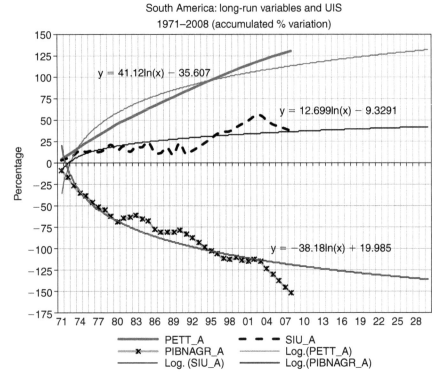

*Figure 12.A.1* ARMA model of UIS employment growth and projections to 2028 (source: author's calculation).

# Notes

1 I would like to thank William Sanchez, for his collaboration in the construction of comparable series and the graphs and tables. Thanks also to Alex Carbajal for his assistance in the estimations in the sixth and seventh sections of the chapter. Thanks, finally, to Hazel Geatches, Tina Malaney, Helio San Miguel and Ruth Simmons for their useful suggestions.
2 All averages reported are weighted.
3 "In the short run, informal employment is found to be counter-cyclical for the majority of countries, with the degree of counter-cyclicality being lower in countries with larger informal employment and better police and judicial services" (Loayza and Rigolini, 2006).

# References

Boeri, T. and van Ours, J. (2008) *The Economics of Imperfect Labour Markets*, Princeton, NJ: Princeton University Press.

Bourguignon, F. (2010) Interview, International Conference: The informal sector and informal employment, Hanoi, May, pp. 94–98.

Galli, R. and Kucera, D. (2008) Labour Standards an Informal Employment in Latin America, in Berg, J. and Kucera, D. (eds), *In Defence of Labour Market Institutions: Cultivating Justice in the Developing World*, London and Geneva: Palgrave/ILO.

ILO (1972) *Employment, Income and Equality: A Strategy for Increasing Productive Employment in Kenya*, Geneva: ILO.

ILO (1990–2006) *Labour Overview for Latin America and the Caribbean*, Geneva: ILO.

Loayza, N. and Rigolini, J. (2006) Informality Trends and Cycles, *World Bank Policy Research Working Paper*, no. 4078.

Perry, G.E., Maloney, W.F., Arias, O.S., Fajnzylber, P., Mason, A.D. and Saavedra-Chanduvi, J. (2007) *Informality: Exit and Exclusion*, Washington, DC: World Bank.

Solimano, A. (1988) Enfoques alternativos sobre el mercado del trabajo: una evaluación teórica, *Revista de Análisis Económico*, 3(2): 159–186.

# 13 Long term dynamic of the labour market in Thailand

## Transitions between the formal and informal sectors

*Xavier Oudin*

The aim of this chapter is to analyse the evolution of the informal sector in Thailand over a period of more than three decades which were marked by strong growth and rapid industrialisation, with the exception of the crisis years (1997–1999). It is above all a question of explaining the apparent paradox of the continuance of the informal sector while the dynamic of growth stems from industrial investment and the services as well as development of wage labour.

Since the beginning of the 1970s, the rise in the GNP per capita has been rapid: an average of 4.2 per cent per annum between 1970 and 1986 and 8.2 per cent between 1987 and 1996. The sudden fall of the GNP at the time of the Asian crisis did not last long, and there was growth again from 1999 onwards. From 2000 to 2008, the rise of the GNP per capita once again reached an average of 4 per cent per annum. In less than 40 years, the GNP per capita in Thailand tripled, while the population doubled.

We shall first examine the transformations of the labour market which accompanied strong economic growth in Thailand. This growth, which was above all driven by exports and dependent on foreign investment, triggered a rapid increase in salaried work, mainly to the detriment of family work in agriculture. The (non-farm) informal sector has more or less remained stable.

In the second section, we shall examine longitudinal data from surveys carried out by the Centre for Education and Labour Studies (CELS, University of Chiang Mai) and the French Institute of Research for Development (IRD) in 2004 with workers from industry and in 2005 with independent workers and employees of family businesses, with the assistance of the author. From questions about professional trajectories we can better understand the types of evolution which are taking place on the labour market and, above all, explain why the informal sector continues to remain at such a high level in Thailand.

Throughout the whole period of industrialisation and growth between 1970 and 1996, the informal sector remained remarkably stable, in spite of a big demand for labour from formal enterprises. It is more and more apparent that since the Asian crisis, the informal sector has undergone a new period of expansion. This has been to the detriment of agricultural work but cannot be understood without taking into account the aspiration of Thai workers to work independently.

## Evolution of labour market over the last 40 years

This first part is based on data from the Labour Force Survey (LFS) carried out since 1969, first twice then four times a year, by the National Statistical Office (NSO) in Thailand. We have elaborated time series from the tables published in the August survey each year, a peak period for agricultural work. The data have been cleaned and corrected to take into account the changes in concept and nomenclature which took place during the period in question, and smoothed over to mitigate measurement errors. Thus, the surveys allow us to follow the structural changes in the labour market which took place over four decades.

### Demographic transition framework

The changes took place at a time when Thailand was undergoing a period of extremely rapid demographic change. Female fertility fell from seven children per woman in 1965 to two in 1995 (it is currently below replacement level). The result has been a rapid change of the population's age structure and a spectacular fall in the dependency ratio.[1]

The demographic changes have an effect on the labour market, with an abundant supply of labour during a certain period, when the cohorts born before the drop in fertility come to the age of work, that is to say, at the end of the 1980s. From this period onwards, growth on labour supply slowed down, all the more so as an increase in the duration of schooling delayed the age of entry in the labour market. What is more, the 1997 crisis provoked, for some years, a fall in the labour force participation rates, especially for women.

The fall in the fertility rate also had an effect on the demand for education as the legal minimum number of years of schooling rose from four to six years in 1982 and then to nine in 1990. At the beginning of the 1970s the average number of years spent at school was six, whereas this rose to an average of 12 years for the children born in the 1990s who are now arriving on the job market. The net school rate in higher education (for 18 to 24 year olds) rose from 10 per cent in 1975 to 47 per cent in 2005. The young who are now arriving on the labour market are better educated and more skilled than preceding generations.

At the same time, the labour force is ageing, more demanding and less mobile. The ageing of the workforce began to accelerate at the beginning of the 1990s because of the ever growing size of the older age groups and the increase in the average age of people entering on to the labour market. The median age of the labour force rose from 30 years old in 1970 to 39 years old in 2008. The young, who are better qualified and fewer, have expectations which are different from those of preceding generations. They are less ready to accept subaltern tasks, are more demanding, aspire to a higher standard of living and are more sensitive to inequalities. The older generation is more numerous: the over 40s now count for 50 per cent of the labour force compared to 29 per cent in 1970. They are less mobile and suffer from heavy financial constraints as they must pay both for their children's education and for their housing.

**Growth of the labour force**

In less than 40 years, the labour force has more than doubled, from 18 million in 1970 to 38 million in 2008 (Figure 13.1). From 1970 to the end of the 1980s, the labour force grew by an average of more than 3 per cent per annum, which meant 700,000 new jobs each year. In the 1990s, the labour force stagnated and began to grow again at the average moderate rate of 1.3 per cent per annum in the 2000s. Throughout this period, with the exception of the 12-month period which followed the beginning of the crisis (July 1997), unemployment was negligible. The unemployment rate (1 to 2 per cent) was even lower than what would have been expected of frictional unemployment. There is also a low rate of seasonal unemployment.

**Changes in agriculture**

A large part of the population is engaged in agricultural work: 79 per cent of the workforce in 1975, and 63 per cent in 1990. Since this date, this number has fallen rapidly (42 per cent in 2008). Until 1990, that is to say during the high growth period of the labour force, agriculture played an important role in absorbing the workforce. When labour supply weakens, agriculture stops absorbing the workforce. Consequently, it is agriculture rather than the informal sector, as usually postulated (Castells *et al.*, 1989), which has allowed the growth of the workforce to be regulated. At the same time there is an extension of cultivated land (and disappearance of forests) with the result that the average surface of exploited land remains constant (Phélinas, 2001).

The fall in the number of people working in agriculture from 1991 onwards did not take the form of a massive rural exodus of landless peasants, but was caused by the non-replacement of ageing generations. This movement only

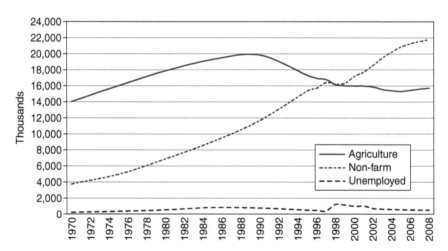

*Figure 13.1* Evolution of the labour force, 1970–2008 (in thousands) (source: CELS database; author's calculations).

concerned family workers. Other categories of workers (employers, self-employed workers and salaried workers) continued to grow. Thus, the number of farms is still increasing (Figure 13.2). On the other hand, the number of jobs per farm has fallen, and the average farm now employs only a couple of farm workers without children working as family workers. The children of farmers no longer work with their parents, but go to the city to seek non-agricultural work. Up until now, the children of agricultural workers have constituted the reservoir of industrial and informal sector workers but there has never been a massive eviction of landless agricultural workers.

If agrarian capitalism has developed in some areas of Thailand (especially on the Central Plain), agriculture remains largely in the hands of the small farmers. Nevertheless, a large increase in the number of salaried agricultural workers and employers occurred. Agricultural holdings with employees (it corresponds to the number of employers in the LFS) rose from less than 60,000 in 1970 to more than 300,000 in 1990, and this number has oscillated between less than 300,000 and 400,000 since this date. However, these count for less than 5 per cent of agricultural holdings. Agricultural salaried workers, who counted for only 3 per cent of the agricultural workforce (half a million workers) in 1970, constituted 10 per cent in 1990 and 16 per cent in 2008 (2.5 million people).[2]

### Regulation of labour market

Until 1990, all types of work contributed to the absorption of the growth of the labour force, a little more for salaried work and a little less for family work. The

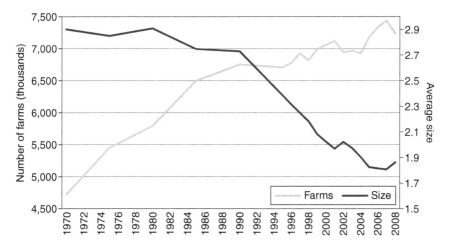

*Figure 13.2* Number of smallholders and average size of smallholdings (source: CELS database; author's calculations).

Note
The number of smallholders is the sum of the number of self-employed workers and employers; the average size is the number of workers employed in agriculture divided by the number of smallholders.

number of independent workers (self-employed or employers) rose at the same rate as the average (Figure 13.3). From 1991, there was a rapid fall in the number of family workers, especially in agriculture. The growth in the number of employees accelerated until 1997. After a sudden slowing down at the time of the crisis, this growth continued until 2008, although at a slower rate than before the crisis. In 2006, there were 16 million employees, compared to two million in 1970. The number of independent workers is continuing to increase at a constant but slow rate and has not been interrupted by the crisis.

In 2008, employees counted for less than half the workforce. Employees in the private sector accounted for 35 per cent and public sector workers 9 per cent of the employed workforce. Independent workers have continued to make up one-third of the employed for more than three decades (Table 13.1). This proportion, which weakened in the 1980s, has risen and slightly overtaken its 1970 level. Finally, the number of family workers fell from 12.5 million in 1990 to

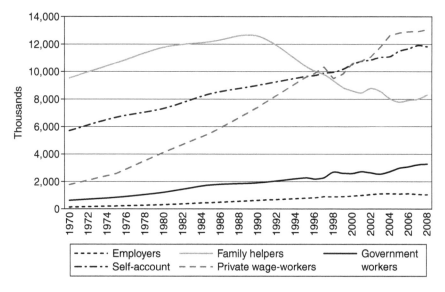

*Figure 13.3* Evolution of the employed labour force by status, 1969–2008 (thousands) (source: CELS database; author's calculations).

*Table 13.1* Distribution of the employed labour force by status, 1970–2008 (%)

|  | *1970* | *1990* | *2008* |
| --- | --- | --- | --- |
| Employees | 13.6 | 29.6 | 43.6 |
| Employers and independent workers | 32.9 | 30.5 | 34.3 |
| Family workers | 53.5 | 39.9 | 22.1 |
| *Total in thousands* | *17,784* | *31,531* | *37,499* |

Sources: CELS database; author's calculations.

less than eight million in 2008. This fall corresponds to the increase in salaried work during the same period.

Owing to an economic growth which depended particularly on labour intensive industries, labour demand has remained constant, except for the end of 1997 to 1999 period. However, labour supply was exceptionally high between 1970 and 1990 because of the arrival on the labour market of the large classes of age born before the fall in fertility. It was only thanks to family labour in agricultural exploitations that unemployment was avoided and high levels of activity were maintained.

### Situation of non-farm work and estimations about work in the informal sector

Owing to the absence of statistics concerning the informal sector,[3] the most pertinent approach consists of examining the status in employment as given by the LFSs: the majority of self-employed workers and family workers are employed in the informal sector, as well as employers who are nearly all heads of family enterprises employing some employees. Other categories (private sector workers, government employees) are generally employed in the formal sector (OECD, 2002).

As is always the case, this approach is not satisfactory for two reasons: there are employees in the informal sector and independent workers in the formal sector. Existing statistics do not allow us to distinguish between employees in formal businesses and those in informal ones. The size of the establishment can then be used as "proxy", but this information is not published (though captured by the LFSs). The Ministry for Labour publishes labour statistics with the number of workers by size of establishment. Thus, in 2003, 16 per cent of private sector employees worked in establishments with fewer than ten employees. Finally, independent workers in the formal sector (registered self-employed workers) account for a very small part of the 12 million (in 2008) self-employed workers.[4]

In August 2008, the labour force numbers 38 million, of which half a million are unemployed. The employed population thus numbers 37.5 million, of which 15.7 million (42 per cent) are employed in agriculture. A total of 21.8 million workers are employed in non-farm work. In spite of the decline in agriculture, seasonal variations remain high. The labour force varies by two million during the year and the population employed in agriculture by 3.2 million, that is to say a variation of 22 per cent between the high point (in August) and the low point (in February).[5] The non-farm population varies by 1.2 million between these two months reaching a high point in February. These workers who are employed seasonally in non-farm jobs add to the number of informal workers, as most of them are employed in precarious jobs. However, they do not inevitably join the informal sector. Formal enterprises also employ seasonal workers. As we are using data from each year's August LFS, these people are counted among the agricultural population.

The number of employees in non-farm jobs rose from less than two million in 1975 to 16.3 million in 2008, of which 3.3 million in the public sector. Private sector salaried workers, who accounted for 36 per cent of the non-farm population in 1970 account for 49 per cent in 2008 (Figure 13.4).[6]

If it is estimated that 95 per cent of independent workers and employers are in the informal sector as well as 10 per cent of the employees, which seems to us to be a very low estimate, the non-farm informal sector –including family workers – has a total of 8.7 million people working in it, that is to say 39 per cent of the non-farm labour force. This estimate is certainly a very rough one but the result is plausible and shows that the informal sector continues to play an important part in the Thai economy. The dynamism of the informal sector is remarkable. In 1975 there were a little more than two million independent workers and family workers involved in non-farm activities and more than eight million in 2008.

The growth of the sector cannot be explained by an overabundance of labour supply. Indeed, the informal sector saw its share drop during the high growth years of the labour force. However, in spite of a remarkable increase in the number of employees and the rapid development of formal enterprises in industry and services, work in the informal sector remained at a high level. While the formal sector suffers from a labour shortage, the population employed in the informal sector did not serve as a reservoir of labour. It is, on the one hand, the natural growth of the labour force, and, on the other hand, the transfer from the rural world which have contributed to the growth of formal labour. The formal sector is suffering from a chronic lack of labour and there are very few

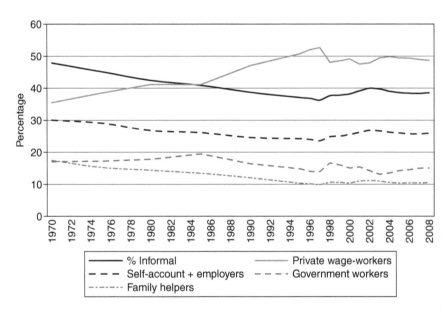

*Figure 13.4* Evolution of the non-farm workforce by status, 1969–2008 (%) (source: CELS database; author's calculations).

barriers which prevent workers acceding to it: required qualifications are within the reach of nearly all the young (however, a small part of informal sector workers remains insufficiently educated to lay claim to a job in the formal sector).

After the crisis, the share of the informal sector rose. The crisis had a stronger impact on the employees of the formal sector. Many were laid off and, at the same time, there was an increase in the number of independent workers. Even though these changes in the labour market during a period of crisis are unexceptional, the fact that independent work and thus informal sector work continued to increase with economic recovery reflects a deep change in the structure of the labour market.

## Mobility of the workforce and professional trajectories

Although this macroeconomic vision provides us with information about structural changes in the labour market, it does not tell us anything about people's mobility. In some regards it is even misleading, as when there is a rapid growth of the labour force, structural changes may result from the higher number of departures of one category (in this case agricultural family workers) and the entrance of other categories (employees), without there necessarily being a movement of workers from one category to another. Inversely, crossovers between statuses cancel each other out in a macroeconomic vision, so well that real mobility can be underestimated.

### Biographical surveys

The following data are from two surveys carried out by the CELS and the IRD, funded by the National Research Council of Thailand, and led by the author. The first survey, carried out in 2004, involved 1,530 workers from 82 formal sector enterprises (principally in the manufacturing sector). Formal enterprises are defined according to the legal status of the company ("borisat") that is corporate enterprises. The second survey was carried out in 2005 and involved 1,550 independent entrepreneurs and 500 employees in the informal sector (individual or family enterprises). If the sample of the first survey is not representative at the national level, the second one is, both for the manufacturing and service sectors. Commercial enterprises, however, were not surveyed.

The two surveys contain a biographical section where educational and professional events in the lives of the interviewees are listed with the help of retrospective questions. After leaving school, their trajectories are divided into sequences. Each change of province, enterprise or work status results in a new sequence. For each sequence the following information is gathered: age at the beginning of the sequence, location (province), status (employee, independent, family worker, etc.). Interviewees were also asked the reasons for leaving a job and the reasons for eventual periods of inactivity between two sequences. Sequences lasting less than six months were not logged, which leads to an underestimating of mobility (Oudin, 2008).

*Measuring mobility*

Mobility on the labour market consists of a change of situation in one's professional life. It may be a change of job, status, enterprise or workplace, etc. We do not measure each of these types of change, but only certain ones: change of enterprise or status (change of status often corresponds to a change of enterprise) and change of province (changes in workplace within a province are not counted).

The analytical framework is inspired by the theory of transitional markets (Schmid and Gazier, 2002). From finishing school onward each change in professional life takes the form of a transition which can be categorised according to its origin and its destination: a period of unemployment to a period of work, for example. In fact, in Thailand almost all transitions, apart from the first from school or university to work, take the form of one job to another. There are no long periods of unemployment and not a lot of periods of inactivity. Thus, the number of jobs during one's professional life, which corresponds more or less to the number of transitions, constitutes the principal indicator of mobility.

The average number of jobs occupied during one's professional career is rather low relatively to the common idea of high mobility, particularly among workers from the manufacturing or service industry (Table 13.2). This idea is based on the declarations of employers or staff managers whom we met at the same time as the survey was carried out among workers. Many of them complained about the high mobility of their personnel and one of the principal problems they evoked was the high turnover rate of the workforce. Wages policy and incentives focus entirely on the development of workforce loyalty, with only a mitigated success.

*Table 13.2* Number of professional experiences by category of workers

| *Sector* | | *Number of experiences* | | | | | | |
|---|---|---|---|---|---|---|---|---|
| | | *1* | *2* | *3* | *4+* | *Total* | *Average* | *Median age* |
| Formal | Managers | 33.0 | 33.5 | 19.6 | 13.9 | 194 | 2.2 | 32 |
| | Skilled workers | 29.6 | 28.3 | 24.4 | 17.7 | 537 | 2.4 | 31 |
| | Non-skilled workers | 27.6 | 34.3 | 23.0 | 15.1 | 688 | 2.3 | 33 |
| Informal | Educated informal workers | 18.1 | 29.7 | 25.9 | 26.3 | 764 | 2.8 | 34 |
| | Non-educated informal workers | 8.8 | 32.1 | 29.7 | 29.5 | 1,257 | 3.1 | 43 |
| | *Total* | *19.2* | *31.5* | *26.1* | *23.2* | *3,440* | *2.7* | *36* |

Sources: Surveys CELS-IRD, 2005; author's calculations.

Note
Managers, skilled workers and unskilled workers in the formal sector are distinguished by their skill (asked in a separate question) or by their educational level if there is no reply to this question. The two categories of workers in the informal sector are distinguished by level of education (above or below nine years of education).

The low figure that resulted from the survey calls into question the supposed excessive mobility of the workforce in Thailand. It is probably more typical of certain types of enterprise (those in industrial zones far from urban centres) or of certain sectors (the hotel industry) where there is much competition and the practice of poaching other people's staff is frequent.

The average number of posts occupied, including the current one, is 2.7 (Table 13.2). This depends, of course, on the age and duration of the working life of the interviewee. Mobility is at its height during the first years of a working life: before the age of 28, the average is two posts whereas for older workers (over 35 years of age), this figure rises to three. A typical worker occupies two posts in his/her 20s and a last one in his/her 30s.

The average number of jobs occupied from leaving school to the time of the survey is truncated, as it only covers a part of the interviewees' lives and mixes people who have been on the labour market for 40 years with others who have just entered it. In order to obtain a better measure of workers' mobility, a synthetic mobility index can be established from the calculation of mobility by generation and by period.[7] This index has been calculated at different periods since 1965. It is more robust for recent periods as there are more observations. It has settled at an average of three jobs during a working life for the period 2000–2004, a fall in relation to the previous decade when there was greater mobility. Over a period of 40 years, it shows contrasting trends in time and by category of workers (Figure 13.5).

However, there is a contrast between the evolution of mobility among workers in the formal sector and those in the informal one. For the latter, mobility seems to have accelerated over the past decade whilst dropping for workers

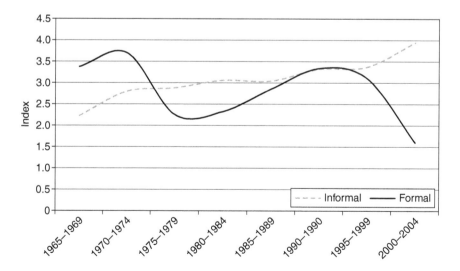

*Figure 13.5* Synthetic mobility index, by period of entering the labour market, 1965–2004 (sources: Surveys CELS-IRD, 2005; author's calculations).

in the formal sector whose mobility was higher in the 1970s. However, it bounced back during the high growth years and at the time of the crisis (1990–1999).

The workers in the informal sector appear to be the most mobile, particularly the least educated workers and employees (less than nine years of education). It is true that on average this category is older than the others. In the formal sector, the unskilled workers are the most mobile, while management staff are the least (two-thirds of them have only one or two experiences). Here, mobility is greater at the beginning of a career, whereas for workers in the informal sector it continues throughout their working life.

The synthetic mobility index gives us an imperfect view of mobility. As mobility can only truly be measured at the end of a career, which is not a great deal of interest for the study of the present labour market, we proceed in the same way as for fertility index, by basing ourselves on current conditions. Nevertheless, this index has the advantage of allowing us to follow changes in time and make comparisons between categories of workers.

### *Agricultural experience*

A little more than one-quarter of the sample group (27.5 per cent) worked in agriculture when young (Table 13.3). But 40 per cent were born in agricultural families, a proportion which is equivalent for workers from the two sectors. In most cases, it was a period of transition between leaving school (at under 15) and entering working life beyond the family smallholding. This population, which corresponds to the presumed flow of agricultural family workers towards a non-farm activity described in the first section, is found as much in the formal sector as in the informal one, but the majority are employees. This is true for all generations.

The agricultural experience, along with educational level, clearly demarcates two categories in the informal sector. Among the least educated workers in the informal sector, there are far fewer who have worked in agriculture and come from agricultural families. On the other hand, a minority segment of the informal sector, principally entrepreneurs (employers), is relatively well educated (19 per

*Table 13.3* Workers with experience in agriculture by category of worker and generation (%)

|  | *Under 35* | *Over 35* | *Total* |
| --- | --- | --- | --- |
| Managers | 19.0 | 17.4 | 18.4 |
| Skilled workers | 31.7 | 18.8 | 27.5 |
| Unskilled workers | 27.0 | 15.0 | 22.2 |
| Educated informal workers | 15.6 | 17.3 | 16.4 |
| Uneducated informal workers | 27.6 | 43.6 | 39.3 |
| *Total* | *24.6* | *30.2* | *27.5* |

Sources: Surveys CELS-IRD, 2005; author's calculations.

cent have a tertiary qualification) and is of urban origin. It is quite remarkable to find a significant proportion of individuals who began their career in agriculture among all the categories of workers. This is proof of a certain social mobility made possible by the rapid development of industry and services.

### Joining the job market

Thanks to biographical surveys, we can now better capture the dynamic of the labour market and understand the transformation which is taking place. In the present section, we concentrate our analysis on the informal and formal sectors.

The non-farm labour market is fed by a flow of workers coming from the educational system or from a period of inactivity. After completing their education, and after a short period of inactivity for some, individuals join the labour market. The majority joins the formal sector. The educational system feeds more the formal sector or, in other words, the majority of individuals (59 per cent) find their first job (except for agriculture) in the formal sector. Logically, those who find work immediately after studying have spent a longer average period studying and are thus – as much in the formal sector as in the informal one – better educated.

Some individuals, particularly those who do not continue studying beyond compulsory education, and on condition that they come from a farmer's family, begin their working life on the family farm. Those who were involved in agricultural work before their first professional experience in the secondary or tertiary sector can be more or less equally divided between the formal and informal sectors. Consequently, it cannot be said that the rural exodus feeds one sector more than another. We are not surprised by this result. It is known that children from agricultural families have abundantly provided flourishing industries with labour, but also that many of them, particularly the less educated, have chosen an informal occupation.

The flow of arrivals (one for each individual) on to the labour market can be broken down as follows:

| | |
|---|---|
| Education or period of inactivity towards formal sector | 42.9 per cent |
| Education or period of inactivity towards informal sector | 29.5 per cent |
| Agriculture towards formal sector | 13.3 per cent |
| Agriculture towards informal sector | 14.3 per cent |

### Internal flow in the labour market

Once they have a job in the formal or informal sector, individuals may want to change their job (change of status or enterprise). A total of 6,021 movements have been recorded knowing that near to one in five individuals who have never changed jobs are not concerned (we ignore the periods of inactivity, return to education and switching of posts within an enterprise, of which there are incidentally not too many). The flows can be divided into two types: those which take place within a sector and those between sectors. Figure 13.6 illustrates the trajectories corresponding to these flows.

Flow within each sector which is not represented in Figure 13.6 is greater than flow between the two sectors. The first represents about three-quarters (half in each sector), the latter a quarter of transitions between posts. This last proportion, however, appears to us to be high. The fact that one-quarter of the workers in the sample group have crossed over from the formal to the informal sector during their working life is a very important result. It goes against the segmentation view of the informal sector described in the dualist theories.

The mobility of employees in the formal sector is principally done within the sector. Employees easily change enterprise while remaining in a similar working environment. The reasons put forward during the interviews are often the desire to improve work experience and have better working conditions. Changing enterprise is very easy in a very fluid labour market where there is a chronic labour shortage. It is necessary to note that this population is young and therefore the mobility indicators, calculated over a relatively short period, are truncated.

Mobility within the informal sector is above all the case of employees and family workers setting up their own businesses. Many independent workers were employed in informal enterprises before starting their own business. Employment changes of informal employees are also very frequent; in this they are not very different from employees in the formal sector.

Transitions from the formal to the informal sector are twice as high as vice versa. Nearly half (46 per cent) of entrepreneurs in the informal sector have previously worked in a formal enterprise (4 per cent in the public sector). They are

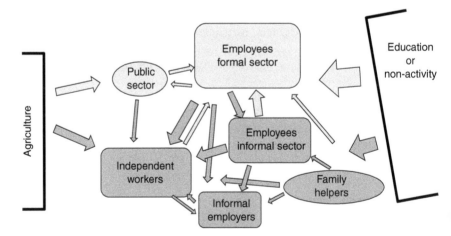

*Figure 13.6* Flow between statuses and sectors (non-farm labour market) (sources: Surveys CELS-IRD; author's calculations).

Note
The thickness of the arrows is proportional to the size of the flow. The flow within a category is not shown.

primarily involved in metallurgy, electronic repairs, laundry, printing and hotel activities which need a relatively large sum of capital, where one finds entrepreneurs with salaried experience in the formal sector.

These informal sector entrepreneurs are, on average, better educated than other independent workers (55 per cent have nine or more years of schooling). Many have attended technical high schools which nowadays is a requirement for the young generation of qualified workers in the formal sector. Thus, we have a population of skilled and dynamic informal entrepreneurs who, what is more, possess some knowledge of management tools (55 per cent keep written accounts).

Transitions from the formal sector, be it private or public, towards the status of employer or independent worker in the informal sector are relatively more common for the older generation. A total of 92.4 per cent of transitions from the formal sector towards the status of employer or independent worker in the informal sector are done by the generation aged 35 and over.

It can be reasonably supposed that the transition from the status of employee towards that of independent worker is usually definitive. There are very few cases of workers returning to the formal sector. Generally, very few of the current workers in the formal sector (2.6 per cent) were once independent workers, whereas the opposite is frequent.

The flow of workers from the informal sector towards the formal one principally concerns informal sector employees (and to a lesser extent family workers). Nearly one in five employees in the formal sector has at one time had some experience as a salaried worker in an informal unit.[8] Current employees in informal units have also often worked in the formal sector (almost 40 per cent). If a minority of employees in the informal sector who have very little chance of working in the formal sector because of their low educational level are excepted, it seems that this population remains indifferent to the type of enterprise (formal or informal) it works in.

The study of these flows throws new light on the labour market in Thailand. It shows that there are frequent passages between the formal and informal sectors. It allows us to trace some types of career of which one of the most significant is that of a worker who begins in a formal enterprise and finishes as an independent worker. However, the survey data only allows us here to formulate hypotheses. As we are not working on completed careers, it is not possible for us to propose a career typology. However, studying the reasons of career changes and especially individual aspirations throws extra light on the subject.

### Reason for job changes

Mobility is most often voluntary. To explain a change of job, only 13.5 per cent of individuals put forward outside events (redundancy, crisis, etc.). Job dissatisfaction is put forward by a large number of employees in the formal sector, but by very few independent workers.

The main reason for changing job, for all categories of workers, is the wish to improve working conditions and, among the other reasons, for more than half of the independent workers, is mentioned the wish to set up one's own business (Table 13.4). This can also mean a return to one's native province. For women, leaving the factory often corresponds to the arrival of a first child. In every case, a change of job brings with it an improvement in working conditions and sometimes living conditions and this often means setting up one's own business. For employees in the formal sector, a change of job is sometimes a strategy to become better qualified as promotions and educational opportunities are very rare in most enterprises. It is also a way of improving one's salary.

These strategies are of course only possible when there is a high demand for labour and there is no unemployment. However, the high demand of formal enterprises for labour should attract workers from the informal sector who are looking for more job stability, better pay and the right to social security benefits. This is not the case because these advantages are not guaranteed and working conditions in formal enterprises are not so attractive. The average salary of independent workers is similar to that of unskilled employees in the formal sector. Even when the enterprise has a favourable policy towards its workers, the latter suffer from being far from their homes (particularly in industrial zones) and the difficulty to reconcile family and professional life.

### Career perspectives

The population of employees in the sample group is young. Among the employees in the formal sector, two-thirds are 35 and younger. They are thus in the first part of their professional career and have a great chance of having new experiences. Several questions have been raised in the same way about the vision of the future and professional prospects in the two surveys. The results show a very strong inclination for independent work (Table 13.5).

The ideal career for the majority is to own one's own family enterprise. The majority of Thais aspires to having good living conditions, not being too far from home, not having to respect an imposed timetable and not having to obey a hierarchy. This ideal is shared by all the categories of workers in the sample group. The majority both of managers and of unskilled formal sector workers, as well as employees from the informal sector, would like to set up their own business. This aspiration is shared by both men and women of all generations. For many employees in formal enterprises, wage work is a temporary experience (often the first after leaving education) done before setting up their own business. One of the commonest types of career is one that consists of between one and three experiences in large enterprises, often far from home, followed by a return to the family enterprise. In certain cases, particularly in the clothing industry, links may exist with the initial employer through subcontracting.

The ageing of the workforce and the implied change in its characteristics, as we have already mentioned in the first section, probably contribute to explaining

Table 13.4 Reasons for last job change

| | Formal salaried worker | Independent worker | Informal salaried worker | Total | (obs) |
|---|---|---|---|---|---|
| Personal or family reasons (marriage, pregnancy, children, change of residency…) | 11.0 | 26.6 | 26.6 | 20.6 | 587 |
| Wish for a better job (better qualified, higher salary, setting up one's business…) | 42.3 | 52.7 | 45.4 | 47.9 | 1,361 |
| Dissatisfied (work too hard, problems at work, health problems, low salary, no welfare benefits) | 28.1 | 7.2 | 15.7 | 16.2 | 461 |
| Redundancy, end of contract, crisis… | 16.2 | 12.2 | 10.6 | 13.5 | 384 |
| Other | 2.5 | 1.3 | 1.7 | 1.8 | 51 |
| Total | 100 | 100 | 100 | 100 | 2,844 |

Sources: Surveys CELS-IRD; author's calculations.

Note
Prior to current post; this only concerns those who have had previously had other professional experience (except in agriculture), that is to say 70% of formal sector salaried workers, 90% of independent workers and 77% of employees in the informal sector.

*Table 13.5* If you had to leave your job, what would you like to do?

| | Formal salaried worker | Independent worker | Informal salaried worker | Total |
|---|---|---|---|---|
| Work in a family enterprise | 71.5 | 63.6 | 69.1 | 67.7 |
| Take care of my family and children | 2.6 | 2.0 | 1.6 | 2.2 |
| Have a similar job | 4.2 | 1.6 | 4.2 | 3.0 |
| Have a new experience and acquire new skills | 4.9 | 0.6 | 2.7 | 2.7 |
| Have a job which corresponds to my qualifications | 8.0 | 3.6 | 8.0 | 6.1 |
| Have a better salary | 1.9 | 0.5 | 3.1 | 1.4 |
| Do not wish to leave | 7.0 | 28.1 | 11.3 | 16.9 |
| *Total (=100)* | *1,505* | *1,546* | *450* | *3,501* |

Sources: Surveys CELS-IRD; author's calculations.

why employees in the formal sector form so few attachments to their work and their enterprise. Relationships between employees remain hierarchical and salaries low. There is no real wage labour culture, apart from in a few segments of the formal sector (public enterprises, for example).

Independent workers express no wish to become wage workers. This question has been explicitly asked to all independent workers. The answer is unambiguous: nearly nine out of ten independent workers would not wish to be a wage worker in an enterprise, even for a salary of 10,000 baht (two-and-a-half times the minimum wage), and this is true whatever the amount of their income (63 per cent earn between 5,000 and 10,000 baht per month and 15.5 per cent more than 10,000 baht). Among the poorest, who have a monthly income below 5,000 baht, less than 20 per cent would accept having a wage position with a salary of 10,000 baht (half of them would even accept for 5,000 baht).

## Conclusion

During the four decades of rapid economic growth in Thailand, with the exception of the 1997 economic crisis, the labour market has undergone profound changes. The rapid growth of wage labour which went hand in hand with investments in the formal sector was principally fed by the natural growth of the labour force until 1990, then by the fall in the number of family workers in agriculture. The urban informal sector has continued to develop during this period.

It appears that this sector has not fulfilled the role of "waiting room" for workers wishing to enter a formal enterprise. On the contrary, it continues to develop because of the frequent passages from a wage labour position in the formal sector towards an independent status in the informal sector. This also shows that the two sectors are not cut off from one another.

The informal sector was able to keep up and even to grow because of the absence of a significant wage labour culture and because of the attachment of the

Thai to a certain way of life which favours independence, family life, not to mention their attachment to the land. The maintaining of the informal sector in a context of economic growth that favoured wage labour cannot be explained without taking in account these cultural traits.

## Notes

1 The dependency ratio is the ratio of the population under 15 and over 65 years of age over the working age population (15–64 years).
2 It is however possible that the number of agricultural employees has been underestimated. Indeed, more and more salaried immigrant workers (Burmese, Cambodian and Laotian) are nowadays found in agriculture. However, this population is largely underestimated in the work surveys.
3 Surveys about the informal sector or about informal sector job categories exist (homeworkers for example), but it is not possible to compare these results with those of the LFSs (non-correspondence of categories used). For some years now (2007), questions concerning affiliation to social security have been added to the LFS questionnaire, which allows us to characterise informal work (and not informal sector work).
4 Professions in groups I and II (management and liberal professions) in the ILO professions classification only account for 0.8 per cent of the total number of self-employed. Those among them who could be counted in the formal sector, a minority, are not, all things considered, very many. However, many more of them have employer status, most of them being the managers of small enterprises.
5 Our own calculations. Average 2003–2008; uncorrected data from the NSO (http://web.nso.go.th/en/survey/ifs/ifs2011.htm).
6 In relation to the non-farm labour force, the number of employees in the public sector varies very little, falling from 17 per cent in 1975 to 15 per cent in 2008.
7 This index can be read in the same way as a synthetic fertility index. It is the sum of the average number of job changes year by year (we calculate here by five year period) of each generation of workers (the generations are the cohorts by year of entry on the labour market). For example, to calculate the index for the years 2000–2004, we sum the average number of job changes of the generation who started working in 1965–1969, the same for generation 1970–1975 and so forth.
8 Unable to determine the formal or informal status of the enterprises of workers' past experience, we have based ourselves on the size of the enterprise: past posts occupied in enterprises employing fewer than ten people are considered as experiences of informal salaried work.

## References

Castells, M., Portes, A. and Benton, L.A. (1989) *The Informal Economy: Studies in Advanced and Less Developed Countries*, Baltimore, MD: The Johns Hopkins University Press.

OECD (2002) *Measuring the Non-Observed Economy: A Handbook*, OECD, IMF, ILO, Paris: OECD Publishing.

Oudin, X. (2008) "Surveys on the Labour Force in Thailand: Characteristics of the Labour Force", CELS Working Paper 5, Chiang Mai University.

Phélinas, P. (2001) *Sustainability of Rice Production in Thailand*, Hauppauge, NY: Nova Science Publisher.

Schmid, G. and Gazier, B. (eds) (2002) *The New Dynamics of Full Employment: Social Integration through Transitional Labor Markets*, Northhampton, MA: Edward Elgar.

# 14 Dynamics of informal microenterprises and poverty in Peru

## A panel approach

*Javier Herrera and Nancy Hidalgo*

The aim of this chapter is to go beyond the poverty studies which concentrate exclusively on the socio-demographic characteristics linked to the conditions of poverty. These studies only allow us answer the question as to who the poor are, but not the question about why they are in such a situation. Knowing how many people are poor and who they are certainly allows us to evaluate the efficiency of poverty reduction policies and to implement more efficiently these policies, but at the same time tends to orient these policies in a certain way towards transfer policies and not towards policies favouring an increase in productivity.

Studies into poverty or into the labour market have generally been carried out using static unconnected approaches. However, the link between poverty and the labour market is implicit in the reflections about the impact of growth on the creation of quality jobs but also in policies in the fight against poverty which focus on credit access for micro-enterprises, or which seek to increase their productivity through professional training within enterprises. Beyond the conception of the policies, the examination of the link between the labour market and poverty is just as justified given the utmost importance of labour income in total household income and predominance of informal sector workers among poor households.

These observations lead us to ask questions about the links between poverty dynamics on the one hand and micro-enterprises on the other. Even though Informal Production Units (IPUs) make up a distinct segment sharing the same common characteristics (small size, small amount of capital, low productivity, predominance of the tertiary sector, etc.) compared to formal enterprises, they group together heterogeneous characteristics not only for the incomes they are capable of generating but also for their capacity to survive and develop. For this reason, beyond the individual characteristics of the households and the workers (supply factors), it is necessary to include among the determinants of primary incomes in the analysis of the labour market the characteristics of the production units in which the workers exercise their productive activity (demand factors). Such an analysis may help reorient policies aimed at fighting poverty towards an increase in productivity, which might ensure a greater sustainability of results compared to policies centred on social transfers.

This chapter examines the links between the labour market and poverty dynamics by focusing on informal microenterprise dynamics. In the first section, we shall review the principal academic work linking workers' characteristics to those of their production units. The second section will present the principal characteristics of IPUs. The third section will examine the micro-dynamics of the informal enterprises included in the panel. Particular attention will be paid to the creation, survival and failure of informal microenterprises throughout the growth phase of the last decade. First, we shall examine the transitions in employment of all the individuals by focusing on those concerning the informal sector worker. Second, the principal characteristics of microenterprises (as a whole compared to those which survive and those which disappear or have just been created) are examined from a descriptive point of view. Finally, we shall examine the link between microenterprise dynamics, their productivity and household poverty. The principal conclusions and implications for the policy for the combat against poverty through the promotion of productive jobs are set out in the final section.

## Studies into the dynamics of micro-enterprises and poverty

The recognition of the importance of taking into consideration jointly the characteristics both of production units and of workers is relatively recent in empirical economic studies and stems from the fact that workers with similar individual characteristics, but working in production units with different characteristics, have different wages (Abowd *et al.*, 1999; Mortensen, 2003). In the case of developing countries the theme has been indirectly addressed, through strategies of diversification towards non-agricultural productive activities in the case of rural households (Lanjouw, 2008).

The explanations for this phenomenon have sought to consider conjointly the factors linked to labour supply and demand and in particular the characteristics of enterprises. According to Hamermesh (2008: 664), 'One of the most interesting developments in labour economics in the past decade has been the new ability to study both the demand and the supply side of the labour market'. For Hamermesh, a crucial question in the income's equation is to know the relative importance of the characteristics of enterprises compared to those of the workers. This is important for public policies as these two factors call for two different types of intervention. It rapidly transpired that there was a strong correlation between wages and the size of firms. Oi and Idson (1999) have found three hypotheses to explain this: (1) the most productive employees pair off with the most skilful entrepreneurs in order to minimize the total amount of salaries and supervision costs; (2) the biggest enterprises pay the highest salaries in order to retain them; (3) the biggest enterprises adopt a discretionary salary policy in order to participate in the annuities. The size of the enterprises, a factor which is closely linked to their productivity, is considered in several empirical studies as the principal determinant for inequalities in wages.

Brown and Medoff (1989) remarked, in the case of the United States, a positive correlation between the size of the firm and workers' salaries. These disparities between wage levels persist even when controlling the effects of observable characteristics as much for workers as for enterprises. Groshen (1991) also investigated the sources of the intra-branch wage dispersion of North-American workers by taking into account the differences linked to the occupation and the establishment (size, presence of unions, branch, per cent of women, etc.) and found that the characteristics of establishments explain nearly half of the salary disparities.

Brunello and Colussi (1998) studied the case of Italy which is more similar to that of developing countries because of the relative importance of small- and medium-sized enterprises. The authors estimated mincerian income equations by considering the allocation of workers in enterprises of different size as being explicitly endogenous. The authors found that the differential linked to the size of the enterprise is not different from zero: but this result is sensitive to subjacent hypotheses of worker distribution in the enterprises. Disparities in salaries might be explained by individual characteristics observed among the workers and by selection effects.

The informal sector has been generally considered to be a subsistence sector, a refuge during periods of crisis. Another vision describes the informal sector as a hive of activity, where micro-entrepreneurs carry the torch of the capitalist spirit (de Soto, 1986). Although the incomes of informal entrepreneurs are on average relatively low, they are also quite dispersed and, for one segment of them, quite near to, if not higher than, formal sector salaried workers. In the 'choice' motive explanation for becoming an informal entrepreneur two antagonistic visions coexist. For some it is a choice linked to expected advantages (and not only pecuniary ones), while for others it is a situation which is not freely chosen and is linked to the fact that workers have insufficient qualifications to access salaried work. According to Cunningham and Maloney (2001), these opposing visions can be reconciled once the existence of a high level of heterogeneity within the informal is acknowledged.

Very few studies have examined the links between workers' incomes and the characteristics of enterprises in developing countries. Funkhouser (1998) studied a small sample of enterprises in Guatemala (data for 256 big enterprises gathered by the Labour Ministry). The results of the regressions show that half of salary dispersion is linked to the observed heterogeneity of the enterprises and that about 15 per cent is linked to the fixed effects of the enterprises. By using a representative sample of micro-enterprises, Cunningham and Maloney (2001) showed that in the case of Mexico, the high level of heterogeneity of micro-enterprises does not correspond to a segmentation of the labour market but rather to the disparities specific to a sector where small enterprises proliferate. The observed disparities in terms of enterprise size, permanence and degree of formality are argued to be due to the unequal distribution of human and physical capital and not to any dualism whatsoever in the labour market.

The factor and cluster analysis applied to the survey of Mexican micro-enterprises data effectively reveals that micro-enterprises serve as a refuge for those unable to find salaried work but the authors also point out that this is nevertheless a small phenomenon compared to the vast majority who have chosen voluntarily this type of work out of a desire to be independent and because of the perspective of a higher income. The profile of those who leave it corresponds more to that of workers who have failed and voluntarily quit the micro-enterprise sector. The authors conclude that there exists only a weak link between capital intensity, size and human capital returns (Cunningham and Maloney, 2001).

For Tokman (1989), workers in the informal sector are part of the workers who do not possess the required qualifications to accede to the salaried jobs which are insufficient in number owing to low productive investment. Conversely, for Soto (1986), the micro-entrepreneurs in the informal sector could develop and manage bigger enterprises. Regulations and the weight of administrative costs constitute a serious barrier to their development.

Even if there is no doubt about the existence of a dynamic segment of micro-enterprises capable of evolving into bigger ones in developing countries, very few studies have examined the micro-economic determinants which make these transitions possible and the few rare existing studies show contradictory results which are very sensitive to the methodological approach used. Thus, de Mel *et al.* (2008), basing themselves on panel data from households surveys in Sri Lanka, show that about two-thirds to three-quarters of self-employed workers have characteristics similar to those of salaried workers rather than those of the managers of big enterprises. The authors conclude that credit access is not the only constraint to the growth of micro-enterprises. The analysis of the panel data from the Chilean household survey (CASEN) serves as an empirical base for Ñopo and Valenzuela (2007) for the analysis of the consequences of the reconversion of salaried workers into entrepreneurs. Using matching techniques to construct a counterfactual, the authors show that the gains are positive and significant while for the cases of inverse transition there is loss of income.

## Characteristics of the informal sector in Peru

In this section we shall examine the characteristics of informal sector production units and the workers' profiles and evolution over a period of time. The small size (measured by the number of workers) of the IPUs is perhaps the most visible characteristic, to such a point that this criterion served for a long time as a 'marker' of the informal sector. The average size of urban IPUs remained constant throughout the 2004–2010 period (1.6 workers on average by IPU). What is more interesting is the fact that in 2010 remunerated workers represented 13 per cent of the total of workers in IPUs, a proportion which remained stable for practically all the analysed period.

The other main characteristic of the IPUs is their high heterogeneity. IPUs with characteristics similar to those of formal enterprises coexist with others which are closer to survival jobs. IPUs without premises represent a little more than half the total. The low rate of access to public services reflects the precariousness of working conditions and is a factor which weighs negatively on the productivity of IPUs. No significant improvement was visible during the period of high macro-economic growth.

A relative young age is also a shared trait among most IPUs, which is also testament to their fragility. The average age of IPUs was 6.5 years in 2010. A high dispersion was observed judging by the difference between the average and the median age (four years). The period of growth seems to have had a 'rejuvenating' effect on the IPUs: the average age fell by almost one year between 2004 and 2010 (falling from 7.3 to 6.5 years and half the IPUs were three years old instead of four). Only one-fifth of IPUs succeed in surviving beyond ten years, one-third are not yet one year old and less than one-quarter are between five and ten years old. A more disaggregated analysis of the age of IPUs revealed that for households which were not poor the age of their IPUs was systematically higher than those of poor households.

The examination of the average structure (2006–2010) of income in urban Peruvian households (Table 14.1) confirms that income from work constitutes by far their principal source of income (64.6 per cent of the total). While formal work represents less than 40 per cent of the total, it accounts for more than half (56.9 per cent) of income from work, if agricultural income is excluded. The gaps in remuneration between the formal and informal sectors are thus considerable. Poor households have an income structure different from that of non-poor households: the share of income from the informal sector there is a lot bigger (72.5 and 41 per cent of salaries from work, excepting agriculture, respectively).

The heterogeneity of the repartition of informal sector workers' incomes with a large segment of low incomes, an intermediate segment with salaries around the poverty line and a minority with high incomes also finds its expression in a diversity of situations regarding the motivations which drove heads of production units and self-employed workers to create their own jobs. The results concerning the reasons for informality in the case of Peru reinforces both the idea of

*Table 14.1* Structure of urban household incomes according to source, average 2006–2010

|  | Structure according to source of income | | | Breaking down of inequalities (Shorrocks' decomposition) |
|---|---|---|---|---|
|  | Total households (%) | Poor households (%) | Non-poor households (%) | |
| Working income | 64.6 | 61.0 | 58.7 | 66.0 |
| • formal sector | 33.5 | 16.8 | 34.6 | 55.4 |
| • informal sector | 25.3 | 44.2 | 24.0 | 10.6 |
| • agricultural sector | 5.8 | 11.9 | 5.4 | 7.5 |
| Private transfers | 10.7 | 10.6 | 10.7 | 3.6 |
| Public transfers | 9.1 | 6.3 | 9.3 | 8.4 |
| Private income | 3.3 | 0.9 | 3.5 | 6.7 |
| Imputed rent | 10.4 | 7.7 | 10.6 | 6.7 |
| Others | 1.9 | 1.7 | 1.9 | 1.3 |
| Total | 100.0 | 100.0 | 100.0 | 100.0 |

Sources: ENAHO 2006–2010, INEI; author's calculations.

an informal sector chosen by default when faced with the difficulties of acceding to salaried work and that of a voluntary choice in the hope of obtaining a higher income. More than half workers (56 per cent in 2010) hold a job in the informal sector because they haven't found salaried work. The results also confirm the existence of a non-negligible segment who deliberately chose to create an IPU either because it would allow them, according to the individuals surveyed, to earn higher incomes (28.3 per cent in 2010), or because of the wish to be independent (12.5 per cent) or because of family tradition (3.2 per cent).

## Informal micro-enterprise dynamics

### *Macro-economic dynamics*

Since the beginning of the 2000s Peru has been undergoing a period of strong uninterrupted growth which accelerated during the 2004–2010 period (5.6 per cent of annual average growth of real per capita GNP). This growth was accompanied by a significant reduction in poverty, particularly in urban areas (from 37.1 to 19.1 per cent during the same period). In cities, the unemployment rate did not begin to perceptibly fall until 2006, when the average GNP growth rate rose above 6 per cent. The fall in the total number of unemployed (including discouraged workers) over the same period was also significant (from 13.2 to 7.7 per cent).

Several authors have underlined the anti-cyclical behaviour of the informal sector: swelling during periods of crisis and shrinking during periods of growth. In the case of Peru, this stylized fact seems to be confirmed with one nuance: the share of the informal sector in employment only diminishes when growth goes beyond a certain threshold (about 4 per cent). This share thus fell from 69 per cent in 2004 to 62.3 per cent in 2010 (Figure 14.1).[1] On the contrary, between 2004 and 2010, the part of salaried workers in the formal private sector rose significantly (from 17.3 to 22.5 per cent) while a reconstitution of employment took place within the informal sector. Thus, while the number of self-employed workers only rose by 12 per cent between 2004 and 2010, the number of informal sector managers and salaried workers rose by 25.4 and 33.2 per cent respectively. The phase of high growth seems to have induced a greater heterogeneity in the informal sector, the 'top of the range' segment (production units with salaried workers) developing more rapidly than the 'bottom of the range' segment (here self-employed workers and PUs without salaried workers).

### *Micro-economic dynamics*

Two antagonistic visions of the dynamics of the informal sector are the object of much debate and controversy. On the one hand, certain researchers such as Tokman (1989) consider that the high number of jobs in the informal sector is the result of the segmentation of the labour market which excludes the less qualified workers from salaried work. On the other hand, according to the analysis proposed by de Soto (1986), there is the perception according to which

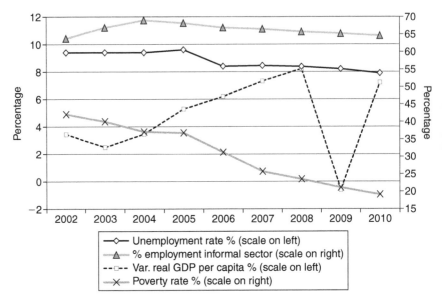

*Figure 14.1* Economic growth, poverty, unemployment and employment in the informal sector, 2002–2010 (sources: ENAHO 2002–2010, INEI; authors' calculations).

micro-entrepreneurs have the abilities required to grow and develop and that the obstacles to this development stem essentially from regulations which make it difficult to create enterprises (the 'cost of formality') and other institutional 'inflexibilities' concerning the labour market. To this can be added the low opportunity costs of entering the informal sector, which leads to the predominance of enterprises with very low productivity, slim chances of growth and high failure rates (Fajnzylber and Maloney, 2007).

Fajnzylber *et al.* (2006) also analyse the dynamics of Mexican micro-entrepreneurs and micro-enterprises through the national survey of Urban Employment (ENEU) and the National Survey of Micro-enterprises (ENAMIN). Their analysis of working transitions concludes that salaried workers are found among those who become self-employed or set up micro-enterprises. What's more, once the probability of having an employment transition is taken into account, salaried workers are more likely to become self-employed than are the unemployed and inactive population. According to the authors quoted, the informal sector is only a survival refuge for workers who have not succeeded in finding salaried work (Fajnzylber *et al.*, 2006).

Ñopo and Valenzuela have shown in the case of the Chilean household panel (CASEN) that the gains in terms of income when a worker changes statute from salaried worker to micro-entrepreneur are substantial and statistically robust (as much with regard to extreme cases than as to possible skews linked to unobservable factors).[2] Conversely, the transition from micro-entrepreneur to salaried worker is associated with a drop in income. The gains linked to the change of status from salaried worker to micro-entrepreneur are moreover higher for women than for men, just like the losses in the case of transitions in the opposite direction.

Do independent workers resemble salaried workers or are they rather like heads of enterprise? A discriminant analysis carried out on the data from the Sri Lanka Survey of Micro-Enterprises lead by de Mel *et al.* (2008) concludes that about two-thirds of independent workers should be classed among salaried workers and not among entrepreneurs.

A study based on the *1-2-3 Surveys* on the informal sector in Vietnam estimates the failure rate of informal enterprises at 14.7 per cent in Hanoi and 21 per cent in Ho Chi Minh City over the period 2007–2009 (Demenet *et al.*, 2010). These results were close to those obtained by Vijverberg *et al.* (2006) using the Vietnamese panel Vietnam Household Living Standard Survey (VHLSS) 2002 and 2004.

Table 14.2 presents the average annual employment transitions over the 2002–2010 period. In first place, we can remark that unemployment is the most transitory state as only one unemployed worker in five remains in this situation for more than one year. Most of them (34 per cent) switch to a state of inactivity (of which a proportion of about 40 per cent is made up discouraged workers). A little less than one-third (31.7 per cent) enter into salaried work, thus reinforcing the hypothesis of a 'waiting room' (or 'luxury') unemployment which allows workers to find work better suited to their qualifications and/or expectations. Only 14.6 per cent leave unemployment to become micro-entrepreneurs. The inactive and unemployed who change their situation represent only 15.3 per cent of the total number of entrepreneurs, while salaried workers who become micro-entrepreneurs represent 19.8 per cent. Spending time in salaried work appears to thus be the most popular way of becoming a micro-entrepreneur while for a relatively small proportion of workers becoming self-employed constitutes a way of escaping from unemployment or inactivity. The idea according to which the

*Table 14.2* Individual status transitions in employment, average 2002–2010 (%)

|  | With 2 IPUs | With 1 IPU | Salaried worker | Unemployed | Inactive | Total | Total |
|---|---|---|---|---|---|---|---|
| With 2 IPUs | **24.8** | 52.5 | 13.3 | 1.7 | 7.8 | 100 | 1.9 |
| With 1 IPU | 4.5 | **62.4** | 19.0 | 3.8 | 10.3 | 100 | 23.2 |
| Salaried worker | 0.7 | 14.1 | **68.9** | 5.5 | 10.8 | 100 | 35.2 |
| Unemployed | 1.0 | 13.6 | 31.7 | **19.8** | 34.0 | 100 | 7.3 |
| Inactive | 0.5 | 8.6 | 15.8 | 8.6 | **66.5** | 100 | 32.3 |
| Total | 2.0 | 24.2 | 36.4 | 7.1 | 30.3 | 100 | 100 |

Sources: ENAHO 2002–2010, INEI; authors' calculations.

Note
The data is missing for 2007/2006 because of a new survey design containing a total renovation of the panel.

informal sector of micro-enterprises is exclusively a 'refuge' for the unemployed and the inactive has only been partially verified; it is probable that the transition to entrepreneurship from salaried work allows workers to constitute a bigger amount of starting capital and to gain experience and qualifications: factors which in all likelihood constitute a form of protection against failure. Finally, only one-quarter of individuals with two IPUs succeed in maintaining them both in activity one year after; half keep only one IPU and 22.8 per cent call a complete halt to their activity of micro-entrepreneur.

Table 14.3 shows the evolution of the rates of creation, failure and survival, calculated from the 2002–2010 panel. We can observe first that the failure rate is very high since, on average, a little more than one-third (35.4 per cent) of the IPUs disappear from one year to the next. However, a creation rate that is a little higher (38 per cent on average) counterbalances the effect of these disappearances. In this period of sustained economic growth we can also observe that the creation rate is systematically superior to the failure rate. However, an inflexion point seems to appear at the turn of 2004/2005, at the moment when growth accelerates: the failure rate falls a little more than four points (from 39.5 to 35.2 per cent). During the same period of strong growth, the creation rate of IPUs suffered a downturn from 2007/2008, as opportunities for better paid salaried work multiplied. The strong and sustained period of growth seems to have thus had a double effect: on the one hand it heightens the survival chances of IPUs and on the other it slows down the creation of micro-enterprises because of the increase in number of better remunerated salaried work. What's more, and although there are relatively few of them (8 per cent), informal entrepreneurs who own two IPUs register much higher failure rates (49.1 per cent) than those who manage just one IPU (33.1 per cent).

The great majority of those who close an IPU remain occupied (63.8 per cent) while those who leave the labour market represent 26 per cent. Only one in ten (10.2 per cent) become visible unemployed or hidden unemployed ('discouraged' unemployed). A higher proportion (53 per cent) of workers who succeed in keeping their IPUs active manage to generate a working income above the poverty line than workers who create or close one (or two) IPUs (44.6 and 43.9 per cent on average, respectively, over the period 2002–2010). One in five (19 per cent) of

*Table 14.3* Evolution of failure, creation and survival rates of IPUs, 2002–2010 (%)

|  | Average 2002/2010 | 2003/ 2002 | 2004/ 2003 | 2005/ 2004 | 2006/ 2005 | 2008/ 2007 | 2009/ 2008 | 2010/ 2009 |
|---|---|---|---|---|---|---|---|---|
| Failure rate | 35.4 | 31.0 | 34.8 | 39.5 | 37.9 | 35.9 | 36.1 | 35.2 |
| Creation rate | 38.0 | 40.8 | 37.9 | 40.7 | 40.4 | 36.9 | 37.3 | 36.8 |
| Survival rate | 64.6 | 69.0 | 65.2 | 60.5 | 62.1 | 64.1 | 63.9 | 64.8 |

Sources: ENAHO 2002–2010, INEI; authors' calculations.

Note
The data is missing for 2007/2006 because of a new survey design implying a total renovation of the panel.

those who create an IPU do not succeed in generating a sufficient number of working hours ('visible' under employment) in their principal activity. This is doubtlessly proof of the weakness of the means of production implemented.

## Impact of informal sector dynamics on poverty dynamics

In this section, we seek to analyse in greater detail informal enterprise dynamics by asking two major questions studied in succession:

- First, which factors are associated with the failure, creation or survival of micro-enterprises? Answering this question leads us to compare the profiles of micro-entrepreneurs according to whether their IPU was created during the year of the survey, failed or, on the contrary, succeeded in surviving.
- Second, what is the link between informal micro-enterprise dynamics and poverty? A question which is still much neglected due to the absence of panel data.

### *Profile of the micro-entrepreneurs according to the conditions of creation, failure and survival of IPUs*

The typical profile of the IPUs and the entrepreneurs that fail (compared to those that survive) is as follows: they are most often single younger women who live in extended, larger households and they have less professional experience (6.2 years vs 8.9 for those whose IPUs survive). Paradoxically, these micro-entrepreneurs have a slightly higher level of education, a greater proportion having been in higher education. The human capital of the household (measured by the total number of cumulated years in education compared to the potential total given the age of the members of the household) is also higher than for households whose IPU survives for two consecutive periods. These results can be explained by the fact that the better educated are also those who can 'escape' more easily from the informal sector, either by obtaining salaried work or by 'choosing' unemployment while awaiting better opportunities in the formal sector. Finally, a greater proportion of them reside in big and medium-sized cities, which may be linked to the fact that they offer greater prospects of mobility.

However, no significant difference can be found concerning the incidence of poverty at the household level, or for access to public services. As for the characteristics of the IPUs and in conformity with expectations, the IPUs which survive have a higher productivity. Thus, the added value by hour worked is 27 per cent higher in the case of IPUs which survive compared to that of micro-entrepreneurs who close their IPUs (7.4 soles/hour vs 10.1 soles/hour). There is a close correlation between the type of premises and the chance of survival and creation of the IPUs. More than half of the micro-entrepreneurs who shut down their IPU do not have working premises. Among those who create IPUs there are only 38 per cent in this situation and 48.6 per cent in the case of IPUs which survive two consecutive periods.

If the typical profiles of informal micro-entrepreneurs who cease their activity is rather different from those who survive, the former are very much like those who create IPUs. The only factors which appear to differentiate them are the branch of activity (IPUs with commercial activities are more likely to close), human capital and productivity (less in the IPUs which fail). Logically, the comparison between the profile of the creators of IPUs and the profile of those whose IPU holds steady gives globally the same contrasts than those between those who close their enterprise and those who survive. A few notable exceptions lie within the branch of activity (more in industry and the services) and the absence of any difference in their hourly productivity rate.

### Dynamics of informal micro-entrepreneurs and poverty

In Table 14.4 poverty transitions are crossed with individuals' different trajectories as regards their IPU. Here it is not a question of poverty at a household level but rather at an individual level. Workers are considered to be poor at the period $t$ if their working income is below the cost of the basic consumption basket given the size of the household and the number of income earners. It was observed that the individuals whose IPU closes finds themselves overrepresented in the category of those who make the transition towards poverty compared to those who succeed in keeping their IPU alive. On the other hand there is no statistically significant difference between individuals who create and those who close their IPU, whatever their poverty transition.

Few studies exist concerning poverty dynamics in developing countries and few among them have considered conjointly analysing this with the dynamics of micro-enterprises.[3] One exception is the study by Devicienti et al. (2009) which used the panel of Argentine households from the Permanent Employment Survey carried out by the Institute of Statistics over the period 1996–2003. The authors estimated a dynamic bivariate probit random effect model which simultaneously considered the risk of poverty and the probability of having a job in the informal

*Table 14.4* Poverty transitions and dynamics of micro-entrepreneurs (%)

| Transitions | Cease activity | Create | Survive | Total |
|---|---|---|---|---|
| Non-poor–non-poor | 45.2 | 45.9 | 44.0 | 44.8 |
| Poor–non-poor | 19.2 | 20.6 | 20.9 | 20.4 |
| Non-poor–poor | 20.4** | 18.6 | 17.8 | 18.6 |
| Poor–poor | 15.2* | 14.9*** | 17.4 | 16.2 |
| Total | 100 | 100 | 100 | 100 |

Sources: ENAHO 2002–2010, INEI; authors' calculations.

Notes
Poverty transitions based on individuals' working incomes.
*       significant at a 10% level.
**    significant at a 5% level.
***  significant at a 1% level.

sector. The authors show that individuals working in small production units are more likely to find themselves in a situation of poverty and employed in the informal sector enterprises characterized by their low productivity.

We propose next to examine in the case of Peru the correlation between poverty transitions while taking into account the dynamics of informal micro-enterprises. To what extent is the observation made in the bivariate framework confirmed in the multivariate framework of the estimation of a multinomial logit model explaining poverty transitions in function of individuals' characteristics, their household and their production unit? We do not here seek to establish links of causality between poverty and micro-enterprise dynamics (it is just as easy to imagine that the direction of causality goes in both directions, the two phenomena feeding each other). The more modest objective here is to verify if this correlation continues or not after having taken into account other variables which might also have an impact on poverty transitions. We shall restrict our analysis to urban workers.

The dependent variable is a qualitative variable with four modalities, each one corresponding to possible poverty transitions: non-poor–non-poor; poor–non-poor; non-poor–poor; poor–poor. In so far as the probability of the four united cases is equal to one, the estimation of a multinomial non-ordered logit model is the best adapted and one modality will serve as a reference for the others. We chose the situation non-poor–non-poor in order to make easier the reading of results concerning entry into poverty and permanence in poverty and the modality poor–poor as the reference modality for the 'out of poverty' transition. The estimated coefficients will be expressed in the form of odds ratios. A value inferior to 1 indicates a negative impact of $(1-\beta)$ per cent in the probability of finding oneself in a transition compared to the state of transition serving as a reference model. Among the 'explanatory' variables we retained variables connected to individual characteristics (gender, age group, marital status, level of education), household characteristics (size, type, access to public services), production unit characteristics (size, branch, type of premises, ownership) and geographical variables (size of the town).

The results presented in Table 14.5 indicate that those who close their IPUs have a 42 per cent greater risk of slipping into poverty compared to those who keep their IPU going. The failure of IPUs is also positively associated with a greater risk of remaining in a situation of poverty (23 per cent more risk compared to those whose IPU survived). Finally, it is always more difficult for an individual who has had to close down his/her IPU to escape poverty than for those whose IPU continues operating (16 per cent less chance of escaping poverty). These results are all statistically significant. Regarding the individuals who create an IPU, their chance of escaping poverty is 25 per cent higher relative to those who remain in poverty. They also run less risk (–21 per cent) of remaining two consecutive periods in poverty or of falling into poverty (–14 per cent) compared to non-poor individuals. However, these results are not statistically robust.

Men have twice as high a chance as women (+2.12) of escaping poverty whereas individuals in nuclear households (–26 per cent) and bigger ones (–6 per

*Table 14.5* Poverty transitions and demographic dynamics of IPUs, 2002–2010

| Variables | Poverty transitions | | | |
| --- | --- | --- | --- | --- |
| | Poor–non-poor (ref. poor–poor) | Poor–poor (ref. non-poor–non-poor) | Non-poor–poor (ref. non-poor–non-poor) | |
| Male (ref. female) | 2.12*** | 0.49*** | 0.48*** | |
| *Age group* (ref. 65 and over) | | | | |
| 13–24 years | 2.14*** | 0.42*** | 0.81 | |
| 25–44 years | 1.80*** | 0.51*** | 0.51*** | |
| 45–64 years | 2.10*** | 0.38*** | 0.49*** | |
| *Marital status* (ref. single) | | | | |
| Married | 1.12 | 0.83** | 1.07 | |
| Cohabitation | 0.99 | 1.07 | 1.16 | |
| *Level of education* (ref. primary or less) | | | | |
| Secondary | 1.35*** | 0.60*** | 0.83** | |
| Higher non-university | 1.94*** | 0.33*** | 0.57*** | |
| Higher university | 2.30*** | 0.25*** | 0.40*** | |
| *Household characteristics* | | | | |
| Size of household | 0.94*** | 1.17*** | 1.11*** | |
| *Type of household* (ref. compound, one-person, without nucleus) | | | | |
| Extended household | 0.83 | 1.86*** | 1.61*** | |
| Nuclear household | 0.74** | 1.79*** | 1.48*** | |

| | | | |
|---|---|---|---|
| *Access to public services* (1=yes; 0=no) | | | |
| Drinking water | 0.81 | 1.21 | 1.11 |
| Drains | 1.15 | 1.00 | 1.17 |
| Electricity | 1.15 | 0.86 | 0.78 |
| Fixed telephone | 1.65*** | 0.43*** | 0.69** |
| *Size of town* (ref. town with more than 100,000 dwellings) | | | |
| More than 100,000 dwellings | 1.59*** | 0.47*** | 0.76*** |
| 20,001 to 100,000 dwellings | 1.16 | 0.83** | 1.09 |
| 10,001 to 20,000 dwellings | 1.31** | 0.63*** | 0.91 |
| *Creation, failure of IPUs* (ref. IPU survive) | | | |
| IPU cease activity | 0.84* | 1.23** | 1.42*** |
| Create IPU | 1.25 | 0.79 | 0.86 |
| *Size of IPU* (ref. 5 or more) | | | |
| Only 1 worker | 0.23*** | 3.49*** | 2.57*** |
| 2 workers | 0.37*** | 2.68*** | 1.97*** |
| 3 workers | 0.44*** | 2.12*** | 1.73*** |
| 4 workers | 0.53** | 1.96*** | 1.27 |
| Without premises | 0.94 | 1.15 | 1.05 |
| Owner of the IPU premises | 1.03 | 1.03 | 1.08 |
| *Branch of activity* (ref. services) | | | |
| Manufacturing | 0.95 | 1.16 | 1.06 |
| Commerce | 0.82** | 1.45*** | 1.27*** |
| Constant | 1.42 | 0.30*** | 0.29*** |
| Observations | 7,211 | 7,211 | 7,211 |

Sources: ENAHO 2002–2010, INEI; authors' calculations.

Notes
*      significant at a 10% level.
**    significant at a 5% level.
***  significant at a 1% level.

cent for each member) have less chance of doing so. No notable differences were observed according to age for individuals under the age of 65. Education pays, even in the informal sector. The chance of escaping poverty rises greatly with the level of education (+1.35, +1.94, +2.30 compared to primary education).

The size of the IPU is strongly correlated with the chance of escaping poverty: the smaller the size, the lesser the chance of escaping it. The absence of premises reduces the chance (–6 per cent) of escaping poverty whereas being the owner of the premises increases it by 3 per cent. These two last results are not statistically significant. The informal sector workers in the trade branch see their chance of escaping poverty reduced (–18 per cent). The size of the town also counts: it is better to live in a big city (more than 100,000 dwellings) than a small town (+59 per cent chance of escaping poverty).

There is some symmetry between the factors associated with entering and escaping poverty: men run less risk than women (–52 per cent). The same is true for workers of prime-age (25–44 years): –50 per cent. Likewise, the higher a worker's level of education, the less chance he/she has of experiencing a transition towards poverty. It is the same thing regarding the residents of big cities and workers in large-sized units. Those working in the retail trade branch will run a greater risk (+27 per cent) of following an unfavourable trajectory.

No specific factors were found linked to permanence in poverty. The same variables having an incidence on an unfavourable poverty transition here also have an impact in the same direction. Thus, the fact of working in the trade branch brings with it an increased risk of remaining in poverty (+45 per cent risk compared to the non-poor) and the same is true for the smallest-sized IPUs. Having a higher level of education, living in a big city, being of prime-age, married and male diminish the risks for workers of remaining beneath the poverty line for two consecutive periods.

## Conclusion

The accumulation of more than ten successive years of surveys gathering together information about households, individual socio-demographic characteristics and characteristics of the labour market as well as about informal micro-enterprises has allowed us to establish the actual situation and the importance of the informal sector, its principal characteristics and its macro dynamics. We have also examined the employment transitions and the trajectories of micro-entrepreneurs over short periods (panels of two consecutive years). It was observed that nearly nine out of ten urban workers employed in the informal sector and nearly six out of ten workers in the informal sector are poor. This double observation justifies the interest of conjointly analysing poverty and informality. Beyond the individual and household characteristics generally considered (human capital, size and type of household, etc.) few studies have addressed the impact of the characteristics of the IPUs and their demography on transitions towards poverty.

The period studied was characterized by strong macro-economic growth, a big reduction in poverty and a fall in unemployment. The proportion of informal urban workers diminished moderately, thus supporting the hypothesis of an anti-cyclical behaviour generally observed in periods of recession. The IPUs' characteristics are quite heterogeneous; IPUs with characteristics similar to formal enterprises coexist with others which are closer to survival jobs. The results regarding informality in the case of Peru reinforce at the same time the idea of an informal sector chosen by default when faced with the difficulties of acceding to the salaried work and that of a voluntary choice made with the prospect of obtaining a higher income.

The very high rate of IPU failure observed in the case of Peru (a little more than one-third of IPU heads close their unit each year) tempers the often optimistic vision of micro-entrepreneurship as a vector of growth in developing countries. The creation rate is also very high (38 per cent). Given the relative importance of labour income in total income and the high proportion of jobs in the informal sector, micro-enterprise dynamics is closely linked to the dynamics of poverty. Indeed, among the most striking results can be mentioned the role of micro-enterprise dynamics (creation, survival and failure of IPUs) on individual poverty transitions. The estimated econometric model corroborates the hypothesis of a greater vulnerability to poverty in the case of workers who close down their IPU: they run a 42 per cent higher risk of falling into poverty compared to individuals whose IPU succeeds in surviving but also a higher risk (23 per cent) of remaining in poverty.

Public policies have generally highlighted the positive aspects of micro-enterprise dynamics and have sought to encourage their extension and development often in the framework policies fighting poverty. The relatively high failure rate of IPUs implies a loss of household productive assets rendering them more vulnerable to poverty. Public policies must take into account the high rate (and its impact) of failure of micro-enterprises. The characteristics of production units and the branches of activity play a decisive role in the differences in productivity, incomes and thus on household poverty. Micro-enterprise dynamics is thus important if one wishes to understand poverty dynamics and poverty alleviation. Public policies should also pay attention to the factors linked to the risks of failure in order to attenuate household vulnerability.

## Notes

1 This evolution is robust whatever the operational definition of the informal sector.
2 The estimation method relies on 'matching' non-parametric differences-in-differences which allow addressing the question of bias due to observables and non-observables and creating an appropriate counterfactual.
3 See Herrera and Roubaud (2007) for the results of these studies.

## References

Abowd, J., Kramarz, F. and Margolis D. (1999) 'High-wage workers and high-wage firms', *Econometrica* 67(2): 251–333.
Brown, C. and Medoff, J. (1989) 'The employer size–wage effect', *Journal of Political Economy* 97(5): 1027–1059.

Brunello, G. and Colussi, A. (1998) 'The employer size–wage effect: evidence from Italy', *Labour Economics* 5(2): 217–230.

Cunningham, W. and Maloney, W. (2001) 'Heterogeneity among Mexico microenterprises: an application of factor and cluster analysis', *Economic Development and Cultural Change* 50(1): 131–156.

de Mel, S., McKenzie, D. and Woodruff, C. (2008) 'Who are the micro-enterprise owners? Evidence from Sri Lanka on Tokman v. de Soto', Policy Research Paper No. 4635, World Bank.

de Soto, H. (1986) *El Otro Sendero: la revolución informal*, Lima: Ed. El Barranco.

Demenet, A., Nguyen, Thi Thu Huyen, Razafindrakoto, M. and Roubaud, F. (2010) 'Dynamics of the informal sector in Hanoi and Ho Chi Minh City 2007–2009', GSO-IRD, UKaid, World Bank, Hanoi (www.worldbank.org/en/country/vietnam/research).

Devicienti, F., Groisman, F. and Poggi, A. (2009) 'Informality and poverty: are these processes dynamically interrelated? Evidence from Argentina', ECINEQ Working Papers 146, Society for the Study of Economic Inequality.

Fajnzylber, P. and Maloney, W. (2007) 'Micro-firm dynamics and informality', in *Informality: Exit or Exclusion?* G.E. Perry, W.F. Maloney, O.S. Arias, P. Fajnzylber, A.D. Mason and J. Saavedra-Chanduvi (eds), Washington, DC: World Bank, 133–156.

Fajnzylber, P., Maloney, W. and Montes, G. (2006) 'Micro-firms dynamics in less developed countries: how similar are they to those in the industrialized world-evidence from Mexico', *World Bank Economic Review* 6: 1–31.

Funkhouser, E. (1998) 'The importance of firm wage differentials in explaining hourly earnings variation in the large-scale sector of Guatemala', *Journal of Development Economics* 55(1): 115–131.

Groshen, E. (1991) 'Sources of intra-industry wage dispersion: how much do employers matter?' *Quarterly Journal of Economics* 106: 869–884.

Hamermesh, D. (2008) 'Fun with matched firm-employee data: progress and road maps', *Labour Economics* 15(4): 663–673.

Herrera, J. and Roubaud, F. (2007) 'Urban poverty dynamics in Peru and Madagascar', *International Planning Studies* 75(1): 70–95.

Lanjouw, P. (2008) 'Does the rural non-farm economy contribute to poverty reduction?' in *Transforming the Rural Non-farm Economy: Opportunities and Threats in the Developing World*, S. Haggblade, P. Hazell and T. Reardon (eds), Baltimore, MD: Johns Hopkins University Press, 55–79.

Mortensen, D. (2003) *Wage Dispersion: Why Are Similar Workers Paid Differently?* Cambridge, MA: MIT Press.

Ñopo, H. and Valenzuela, P. (2007) 'Becoming an entrepreneur", IZA Discussion Paper No. 2716.

Oi, W. and Idson, T. (1999) 'Firm size and wages', in *Handbook of Labor Economics*, O. Ashenfelter and D. Card (eds), Amsterdam: Elsevier, edition 1, vol. 3B, 2165–2214.

Tokman, V.E. (1989) 'Policies for a heterogeneous informal sector in Latin America', *World Development* 17(7): 1067–1076.

Vijverberg, W., Hoang, H., Nguyen, T., Nguyen, Q., Nguyen, Q., Phung, T. and Vu, M. (2006) 'Non-farm household enterprises in Vietnam: a research project using data from VHLSS 2004, VHLSS 2002 and AHBS 2003', Hanoi.

# 15 Informality, crisis and public policies in Vietnam

*Jean-Pierre Cling, Mireille Razafindrakoto and François Roubaud*

In spite of their predominant weight in developing countries and countries in transition, the informal economy remains largely neglected by public policies. Vietnam is no exception to this rule, quite the contrary. In the euphoria which accompanied the exceptional success of the policy of opening up and the implementation of a market economy (*Doi Moi*) in 1986, the Vietnamese authorities acted as if the informal economy did not exist, or was about to rapidly disappear. Inspired by a simplified and "developmentalist" conception of structural change, they consider that economic transition would entail a huge movement of the workforce from the agricultural sector towards the sector of big enterprises. In these conditions, there was no need to implement specific support policies for the informal sector, which remains to this day a veritable no man's land for the country's authorities. The financial crisis which hit Vietnam in 2009 might have been an opportunity to take into account the role of the informal sector as a cushion to limit induced tensions in the labour market. This opportunity was not taken. Once again, all attention focused on the rise of visible unemployment and the support to be provided to the formal sector to kick start the economy and create jobs. In fact, the only existing measures concerning the informal economy are of a repressive nature, notably operations to drive away itinerant sellers, which are both inappropriate and inefficient, undertaken in the framework of urban "beautification" policies in Vietnam's big cities.

The aim of this chapter is to give guidelines for public action about how to address the informal economy issues. We use a rich corpus of quantitative data collected at the authors' instigation in order to measure its weight, analyse its characteristics, functioning and dynamism, especially in times of crisis. Too often, policy recommendations concerning the informal economy are not supported beforehand by a real accurate diagnostic of this sector, because of a lack of representative statistical information.

In conformity with international recommendations, we distinguish two components in the informal economy. Informal sector is defined as all private unincorporated enterprises that produce at least some of their goods and services for sale or barter, are not registered (no business licence) and are engaged in non-agricultural activities. Informal employment is defined as employment with no social security. Thus, informal employment is made up of two distinct components, namely employment in the informal sector, as well as unprotected work in the formal sector. The broader "informal economy" concept covers both the informal sector and the different forms of informal employment found in the informal and formal sectors (ILO, 2003). The principal empirical results draw on the results of the latest available statistical surveys conducted with support from the authors and refers to different studies (Cling *et al.*, 2010a, 2010b; Nguyen Huu Chi *et al.*, 2010; Demenet *et al.*, 2010) undertaken in the framework of an international programme.[1] It is based on the results of two rounds of the Labour Force Survey (LFS) implemented nationwide in 2007 and 2009 and on a specific Household Business and Informal Sector Survey (HB&IS) carried out twice in the same years in Hanoi and Ho Chi Minh City.

The first section of this chapter highlights the major role played by the informal economy in employment in Vietnam, describes its principal characteristics and future prospects. The second section explores the adjustment mode on the labour market in times of crisis, and more particularly the impact of the crisis on the informal sector. The third section is focused on the two main cities, Hanoi and Ho Chi Minh City, where detailed information on the informal sector dynamics is available. Finally, the fourth section draws some policy recommendations to provide support for household businesses in the informal sector. Although our analysis concerns the case of Vietnam, it has a wider scope and aims to contribute to the global debate on the informal economy in developing countries.

## The informal economy, first source of non-agricultural employment

The Labour Force surveys carried out by the GSO since 2007 have provided for the first time accurate and representative data at a national level about the informal economy. Therefore the questionnaire for the survey was defined with the help of the authors in conformity with international recommendations in order to measure the informal economy (Cling *et al.*, 2010a). These surveys highlight the preponderant weight of the informal economy in employment and the fact that the informal sector is characterized by badly remunerated, precarious and unprotected jobs.

### *The informal economy, a predominant sector where precarious conditions prevail*

The informal sector represents nearly a quarter of total employment and is the first source of non-agricultural jobs (Table 15.1). Although the socio-economic characteristics of the labour force working in the informal sector are not that different from the rest of the labour force (except for their level of education), job characteristics in the informal sector are very different and usually much worse than in other sectors, except agriculture. The rate of wage workers is low (27 per cent) and the forms of wage work are clearly more precarious: more than 99 per

*Table 15.1* Characteristics of the workforce and of employment by institutional sector in Vietnam, 2009

| Institutional sector | Number of jobs (1,000) | Structure (%) | Migrant (%) | Head of household (%) | Salaried workers (%) | Average monthly income (1,000 VND) | Professional premises (%) | Informal job (%) |
|---|---|---|---|---|---|---|---|---|
| Public sector | 4,615 | 9.7 | 10.4 | 43.6 | 99.7 | 1,964 | 96.4 | 12.5 |
| Foreign enterprise | 1,376 | 2.9 | 32.1 | 25.4 | 99.9 | 1,735 | 97.6 | 12.9 |
| Domestic enterprise | 3,669 | 7.7 | 16.0 | 33.0 | 93.6 | 2,093 | 86.4 | 48.1 |
| Formal household business | 3,688 | 7.8 | 8.4 | 37.6 | 36.4 | 1,805 | 33.8 | 51.5 |
| Informal sector | 11,313 | 23.8 | 5.6 | 42.9 | 26.7 | 1,273 | 7.8 | 100 |
| Agriculture | 22,838 | 48.0 | 2.4 | 39.7 | 9.6 | 703 | 1.1 | 98.6 |
| Total | 47,548 | 100 | 6.3 | 39.7 | 33.6 | 1,185 | 23.8 | 80.5 |

Sources: LFS 2009, GSO; authors' calculations.

cent have at best a verbal contract (25 per cent have no contract at all); only 10 per cent are paid on a monthly basis (which constitutes the norm in the other sectors), the majority being remunerated on a daily or hourly or piece-rate basis.

For the workers in this sector, the rate of social protection is negligible (0.1 per cent), whereas it reaches 87 per cent in the public sector and in foreign enterprises. Workers in the informal sector earn the lowest salaries outside agriculture. Almost all of the jobs in the informal sector are carried out without specific professional premises (at home or in the street), which constitutes another indicator of the precariousness of jobs in this sector.

The survey also provides a measure of informal employment which represented 80.5 per cent of total employment in 2009 in Vietnam. Thus, only nine million workers are covered by social security (obligatory or voluntary; VASS, 2010). The rate of informal employment varies a great deal by institutional sector. Informal employment peaks at more than 99 per cent in agriculture and 100 per cent in the informal sector. But informal employment exists in all institutional sectors (including the public sector): nearly half of domestic enterprise jobs and more than 10 per cent in foreign enterprises and in the public sector are informal (Razafindrakoto *et al.*, 2011).

### The informal sector will tend to grow

In the long term, it is expected that the weight of the informal sector decreases progressively with the country's development progress, in conformity with the observation of the negligible weight of this sector in developed countries (La Porta and Schleifer, 2008; Bacchetta *et al.*, 2009). Indeed, these countries have relatively efficient regulation and fiscal control from which it is difficult to escape for small entrepreneurs. However, this mechanism only works in the long run, as Bacchetta *et al.* stated: "informality rates can be shown to be highly persistent over time, responding only weakly to accelerations in economic growth or trade openness". Given the rapid growth of the Vietnamese economy since the 1980s and the launch of *Doi Moi*, we could expect at least a slightly decreasing trend of the informal sector's weight. However, at odds with expectations, Nguyen (2012) shows that the share of the informal sector in total employment rose from 23.2 to 26.6 per cent between 1998 and 2008. Moreover, the share of this sector is the highest in the two most industrialized regions in the country, the Red River Delta (Hanoi region) and the south-east (Ho Chi Minh City region). In spite of the rise in the rate of salaried workers and the expansion of the private formal sector, the informal sector will thus continue to grow in Vietnam, the consequence of a phenomenon of rapid agrarian, urban and demographic transition.[2]

Besides, forecasts for employment in 2015 that we made using past trends – before the crisis – show that employment in the informal sector and its relative weight in total employment are going to keep growing over the next few years (Cling *et al.*, 2010c). Regarding labour supply, Vietnam is experiencing a "demographic dividend" which impact is the arrival of a huge number of young people as new entrants on the labour market (more than one million per year), and this situation is going to last until 2015 (Oudin *et al.*, 2013). At the same time, given that agricultural employment (which represents nearly half of total employment) is in a decreasing trend, a rapid growth of the formal private sector cannot create enough jobs for all the new arrivals on the labour market. When the Vietnamese economy recovers from the crisis, even if we suppose a strong growth scenario, the share of the informal sector in total employment will still be predominant in the years to come (about 27 per cent in 2015): indeed, employment in foreign enterprises will grow by 180 per cent between 2007 and 2015 (i.e. it will increase almost threefold), the equivalent growth rate is 124 per cent in domestic enterprises, 6.8 per cent in formal household businesses, but employment in the informal sector will increase by 33.8 per cent during the same period, the trend in the agricultural and the public sector being negative.

## The impact of the crisis on employment and the informal sector at a national level

Vietnam has been affected by the international crisis which began in 2008. This crisis triggered a slowing down of growth which was however less acute than in many other Asian countries which suffered a recession in 2008–2009. The impact of the crisis on the principal macro-economic aggregates has been analysed in many studies (see for a synthesis, Cling *et al.*, 2010c). All these studies adopt a macro-economic approach to conclude that the impact of the crisis on household income could be quite harmful as some workers had to experience job loss and/or a shift to lower paid jobs in the informal sector or to return to agricultural activities.

However, these studies did not investigate precisely the repercussions of the crisis on the labour market. The impact of the crisis on the informal sector in particular is virtually unknown. A few qualitative studies focused on some specific sub-sectors or population categories concluded that many workers have lost their job (see Cling *et al.*, 2010c, for a review). On the quantitative front, only two studies launched by UNDP (Warren-Rodriguez, 2009; Nguyen Viet Cuong *et al.*, 2009) intend to measure the global impact of the crisis on the labour market. Using a similar methodology, based on employment elasticities to growth, both studies converge in forecasting a significant slowdown in job creation and consequently strong increase of the unemployment rate, in particular in urban areas. At odds with all these studies, Cling *et al.* (2010c) suggest that unemployment will not be the main labour market response to the crisis, the informal sector and the quality of jobs being the key components in the adjustment process between supply and demand of labour like in a wide range of middle income countries (Khanna *et al.*, 2010). Analysis of the LFS carried out in 2007 and 2009 allows us to assess the effective impact of the crisis on the informal economy.

*A rather stable employment structure by institutional sector*

In Vietnam, as in many other developing countries, the unemployment rate is rather inelastic to the variations of GDP growth (Figure 15.1). Not only was there no burst in unemployment, but it actually decreased: the unemployment rate went down from its structurally low level of 2.4 per cent in 2007 to 1.9 per cent in 2012 (a too small change to be statistically significant). The decline is noteworthy for the urban unemployment (from 4.7 per cent in 2007 to 3.5 per cent in 2012), a more meaningful indicator than the rural one in a developing country like Vietnam. It is nowadays widely acknowledged that open unemployment is not the best indicator of market clearing in developing countries. In such countries where wage relations cover a low percentage of the labour force and where unemployment risk is not covered by social institutions, the shortage of labour demand passes through other mechanisms than unemployment.

Between 2007 and 2009, almost two million jobs were created. The distribution by institutional sector did not change significantly with the crisis. Agricultural jobs continued their declining pattern (from 50.4 to 48.1 per cent of total employment). The informal sector slightly increased its share of total employment (from 23.4 to 23.8 per cent), with the creation of 639,000 new jobs. However, it was the private formal sector in particular which was the most dynamic: more than one million additional jobs (+41 per cent) in domestic enterprises and 480,000 jobs (+53 per cent) in foreign direct investment sector. Regarding formal household businesses, with the creation of 183,000 jobs, their share of total employment did not change significantly. If we turn to the analysis of labour conditions, the rate of wage workers keeps growing (29.8 to 33.6 per cent). Informal employment still represents 80.5 per cent of total jobs in 2009, which means that the great majority of

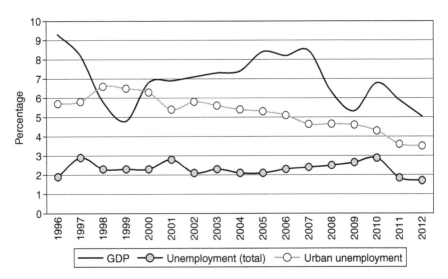

*Figure 15.1* Unemployment rates and GDP growth in Vietnam, 1996–2012 (sources: MoLISA and GSO (1996–2013); authors' calculations).

workers are not covered by the social insurance scheme. But, this figure corresponds to a small drop compared to 2007 (81.9 per cent).

*Adjustments on the labour market: underemployment and multi-activity*

While the main structures of the labour market remained globally unaffected, the principal variable of adjustment during the economic slowdown has been the working hours. The average working time has been reduced (from 43.9 to 42.6 hours per week between 2007 and 2009). Part-time workers' share has doubled. Paradoxically, whereas more workers had to work less, at the other side of the hours ladder, an increasing share of workers had to work more hours to make a living, which is usually considered as another form of "invisible" unemployment. Finally, to compensate for this contraction in available hours, more workers had to find additional sources of income by getting a second job. The multi-activity rate gained 7.2 percentage points, from 18.2 per cent in 2007 to 25.4 per cent in 2009.

## The impact of the crisis in Hanoi and Ho Chi Minh City

This section focuses on the dynamics of the informal sector in Hanoi and Ho Chi Minh City. Actually, two specific sets of surveys have been conducted in these two cities in 2007 and 2009, in parallel with the LFS. Three main advantages of these surveys should be underlined: first, they enlarge the perspective from only considering labour market issues, to address the supply side (production, investment, etc.) of the informal firms. Second, they provide more reliable measures of income than those captured in the LFSs. Finally, they include a panel component to assess individual demographic and economic dynamics of HBs.

Two key messages come up from the analysis of the survey results: on the one hand, the important growth of employment in the informal sector between 2007 and 2009, as well as of the number of informal household businesses, which has been stimulated by the crisis; on the other hand, the striking difference between Hanoi and Ho Chi Minh City, the informal household businesses in the south being by far the most affected on the whole, especially in terms of incomes. Although this latter result should be checked further, one can hypothesize that Vietnam's economic hub has suffered more on the whole from the crisis due to its dependency on world markets, and that this greater openness directly impacted on the informal sector.

*The phenomenon of informalization at work*

In 2009, Hanoi counted 3.3 million (main) jobs, while there were 3.7 million in Ho Chi Minh City. Among these jobs, respectively, 32 and 34 per cent of total employment were in the informal sector. This makes the informal sector the number one employer in both cities. The total number of informal household businesses (IHBs) comes to 725,000 in Hanoi in 2009, and the corresponding figure in Ho Chi Minh City is 967,000. The growth of the number of informal HBs is estimated at 23 per cent in Hanoi and 29 per cent in Ho Chi Minh City from 2007 to 2009, whereas employment in this sector has increased, respectively, by 6 and 19 per cent within the two-year period. With this quite rapid growth pace, the persistence and dynamism of this sector cannot be denied. However, without any comparable figures from another time period or from other similar countries, the diagnosis which can be made is limited. On the one hand, this evolution could just result from the usual rhythm of expansion of the informal sector given the demographic growth of the population in the cities. It even could have been slowed down by the lower growth of the economy in general and the contraction of demand. On the other hand, the informal sector could evolve in a countercyclical way compared to the rest of the economy.

The economic crisis in 2008–2009 has induced a phenomenon of informalization which has affected the two cities and almost all industries. This hypothesis is confirmed by the diminution of the rate of formalization: in 2009, formal HBs represent 15.3 per cent of HBs in Hanoi and 17.6 per cent in Ho Chi Minh City (the percentages were, respectively, 19.5 and 25.4 per cent in 2007). Panel data analysis based on a survey sub-sample confirms also this informalization process (Table 15.2): a huge 31 per cent of FHBs in Hanoi and 15 per cent in Ho Chi Minh City entered the informal sector, while on the reverse only around one IHB out of ten got formalized, in both cities. The HBs which became informal were smaller (value added, number of jobs), less productive and more precarious (no professional premises).

### The impact of the crisis on economic performance and on living conditions in Hanoi and Ho Chi Minh City

Changes in income are particularly difficult to analyse during periods of high inflation. Results might differ depending on the indicator used. In *Hanoi*, an impressive

*Table 15.2* Formalization and informalization rates between 2007 and 2009 (%)

| Economic activity (2007) | Formalization rate | | Informalization rate | |
|---|---|---|---|---|
| | Hanoi | Ho Chi Minh City | Hanoi | Ho Chi Minh City |
| Manufacturing | 4.5 | 9.5 | 25.4 | 9.0 |
| Trade | 10.9 | 12.9 | 26.1 | 10.6 |
| Services | 7.7 | 8.5 | 47.3 | 26.1 |
| Total HBs | 8.3 | 10.2 | 31.1 | 15.3 |

Sources: HB&IS survey, Hanoi and Ho Chi Minh City, 2007 and 2009, panel survey, GSO/IRD-DIAL; authors' calculations.

Note
"Formalization" means that the HB was informal in 2007 and became formal in 2009. "Informalization" means that the HB was formal in 2007 and became informal in 2009.

growth of the average level of income can be observed. In *Ho Chi Minh City*, if we look at the evolution of the average income, the situation has worsened in the informal sector from 2007 to 2009 (–3.5 per cent in real terms). But the median income has clearly increased (+10.9 per cent). Contrarily to Hanoi, the units with higher level of income (the bigger or the most efficient ones) tend to pull down the average income. It appears that since they are more connected to the formal economy, they are the main victims of the crisis.

The fact that the informal sector met more serious difficulties in Ho Chi Minh City is confirmed by qualitative answers to the survey. Almost one half (46 per cent) of IHBs in Ho Chi Minh City declared that they have suffered from a decrease in income between 2008 and 2009. This proportion is much inferior in Hanoi, where one-quarter (23 per cent) of Hanoi's IHBs suffered from such a decrease. These results tend to prove the reality of the crisis, particularly hard in Ho Chi Minh City. The contrast between the two cities is consistent with previous findings.

## Implications in terms of public policies

Structurally, the informal economy remains a huge component of the labour force in Vietnam, characterized by poor labour conditions. This section presents the policy implications which can be drawn from the survey results. Three types of measure can be put forward: the first type of measure aims at recognizing officially the existence of the informal sector, which means that it has to be defined, measured and monitored regularly in official statistics; the second type concerns the clarification and simplification of the law regarding household businesses and the registration formalities; the third type regroups targeted policy measures for the informal sector (tax policy, incentives, support programme).

### *Recognition of the informal sector*

In spite of a recent higher awareness about informality in Vietnam, the informal sector still remains a *terra incognita* from a policy perspective, largely ignored by the authorities. None of the temporary measures considered in the stimulus package to mitigate the negative impact of the global crisis has benefitted the informal sector (Razafindrakoto *et al.*, 2011). It is all the more problematic that poverty is progressively changing face, from its traditional rural and agriculture profile to a more urban and informal phenomenon. But, the lack of support policies for informal household businesses does not concern only the period of crisis. For example, the socio-economic development plan for the 2011–2015 period never mentions the informal economy and still focuses on the target of lowering unemployment (MPI, 2010).

In order to put in place specific policies, the very concept of the informal economy (sector and employment) needs to acquire a legal and recognized existence in Vietnam, which is not currently the case. It must be defined in a relevant and juridically recognized document (law, decree, circular, etc.). It is a preliminary condition so that the different institutions (public and private) may target the informal sector with their interventions. This legal recognition is also a prerequisite to allow regular measurement and monitoring of the sector by the GSO and thus allow the elaboration of efficient policies founded on robust empirical information. This official recognition would not mean that the informal sector is legalized. Indeed, a large number of household businesses operate "illegally" since their income is higher than the legal threshold above which they should get a business licence (Cling *et al.*, 2012).

The recognition of the informal sector would also permit avoidance of the exclusion of millions of workers from economic and social life. To some extent, the informal sector workers would become real citizens. Such a situation would favour the creation of associations which can help workers in negotiations and in the policy dialogue with the government (see below). The informal sector would forge the missing link between the shiny, globalized face of Vietnamese growth (foreign direct investment, exports, new technologies, etc.) and the peasantry, which should be a priority target of poverty reduction and development policies.

### Suppressing the grey lawless zone

In fact, if the state does not really understand the informal sector, the reverse is also true. No one really knows who should register (get business licence) and pay taxes. This fuzzy frontier between formal and informal HBs and lack of transparency create a grey zone prone to informal arrangements and negotiation, including corruption. As a street seller declared, "I know nothing about the regulation except one rule: when I see policemen coming, I have to run" (Razafindra-koto and Nguyen Huu Chi, 2010). Enacting clear rules would help reducing discretionary decisions and harassment by public officials, as well as allowing them to enforce legal regulations on a clear-cut basis.

Nearly all household businesses should be registered in Vietnam if the legislation was strictly enforced. But the applied criteria which determines whether an HB has to register or not is fuzzy. Therefore, the fact that almost no IHBs (less than 1 per cent) know the threshold above which HBs have to register is not a surprise (Demenet *et al.*, 2010). Even among the formal HBs, only a minority claims that they know the registration legislation (10 per cent of FHBs in Hanoi and 20 per cent in Ho Chi Minh City), and their knowledge appears to be limited since the magnitude of the registration threshold that they put forward varies substantially (from two million to 15 million VND per month). One might as well say that the application of the law is totally discretionary, thus creating an unpredictable business environment which is a source of economic inefficiencies.

Enacting clear, simple and available rules would encourage formalization. Regarding the criterion to be chosen, among the two possibilities (size and revenue threshold) currently used in Vietnam and which differ from one commune to another, each one has its advantages and disadvantages, consequently trade-offs must be considered (for example between economic relevance and ease-of-use for the controlling system). Besides, formal and informal sectors are no definitive status: the dynamic approach shows that a far from negligible part of IHBs get formalized and vice versa. Given the advantages of formalization (access to credit, lower risks of corruption, better economic performances, etc.; Rand and Torm, 2012), the design of incentive policies alongside clear rules would favour the flow from informal to formal sector. Regarding migrants, the residential registration regulation seems to be an obstacle for some household businesses which cannot register because their migration status is precarious. One may think that simplifying migration registration could also be an incentive for formalization.

Outlining the contours of the informal sector and the precise rules regarding registration should facilitate the implementation of an incentive fiscal policy tailored to the specific circumstances of this sector. Fiscal and support policies are complementary: on the one hand, the tax burden acceptability will depend on the existence of support policies that household businesses can benefit from, the implementation of relevant support policies being to a certain extent the necessary and logical counterpart to the taxation system; on the other hand, the taxes collected from household businesses (despite the usual principle of "fungibility" of the public budget) should naturally contribute, at least partially, to funding these support policies.

The informal sector can constitute a potential tax pool which is far from negligible: out of the 8.4 million household businesses in Vietnam, only 1.2 million are on a tax register. Actually, the number of HBs which effectively contribute is higher given the multiplicity of local taxes. For example, in Hanoi and Ho Chi Minh City, about a quarter of informal HBs already pay at least one kind of tax, whereas it is the case of almost all formal HBs. But the empirical evidence suggests that the correlation between taxation and the true level of activity is quite low, the most "visible" ones being more often taxed, whatever their income. Besides, a significant percentage of the heads of HBs declare that they are prepared to pay taxes, and their number could increase if they have a guarantee that at least a part of the funds collected would be used to remove the constraints weighing heavily on the sector.

Three principles should guide the informal sector taxation strategy. On the one hand, it should be equitable and depend on the HBs' ability to contribute. On the other hand, given the meagre profitability of most IHBs, the amount of tax should be sufficiently low to prevent HBs from being driven to "evade" legislation. Finally, it should be based on "a new social contract" between the state and the informal sector so that the latter is not only (or does not have the impression of being just) taxed but also receives tangible benefits from its contributory efforts. According to HBs' head, a single tax, based on the "one-stop shop" model, which would be both easy to calculate and collect, managed by the local/decentralized authorities (commune, district) and not by the central level would be the most appropriate one.

## The implementation of targeted support policies

The problems and the demands expressed by the heads of informal HBs constitute a valuable guide to identify the different constraints they face and to define adequate support policies. Nevertheless, additional suggestions can be put forward since informal HBs only perceive the world as it functions (or dysfunctions), and not as it could function. Consequently, since the latter feel isolated and ignored by the state, they are inclined to expect nothing and to count only on their own force (the famous *exit option* developed by Hirschman). Indeed, the proportion of those who ask for state support is surprisingly low given the difficulties they face. More formal HBs are complaining of difficulties and call for assistance, although these establishments are more successful; this is an example of the preference attrition phenomenon, the capacity to protest being proportional to the level of ambition. The restoration of a climate of confidence between the informal sector and the state is a prerequisite for any support policy.

Figures 15.2 and 15.3 compare and contrast the difficulties faced by informal operators and their demand for assistance addressed to the authorities, these two dimensions being closely linked.

Drawing on empirical data and existing research in this domain, it is possible to outline the guiding lines for a policy package to be prioritized. The main challenges are, on the one hand, to increase the informal sector's productivity and, on the other, to improve labour protection while maintaining the flexibility of the sector and its job creation potential. On the first front, three types of action should be favoured.

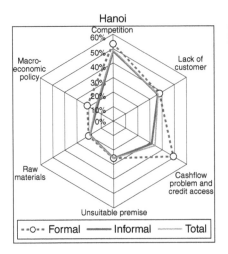
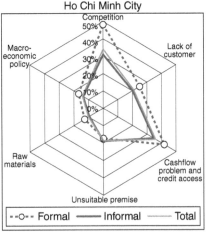

*Figure 15.2* The main problems encountered by household businesses (sources: HB&IS surveys, Hanoi and Ho Chi Minh City, 2009, GSO/IRD-DIAL; authors' calculations).

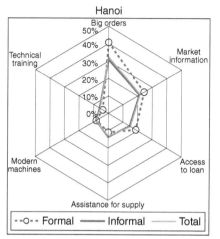

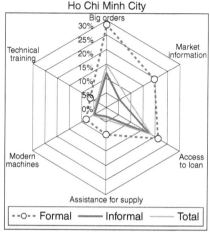

*Figure 15.3* The main needs for assistance expressed by household businesses (sources: HB&IS surveys, Hanoi and Ho Chi Minh City, 2009, GSO/IRD-DIAL; authors' calculations).

## Access to market information, to big orders and promotion of associations

The informal sector is only marginally integrated into the rest of the economy, whether it be through subcontracting or access to big orders. Consistently, this point became one of the main demands for assistance expressed by the IHBs. Therefore, there is room for policies to enhance access to market, in particular through market information. Actually, competition and lack of customer are among the main difficulties reported by the HBs, and these problems are related to the low level of aggregate demand. Nevertheless, a stronger link with the formal sector, which potential (and dynamic) demand could be satisfied partially by informal HBs, would be likely to reduce market constraints. Thus, the informal sector should be given preferential access to some specific public markets from which it is currently completely excluded. Likewise, the reinforcement of subcontracting links with big enterprises (on the domestic market or for export) is likely to provide market opportunities for the informal sector, as it happens in the craft villages (Fanchette and Nguyen, this volume). However, given the size of informal HBs, contracts cannot be negotiated at their individual level. In order to reduce transaction costs the latter should organize themselves and form professional associations which are currently almost inexistent (only 1 per cent of informal HBs are members of an association). International experience shows that these associations play an essential role to build professional networks and social capital, a factor of production which determines entrepreneurial success. Alongside the emergence of groups of operators, these networks would also give a voice to workers in the informal sector and stand up for their interests in front of other organized forces (public authority, employers' associations, NGOs, etc.).

### Access to credit

Informal HBs appear to be excluded from the financial system as only 2 per cent have been able to obtain bank loans in order to create their own business (essentially financed by individual savings); less than 10 per cent (7 per cent in Hanoi and 4 per cent in Ho Chi Minh City) managed to get loans in 2009, as in 2007; finally, a negligible proportion (between 2 and 3 per cent) received loans from microfinance institutions. Easier access to credit would help to improve equipment and productivity. It is all the more important as more and more IHBs are facing credit constraints. Credit constraints (cash flow problems and access to credit) are among the sources of difficulties stressed by HBs while easier access to credit is the first need for assistance requested (Figures 15.2 and 15.3). Since the complexity of procedures or the level of collateral might be a major obstacle to credit demand by the informal sector, it could benefit from the development of microfinance organizations, building on the experience of other developing countries where these organizations play a significant role.

### Developing training

Alongside access to credit, the lack of capacities to manage businesses on a rather larger scale is another major obstacle to the development of small informal production units. Surprisingly, informal HBs do not call for assistance in this domain. Yet, the great majority does not keep any account to manage their business: 62 per cent of HBs in Hanoi and 79 per cent in Ho Chi Minh City do not keep any form of written account, even just a personal book. The implementation of training programmes to improve accounting and financial literacy, and, more generally, technical training with specific curricula adapted to informal sector conditions, should be developed to improve returns to skills. Up to now such programmes have been marginal (if any) in Vietnam; existing professional training programmes are exclusively targeted towards big formal enterprises highly capitalistic or agriculture, the informal sector being once again the missing link. Thus, only one-quarter (23 per cent) of workers in the informal sector have participated in any professional training (8 per cent if only training which lasted more than three months is considered). Moreover, evidence is lacking on the link between the training they followed and the jobs they have exercised.

In parallel, a reorientation of the general education system might be necessary since it does not give any consideration to activities in the informal sector. Consequently, the young consider wage work in the formal sector (in particular in the public sector) as the only conceivable finality of a successful school cycle, in spite of the limited opportunities in this sector (see Razafindrakoto *et al.*, this volume). In order to ensure that training matches with work opportunities, the informal sector specificities should be considered in the curriculum (especially regarding technical training). Training periods in "enterprises" could be organized, heads of informal HBs could share their experiences, etc. These policies would prepare better the majority of the young who will work in this sector. It would also help to struggle against the negative image of the sector which the education system contributes currently to create.

On the second front, *labour force protection* schemes adapted to the characteristics of the informal sector should be put in place. Almost all workers in the informal sector (and informal employment within the formal sector by definition) do not benefit from any social protection. Including the informal sector in the social protection system would lead to the reduction of the precariousness and vulnerability of workers in this sector. In 2008, a voluntary social protection scheme was implemented in Vietnam for all workers not covered by

---

**Ten commandments of economic policy for the informal sector**

*Recognition, monitoring of the informal sector and policy evaluation*

1  Official adoption of an international definition of the informal sector in all the ministries concerned (mainly the Ministry of Economy, the Ministry for Finances and the Ministry of Labour), as well as in the National Statistics Office.
2  Implementation of a regular survey to monitor the informal sector and integration of the results into the national accounts.
3  Assessment of the impact of targeted policies on the informal sector using impact evaluation methods.

*Transparency, clarification and simplification of administrative procedure*

4  Enacting simple rules for the registration procedure for all HBs in Vietnam.
5  Applying a single tax to all HBs fixed at a low level.

*Targeted policies*

6  Developing finance and micro-finance organizations.
7  Defining training programmes aimed at attracting micro-entrepreneurs and workers in the informal sector.
8  Promoting the establishment of professional networks within the informal sector, with the aim of reinforcing integration into the formal sector (public and private), improving access to information and markets and strengthening informal workers' voice.

*Extending social protection*

9  Adapting the voluntary social security programme to the needs of the informal sector.
10  Involve workers and enterprises in the process of social security reform in order to reduce informal employment.

---

the compulsory system (salaried workers whose contract is for less than three months and non-salaried workers). This policy has the ambitious objective of providing universal social protection by 2020. Yet, in 2010, 41.4 million out of the 50 million workers did not benefit from any protection, that is to say 83 per cent of the workforce. Less than 50,000 workers had joined the voluntary scheme. Actually, the current voluntary system does not correspond to the informal sector workers' needs. Besides, its financial viability is questionable. Therefore, an assessment and an adaptation of this voluntary social insurance seem necessary.

*A more systematic evaluation of policies*

Conducting more systematic impact evaluations of policies targeting the informal sector would be helpful. Such procedures still remain exceptional in Vietnam. Besides, given the extent of the needs to support the informal sector, the limited available resources and the lack of previous experience, any implemented policies should be tested on small-scale pilot schemes, before scaling up (depending on the results) is considered. This progressive temporal sequencing of policy coverage is also a favourable condition for the elaboration of rigorous impact evaluation measures.

## Conclusion

Whatever the growth hypotheses for the coming years, the informal economy will keep playing a predominant role in Vietnam. Survey results show the remarkable resilience of the Vietnamese labour market during the crisis. The main features observed are at odds with the expectations: stubbornly low unemployment, resilience of job structure and past trends, informalization, etc. These unexpected figures may be explained by the formidable (and understated) flexibility of the labour market in Vietnam (both in the formal and informal sector), which allows it to mitigate the negative impact of the global crisis. While the main structures of the labor market remained unaffected overall, the principal variable of adjustment during the slowdown has been the working hours and the multi-activity. Unfortunately, we will never be able to evaluate the real impact on employment of the crisis, when it hit Vietnam the hardest, as no appropriate surveys were conducted during this period. This point reinforces the necessity to design a higher frequency survey scheme.

The impressive labour flexibility, even in the formal sector, plays a great role for Vietnam in absorbing the shocks at the macro level. However, at the individual level, the affected workers and households have fully endured the negative impact of the crisis. In spite of its intrinsic flexibility, the informal sector suffered significantly from the difficult economic situation in 2008 and 2009. This is specially the case in Ho Chi Minh City, where clear recessive patterns were observed. The greater vulnerability of the economic capital of Vietnam compared to Hanoi may be explained by the very nature of the shock which affected the megalopolis which is more open to international markets.

This chapter points out some policy implications drawn from these survey results. Compared to 2007, when the first surveys were conducted on behalf of the GSO-IRD project, the informal economy is not a huge black hole any more in Vietnam. Reliable and comprehensive data are now available, and time series began to be available to monitor this key component of the national economy. However, in spite of a recent higher awareness about informality in Vietnam, the informal economy still remains a non-tackled issue from a policy perspective, largely ignored by the authorities. It is all the more problematic that poverty is progressively changing face, from its traditional rural and agriculture profile, to a more urban and informal phenomenon. Designing adequate targeted policies remains a major challenge. The measures outlined in this chapter are not only limited to the specific case of Vietnam but have a broader scope since the characteristics of the informal economy in Vietnam are similar to those observed in other developing countries.

## Notes

1 It concerns a research programme carried out by the General Statistics Office (GSO) in Vietnam and the French Institute for Research and Development (IRD) between 2006 and 2011. The authors of this chapter have been posted in Vietnam throughout this programme.
2 This conclusion is not shared by McCaig and Pavcnik (2011) who, on the contrary, conclude that the number of jobs in the informal sector decreased at the beginning of the 2000s thanks to an increased opening up to international markets.

## References

Bacchetta M., Ernst E., Bustamante J. (2009) *Globalisation and Informal Jobs in Developing Countries*, Geneva: ILO and WTO.

Cling J.-P., Nguyen Thi Thu Huyen, Nguyen Huu Chi, Phan T. Ngọc Trâm, Razafindrakoto M., Roubaud F. (2010a) *The Informal Sector in Vietnam: A Focus on Hanoi and Ho Chi Minh City*, Hanoi: The Gioi Editions.

Cling J.-P., Nguyen Huu Chi, Razafindrakoto M., Roubaud F. (2010b) "How deep was the impact of the economic crisis in Vietnam? A focus on the informal sector in Hanoi and Ho Chi Minh City", Policy Brief, GSO-IRD, UKaid, World Bank, Hanoi (www.worldbank.org/en/country/vietnam/research, WP 6176, 1 December 2010).

Cling J.-P., Razafindrakoto M., Roubaud F. (2010c) "Assessing the potential impact of the global crisis on the labour market and the informal sector in Vietnam", *Journal of Economics and Development*, 38 (June): 16–25.

Cling J.-P., Razafindrakoto M., Roubaud F. eds (2012) "To be or not to be registered? Explanatory factors behind formalizing non-farm household businesses in Vietnam", *Journal of the Asia and Pacific Economy*, 17(4): 632–652.

Demenet A., Nguyen Thi Thu Huyen, Razafindrakoto M., Roubaud F. (2010) "Dynamics of the informal sector in Hanoi and Ho Chi Minh City 2007–2009", GSO-IRD, UKaid, World Bank, Hanoi (www.worldbank.org/en/country/vietnam/research, WP 6174, 1 December 2010).

GSO (2008, 2010) "Report on labour force and employment survey: Vietnam (2007 and 2009)", Ministry of Planning and Investment, Hanoi.

ILO (2003) "Guidelines concerning a statistical definition of informal employment", 17th ICLS, ILO, Geneva.

IPSARD (2009) "Impact of economic slowdown on labourers, employment and life of rural people", Reference Report 1, Hanoi.

Khanna G., Newhouse D., Pacci P. (2010) "Fewer jobs or smaller paychecks? Labor market impacts of the recent crisis in middle-income countries", *Economic Premise* 11, World Bank, Washington DC.

La Porta, R., Shleifer, A. (2008) "The unofficial economy and economic development", NBER Working Papers 14520, National Bureau of Economic Research, Cambridge MA.

McCaig B., Pavcnik N. (2011) *Export markets, household businesses, and formal jobs; Evidence from the US–Vietnam Bilateral Trade Agreement*, processed.

Ministry of Planning and Investment (2010) "Socio-economic development plan 2011–2015", Hanoi.

MoLISA (2010) "Viet Nam employment strategy 2011–2020", First Draft, Hanoi, December.

Nguyen Huu Chi (2012) "Secteur informel, emploi pour les travailleurs ruraux, et processus d'integration economique: le cas du Delta du Fleuve Rouge (Vietnam)", PhD thesis, Université Paris 13, Paris.

Nguyen Huu Chi, Nguyen Thi Thu Huyen, Razafindrakoto M., Roubaud F. (2010) "Vietnam labour market and informal economy in a time of crisis and recovery 2007–2009: main findings of the labour force surveys (LFS)", Hanoi: GSO/IRD, UKaid, World Bank, Hanoi (www.worldbank.org/en/country/vietnam/research, WP 6175, 1 December 2010).

Nguyen Viet Cuong, Pham Thai Hung, Phung Duc Tung (2009) "Evaluating the impacts of the current economic slowdown on (un)employment in Vietnam", UNDP, Hanoi.

Oudin X., Pasquier-Doumer L., Pham Minh Thai, Roubaud F. and Vu Hoang Dạt (2013) "Adjustment of the labour market in time of economic fluctuations and structural changes", in Nguyen Duc Thanh (ed.), *Vietnam Annual Economic Report 2013: On the Bumpy Road to the Future*, Hanoi: Vietnam National University Publisher.

Rand J., Torm N. (2012) "The benefits of formalization: evidence from Vietnamese SMEs", *World Development*, 40(5): 983–998.

Razafindrakoto M., Roubaud F. (2007) "Towards a better monitoring of the labour market", in World Bank (ed.), *Vietnam Development Report 2008: Social Protection*, Hanoi: World Bank.

Razafindrakoto M., Nguyen Huu Chi (2010) "Household business and informal sector in Hanoi and Ho Chi Minh City: first results from a qualitative survey (2009)", DIAL, Hanoi.

Razafindrakoto M., Roubaud F., Nguyen Huu Chi (2011) "Vietnam labor market: an informal sector perspective", in Nguyen Duc Thanh (ed.), *Vietnam Annual Economic Report 2011: The Economy at a Crossroad*, Hanoi: Tri Thuc Edition.

Vietnam Academy of Social Sciences (2010) "Poverty reduction in Vietnam: achievements and challenges", Vietnam's Poverty Assessment 2008–2010, Synthesis report, Hanoi.

Warren-Rodríguez A. (2009) "The impact of the global crisis downturn on employment levels in Viet Nam: an elasticity approach", UNDP Viet Nam Technical Note, Hanoi.

# Index

Page numbers in *italics* denote tables, those in **bold** denote figures.

For Product Safety Concerns and Information please contact our EU
representative  GPSR@taylorandfrancis.com
Taylor & Francis Verlag GmbH, Kaufingerstraße 24, 80331 München, Germany

www.ingramcontent.com/pod-product-compliance
Ingram Content Group UK Ltd.
Pitfield, Milton Keynes, MK11 3LW, UK
UKHW021623240425
457818UK00018B/700